BASEBALL'S DYNASTIES AND THE PLAYERS WHO BUILT THEM

BASEBALL'S DYNASTIES AND THE PLAYERS WHO BUILT THEM

Jonathan Weeks

ROWMAN & LITTLEFIELD
Lanham • Boulder • New York • London

Published by Rowman & Littlefield
A wholly owned subsidiary of The Rowman & Littlefield Publishing Group,
Inc.
4501 Forbes Boulevard, Suite 200, Lanham, Maryland 20706
www.rowman.com

Unit A, Whitacre Mews, 26-34 Stannary Street, London SE11 4AB

British Library Cataloguing in Publication Information Available

Library of Congress Cataloging-in-Publication Data

Names: Weeks, Jonathan, author.
Title: Baseball's dynasties and the players who built them / Jonathan Weeks.
Description: Lanham : Rowman & Littlefield, [2016] | Includes bibliographical references and
index.
Identifiers: LCCN 2015045357 | ISBN 9781442261563 (hardcover : alk. paper)
Subjects: LCSH: Baseball teams—United States—History. | Baseball—United States—History.
Classification: LCC GV875.A1 W4 2016 | DDC 796.357/640973—dc23
LC record available at https://lccn.loc.gov/2015045357

♾™ The paper used in this publication meets the minimum requirements of
American National Standard for Information Sciences Permanence of Paper
for Printed Library Materials, ANSI/NISO Z39.48-1992.

Printed in the United States of America

For my mom and dad. In loving memory

CONTENTS

ACKNOWLEDGMENTS

I'd like to offer a quick word of thanks to my editors at Rowman & Littlefield—Christen Karniski and Andrew Yoder, who were charged with the task of fixing my mistakes and answering all of my stupid questions. Together, they helped make this book a lot better than it was when it first landed on their desks.

Thanks guys—You're the best!

INTRODUCTION

What makes a dynasty? That depends on who you ask.

By strict definition, a dynasty is established when a team wins three consecutive world championships. But since the Yankees and A's are the only clubs to have accomplished the feat, this project would have been far less diverse had I accepted that rule. In the interest of adding some spice, I created a few guidelines of my own. The "dynasties" in this volume were weighed and measured by the following criteria:

- Frequent postseason appearances in a short time span with something to show for it (multiple pennants and world championships)
- The presence of several Hall of Fame–caliber players
- A relatively stable lineup during the period of dominance

According to my expanded definition, there have been at least 22 "dynasties" in baseball history dating back to the nineteenth century. Several teams in the present millennium have come up just short, and you will find them listed in the "Honorable Mentions" section at the end of this book. That having been said, I feel I owe an advance apology to Giants fans.

When the Giants captured their third championship in a five-year span during the 2014 season, I resigned myself to include them in this project. But as I was conducting the research, I was somewhat surprised to discover that they failed to meet two of the three requirements I had established. Not only did they miss the playoffs in 2011 and 2013, but they also spent most of the 2014 campaign behind the Dodgers before emerging with a last-minute wild-card berth. The lineups were some-what unstable as well, with Buster Posey and Pablo Sandoval being the only positional players to maintain full-time status in all three cham-pionship seasons. In regard to Hall of Fame prospects, there were none to be found (although perhaps it's too early to tell in the case of Posey).

This left me in a bit of a bind: Should I add another chapter to my book? Could I exclude the Giants with good conscience? What would fans in San Francisco think?

In the end, I decided to err on the side of recklessness. If the wild-card playoff format has taught us anything, it's that the greatest teams don't always win. I hope this inconvenient fact does not detract from your reading experience in any way.

1

BALTIMORE ORIOLES

1894–1897

Although the accomplishments of players in the game's earliest days should in no way be disregarded, multiple rule changes in the late nineteenth century helped lend more credibility to the sport. When the National League was founded in 1876, there were a host of curious guidelines in effect. For instance, umpires worked alone and catchers did not have to catch a pitch on the fly in order to register an out on a third strike. Both of those conventions would soon be modified.

Another dramatic revision occurred in 1893, when the pitching rubber was moved to a distance of 60 feet, six inches. Pitchers had previously been throwing at batters from a claustrophobic span of 50 feet. Two seasons later, the infield-fly rule was established, and held foul tips were counted as strikes. Only then could the game be considered truly modernized.

Using these developments as a starting point, the Baltimore Orioles can be cited as the first dominant team of the "modern era." The Orioles were founded in 1882, as charter members of the American Association—a second major league designed to challenge the monopoly of the NL. The AA undercut National League profits by charging lower admission prices, playing games on Sundays, and allowing alcohol to be served at ballparks. Alarmed by this new threat to their livelihood, puritanical NL owners disparagingly referred to the rival confederacy as the "Beer and Whiskey League."

According to historian Fred Lieb, Orioles owner Harry Von der Horst entered baseball for the sole purpose of elevating his beer sales. Proprietor of the Eagle Brewery and Malt Works, Von der Horst built a 6,000-seat stadium (originally known as Union Park) on East 25th Street in the Barclay section of Baltimore. The suds flowed freely during games as Von der Horst offered various innovative promotions. On holidays, picnic lunches and schooners of Eagle Beer were offered to fans, with dancing under the stars following.

Although Von der Horst turned a sizeable profit, the Orioles fared poorly in the standings, placing no higher than sixth from their year of inception through the 1886 slate. After a third-place showing in 1887, they dropped back out of contention. The turning point for Baltimore came after the 1891 campaign, when the AA folded. Von der Horst moved the club into the NL and granted able-bodied player-manager Ned Hanlon authority over baseball operations. Hanlon's official Hall of Fame biography paints him as a "shrewd trader, innovative tactician, and master of inside baseball." He perfected the art of "small ball," manufacturing runs the hard way—by bunting, stealing, and sacrificing. Defensively, Hanlon's Orioles were among the first to use relays and cutoffs.

While the team finished dead last in 1892, the rudiments of a championship squad were in place, with Wilbert Robinson doing the catching and John McGraw serving as a utility player. Both ended up in the Hall of Fame as managers. During the next two seasons, Hanlon imported an eclectic mix of established veterans and budding prospects to Baltimore. From 1894–1897, there were no fewer than six future Cooperstown inductees in residence.

With a roster full of superstars, the Orioles captured three straight pennants from 1894–1896. They followed with a pair of near misses, placing second in 1897 and 1898. Along the way, they developed a reputation as one of the nastiest teams in baseball. John Heydler, an umpire who would later ascend to the NL presidency, described the Orioles of the 1890s as "mean, vicious, ready at any time to maim a rival player or an umpire." Infielder John McGraw was proud of that distinction. "We'd go tearing into a bag with flying spikes as though with murderous intent," he boasted. "We were a cocky, swashbuckling crew and wanted everybody to know it."

Pirates great Honus Wagner manufactured a tall tale about a harrowing trip around the bases against the Orioles. After driving a ball deep into the outfield, he claimed to have been tripped at first base by Jack Doyle and then knocked flat by Hughie Jennings at second. Climbing to his feet, he lumbered toward third, only to find John McGraw holding a shotgun on him. "You stop right there!" McGraw allegedly bellowed. Although Wagner's story is obviously apocryphal, numerous reliable accounts confirm the fact that the Orioles resorted to underhanded tactics regularly. When they weren't physically accosting opponents, they were treating them to streams of verbal abuse. Baltimore players were so free in their use of profanity that a resolution was adopted in 1898, imposing mandatory expulsions upon anyone using "villainously foul" language.

Even the groundskeepers at Baltimore were deceitful. Soap flakes were mixed with the soil around the pitcher's mound to make the hands of opposing hurlers slippery when they reached into the dirt. Orioles moundsmen knew to keep untainted soil in their pockets. The infield was mixed with clay and rarely watered, creating a surface not unlike cement. Baltimore players chopped down on the ball, creating dramatically high hops that gave them a head start to first base (hence, the origin of the term *Baltimore chop*). The outfield was ruddy and riddled with weeds. Outfielders allegedly kept extra balls hidden out there in the event that the ones in play eluded them.

During the mid-1880s, the AA champions met the NL champions in an unofficial version of the World Series. The affairs ranged from three to 15 games, with two of them ending in ties. The practice was terminated in 1891, when the AA disbanded. After the Pittsburgh Pirates finished second in 1893, owner William Chase Temple donated a 30-inch silver chalice to the league in the interest of reviving a playoff scenario. The Temple Cup Series was born.

From 1894–1897, the NL championship was determined by a best-of-seven showdown between the first- and second-place clubs. The Orioles appeared in all four series, losing the first two and winning the ones that followed. Players became disillusioned from the onset after New York Giants representatives allegedly cheated several members of the Orioles out of their gate receipt shares in 1894. The series continued nevertheless, with fan interest reaching a peak the following year. The 1895 playoff pitted the Orioles against the Cleveland Spiders. Both clubs were known for their overtly aggressive style of play, and fans behaved accordingly.

Patrons from both cities came armed with fruit, cabbage, and rotten eggs to pelt opposing players with. Wagering, drunkenness, and hooliganism were the order of the day. Before Game 4 in Baltimore, the Spiders required a police escort into the stadium. They tried to slip beneath the grandstand but ended up getting showered with assorted projectiles. Numerous arrests were made before the game was even underway. The Orioles won that day to avoid a sweep but ended up dropping the series in five games.

The behavior of fans in Baltimore and Cleveland did nothing to enhance the reputation of the Temple Cup Series. With the second-place team winning both of the first two matchups, the affair seemed "artificial" to many fans anyway. Attendance sagged dramatically during the next two series, and player apathy was rampant. After 1897, the championship playoff format was again abandoned.

The demise of the NL Orioles came rapidly, as owner Harry Von der Horst—alarmed by slumping attendance in Baltimore—orchestrated a merger with the Brooklyn Superbas and transferred most of his top players to New York. The Superbas finished first in 1899, while the Orioles, with a depleted roster, slipped to fourth place. Unable to handle a cumbersome aggregation of 12 teams, NL officials eliminated four franchises at the turn of the century. Baltimore was ousted, along with the Louisville Colonels, Washington Senators, and Cleveland Spiders. The Orioles would reappear in the American League briefly during the 1901 and 1902 campaigns, before moving to New York and becoming the Highlanders. The modern-day Orioles entered the AL in 1954, when the lowly St. Louis Browns moved to Baltimore and changed their identity.

Even though many of the player names have been forgotten throughout time, the Orioles of the 1890s were among the most star-studded clubs ever assembled. The following men were instrumental in establishing the game's first true dynasty.

JOHN MCGRAW, INFIELD

McGraw had a rough childhood, losing his mother and several siblings to a diphtheria epidemic during the winter of 1884–1885. Beaten severely by his alcoholic father, he ended up being raised by a neighbor who ran a hotel across the street. The experience may or may not have contributed to his pugilistic nature on the field. As a player, McGraw broke rules, instigated fights, and did everything in his power to prevent opponents from scoring runs. One writer commented, "McGraw uses every low and contemptible method that his erratic brain can conceive to win a play by a dirty trick." As a manager, he became one of the most despised figures in the NL. Hall of Fame pitching great Christy Mathewson once remarked, "I have seen McGraw go onto ball fields where he is as welcome as a man with the black smallpox."

After becoming a star pitcher at the age of 16 for his hometown Truxton Grays, McGraw moved on to the Western New York League, where he was converted to an infielder. He spent one season in the Illinois-Iowa League before joining the Orioles—then of the AA—in 1891. He played in just 33 games under manager Billy Barnie that year, but when Ned Hanlon took over the following season, McGraw blossomed into one of the top leadoff hitters in the game. Choking up high on the bat, he used a chopping motion to put the ball in play. From 1893–1899, he hit no lower than .321. A patient batsman, he was a nuisance to opposing pitchers. During one spring training game, he allegedly fouled off more than two dozen pitches in a single at-bat. He led the league twice in on-base percentage, and his lifetime mark of .466 is third on the all-time list.

McGraw spent nine seasons with the NL Orioles, serving primarily as a third baseman and shortstop. When Harry von der Horst tried to send him to Brooklyn in 1899, McGraw refused to report. He was allowed to stay one more season, but when the Orioles were ousted from the NL lineup before the 1900 slate, he ended up with the Cardinals. He returned to Baltimore in 1901, as a player-manager.

After quarreling with AL president Ban Johnson repeatedly, McGraw jumped to the New York Giants in 1902, taking several high-profile players with him, including future Hall of Famers Joe McGinnity and Roger Bresnahan. McGraw remained at the helm in New York for 31 years, guiding the club to 10 pennants and three World Series titles. His last appearance as a player came in 1906.

During his tumultuous career as manager, he fought with fans and security guards, and even inspired a police officer to take a swing at him once. Although many of his players came to resent him, he was immensely popular with luminaries outside the baseball establishment. A big-time celebrity, he even toured the vaudeville circuit for three months in 1912.

McGraw won his last NL pennant in 1924. During the next several seasons, he grew increasingly impatient and irritable. Hall of Famer Freddy Lindstrom commented that McGraw "could be very unfair at times." According to multiple sources, McGraw (or "Little Napoleon," as he was known to some) avoided the Giants clubhouse altogether and didn't even bother to show up for games sometimes. In June 1932, he turned over managerial duties to first baseman Bill Terry. Terry led the Giants to a World Series victory the following year.

McGraw was summoned from retirement to manage the first NL All-Star Team in 1933. The NL lost by a score of 4–2. It was McGraw's last major public appearance. He died of cancer and uremia in February 1934. He was voted into the Hall of Fame as a manager three years later.

WILBERT ROBINSON, CATCHER

As a kid, Robinson worked for a fish merchant. One day, an irate woman yelled, "Come back here, Billy Fish, and take away your fish. They stink!" From then onward, he was known to close associates as "Billy Fish." At 5-foot-8, 215 pounds, Robinson was oddly proportioned for a ballplayer. When he worked with staff ace Sadie McMahon, the two were referred to as the "Dumpling Battery." Robinson formed a lasting friendship with longtime teammate John McGraw, who was his polar opposite. McGraw was aggressive and universally disliked, while Robinson was laid-back and widely admired by fans. Historian Fred Lieb described Robinson as "big, gruff, genial, and kindly." During his later days as Brooklyn manager, he was referred to affectionately as "Uncle Robbie."

Robinson followed his older brother's example when he joined the Eastern New England League in 1885. Fred Robinson had gotten a cup of coffee with the Reds of the Union Association the previous year. Obviously the more talented of the two, Wilbert would spend more than three decades as a player, manager, and coach. During his four full seasons with the American Association A's, Robinson's highest batting average was .244. Released by Philly in September 1890, he became a star with the Orioles, topping the .300 mark at the plate four times between 1893–1897. He had little power, never collecting more than 27 extra-base hits in any season. His finest single-game performance came in 1892, when he went 7-for-7 in a June match against the St. Louis Browns. The seven hits were a NL record that would later be tied.

A sizeable target behind the plate, Robinson was as good as most of his contemporaries defensively. He led the league in stolen bases allowed twice but compensated for this by pacing the circuit in putouts the same number of times. He also posted the highest fielding percentage in the NL during the 1895 slate. Following McGraw's lead, Robinson refused to report to Brooklyn in 1899. Both players ended up in St. Louis when the Orioles were expelled from the league at the turn of the century. Both returned to Baltimore for the O's fledgling AL run in 1901. When McGraw left for New York partway through the 1902 slate, Robinson took over as manager. He spent several seasons with Baltimore's minor-league team before ending his playing days at the age of 44.

For years, Robinson ran a saloon in Baltimore and worked in his family's butcher shop. He worked as a Giants spring training instructor for two years before returning to baseball as a full-time coach in 1911. Robinson has been given a lot of credit for developing Hall of Fame pitcher Rube Marquard, who was initially considered a bust. McGraw and Robinson parted ways after the 1913 campaign when McGraw claimed that Robinson had failed to relay a sign to one of his players at a crucial juncture in the World Series. Robinson signed on as manager with Brooklyn the following year.

During his 18 seasons in Flatbush, Robinson became a revered figure. The team was renamed the "Robins" in his honor. They captured pennants in 1916 and 1920, but lost in the World Series both years. Robinson was known for his ability to work with pitchers. His philosophy was simple. "There's only one theory on pitching," he once said.

"Get the biggest guy you can find who can throw a ball through a two-inch plank and you got yourself a pitcher."

During the 1920s, the club fell on hard times while gaining a reputation for overtly sloppy play. Even so, fans flocked to the stadium to watch their "Daffiness Boys" in action. Robinson tried to discipline his players as best he could, establishing a "Bonehead Club" with a schedule of fines for various transgressions. It didn't help much, as the team finished below .500 six times during the 1920s. Robinson stayed on as manager through the 1931 slate. He served as president of the Atlanta Crackers of the Southern Association until he died after a serious fall in his hotel room. He was elected to the Hall of Fame as a manager in 1945.

WILLIE KEELER, OUTFIELD

Keeler was passionate and almost childlike in his enthusiasm for the game. In later years, he told a reporter, "I was just thinking of those suckers, the club owners, paying me for playing ball. Why, I would pay my way into their ballparks if it was the only way I had to get into a game." In Keeler's era, most parks had 25-cent bleacher seats that were usually filled with kids. Keeler was known to stand near the fence and keep up a running dialog with the children, explaining to them what was going on in the game.

Born in Brooklyn, Keeler was the son of a trolley conductor. Obsessed with baseball from an early age, more than one of Keeler's teachers remarked that he would amount to nothing. He had a breakthrough season with Binghamton of the Eastern League in 1892. The Giants signed him, but after he broke his ankle early in the 1893 campaign, New York manager John Montgomery Ward considered him too frail for major-league play. He was dealt to Brooklyn and ended up joining the Orioles in 1894.

At 5-foot-4, 140 pounds, Keeler wasn't much bigger than the average batboy. He was shy and reserved, unlike many of the rowdy players surrounding him in Baltimore. Despite his diminutive stature, he used one of the heaviest bats available—reportedly weighing 46 ounces. Pirates great Honus Wagner was enamored with Keeler's bunting skill. "If the third baseman came in for a tap, he invariably pushed the ball past the fielder. If he stayed back, he bunted," said Wagner. Keeler became famous for his hitting philosophy, which was to "hit'em where they ain't." At the height of his career, he occupied the top spots in the Orioles batting order, along with John McGraw.

From 1895–1901, Keeler gathered no fewer than 202 hits each year. He led the league in that category three times, while claiming a pair of batting titles. His greatest offensive season came in 1894, when he hit safely 239 times, while compiling a batting average of .424—among the highest single-season marks in history. In 1897, he started the season with a 44-game hitting streak, breaking the NL record set by Bill Dahlen.

Like most of his teammates, Keeler was not above breaking the rules. The grass was deliberately kept high in right field at Oriole Park, and "Wee Willie" allegedly kept extra balls hidden out there just in case. He finished among the league leaders in fielding percentage several times, posting the highest mark in the NL on two occasions.

Transferred to Brooklyn in 1899, Keeler stayed there until 1903, when the Highlanders (later known as the Yankees) claimed him for their inaugural campaign. He remained in the Bronx for seven seasons, and although his batting average dropped off sharply, his superior bunting skills proved highly useful. He averaged 30 sacrifice hits per year between 1903–1909. In 1905, he set a team record with 42 sacrifices. Keeler finished his career with the Giants in 1910. He was third on the all-time hit list, behind Cap Anson and Jake Beckley, when he retired.

After his death in 1923, and induction into the Hall of Fame in 1939, he was immortalized in a poem by Ogden Nash, entitled "Line-up for Yesterday." It contains the following lines:

> K is for Keeler,
> As fresh as green paint,
> The fastest and moistest
> To hit where they ain't.

HUGHIE JENNINGS, SHORTSTOP

Hughie Jennings is remembered as one of the game's most lively characters—and one of the luckiest. A lifetime .312 hitter, he escaped debilitating injury and death on numerous occasions. His major-league career began in 1891, with the Louisville Colonels of the AA. He put up pedestrian numbers until a trade sent him to Baltimore near the end of the 1893 slate. It was there that he emerged as a major star. In 1896, he collected 121 RBIs without the benefit of a single homer—a major-league record. From 1894–1898, he scored an average of 137 runs per year. In that same span, his on-base percentage never dropped below .411. Extremely gifted with a glove, Jennings was one of the premier defensive shortstops of the era as well, leading the league in fielding percentage and putouts four times apiece.

Jennings was not afraid to mix it up with opponents and umpires. Along with John McGraw, he became one of the most detested players in the NL. Jennings and McGraw would often take turns shouting obscenities and spraying tobacco juice on umpires. Crews were much smaller in those days, and both men were known to take advantage of the situation, tripping opposing runners or taking a shorter route on the base paths by cutting across the diamond when umpires had their backs turned.

Jennings's career was marred by injuries. He tempted fate time and again by leaning into pitches. During one particular five-year span, he was hit more than 200 times. In 1896, when he set the all-time record with 51 beanings, his on-base percentage was an incredible .472. He didn't always get off so easily, however, as his skull was fractured on three separate occasions. In 1897, he was unconscious for four days after being hit by an offering from Giants ace Amos Rusie. His career continued nevertheless. Transferred to Brooklyn in 1899, he spent portions of two seasons there before ending with the Phillies. Injuries began to take their toll, and, by 1901, he was finished as a full-time player. In 1904, Jennings was seriously hurt yet again when he dove into Cornell University's pool after it had been drained of water. He missed the entire season and made just 12 appearances as a player after that. He eventually earned a legal degree and became a practicing lawyer.

Jennings moved on to a long and prosperous managerial career, guiding the Tigers to three straight AL championships beginning in 1907. He displayed a host of odd behaviors on the diamond. When his players were at bat, he would stand in the coaching box and needle opposing pitchers with an ongoing dialog punctuated by piercing shouts and whistles. Numerous photos show him standing on one leg with his fists in the air and his mouth agape. His nickname "Ee-Yah!" is derived from the sound he would make when one of his players did something that pleased him. According to a 1910 article in *Outing* magazine, Jennings was fond of plucking large patches of turf and stuffing them into his mouth. "During the course of the season, he eats enough grass to stuff a mattress," writes C. E. Van Loan. "He is a thorn in the side of all greenskeepers. Some of them say they are going to sprinkle Paris Green (a toxic insecticide) around the coaching lines to discourage Hughie's appetite."

The resilient Detroit skipper suffered yet another perilous mishap in 1911, when his car plummeted from a bridge above the Lehigh River. He narrowly escaped drowning and was left with two broken legs, along with a broken arm. He remained at the Detroit helm until 1921, when he was replaced by Ty Cobb. That same year, Jennings took a job as a coach for the Giants. His enthusiasm was contagious, as the New Yorkers ran off a string of four consecutive pennants. When John McGraw fell ill with various ailments in 1925, leaving Jennings in charge, the club slipped to second place. That winter, Jennings was diagnosed with tuberculosis. The illness ended his baseball career, but he hung on until a bout of meningitis finally claimed his life at the age of 58. He was posthumously elected to the Hall of Fame in 1945.

JOE KELLEY, OUTFIELD

According to multiple sources, Kelley had movie star good looks and was popular with the ladies. Emminently aware of this, he kept a comb in his back pocket at all times to maintain his appearance. The left-field bleacher section of Oriole Park, which was often filled with female fans, came to be known as "Kelleyville." Kelley's birth name was actually "Kelly." The "e" was added by journalists because it inferred higher status in Ireland. Kelley approved of the change and adopted it.

Kelley began his career as a pitcher. In 1891, he posted a 10–3 record in the New England League with a healthy .331 batting average. He ended up signing with the Boston Beaneaters as an outfielder. Kelley's major-league career got off to a slow start. He hit .244 in his debut. With the Pirates in 1892, he managed a lowly .239 average before a trade landed him in Baltimore. The deal was risky, since Kelley was an unknown, and George Van Haltren, whom the Pirates received in return, was one of the Orioles' better hitters. But Kelley quickly established himself as one of the most productive members of the Oriole offense, justifying the transaction.

From 1894–1897, Kelley's batting average ranged from .362 to .393. He reached the 100-RBI threshold each year. Demonstrating superior speed on the bases, he led the NL with 87 steals in 1896. During the 1894 campaign, he gathered 74 extra-base hits, second in the league to Hugh Duffy. His finest afternoon with the Orioles came in September of 1894, when he went 9-for-9 in a doubleheader.

Kelley denied that the Orioles played dirty baseball. He once told a reporter, "We bathe as much as the next, and this talk is all nonsense." But like his outfield mate, Willie Keeler, he was accused of keeping extra baseballs hidden in the grass in case the ones hit to him eluded his grasp.

Kelley was among the gaggle of stars transferred to Brooklyn in 1899. He continued his success in Flatbush, compiling a .317 batting average in portions of three seasons. He returned to the Orioles for part of the 1902 campaign, but he was released in spite of his .311 average. The Reds made him a player-manager, and he served in that capacity for the better part of four seasons, never guiding the club to a finish higher than third. He resigned as Reds manager in November 1905, telling reporters that he was "tired of being roasted."

Kelley remained in Cincinnati through the 1906 slate. The following year, he accepted a position as player-manager of the Toronto Maple Leafs—an Eastern League franchise. The contract he signed made him the highest-paid minor-league player in history to that point. He more or less earned his pay by piloting the club to a first-place finish, while hitting .322 in 91 games. The following year, Kelley took over the helm of the Boston Beaneaters. The team played lackluster ball, as Kelley managed a meager .259 average in 73 appearances. It was his last major-league season.

Kelley returned to the Maple Leafs as manager for three more seasons. He later worked as a scout for the New York Yankees. In 1926, he returned to Brooklyn as a coach. He died in 1943, and was posthumously elected to Cooperstown via the Veteran's Committee.

STEVE BRODIE, OUTFIELDER

Born in Warrenton, Virginia, Walter Scott Brodie got his first taste of organized ball in the state's semipro industrial leagues. He picked up the nickname of "Steve" from a famous daredevil who had jumped off the Brooklyn Bridge in 1886, and lived to tell the tale. Brodie shuffled around the minors until 1890, when a large group of disgruntled major leaguers formed their own short-lived circuit, which was known as the Players League. With their roster severely depleted, the Boston Beaneaters called up Brodie from Hamilton of the International League. He won the starting job with a .296 batting average, 67 RBIs, and 77 runs scored. He would spend portions of four seasons in Boston and St. Louis before joining the Orioles.

A fun-loving jokester, Brodie became known as "one of the premier clowns of the game." To the delight of fans, he carried on conversations with himself in the outfield, quoted Shakespeare at the plate, and caught balls behind his back during practice. One writer labeled Brodie a "flake . . . who delights in zany behavior." John McGraw once commented that Brodie was "unconsciously funny" and that he actually took baseball quite seriously.

Before a game one day, Ned Hanlon chewed out players for their impatience at the plate. "That goes especially for you, Steve," he said to Brodie. "There is no harm in having a strike called on you once in a while." Brodie didn't appreciate being singled out, and in his first at-bat of the afternoon, he deliberately watched three strikes go past. "Don't tell me I can't take 'em," he shouted at Hanlon afterward. "I could have knocked any one of them pitches out of the park!"

Highly durable, Brodie played in 727 consecutive games—a nineteenth-century record. He enjoyed his best seasons with the Orioles in 1894 and 1895. He hit .358 in that span with 247 RBIs and 77 stolen bases. The outfield combination of Brodie, Joe Kelley, and Willie Keeler has been rated as one of the best of the nineteenth century. From 1894–1896, the trio collectively hit .363 and averaged more than 300 RBIs per year.

Brodie's offensive numbers tailed off in 1896, and he was traded to Pittsburgh. He returned to Baltimore in 1899, and played well, hitting .309 with 87 RBIs. Unfortunately, the O's had lost most of the players that had made them a powerhouse and finished in fourth place. Brodie played in the minors through 1910. He later became a coach for Rutgers, Princeton, and the U.S. Naval Academy. He was inducted into the Salem-Roanoke Hall of Fame in 1992.

JACK DOYLE, FIRST BASE

By the time Doyle joined the Orioles in November 1895, he was a veteran of seven major-league seasons. He had played for the Giants in the 1894 Temple Cup, hitting .588 and leading the New Yorkers to a four-game sweep of the Orioles. Many Baltimore players still held a grudge, but when they saw how Doyle could help the team they reluctantly accepted him.

Doyle hit .339 with 101 RBIs for the O's in 1896, and followed with a lofty .354 average the following year. He stole 135 bases in that span, while scoring 207 runs. Defensively, he was competent but not exceptional, finishing among the top five in putouts and double plays both seasons. He committed his fair share of errors, leading the league during the 1896 slate, while placing second in 1897.

Some say that Doyle earned the nickname "Dirty Jack" because his uniform was always filthy. Others attribute the moniker to his aggressive behavior. "I was a hard baserunner," he admitted in his later years. "You had to be in those days. It wasn't a matter of being rough or dirty." Despite that testimonial, Doyle was one of the most notorious hotheads of the era, fighting with almost anyone who crossed him. He went into the stands to confront fans on numerous occasions, resulting in multiple arrests. He also tangled with umpires Tom Lynch and Bob Emslie.

Doyle began his career as a catcher. No stranger to underhanded tactics, he was known to stuff rocks in the shoes of opponents while they were batting. His actions often went unnoticed until the victimized player was running the bases. Doyle eventually received a reprimand from NL officials for the practice. Although he served mostly as a first baseman after the 1893 campaign, he made sporadic catching appearances for several years.

Doyle was named captain of three different teams in New York, Baltimore, and Chicago. Despite his prior arrest record, he served as a police commissioner for two years. He got to see what the game was like from the other side when he later became a minor-league umpire.

FAST FACT: In 1894, the Orioles scored 1,171 runs—an average of more than nine per game.

2

PITTSBURGH PIRATES

1901–1903

The first organized ballclubs in Pittsburgh played in Allegheny City, a neighboring municipality located across the Ohio River. In 1882, the strongest outfit in the area joined the newly formed American Association. Originally referred to as the Alleghenys, the team remained affiliated with the league for five seasons and finished out of the running almost every year. On the heels of a dispute with AA officials regarding player contracts, the Alleghenys migrated to the National League in 1887. The American Association folded not long afterward.

When the short-lived Players League was founded in 1890, most of the Allegheny regulars jumped to the Pittsburgh Burghers club. Among the stars to depart were pitcher Pud Galvin, first baseman Jake Beckley, and center fielder Ned Hanlon—all of whom would be enshrined at Cooperstown. The results were disastrous, as the Alleghenys compiled the worst record in franchise history, at 23–113. The Players League disbanded after just one season, and the three previously mentioned luminaries returned to their point(s) of origin.

Before the 1891 campaign, Pittsburgh owners lured several players away from the floundering AA, including Philadelphia's star second baseman Lou Bierbauer. The Athletics complained quite loudly, and one AA official referred to the transaction as "piratical." Poking fun at their detractors, the Alleghenys changed their name to the Pirates—a handle that has survived to the present day.

Aside from one second-place showing in 1893, the Pirates finished no higher than sixth from 1891 through the 1899 slate. When the NL downsized to eight teams before the 1900 campaign, Louisville Colonels owner Barney Dreyfuss purchased half of the Pirates shares. He then transferred his best players to Pittsburgh, including future Hall of Famers Honus Wagner and Fred Clarke.

Dreyfuss had immigrated to the United States from Germany in the 1880s. His cousins, the Bernheim brothers, had arrived in the United States shortly after the Civil War and opened a successful bourbon distillery. A former bank clerk in his hometown of Freiburg, Dreyfuss was recruited to work for them. With little money and a limited grasp of the language, he studied English at night while working six days a week in the distillery.

The ambitious Dreyfuss eventually secured a loan from his cousins to become sole owner of the Pirates. He would maintain possession of the club for more than three decades, enjoying multiple periods of success. NL president John Heydler once commented, "[Dreyfuss] discovered more great players than any man in the game." This was certainly true at the turn of the century, when the Bucs first rose to supremacy.

On the heels of a disappointing seventh-place finish, the Pirates ended up just four and a half games behind the Brooklyn Superbas in 1900. They had stood within a game and a half of the NL lead in late September before a sudden swoon derailed their pennant run. The season featured breakout performances from a pair of future Hall of Fame pitchers—Jack Chesbro and Rube Waddell.

Chesbro had made his Pirates debut in July 1899. He was mediocre in 19 appearances but came back strong the following year, contributing 15 wins to the Pittsburgh cause. Waddell—another one of Dreyfuss's Louisville transfers—posted the lowest ERA in the NL during the 1900 campaign, while finishing second in strikeouts. Impressive numbers aside, the erratic hurler demonstrated an alarming lack of discipline during his career. He had a penchant for turning up missing during spring training, investing his energy in a host of inane pursuits (among them alligator wrestling). Multiple sources claim that he would stroll through the stands in street clothes before game time, drinking beer, eating red hots, and instigating fights. He would sometimes play the role of a celebrity bartender at local taverns prior to arriving at the ballpark. It has been suggested by many that he was either mentally ill or developmentally disabled. Whatever the case, Pittsburgh player-manager Fred Clarke quickly tired of Waddell's antics and sold him to the Chicago Orphans (later known as the Cubs) in May 1901.

With Wagner and Clarke leading the offensive charge, the Pirates captured the NL pennant every year from 1901–1903. They posted the highest winning percentage of all time in 1902, with a .741 mark. The achievement would be short-lived, as the Cubs eclipsed it in 1906 (details of which can be found in the next chapter).

Things were less than blissful between the two rival circuits at the turn of the century. American League owners sought to undermine their NL rivals by engaging in frequent roster raids. The bickering became so intense that a National Commission was established to preside over the operations of both leagues. After keeping the Pittsburgh lineup largely intact, Barney Dreyfuss took great strides toward a peaceful accord in 1903, when he challenged the AL champion Boston Americans to a best-of-nine postseason showdown.

Baseball's first official World Series began with the Pirates taking two out of three at Boston. The third game was a nightmare for both clubs, as fans kept showing up at the Huntington Street Grounds, even after tickets were sold out. By midafternoon, the field was crowded with trespassers. Thousands of fans broke through a cordoned-off area and headed toward the reserve grandstand, where they fought with Boston players and police. Armed with a fire hose and bats (supplied by the home team's business manager), police reinforcements were able to secure a 50-foot stretch beyond the diamond and a 30-foot span behind home plate. The game started a few minutes late with special ground rules in effect. It was decided that balls hit into the crowd (a meager 150 feet from home) would count as doubles. Seven of them were hit that day as Pittsburgh came away with a 4–2 victory.

In Lawrence Ritter's classic work *The Glory of Their Times*, infielder Tommy Leach refers to the 1903 affair as the "wildest" World Series ever. "The fans were part of the game in those days," he said. "They'd pour right out onto the field and argue with the players and the umpires. [It] was sort of hard to keep the game going sometimes to say the least."

The Pirates were treated to an entirely different scenario when they returned home for Game 4. A meager crowd of 7,600 turned out to see a dramatic Boston rally fall short in the ninth, giving Pittsburgh a 3–1 Series edge. It was the last game the Bucs would win that year as they inexplicably dropped the next four contests by a combined score of 27–8. Pittsburgh batters had a particularly difficult time against hard-throwing right-hander Bill Dinneen, who made four starts for Boston and struck out 28 opponents. The Bucs would not return to the postseason until 1909, when they finally captured an elusive championship with a seven-game victory over the Tigers.

The Pirates carried multiple Hall of Famers on their roster during the early 1900s. While Honus Wagner invariably soaks up most of the attention when tales of the Deadball Era are told, other lesser-known greats had a major impact on the club's success during that period.

HONUS WAGNER, SHORTSTOP

If Wagner's on-field accomplishments are ever forgotten, he will at least be remembered for the value of his baseball cards. From 1909–1911, the American Tobacco Company issued its T206 series. Wagner objected to the distribution of his own card, likely because he didn't want kids to buy cigarettes. Although the exact number is not known, somewhere between 50 to 200 cards were issued before production was stopped. Since the cards are so rare, they fetch incredible prices at auction. Even in poor condition, they have been sold to collectors for more than a quarter of a million dollars. In 2013, a card of high quality netted $2.1 million.

Within the existing body of baseball literature, there are few writers who consider Wagner to be anything less than the greatest shortstop of all time. After toiling in the minors for portions of three seasons, he joined the Louisville Colonels as a midseason call-up. He hit .335 in 62 games and, by 1899, had emerged as the brightest star on the club. The biggest issue faced by Louisville management was finding a defensive position for him to play. When the franchise folded after the 1899 campaign, Barney Dreyfuss orchestrated a merger with the Pirates. By the time Wagner was permanently installed at shortstop by player-manager Fred Clarke in 1903, he had tried out every position except catcher.

Wagner was not the most handsome man to grace the diamond. Barrel-chested and bowlegged, he had a prominent nose, long arms, and uncommonly large hands. His defensive play was commensurate with his outward appearance—somewhat rough around the edges. He used a pancake-shaped glove with a hole cut in the palm to give him a better feel for the ball. According to one source, "He was often likened to an octopus. When he fielded grounders, his huge hands also collected large scoops of infield dirt, which accompanied his throws to first like the tail of a comet." Wagner's defensive skills improved with age. He captured his first fielding title at the age of 38 and hung onto it for the next three seasons.

Wagner has gained more acclaim for his wondrous batting feats. He led the league in every major offensive category except homers at least twice. Between 1900–1911, he captured eight batting crowns. He currently ranks among the top 10 of all time in doubles, triples, and base hits. While he looked a bit awkward doing it, he could run with the best of them, stealing 20 or more bases in 19 consecutive seasons. His lifetime total of 723 is 10th on the all-time list. Although he fizzled in the 1903 World Series against Boston, he handled Detroit pitching at a torrid .333 clip during the Bucs' championship season of 1909.

Wagner played hard but never instigated fights or baited umpires. He loved spinning tall tales about his baseball experiences, even though some of them may seem rather corny to modern readers. He claimed to have once picked up a rabbit that was running across the infield and thrown it to first, where the umpire ruled that the runner was "out by a hare."

Wagner played until 1917, the same year he logged his only major-league managerial experience. The Pirates were 1–4 during his brief stint. In 1932, he vied for the manager's job in Cincinnati but ended up as a coach. The Pirates brought him back as a coach many years later and kept him around until severe arthritis finally forced him to retire in the early 1950s. Wagner died in 1955, at the age of 81. A bronze statue was erected at Forbes Field in his honor. An inscription on the base of the statue hailed him as a "champion among champions." It was rededicated in 1972, at Three Rivers Stadium.

FRED CLARKE, OUTFIELD

Born in Iowa, Clarke found adventure early in his life when he traveled
with his family in a caravan of covered wagons to Kansas. Multiple
stories exist as to how he eventually got his start as a professional player.
In one version, he impersonated another prospect to get a tryout with a
team in Hastings, Nebraska. His minor-league career was brief. After
hitting .311 in the South Atlantic League, he was summoned by Louisville owner Barney Dreyfuss in June 1894. Dreyfuss had promised
Clarke $100, and Clarke refused to play until he received it. Dreyfuss
reportedly settled the debt with cash. Clarke proceeded to go 5-for-5 at
the plate in his debut.

Clarke was no stranger to rough play and didn't understand all the
fuss about beanballs in his later years. "In my day, we used to invite
them to throw at us," he told a reporter. "That was a good way to get on
base." Clarke began his career as a drinker and hell-raiser but stopped
when Dreyfuss warned him that it would impede his development as a
player. He allegedly became an impulsive chewer of toothpicks instead.

Clarke was entering his fourth season with the Colonels when he was
promoted to manager. The Colonels were a poor team in those days and
never finished above .500 during Clarke's three years at the helm.
When the club was ousted from the NL before the 1900 slate, Clarke
was installed as Pirates skipper. With a strong pitching staff, the Pirates
were in contention for the first time in several years.

Clarke had a knack for working with pitchers. During his 19 years as
manager, his moundsmen posted 20-win seasons on more than two
dozen occasions. Described by one source as "a tough competitor, an
aggressive baserunner, and a manager who communicated a positive
attitude to his players," Clarke led by example. A lifetime .312 hitter, he
scored at least 80 runs in 13 seasons. He also stole more than 500 bases.
One of those steals occurred by accident. In 1906, he was on third with
the bases loaded and Jim Nealon at bat. With a 3–1 count, Nealon took
a pitch that appeared to be outside the strike zone. Umpires didn't
signal strikes in those days, they called them. When Hank O'Day didn't
say anything right away, Clarke trotted home. By the time O'Day
cleared his throat and made a strike call, Clarke had crossed the plate.
He didn't even realize he had stolen home until he was in the dugout.

Clarke's best offensive season came in 1897, with Louisville, when he hit .390 and compiled an on-base percentage of .461. In 15 postseason games, he collected 13 hits (five for extra bases) and six walks, while driving in nine runs. The 1911 season was his last as a full-timer, and he went out with a bang, hitting .324 in 110 games. When he retired, his 1,602 managerial wins were a record.

Presumably finished with baseball, Clarke returned to his farm in Kansas. But the Bucs brought him back as a coach in 1925. The team responded well, capturing their first pennant since Clarke's playing days. The 1926 club was not as good, and Clarke was accused of undermining manager Bill McKechnie. In a secret ballot, players voted to keep Clarke on the bench by a margin of 18–6. The three men who had rallied for Clarke's dismissal—Babe Adams, Max Carey, and Carson Bigbee—were quickly no longer Pirates.

Clarke's retirement was almost as exciting as his baseball career. While on a fishing trip, his boat capsized in a storm. He and his wife remained in the water for hours before they were rescued. While hunting quail one day, Clarke avoided a serious mishap when the bill of his cap deflected pellets from a companion's misfire. Upon arriving home after the incident, he turned on his gas furnace and it exploded, sending him flying across the basement. Remarkably, he survived. Clarke once commented aptly that, "[L]ife is a funny game, and a little thing, almost a trifle, may make a splash in your affairs so big that the ripples will be felt as long as you live."

JACK CHESBRO, PITCHER

Prior to turning pro, Chesbro acquired the nickname "Happy Jack" while working at a state mental hospital in Middletown, New York. The moniker referred to his cheerful disposition. His early days in baseball were star-crossed, as several of the clubs he played for were unable to stay afloat. He pitched for Albany and Johnstown of the Eastern League, posting a cumulative 7–10 record before both teams folded. Later, he played for the ill-fated Roanoke Magicians, who disappeared from the Virginia League like the original colony. In 1899, Chesbro went 17–4 in the Atlantic League, earning a promotion to the Pirates.

Chesbro relied heavily on his fastball in the early days. He later added a spitball, which became his bread and butter pitch. Always a bit reluctant to commit to a particular club, Chesbro initially refused to follow the Pirates south for spring training in 1900. He eventually reported, but his holdouts and threats to quit were a habitual routine during his career.

A difficult pitch to control due to its dramatic movement, Chesbro gradually became a master of the "wet one." The results were dramatic, as he won 28 games for the Pirates in 1902—a league high. He paced the circuit in shutouts for two straight seasons.

Before the conclusion of the 1902 slate, Chesbro signed a contract to jump to the AL. He was subsequently banned from playing in a series of exhibition games in Pittsburgh that netted Pirates players a fair amount of cash. Chesbro went on an all-star barnstorming tour of the West Coast instead.

In 1903, the stocky right-hander (5-foot-9, 185 pounds) collected 21 victories for the fledgling New York Highlanders, representing 29 percent of the club's total win shares that year. New York manager Clark Griffith disliked the spitball and limited its use. But when Chesbro got off to a slow start in 1904, Griffith gave his star hurler the green light. Chesbro enjoyed one of the most spectacular seasons in history, winning 41 games and posting a 1.82 ERA. He completed 48 of his 51 starts that year. Despite those impressive numbers, his season was remembered for one pitch.

The Highlanders had led the AL for most of the season, but a late-season surge put Boston ahead with two games remaining. Chesbro took the mound in the first game of a must-win doubleheader between the two clubs. With the score tied in the ninth, Boston catcher Lou Criger reached base on a slow roller to short. Boston pitcher Bill Dinneen sacrificed Criger to second, and a groundout by Kip Selbach moved the runner to third. Facing the dangerous Freddy Parent, Chesbro worked the count even. The next pitch was a spitball that sailed over the head of New York catcher Red Kleinow. Criger scampered home with the go-ahead run. When the Highlanders failed to score in the bottom of the inning, the pennant went to Boston.

Chesbro had a couple of decent seasons after that but never came close to matching his 41 victories in 1904. After retiring in 1909, he coached at the college level briefly before moving on to other pursuits.

He coached for the Washington Senators in 1924. The wild pitch haunted Chesbro for the rest of his life, as he was asked about it constantly. Some of his friends reportedly tried to get the ruling changed to a passed ball, but their efforts were fruitless. Chesbro died in 1931, at the age of 57. He was elected to the Hall of Fame in 1946.

TOMMY LEACH, THIRD BASE/OUTFIELD

Leach spent portions of four seasons in the minors before earning full-time playing status with the Louisville Colonels in 1899. Transferred to Pittsburgh the following year, he slowly emerged as one of the Pirates' most reliable hitters. Despite his diminutive stature (5-foot-6, 150 pounds), he finished among the top 10 in triples and homers six times apiece. He was modest about his power numbers, commenting in later years, "Sometimes they played me right in back of the infield. Every so often, I'd manage to drive a ball between the outfielders and it would roll to the fence . . . I don't ever recall getting a home run on a ball that hit outside the park."

In 1905, Leach sustained an injury in a collision at home plate. He had difficulty throwing across the diamond after that, and Fred Clarke moved him to the outfield. During the course of his career, Leach spent roughly equal portions of time at third base and in center field. He covered a lot of ground, posting the highest range factor among outfielders four times and third basemen on three occasions.

While stationed at third during a 1904 exhibition game, Leach made an embarrassing mistake. Chasing a popup behind the bag, he was temporarily blinded by the sun. "I seemed to see two little specks of white up above the blinding rays, but I put up my hands as I ran and a few seconds later had the ball in my glove," he told a *Cleveland Press* reporter. Immediately following the catch, the sure-handed infielder was surprised to find teammate Honus Wagner standing near third base with another ball in his possession. Wagner politely explained that the one Leach had caught was a foul ball thrown back onto the field by a fan. The other had dropped behind the bag for a double.

Leach's 172 career triples are among the top 25 totals of all time. His first-inning triple in Game 1 of the 1903 Fall Classic (off of Cy Young) was the first base hit in World Series history. Honus Wagner singled

Leach home, making him the first player to score a run in the Series as well. He collected nine hits and seven RBIs that October. Returning to the Fall Classic with the Pirates in 1909, he hit .360 and scored eight runs in Pittsburgh's seven-game win over the Tigers.

Leach's tour of the majors lasted for 19 years. In 1920, he helped organize the Florida State League and spent three seasons as a player-manager for the Tampa Smokers. He later scouted for the Boston Braves. After leaving baseball behind, he invested in the citrus trade in Haines City, Florida. He lived to the ripe old age of 91.

DEACON PHILLIPPE, PITCHER

Charles Phillippe was given the nickname "Deacon" early in his career due to his humble manner and orderly behavior on and off the field. Unlike many players of the era, he didn't drink, smoke, or swear. He was blessed with a sharp curve and exceptional control. Asked about his success on the mound, he remarked that he liked to "keep batters guessing." He added, "I study the batsman in every way, his position in the box, his general attitude, the way he holds the bat."

Phillippe got a late start in baseball. He was 26 years old when he made his big-league debut with Louisville in 1899. The Colonels finished below .500 that year, but Phillippe managed to win 21 games anyway. Transferred to Pittsburgh in 1900, he would string together four consecutive 20-win seasons with the Bucs, reaching a high of 25 victories in 1903. From 1900–1903, his ERA never progressed beyond the 3.00 mark.

Aside from his one season in Louisville, Phillippe spent his entire career in Pittsburgh. He retired with a total of 189 wins—an average of 15 per year. His strikeout-to-walk ratio was the best in the NL on four occasions. His lifetime ERA of 2.59 is among the top 100 totals of all time among pitchers with at least 1,000 innings of work.

In Game 1 of the 1903 World Series, Phillippe beat Cy Young, 7–3. He had 10 strikeouts that afternoon. Fred Clare kept handing him the ball throughout the Series, and he ended up winning three of his five starts. When Pittsburgh returned to the postseason in 1909, Phillippe was 37 years old and suffering from arm trouble. In a diminished role, he performed admirably, tossing six shutout frames. He retired with a serviceable 2.70 ERA in seven World Series appearances.

By 1910, Phillippe was employed mostly as a closer, winning 14 of 16 decisions for a league-leading .875 percentage. It was his last great season. He fell from the major-league ranks on the heels of multiple ineffective appearances the following year. Finished as a player after the 1913 slate, he scouted for the Pirates and held various odd jobs in Pittsburgh. He lived to the age of 79.

GINGER BEAUMONT, CENTER FIELD

Ginger Beaumont didn't look like someone who was capable of stealing bases and scoring runs. He carried 190 pounds on his 5-foot-8 frame. But appearances were deceiving. Beaumont was once clocked at 4.4 seconds from home to first. He navigated the bases with remarkable agility, scoring at least 90 runs in six consecutive seasons from 1899–1904.

During his debut season with the Pirates in 1899, Beaumont proved he belonged in the majors with a .352 average in 111 games. On his birthday that year, he beat out six infield hits. He remembered the game quite clearly long after his retirement, commenting, "My fourth time at bat, the third baseman stood 10 feet from home plate and I still beat my bunt out."

Beaumont quickly became the NL's premier leadoff man. A columnist for the *Pittsburgh Press* recounts that the somewhat paunchy center fielder was one of the "slowest-moving men" when walking to and from his position. According to the same writer, "[H]e lost every semblance of laziness and was a regular greyhound on the base paths" when it was his turn to bat. Beaumont participated in a pregame running competition one day in Cincinnati and was allegedly clocked at three seconds from home plate to first base.

While playing for the Pirates from 1899–1906, Beaumont led the league in hits three times. He won a batting crown in 1902, with a .357 mark. During Pittsburgh's pennant run of 1903, he paced the circuit in total bases. Although he failed to hit in the first three games of the World Series that year, he went 9-for-18 in the next four contests. This included a 4-for-5 performance in Game 6.

As time wore on, Beaumont developed leg problems, which led to his eventual trade to Boston. After leading the league in hits again while playing for the Doves in 1907, he began a rapid decline. Lacking the speed to beat out infield hits, his batting average hovered in the .260 range for the next three seasons. He finished his big-league career with the Cubs in 1910, and then spent one year with the St. Paul Saints of the AA. He retired to his 180-acre farm in Wisconsin.

SAM LEEVER, PITCHER

Born in Goshen, Ohio, Leever received the nickname the "Goshen Schoolmaster" because he taught high school for several years before signing his first professional contract. He was never a hard thrower, relying instead on superb control and an excellent curveball. He spent his entire 13-year career in Pittsburgh, reaching the 20-win plateau on four occasions. From 1899–1908, he averaged 18 victories per year and placed among the top 10 in shutouts on seven occasions. He led the league in that category during the 1903 campaign.

Like his talented staff mate Deacon Phillippe, Leever was a late arrival to Organized Baseball. He was already in his mid-20s by the time he made his minor-league debut for the Richmond Giants of the Atlantic League in 1897. He performed well, earning himself a call to Pittsburgh the following year. He reported to camp with a sore arm and was promptly sent back to Richmond, where he won 14 more games and helped the club to a league championship. He was recalled by the Pirates near the end of the 1898 campaign.

In 1899, Leever was a workhorse for Pittsburgh, tossing a league-high 379 innings. The team was mediocre that year, and he posted a sub-.500 record. As the Pirates improved dramatically through time, so did Leever's winning percentages. From 1901–1905, the right-hander led the league three times in that department. His lifetime mark of .660 is among the top 20 totals of all time for pitchers with at least 100 decisions.

During the Pirates' World Series run of 1903, Leever injured his arm while competing in a Pennsylvania trapshooting contest. He started Game 2 of the Series but was removed after surrendering two runs, three hits, and a walk in one inning of work. He returned for Game 6 and went the distance in a 6–3 loss. He was later unfairly accused by some of slacking off on the mound.

After his 36th birthday, Leever was used increasingly in relief. He closed 40 games for the Pirates from 1908–1910, posting a 29–13 record and a 2.43 ERA. He logged his last professional season in 1911, with the Minneapolis Millers of the AA. When his playing days were over, he returned to teaching and served as postmaster in his hometown of Goshen.

In 1924, it was falsely reported that Leever was dead. Upon reading his own obituary in the newspaper, he felt compelled to dispel any rumors of his demise. He told the *Sporting News* with tongue in cheek that he had never felt better and had "no thought whatsoever of cashing in."

FAST FACT: From June 2–June 8, 1903, Pittsburgh moundsmen threw six consecutive shutouts, beating the Giants, Beaneaters, and Phillies by a combined score of 32–0, establishing a major-league record that still stands.

3

CHICAGO CUBS

1906–1910

Long before billy goats and June swoons, the Cubs were among the most powerful teams in the majors. Their origins can be traced back to the 1860s, when a number of all-professional clubs were formed. Many of the early organizations adopted names from their uniform colors. Chicago's squad, originally known as the "Chicago Baseball Club," chose white uniforms and began referring to themselves as the "White Stockings." They joined the National Association of Baseball Players in 1870 and won a championship that year.

In 1871, the first all-professional league was formed, and the White Stockings became charter members. Financed by businessman William Hulbert, a stadium known as the Union Baseball Grounds was built in the northeast corner of Grant Park. The structure was destroyed during the Great Chicago Fire, which raged for two days and killed hundreds of people. The homeless White Stockings finished the season on the road in borrowed uniforms, coming up just two games shy of another championship. They withdrew from the league while the city was being rebuilt but returned in 1874, playing games at the 23rd Street Grounds.

Disgruntled by an absence of enforceable contracts, which led many Chicago players to jump to other clubs, William Hulbert rallied for the establishment of a more organized league. He vowed that the new circuit would have a stricter code of ethics to discourage gambling and alcohol abuse, which had pervaded the sport. Before the 1876 slate,

Hulbert convinced a number of teams to join the new alliance, among them the St. Louis Brown Stockings, Philadelphia A's, and Hartford Dark Blues. Those who refused to make the change either folded or assumed minor-league status.

The White Stockings quickly emerged as one of the most powerful teams in the National League, capturing a championship during the inaugural season of 1876. Led by nineteenth-century icons Cap Anson and King Kelly, five more championships would follow between 1880–1886. When Hulbert died before the 1882 campaign, sporting goods mogul (and former pitcher) Albert Spalding assumed ownership. The team would undergo several name changes throughout the next two decades, playing as the Colts from 1890–1897, the Orphans from 1898–1902, and the Cubs thereafter.

After a rough patch during the 1890s, Chicago slowly climbed back into contention. By the time former baseball writer Charles Murphy bought the franchise in 1905, the Cubs were on the cusp of greatness. From 1906–1908, they compiled a winning percentage of .703—the most successful three-year run in team history. At the root of their success was a trio of talented infielders.

In 1910, the double-play combination of Tinker to Evers to Chance was immortalized in a poem written by New York journalist Franklin Pierce Adams. Years later, all three subjects were inducted into the Hall of Fame together. But despite the lavish praise, Adams's "trio of bear cubs" (which he described as being "fleeter than birds") was actually a dysfunctional unit. Frank Chance, who served as player-manager for eight seasons in Chicago, was a strict disciplinarian who was widely disliked by his players. Joe Tinker and Johnny Evers went for decades without speaking to one another. The source of their animosity is still under debate. Tinker claimed that the two had squabbled over a cab fare. Evers told a different story, insisting that Tinker had thrown the ball too hard at close range one day and then laughed when the force of his toss bent Evers's fingers back. Whatever the case, the two remained estranged until the 1930s, when both men were invited to help broadcast the World Series. Upon seeing one another, there was an awkward silence, followed by a hug that ended a rift of roughly 30 years.

The Cubs' success in the early Deadball Era was not built entirely upon crisp defense and timely hitting. Their pitching staff was among the most formidable in the majors. From 1906–1910, Chicago hurlers posted a team ERA of 1.97. The liveliest arm belonged to future Hall of Famer Mordecai Brown, who won no fewer than 20 games in six consecutive seasons. Due to a pair of childhood misadventures, Brown's pitching hand was deformed. The irregularity gave his pitches dramatic movement and kept big-league hitters at a disadvantage for 14 seasons.

With a gaggle of all-time greats leading the charge, the Cubs made four postseason appearances in a five-year span. They fell short of a pennant in 1909, finishing second to the Pirates. In 1906, Chicago set the all-time mark for regular-season victories with 116. It was tied in 2001, by the Mariners, who had the benefit of a 162-game schedule (before 1961, teams played 154 games per season). Despite their record-setting .763 winning percentage (still the highest in modern history), the Cubs were upset by the White Sox in the 1906 World Series. They bounced back with a pair of world championships in 1907 and 1908, before dropping another Series to the A's in 1910.

The fact that the Cubs have not won a Fall Classic in more than 100 years (currently the longest dry spell of any major-league club) has consistently drawn attention to their success during the Deadball Era. From 1906–1910, Chicago compiled the best five-year record in baseball history. Aside from the four men who received their just deserts at Cooperstown, the team had one of the most talented rosters ever assembled.

JOHNNY EVERS, SECOND BASE

Evers was generally regarded as one of the smartest players of his era. He had an intricate knowledge of the game and a big mouth to go with it. According to one source, his nightly routine included reading the rule book in bed while eating candy bars. That practice paid off on September 23, 1908, when his appeal to umpire Hank O'Day ultimately robbed the Giants of a pennant. Evers brought O'Day's attention to the fact that New York's rookie first baseman Fred Merkle had not touched second base on an apparent game-winning hit by Al Bridwell. The contest was declared a tie, and a one-game playoff became necessary when the Cubs and Giants remained knotted in first place on the last day of the season. The Cubs won the playoff, 4–2, and the World Series in five games.

An incessant talker who argued with umpires constantly, Evers was suspended multiple times during his 18 years in the majors. According to legend, Cubs owner Charles Murphy once offered him a new suit if he could go two weeks without being ejected from a game. After collecting the prize, Evers was tossed out of the very next contest. Known as "Crab" or "Trojan" to contemporaries, the scrappy infielder was one of the finest bunters in history. He rarely struck out and was an imminent threat to steal, swiping at least 25 bases on seven occasions. Defensively, there were few second basemen who were as adept at turning the 6–4–3 double play.

By his own admission, Evers overcompensated for his small size. His playing weight was listed at anywhere from 100 to 130 pounds. He usually picked out bigger players to spar with, commenting in later years, "Somebody always held them. No one ever thought of holding me." Although Evers claimed that his feud with Joe Tinker ended in 1909, most sources beg to differ. Even so, Evers never let his differences with Tinker stand between them on the field. "What a guy thinks about another guy on a ball team doesn't mean a thing," he once said. "Tinker and myself hated each other, but we loved the Cubs."

A lifetime .270 hitter in the regular season, Evers almost always raised his game to another level in the World Series. Disregarding a poor showing in the 1906 Fall Classic against the White Sox, he compiled a .375 cumulative batting average in three other October showdowns. He peaked at .438 in 1914.

A string of personal tragedies befell Evers in 1910, and he suffered what has been described as a "nervous breakdown." Used sparingly the following year, he compiled a substandard .226 batting average. He bounced back in 1913, with his best offensive season ever, hitting .341 while putting up career-high numbers in several categories. Named player-manager of the Cubs in 1913, he guided the club to a distant third-place finish. He was traded to the Braves in the offseason. Free from the burdens of managing, Evers had an exceptional season, capturing MVP honors and helping the Braves to an improbable World Series victory over the A's.

Evers kicked around the majors for portions of five more seasons before making his last appearance. A native of Troy, New York, he operated a sporting goods store and served as superintendent of

Bleecker Stadium in Albany after leaving baseball behind. He died in 1947, at the age of 75.

JOE TINKER, SHORTSTOP

Born in Muscotah, Kansas, Tinker lost his twin sister at an early age, making him an only child. His family moved to Kansas City when he was quite young, and he finished his schooling there. He spent two seasons in the minors before receiving a summons to Chicago in 1902. In those days, the Cubs were known as the Orphans. Joe's previous baseball experience had been primarily as a third baseman, and he was reluctant to make the switch to shortstop.

Tinker is among the more obscure figures in the Hall of Fame. He didn't hit for average or power. His highest single-season home-run total was six, but only two actually left the park on the fly. Tinker's highest batting average (.317) came in 1913, after he had been traded from the Cubs. Typically occupying the lower third of the batting order, he developed a reputation as a clutch performer. During the infamous "Merkle Game," which ended in a 1–1 tie and necessitated a one-game playoff between the Giants and Cubs in 1908, Tinker's home run off of Christy Mathewson accounted for the only Chicago run of the afternoon. In the one-game playoff that followed, Tinker's third-inning triple ignited a four-run rally. Arguably the greatest pitcher of the era, Mathewson referred to Tinker as the toughest NL batter he had ever faced.

Early in his career, Tinker had a short swing that made him vulnerable to slow curves on the outside corner. As time wore on, he made adjustments, using a longer bat and standing deeper in the box. When the Cubs suffered a slew of injuries in 1908, Tinker rose to the occasion, leading the club in homers, RBIs, and slugging percentage. He drove in no fewer than 64 runs in seven seasons. On the base paths, he had adequate speed, stealing 20 or more bases every year from 1902–1912.

Had the award existed in his time, Tinker would likely have won several Gold Gloves. He led the league in fielding percentage and range factor four times apiece, prompting a writer from *Baseball Magazine* to rank him second to Honus Wagner among NL shortstops.

Traded to the Reds in 1913, Tinker served as a player-manager. He had a lenient approach to the job, remarking to a reporter, "Just because a man is placed in charge of a club does not make it necessary for him to be a task master or a tyrant." Perhaps he should have been more stringent, as the Reds finished well below .500 that year. When owner Garry Herrmann told Tinker that he intended to send a spy on road trips to check up on players, Tinker refused to sign a contract for the following year. He ended up in the Federal League as a player-manager.

In two FL seasons, Tinker guided the Chicago club to a pennant and a second-place finish. He returned to the Cubs when the league folded after the 1915 slate. The Cubs weren't very good, placing fifth in Tinker's return. For several years, Tinker owned and managed the Columbus franchise in the American Association. He moved to Orlando, Florida, when his wife fell ill. Tragically, she committed suicide on Christmas Day 1923. Tinker built two racetracks and a ballpark with real estate earnings but lost it all during the Great Depression. He was still alive when he was selected for the Hall of Fame in 1946.

FRANK CHANCE, FIRST BASE

Chance once received an unusual testimonial from Christy Mathewson. In his book *Pitching in a Pinch*, released in 1912, Mathewson wrote, "If [Chance] has to choose between accepting a pair of spikes in a vital part of his anatomy and getting a putout, or dodging the spikes and losing the putout, he always takes a putout."

Chance was more than content with that distinction. Serving as player-manager of the greatest Cubs squads of all time, he once balked at acquiring Chief Wilson of the Pirates because he felt Wilson was too polite. A writer from the Baseball Hall of Fame once remarked, "Chance was of the win-at-all-costs school of baseball and played at a time when fraternization with the other team might amount to a punch in the mouth or a sarcastic remark." He kept himself in shape as an amateur boxer in the offseason, and his skills were noted by some of the premier pugilists of his time.

Born in Fresno, California, Chance was studying to become a dentist when he was spotted by Cubs star outfielder Bill Lange, who encouraged the club to sign him. Chance hit .279 in his debut and would remain in Chicago for the next 14 seasons. As legend has it, Chance once singled and stole his way around the bases, breaking a late-inning tie with the Cincinnati Reds. In gratitude, Cubs owner Charles Murphy gave him a 10 percent interest in the club. It paid huge dividends, as Chance later sold his share for a vast sum.

Chance picked up two nicknames during the course of his career, "Husk," due to his athletic build, and "Peerless Leader," from players who both respected and resented him. He began his career as a backup catcher, frequently sitting out with broken fingers. When Bill Hanlon left the team abruptly in the spring of 1903, it left an opening at first base. Manager Frank Selee asked Chance to fill the position. In 1905, Selee fell seriously ill, and Chance was installed as his replacement.

Chance was as unsportsmanlike as they come. He once incited a riot at the Polo Grounds in New York when he physically assaulted Hall of Fame pitcher Joe McGinnity. On multiple occasions, he threw beer bottles at fans. Chance had a tendency to crowd the plate and was beaned multiple times. He developed blood clots in his brain and was operated on in 1912. A heated argument with owner Charles Murphy in his hospital room resulted in his release from the Cubs.

The bulk of Chance's playing experience came between 1903–1910. He broke the .300 mark at the plate four times in that span, while leading the league twice in stolen bases—a somewhat remarkable feat for the era considering that nearly every capable player was expected to steal. Chance played in four World Series, accruing a healthy .402 on-base percentage. Against the Tigers and A's in 1908 and 1910, he logged six multihit games and drove in six runs. When the Cubs shockingly lost to their crosstown rivals in the 1906 Fall Classic, Chance remarked bluntly, "There is one thing I will never believe and that is the Sox are better than the Cubs."

Defecting to the Yankees in 1913, he finished his career in New York. His lifetime winning percentage with the Cubs was a lofty .664. He remains the franchise leader in stolen bases. The Veteran's Committee deemed him Hall of Fame worthy in 1946.

MORDECAI BROWN, PITCHER

Due to a childhood mishap, Brown lost most of his right index finger in a piece of farm equipment. Shortly afterward, he fell while chasing a rabbit and broke his other fingers. The result was a permanently bent middle finger, a paralyzed little finger, and a stub for an index finger, which earned him the nickname "Three Finger Brown." The deformity gave his pitches remarkable movement and kept major-league hitters at bay for 14 seasons.

Brown grew up in an Indiana mining town and was taught to pitch by former minor leaguer Legs O'Connell. Although much would be written about his deformed hand throughout the years and how it improved his performance, the burly right-hander told reporters that it "was a terrific handicap. Few know the excruciating pain I suffered when I had to grip the ball in a certain way. I always felt that if I had a normal hand, I would have been a greater pitcher."

As it was, Brown was among the greatest of his generation. In two minor-league seasons, he won 52 games. He was signed by the Cardinals, and despite posting a 2.60 ERA in 1903, Brown finished the season with a sub-.500 record. In December of that year, he was traded to the Cubs in a four-player deal that included right-hander Jack Taylor. In 1904, the Cardinals appeared to have gotten the better end of the transaction when Taylor collected 21 victories to Brown's 15. But throughout the next several seasons, Brown emerged as one of the most successful hurlers in the majors. His 1906 effort was among the finest ever recorded, as he won 26 games—nine by shutout—and compiled an incredible 1.04 ERA.

Brown was one of the hardest-working pitchers in the majors. In addition to the 123 starts he made between 1908–1911, he also closed 65 games, picking up 32 saves (although the statistic did not exist then). He was on the mound for the famous one-game playoff against the Giants in 1908. After the New Yorkers jumped out to a 2–0 lead off of Jack Pfiester in the first inning, Brown was summoned to the rubber. Without even warming up, he slammed the door on the Giants as the Cubs rallied to clinch the pennant with a 4–2 win.

There were times when Brown could have used the extra rest. In the 1906 World Series, he tossed a four-hitter in the opener but lost. He followed with a two-hit shutout in Game 4. Manager Frank Chance tried to turn the tide of the Series by sending Brown back to the mound in Game 6, but it was a mistake. Completely out of gas, Brown was charged with 7 runs in 1.2 innings. He appeared in nine World Series games for the Cubs, winning five of them and posting an ERA below 3.00. In 1907–1908, he tossed a total of 20 postseason innings without yielding an earned run.

Christy Mathewson once referred to Brown as the "perfect pitcher." Teammate Johnny Evers remarked that Brown had "plenty of nerve, ability, and willingness to work under any conditions. He was charitable and friendly to his foes." In 1912, Brown lost his effectiveness and was traded to the Reds. He jumped to the rival FL and led the Chicago club to a championship in 1915. When the league folded, he returned to the Cubs. He later pitched for several minor-league clubs and tried his hand at managing in the Three-I League.

In retirement, Brown owned and operated a gas station in Terre Haute. He died before his Hall of Fame induction in 1949. He still holds modern-era Cubs records for most shutouts (48) and lowest ERA (1.80).

FRANK SCHULTE, OUTFIELD

Schulte's father was a contractor and didn't feel that baseball was a "honest" profession. He offered Frank a lucrative job as a bookkeeper on the condition that he quit playing. Frank's refusal worked in the Cubs' favor, as he patrolled the Chicago outfield for portions of 13 seasons.

Carrying the colorful nickname "Wildfire," Schulte had a number of odd superstitions. He was known to comb the streets looking for hairpins, which he believed could predict his performance at the plate. According to Schulte, the bigger the hairpin, the better his performance was likely to be. He also alleged that a bent pin could forecast the direction of his base hits. If he fell into a slump, he would often blame his shoes for the lack of productivity.

Using bats with unusually thin handles (he reportedly broke as many as 50 of them per season), Schulte hit safely in each World Series game during the 1907 and 1908 campaigns. During his four Fall Classic appearances with Chicago, he assembled a 13-game hitting streak—

among the longest in history. He accrued a lifetime postseason batting average of .321.

Schulte's success was not limited to the World Series. He finished among the top five in homers on five occasions and became the first player to launch four grand slams in one season. He accomplished the feat in 1911, which was his most fruitful year at the plate. He led the league with 21 homers, 107 RBIs, and a .534 slugging percentage, winning the Chalmers Award (the equivalent of the MVP) by a somewhat narrow margin over Christy Mathewson of the Giants.

Schulte was a daring baserunner who stole home 22 times in his career. While he had some power, he was an excellent bunter as well, executing a career-high 31 sacrifices during his MVP year. After finishing third in homers during the 1915 slate, his numbers dropped off, and he was traded to the Pirates. He finished his major-league career in Washington and continued in the minors through the 1922 slate. He retired to Oakland and lived to the age of 67.

JOHNNY KLING, CATCHER

Born in Kansas City, Kling worked in his family's bakery, making deliveries with a horse-drawn wagon. After receiving complaints from a customer about undelivered bread one day, Kling's father became suspicious and tailed the delivery wagon to a field where a ballgame was taking place. Johnny's early infatuation with the sport would lead to a successful major-league career.

Kling was the most dominant defensive catcher of the early twentieth century. From 1902–1911, he led the NL in putouts six times, assists twice, and double plays twice. He also foiled more attempted steals than any of his NL counterparts on three occasions. His lifetime total in that category currently ranks fifth on the all-time list.

The Missouri native began his career in 1895, in the Western Association. He would remain in the minors until September 1900. Catchers were not expected to hit well in the Deadball Era, but Kling was an exception. During his first decade of big-league play, he posted batting averages of .269 or better eight times. He enjoyed his most industrious year at the plate in 1903, when he reached career highs in runs scored (67), hits (146), doubles (29), and RBIs (68). His 13 triples that year were the highest single-season total for a catcher in the 1900s. The mark was tied in 1966, by Tim McCarver of the Cardinals.

Known for his ability to work with batterymates, he kept up an ongoing dialog, a practice that earned him the nickname "Noisy." He was among the first to use pitchouts to break up hit-and-run plays. He rarely argued with umpires and sometimes even alerted them if an unusual play was coming. He maintained a clean lifestyle, avoiding the vices that consumed many players of his era.

After the 1908 campaign, Kling won a world billiards championship and invested in a large pool hall in Kansas City. He arranged for a leave of absence from the Cubs and did not play in 1909. He had a decent regular season in 1910, but a lackluster World Series, managing just one hit in five games. He was never much of a postseason hitter anyway, retiring with a .185 average in 21 October contests.

Kling's productivity dropped off sharply in 1911, and he was traded to the Boston Rustlers. He bounced back with a .317 showing at the plate the following season while serving as a player-manager. The club (renamed the Braves) lost more than 100 games and finished in last place. Kling was replaced at the helm by George Stallings and traded to Cincinnati for the 1913 slate. Platooned with Tommy Clarke, he hit at a respectable .273 clip. It was his last major-league campaign. After his baseball retirement, he moved on to a successful career in real estate. He owned the Kansas City Blues of the AA from 1933–1937.

ED REULBACH, PITCHER

Reulbach was a multisport star at the University of Notre Dame. He opted to skip his senior year there and enroll in med school at the University of Vermont. He got noticed by a Cubs scout while playing for the UVM baseball team and was given a contract offer he could not refuse. He made his Chicago debut in 1905.

The solidly built right-hander (6-foot-1, 190 pounds) was one of the NL's top hurlers for several seasons. He led the league in winning percentage from 1906–1908, posting a stellar 60–15 record. Unbeknownst to teammates and managers, he had a weak left eye that affected his pitching and fielding under certain conditions. He didn't reveal the handicap until after his retirement.

Reulbach was so reliable, he was often called upon in relief. He closed 32 games for the Cubs between 1905–1909. In that span, his ERA never rose above 2.03. Using a dramatically high leg kick, he tossed a pair of one-hitters and six two-hitters during his 13 years in the majors. In 1906, he began a 17-game winning streak that stretched into June of the following year. In 1908, he set a NL record (later broken) with 44 consecutive scoreless frames. He appeared in four World Series with the Cubs, notching a 2–0 record and 3.03 ERA in seven assignments. He held the White Sox to a single hit in Game 2 of the 1906 Fall Classic, a postseason record he would share with two other pitchers until Don Larsen tossed a perfect game in 1956.

A writer from *Baseball Magazine* once referred to Reulbach as "one of the greatest pitchers that the National League ever produced and one of the finest, clean-cut gentlemen who ever wore a big-league uniform." Clean living could not prevent Reulbach's numbers from gradually tapering off, and he was traded to Brooklyn during the 1913 slate. His last great season came in 1915, when he joined the FL and won 21 games for the fifth-place Newark club.

Reulbach skipped part of the 1910 season to attend to his son, who had contracted diphtheria. The years after his retirement were not kind, as he spent a small fortune trying to nurse the lad, who was incessantly ill, back to health. Despite Reulbach's exhaustive efforts, his son died relatively young in 1931.

ORVAL OVERALL, PITCHER

Overall's name sounds like something out of a children's book. He pitched in the majors for just seven seasons, hitting his peak during the Cubs' five-year era of dominance. While wearing a Chicago uniform between 1906–1910, he fashioned a remarkable 82–38 record, leading the league twice in shutouts and once in strikeouts. He was an intimidating presence for the era at 6-foot-2, 214 pounds and knew how to handle himself in a fight.

Following a spring training game in 1904, members of the Cubs attended a professional boxing match along with several of their minor-league opponents. The crowd grew restless when one of the combatants failed to show, and looking to avoid an unpleasant scene, the promoter began combing the audience for potential challengers. Overall, who had pitched for the Tacoma Tigers that day, agreed to trade punches, but despite his imposing size he was paid no respect. "I'll give you two rounds," the experienced fighter said condescendingly. A worthy adversary, Overall literally knocked the man out of the ring. The big right-hander would demonstrate his pitching prowess that year by tossing 510.2 innings and winning 32 games in the Pacific Coast League. By April 1905, he had joined the Cincinnati Reds.

The Reds were a middling squad in 1905, and Overall posted 18 wins against 23 losses. Off to a 4–5 start the following season, he was traded to Chicago. Frank Chance believed that the big right-hander was being overworked and offered him ample rest between starts. The results were dramatic, as Overall went 12–3 with a 1.88 ERA in the second half of the 1906 campaign.

Overall relied heavily on his curveball, which reportedly had a sharp break. He won 14 straight decisions from August 1907 to May of the following year. He was especially effective in World Series play, recording a 3–1 record with a 1.58 ERA in eight appearances (all with Chicago). His finest effort came in 1908, when he completely stifled the Tigers, allowing just seven hits in 18 1/3 innings of work, while striking out 15.

Before the 1911 slate, Overall got into a contract dispute and did not play in the majors. Instead, he pitched in a semipro league and sustained an arm injury. He attempted a comeback with the Cubs in 1913, but failed to make the grade. After his retirement, he took over his family's citrus farm. In 1918, he ran for Congress but was not elected. He was appointed director of the California State Automobile Association in 1936. He died in Fresno, California, at the age of 66.

SOLLY HOFMAN, OUTFIELD/UTILITY

As a 21-year-old rookie in 1904, Hofman had the gumption to tell manager Frank Selee that he could play better than Harry Steinfeldt, Johnny Evers, and Joe Tinker. In the same breath, Hofman told Chance he was slowing up at his position, commenting brashly, "Give me that mitt and I'll show you how first base should be played." As Hofman tried out numerous infield stations and proved his aptitude at each one, other players began to worry that they might lose their jobs. To draw attention away from himself, Evers allegedly pulled Chance aside one day and suggested he use Hofman as a replacement for center fielder Jimmy Slagle. Hofman did become a regular in the Cubs' outfield in 1909, but not before cementing a reputation as one of the best utility men in the NL.

Hofman played every position on the diamond except for pitcher and catcher. Chance put so much stock in his versatile jack-of-all-trades that he refused to allow Hofman to get married until after the 1908 World Series was over, insisting that it was for the "good of the team." Hofman hit .316 in the Series that year.

In 1908 and 1909, Hofman was named to *Collier's* All-American Team. A lifetime .298 hitter in postseason play, he enjoyed his most productive regular season in 1910, when he collected 43 extra-base hits and scored 83 runs, while driving in 86. He finished the campaign with a .325 batting average—more than 50 points higher than his lifetime mark.

Hofman was nicknamed "Circus Solly" after a comic strip character. Some say he earned the moniker with his acrobatic catches in the outfield. In 14 seasons, he fielded his position well above the league average. In 1912, he developed leg trouble and was traded to Pittsburgh. He jumped to the FL in 1914. When the circuit went belly up, he made brief appearances with the Yankees and Cubs. The 1916 season was his last in the majors.

Hofman operated a youth baseball clinic on the West Side Grounds (home of the Cubs during their glory years) and served as a high school coach in 1925. His nephew, Bobby Hofman, played for the Giants from 1949–1957. Solly didn't live to see Bobby's entire career. He passed away in 1956, at the age of 73.

FAST FACT: The Chicago White Sox beat the Cubs in the 1906 World Series despite compiling a miserable .230 team batting average during the regular season—second lowest in the majors. Journalists referred to the ChiSox as the "Hitless Wonders."

4

PHILADELPHIA ATHLETICS

1910–1914

In 1894, Cincinnati sports editor Ban Johnson was appointed president of the struggling Western League—a Class A circuit. Under Johnson's dynamic leadership, the WL became one of the most profitable organizations in the country. By the end of the nineteenth century, some Western League franchises had larger followings than their National League counterparts.

When the NL ousted four teams from its lineup after the 1899 campaign, Johnson saw it as an opportunity to grow. He moved the St. Paul Saints to Chicago and placed them under the control of Charles Comiskey. He planted the Grand Rapids Furnituremakers in Cleveland, where the Spiders had been driven out after fielding one of the worst teams in history. The new alignment—renamed the American League—also featured a Milwaukee franchise, managed by Connie Mack.

Mack began his career as a catcher. Although only moderately talented, he earned abundant praise for his innovative style of play. He was among the first to position himself directly behind home plate. Intimately familiar with the rule book, he exploited any loophole that worked to his advantage. In addition to tipping the bats of opponents with his glove, he was known to deliberately drop pop flies in the interest of turning double plays (both practices were eventually prohibited).

Finished as a major-league player by 1897, Mack took over as manager of the Brewers.

Before the 1901 slate, Johnson announced his intention of directly competing with the NL. He enlisted Mack's help to establish a new franchise in Philadelphia. The team name was borrowed from an American Association club that had operated from 1882–1890. Mack served as treasurer, part-owner, and manager—a post he would occupy for 50 years. With additional franchises added in Boston, Baltimore, and Washington, the AL was officially elevated to major-league status.

There was no maximum AL salary, and many NL players were willing to make the jump. The Athletics' most notable acquisition was second baseman Napoleon Lajoie, who deserted the Phillies for a $1,400 pay raise. Lajoie was dazzling in his AL debut, pacing the circuit in over a dozen statistical categories, including batting average (.426), doubles (48), and RBIs (125). Despite his contributions, the A's finished in fourth place.

In 1902, Mack again used his charms to land Hall of Fame right fielder Elmer Flick—another Phillies standout. Unfortunately, the crosstown franchise obtained a court injunction prohibiting several established stars from playing for the A's. Both Flick and Lajoie were lost to the Cleveland Bronchos (later known as the Indians). Mack's squad did just fine without them, finishing in first place with an 83–53 record. There was no World Series that year.

The Athletics' success in the early years was built primarily around pitching. From 1903–1907, the starting rotation featured a trio of Cooperstown greats. Eddie Plank, Rube Waddell, and Chief Bender collectively won close to 300 games in that span, guiding the A's to a World Series berth and a pair of second-place finishes.

After a disappointing sixth-place showing in 1908, the A's came within three and a half games of a pennant the following year. By then, several members of the old guard had been replaced—most notably Waddell, whose eccentric behavior off the field led many to believe that he was cognitively impaired. Mack later referred to the erratic hurler as the "atom bomb of baseball before the atom bomb was discovered."

With Plank and Bender still anchoring the pitching corps, the A's made numerous upgrades at other positions—especially the infield. Summoned from the minors in September 1908, third baseman Frank "Home Run" Baker was among the game's earliest power hitters. The two he hit in the 1911 World Series earned him his nickname. While Baker was forging a Hall of Fame career at the hot corner, Ivy League graduate Eddie Collins emerged as one of the most gifted second basemen of the era. Ascending to full-time playing status in 1909, Collins impressed teammates and opponents alike with his remarkable glove work and sharp batting eye. He spent six of his best seasons in Philadelphia, capturing multiple fielding titles, while leading the league in runs scored for three consecutive years.

With a star-studded cast, the A's captured back-to-back pennants in 1910 and 1911, making relatively quick work of the Cubs and Giants in the World Series. They "slumped" to third place the following year but came storming back in 1913, to knock off the Giants again in an October rematch. At the peak of the dynasty, Connie Mack quipped to a sportswriter that he wouldn't trade any of his infielders for $100,000 (an enormous sum in those days). The quote became a catchphrase that stuck. Despite their many contributions, Mack's so-called "$100,000 Infield" could not prevent the 1914 campaign from ending in disaster.

After getting off to a lukewarm start in the spring, the A's clawed their way to the top by early June. They built an insurmountable lead over the second-place Red Sox with an incredible 24–2 run that stretched from July 11 to August 13. Meanwhile, in the NL, the Braves staged one of the most improbable pennant bids ever, going from worst to first in a six-week span. Entering the Series as decided underdogs, Boston players remained supremely confident. Infielder Johnny Evers remarked that the A's were "destined to receive the one biggest surprise of their lives." Echoing that sentiment, manager George Stallings declared that his club would "knock Mack's block off." Both prophesies were fulfilled as Braves hurlers limited the A's to a total of five earned runs in 39 innings. The result was a shocking Series sweep and the end of the Athletics' era of dominance.

Disappointed with the outcome, Mack traded off most of his best players. Bender and Plank ended up in the rival Federal League, while Collins was sold to the White Sox. Baker opted to sit out the 1915 slate when his salary demands were not met. As a result of Mack's epic rebuilding project, the A's languished in the AL basement for seven straight seasons. They would return to glory in the late 1920s (details of which can be found in a future chapter).

While discussions of the Athletics' supremacy during the Deadball Era rarely surface nowadays, the club is indisputably among the greatest in baseball history. In addition to the four Hall of Famers who helped carry the club to four pennants in a five-year span, the "Mackmen" (as they were sometimes referred to by journalists) had one of the finest assortments of minor stars ever assembled.

EDDIE PLANK, PITCHER

Plank was not a colorful character and left behind few humorous anecdotes. What he did leave behind was a legacy of smart, reliable pitching. Born in Gettysburg, he once held a job as a tour guide for the famous battlefield. He had little interest in baseball growing up. "I never even read the scores or knew who played in the big leagues until I was 20 years old," he told a journalist. After graduating from Gettysburg College, Connie Mack accepted him on the team without a shred of minor-league experience.

Plank began his career with 17 victories. For the next decade and a half, he would collect no fewer than 14 wins per year. He finished 77 percent of his lifetime starts, while landing among the top 10 in complete games 11 times. He had superb control, averaging just two walks per nine innings in more than 4,000 innings of work. His strikeout-to-walk ratio is the best of all time.

Plank balanced his fastball with curves and assorted off-speed pitches. Using a cross-fire delivery with a three-quarter motion, he painted the outside corners. What set him apart from contemporaries was the time it took him to get the ball to the plate. A writer from *Baseball Digest* once referred to him as the "king of the fidgets." In an era when games rarely lasted longer than two and a half hours, Plank made batters wait between pitches while he pulled at his cap, tugged his belt, shook off signs, and rubbed up the baseball. It has been said that he actually had a negative effect on attendance because fans often worried about missing their train home from the ballpark.

Plank was a tough-luck loser in the World Series several times. Although his lifetime postseason ERA was a highly economical 1.32, he was strapped with a 2–5 record. In the seven games Plank appeared in, the A's managed to score a total of nine runs. His most brilliant performance came in Game 5 of the 1913 World Series versus the Giants, when he tossed a 2-hitter and won, 3–1. He was the first left-hander to record 300 wins, and his 69 shutouts are the most for a southpaw.

After leaving baseball behind, Plank operated a garage in Gettysburg. He died at age 50 from a stroke. In addition to the National Baseball Hall of Fame, he was inducted into the Gettysburg College Hall of Athletic Honor.

CHIEF BENDER, PITCHER

Bender had Native American ancestry and could trace his roots to the Chippewa tribe. Like several other ballplayers with native origins, he was saddled with the nickname "Chief." Bender remembered being teased by teammates and surrounded by children in the streets who greeted him with Indian war cries. He took it all in stride. While he was proud of his heritage, he told a writer from the *Sporting News*, "I do not want my name to be presented in public as an Indian, but as a pitcher." Journalists ignored his request. Even his obituary carried a Native American reference.

Born in Minnesota, Bender spent his early years on the White Earth reservation. He was sent to a boarding school and later ran away from home with his older brother Frank. He ended up at the Carlisle Indian School in Pennsylvania. While at the school, he received athletic instruction from Pop Warner—a famous football icon. While pitching for a semipro outfit in Harrisburg, he fared well in an exhibition against the Cubs. A Philly scout noticed him, and he was invited to join the Athletics in 1903.

Bender was not terribly durable by Deadball Era standards, although he did finish 76 percent of his lifetime starts. He missed portions of multiple seasons with various ailments. He was a control pitcher with a good fastball and effective curve. He also threw a submarine fadeaway—precursor to the modern screwball, which moved away from left-handed batters. Bender used both overhand and sidearm deliveries depending on where he wanted the ball to go. He won at least 15 games on nine occasions and led the league in winning percentage three times. He also hit pretty well for a pitcher, collecting 243 base hits, while keeping his average above .200 in 10 seasons. He peaked at .279.

In 1914, the crafty right-hander won 14 straight decisions and finished the season at 17–3. But in Game 1 of the World Series, he was trounced by the Braves. It was his last appearance in an A's uniform. He defected to the FL the following year and went 4–16 for the last-place Baltimore Terrapins. He spent some time with the Phillies after that league folded. In 1917, he was 8–2 with a 1.67 ERA but ended up getting released anyway. With the outbreak of World War I, Bender went to work in the Philadelphia shipyards to help the war effort.

After the conflict ended, Bender became a minor-league player and manager. He could have returned to the majors but declined multiple offers. He was at the helm of several different minor-league outfits before serving as a coach for the U.S. Naval Academy. He eventually returned to major-league service, working for the White Sox and Giants. Elected to the Hall of Fame in 1953, Connie Mack paid him a high compliment: "If I had all the men I've ever had and they were in their prime and there was one game I wanted to win above all others, Albert would be my man."

EDDIE COLLINS, SECOND BASE

Collins had a knack for making the clubs he played on better. After helping the A's to four World Series berths, he ended up in Chicago, where he was a vital member of two pennant winners. Although he played on the infamous "Black Sox" squad of 1919, he was not involved in the throwing of World Series games. And so, his career continued into the early 1930s.

When ratings of historical players are issued, Collins invariably places among the top second basemen of all time. From a purely statistical standpoint, that distinction is highly justified. Among the second basemen currently in the Hall of Fame, Collins ranks first in hits, runs, and stolen bases. In other major categories, he trails closely behind Rogers Hornsby and Napoleon Lajoie. Beyond the stats, Collins had such immeasurable qualities as leadership and the ability to deliver in the clutch. Most often appearing third in the batting order, he was at his best when the pennant race was in full swing. From 1913 until the end of his career, he compiled a lifetime .363 batting average in the months of September and October (discounting World Series play).

With the pennant already clinched in 1905, A's pitcher Andy Coakley took some time off to get married. While honeymooning in Vermont, Coakley saw Collins play for a semipro team. He recommended Collins—then known as "Eddie Sullivan" to protect his amateur status. Collins made a road trip with the A's, and spotted in a major-league uniform, he was outed as a professional, thereby ending his college baseball career at Columbia University.

When Collins arrived in 1906, Danny Murphy was the incumbent second baseman. Collins remained an understudy until 1908, when Murphy was moved to the outfield. Not only could Collins hit safely and run the bases well, but he was also an outstanding bunter. His career total of 512 sacrifices is an all-time record. On defense, he was as steady as they come, leading the league nine times in fielding percentage, seven times in putouts, and five times in double plays. A reliable post-season performer, he reached base by hit or walk 33 times in 20 World Series games with the A's. Seven of those games were multihit efforts.

Collins was shocked to discover he was being sold to the White Sox after the 1914 slate. When ChiSox owner Charles Comiskey called with the news, Collins's wife reportedly hung up on him, believing it was a hoax. In Chicago, Collins's college education and refined manner kept him out of the crowd of roughnecks that ended up conspiring with gamblers to throw the World Series. In that ill-fated showdown with the Reds, Collins hit just .226, but he was not implicated in any wrongdoing. He stayed with the White Sox until 1926, spending portions of three seasons as a player-manager. He closed out his career with the A's.

From 1933 until his death in 1951, Collins served in the front office of the Red Sox as GM. He presided over a tryout for Jackie Robinson a year before the color barrier was broken. The BoSox were the last team to integrate in 1959.

FRANK BAKER, THIRD BASE

According to historian and statistician Bill James, Baker's temporary retirement in 1915 and again in 1920 prevented him from becoming the greatest third baseman of all time. As it was, his lifetime accomplishments were good enough to land him in the Hall of Fame. Sportswriter

Harry Grayson described Baker as "dark-skinned and dour." By Grayson's account, Baker "had the bowed legs of Honus Wagner and walked like a soft-shelled crab." Baker's awkward gait in no way impeded him from becoming one of the hardest-hitting batsmen in the majors.

Born in rural Maryland, Baker built his muscles working on his father's farm. His mother was allegedly a distant relative of Confederate general Robert E. Lee. Baker played as a pitcher and outfielder in high school. At the semipro level, he got a tryout with the Baltimore Orioles. He was released by manager Jack Dunn on account of his apparent inability to handle pitching at the high minor-league level. In September 1908, Connie Mack promoted him from the Tri-State League.

Baker swung with a violent snapping motion. He used an incredibly heavy bat weighing 52 ounces. Years after his retirement, he remarked that he could have hit at least 50 homers had he been in his prime during the Lively Ball Era of the 1920s and 1930s. Baker led the league in homers four times but never gathered more than 12 in any season. He claimed to have hit the fence at Shibe Park nearly 40 times one year. The dimensions of the park were deep and uniform, with a 500-foot expanse in center field.

With President William Howard Taft in attendance at the home opener in Washington during the 1910 slate, a hot liner off of Baker's unwieldy bat rocketed into the presidential box, hitting Secretary of State Charles Bennett in the head. Bennett was shaken up but otherwise okay.

Baker's popularity soared after he hit homers in consecutive games of the 1911 World Series. The first one came off of Rube Marquard with the score tied at 1–1 and a runner on base in the sixth inning of Game 2. The shot propelled the A's to a 3–1 victory. In the next meeting, Baker victimized future Hall of Famer Christy Mathewson. Interestingly, Mathewson had chided Marquard in the papers for pitching "carelessly" to Baker. No one had ever gone deep in back-to-back games of the Fall Classic, and Baker received hundreds of telegrams from appreciative fans after the Series was over. "I never saw in all my life a ballplayer grow so popular overnight," said New York Highlanders first baseman Hal Chase.

After a salary dispute with Connie Mack, Baker opted to sit out the 1915 campaign. He returned with the Yankees the following year and then missed the entire 1920 slate when his wife died, leaving him with children to care for. Known mostly for his hitting exploits, Baker was a fine fielder as well. He led the AL in putouts seven times, double plays four times, and assists twice.

By the end of the 1922 campaign, Baker's offensive numbers were beginning to taper off. Used sparingly by the Yankees in the 1921 and 1922 World Series, he retired with a .363 batting average in postseason play with 11 extra-base hits and 18 RBIs. When his playing days were over, he managed the Easton team of the Eastern Shore League. He was still alive when he was elected to the Hall of Fame in 1955.

STUFFY MCINNIS, FIRST BASE

When McInnis became the youngest member of Mack's "$100,000 Infield" in 1911, he had big shoes to fill. Veteran Harry Davis had been a mainstay at first base in Philly for 10 seasons, leading the league in homers four times. McInnis didn't have the power of Davis, but he was a highly reliable offensive performer, breaking the .300 mark at the plate in six of seven seasons as a full-timer.

Born John Phalen McInnis, his nickname was derived from the shouts of "That's the stuff, kid!" that reportedly accompanied his performances in the suburban Boston leagues. His youthful appearance and relatively small frame (5-foot-9, 162 pounds) once caused him to be mistaken for a team mascot early in his career. Limited to one appearance in the 1911 World Series due to a late-season wrist injury, McInnis returned to the postseason four more times in his career—twice with Philly, once with the Red Sox, and one last time with the Pirates. His teams were crowned Series champions on four occasions.

Referred to by a wire service writer as "one of the fastest and cleverest first sackers in the league," McInnis was widely known for his sparkling defense. He led the AL in fielding percentage six times between 1913–1922. In 1921, he set a record for most total chances without an error and finished the year with just one miscue. Among the first to use a one-handed grab with his glove hand, he has also been credited with the introduction of the "knee reach," a move that required him to perform a full split in the dirt while reaching for the ball. He currently ranks among the top 10 of all time in the category of putouts. After serving as a player-manager for the Phillies in 1927, he managed in the

New England League. He also coached at Harvard. He died in 1960, at the age of 69.

JACK BARRY, SHORTSTOP

The most seldom-mentioned member of the "$100,000 Infield," Jack Barry has been heralded by some as the most important of the bunch. Offensively, he was a banjo hitter who managed just 10 long balls in his career (three of which were bounce homers). But he was highly skilled at the art of the sacrifice and squeeze. Connie Mack had so much faith in his shortstop's ability to lay down a bunt, he gave Barry permission to execute squeeze plays whenever he saw fit. Although numbers show that Barry was the lightest-hitting player on the squad, he earned a lot of respect from contemporaries for his ability to deliver when it counted most. Historian Fred Lieb commented, "He saved his singles for vital moments when a hit was needed to win a 2–1 or 3–2 game." In his first three World Series with Philadelphia, he compiled a.304 batting average with 9 doubles, 8 runs scored, and 6 RBIs.

Barry worked closely with Eddie Collins in developing a strategy to prevent the dreaded double steal. His unparalleled range allowed Frank Baker to guard the line at third. His ability to turn the 4–6–3 double play was widely celebrated. After the 1910 World Series, several members of the Cubs insisted that Barry had beaten them almost single-handedly with his glove work.

In 1914, sportswriters named Barry to baseball's All-American Team. Commenting on the choice, one columnist offered the following words: "A wonderful and reliable infielder, a clever and intelligent ballplayer, [Barry] has proved one of the strongest points of defense in a great infield . . . he has shown no weakness."

Mack held on to Barry initially after the devastating Series loss in 1914, but when the A's sank to the basement by the end of June 1915, the Philly skipper saw no reason to keep him around any longer. Several teams expressed interest, and in the end it was the Red Sox who landed him. Converted to a second baseman, Barry made the switch with ease. He aided the BoSox to consecutive Series victories in 1915 and 1916, becoming the first player to win four Fall Classics.

Named Red Sox manager in 1917, Barry enlisted in the U.S. Naval Reserve near the end of the season. He missed the entire 1918 slate while on active duty. The following year, he was traded back to the A's. Suffering from leg problems, he opted for retirement. After his major-league days were over, he coached at the College of the Holy Cross for the better part of 41 seasons. More than two dozen of his players made it to the majors.

JOE BUSH, PITCHER

As a boy, Bush reportedly practiced his pitching by tossing rotten apples through the crescent-shaped holes in outhouse doors. By the time he reached the majors, he was one of the hardest-throwing moundsmen in the game, earning the nickname "Bullet Joe." Connie Mack once pro-claimed that, in his prime, Bush was second only to Christy Mathewson. Bush had an effective curveball and later developed a forkball when he was beset by arm trouble. He had a dramatic pirouette delivery and would grunt loudly after every pitch.

Bush logged his first full season with Philly in 1913, notching a 15–6 record. In Game 3 of the Fall Classic that year, he staked the A's to a 2–1 Series advantage over the Giants with a complete-game effort. A *New York Times* correspondent marveled at the achievement, offering the following remark: "Bullet Joe—so they call him—is a mere 'kid' a few years out of high school. . . . Unheralded and practically unknown, young Bush faced the National League champions and displayed a rep-ertoire of curves and speed which held the Giants to 5 hits." Bush would go on to compete in five World Series with three different clubs, compiling a 2.67 postseason ERA.

The hard-throwing right-hander won 17 games in 1914, finishing among the top 10 in strikeouts per nine innings. For the second year in a row, he was called upon to start Game 3 of the World Series. He lasted into the 12th inning and lost a heartbreaker to the Braves on account of his own error. It was the last big game he would pitch for the A's.

By 1915, Connie Mack had dismantled the pennant-winning roster, and his club wallowed in the second division for a decade. Even on dreadful A's teams, Bush managed to win 31 games in a three-year span. During the 1916 campaign, he tossed a no-hitter against Cleveland. He would go on to collect 196 victories for seven different clubs during his career. A respected hitter, he posted a .253 average in more than 1,200 at-bats.

In later years, Bush had a retirement home in Fort Lauderdale, Florida. He worked as a teller at various Florida race tracks just to keep himself busy, maintaining employment until he was in his 70s. He died in Fort Lauderdale at the age of 81.

WALLY SCHANG, CATCHER

Schang arrived in Philadelphia near the end of the Deadball dynasty. Primarily a catcher, he was adept at several positions, including third base and outfield. A hot prospect in the minors, more than a dozen teams tried to draft him before the 1913 slate. The 23-year-old switch-hitter ended up in the capable hands of Connie Mack, who encouraged him to learn from incumbent catchers Jack Lapp and Ira Thomas.

Schang hit .266 in his rookie year and ran his on-base percentage up to .392—tops among major-league backstops. He hit .357 with a triple, homer, and seven RBIs in the World Series. His remarkable performance won him the starting job behind the plate in 1914. He led AL catchers with a .287 batting average and .404 slugging percentage that year. On the downside, he broke the thumb on his throwing hand and committed 30 errors as a result. After the Athletics' shocking loss to the Braves, Schang confessed, "We went into the Series too cocky, and we lived it up too much."

Described by sportswriter Harry Grayson as a "stocky little fellow" who was "agile and tremendously powerful," Schang caught some of the greatest pitchers of his era. In addition to Bender and Plank, he worked with future Hall of Famers Herb Pennock, Waite Hoyt, and Lefty Grove. Commenting on the importance of catchers, Schang once opined, "The catcher is the jockey. The pitcher is the horse. A good horse will lose with a bad rider."

Schang would continue to play well for bad A's clubs after Mack broke up the 1914 squad. On September 8, 1916, he became the first switch-hitter to homer from both sides of the plate. During the 1920s, he cemented his reputation as one of the top offensive backstops in the game. From 1919–1929, he broke the .300 mark at the plate six times, while accruing on-base percentages in excess of .400 on eight occasions. By the time Schang retired from the majors, he had played for five clubs, helping three of them to world championships. He was a .287 lifetime postseason hitter.

FAST FACT: After Connie Mack's roster purge of 1914, the A's became a pitiable club. In 1916, they lost 117 games. This included a streak of 20 straight defeats. The 117 losses were a record for a twentieth-century club in a 154-game season.

5

BOSTON RED SOX
1915–1918

In the first two decades of the twentieth century, the Red Sox went through numerous ownership changes. Half a dozen proprietors laid claim to the club between 1901–1917. Regardless of who was issuing the paychecks, the team fared better than any franchise in the majors, capturing five World Series titles before the 1920s arrived.

They weren't always known as the Red Sox. Making their first American League appearance in 1901, Boston players wore blue socks and were referred to by various names, the most popular being "Americans," in reference to their AL affiliation. After the 1907 slate, owner John I. Taylor issued an official team logo depicting a bright red stocking with the word "Boston" on it. The club has retained that identity ever since.

The BoSox contended from the very beginning, placing no lower than third in their first four seasons. A host of big-name players passed through the Hub in those days, the most prominent being Hall of Famers Cy Young and Jimmy Collins.

Born Denton True Young, the big right-hander's nickname is a shortened version of "cyclone," a flattering reference to the velocity of his fastball. When his speed faded in later years, he mastered a curve, along with various other breaking pitches. By the time Young arrived in Boston for the 1901 slate, he was a 34-year-old veteran of 11 seasons with more than 4,000 innings of work to his credit. The jump from the

National League to the American League rejuvenated his career. as he assembled back-to-back 30-win campaigns. He remained a staple in the Boston rotation until 1909, later retiring with several all-time records, including victories (511) and complete games (749).

Jimmy Collins got a significant pay increase when he jumped from Boston's NL franchise—the Beaneaters—to the city's Junior Circuit squad in 1901. Among the slickest-fielding third basemen of the Dead-ball Era, he has been credited with the invention of the barehanded grab and off-balance throw to first. He was also among the first to play in on the grass to guard against the bunt. Offensively, he was a major contributor, regularly appearing among the league leaders in homers, doubles, and RBIs.

With Collins and Young leading the way, the Red Sox won baseball's first official World Series over the Pirates in 1903. They captured another pennant in 1904, but were denied an opportunity to prove their supremacy when the Giants refused to play them in the postseason. At odds with AL president Ban Johnson, New York owner John T. Brush boldly declared that it would tarnish the reputation of his club to associate with a league he believed was inferior.

Commenting on Brush's decision, the *Sporting News* groused, "Chicanery is the ozone which keeps [Brush's] old frame from snapping and dark-lantern methods the food which vitalizes his body tissues." Seeking to redeem himself and win back fan approval, Brush presented a plan for a World Series against the AL in 1905. The so-called "Brush Rules" outlined a formula for revenue and proposed a best-of-seven format.

By the time Brush's plan was officially adopted, the Red Sox had fallen out of contention. As the original lineup dissolved, the team suffered through some growing pains, placing fourth or lower six times between 1905–1911. Club owners gradually filled the numerous roster gaps with budding new stars. By 1912, the BoSox were poised to capture another pennant. In fact, they ran away with it, gathering 105 wins and leaving the second-place Senators 14 games behind. In the World Series, they beat Giants ace Christy Mathewson twice on their way to claiming the second championship in franchise history.

Boston's new crop featured a trio of outfielders hailed as the best tandem in the game. Nicknamed the "Golden Outfield," Duffy Lewis, Tris Speaker, and Harry Hooper earned glowing praise from sportswriters of the day—especially Harry Grayson, who wrote, "They were smart and fast. They covered every square inch of the park, and they were like three fine infielders on ground balls. They could move into another country if the ball was hit there." Speaker was arguably the greatest center fielder ever to don a Red Sox uniform. During his nine seasons with Boston, he hit at a remarkable .337 clip and set a single-season record for outfield assists. He would remain with the club until 1916, when he was traded to the Indians after holding out for more money in spring training.

Speaker's departure was not well received by fans, although several of his opponents were greatly pleased. Senators pitching phenom Walter Johnson told a reporter from *Sporting Life*,

> With Speaker in the lineup, the Red Sox were almost sure to win. Now they are almost sure to lose. Speaker at the most conservative estimate was worth 10 games to them last year. Take 10 games away from their score and where do they get off? It's a good thing for it gives some of the other clubs a chance.

Johnson's words rang true, as Boston, Detroit, and Chicago engaged in a tight pennant race in 1916. But the Red Sox came out on top without Speaker's services. And a rising young star by the name of Babe Ruth helped fans forget all about the loss of their "Grey Eagle."

Ruth was a 19-year-old unknown fresh off the St. Mary's Industrial School for Boys' schoolyard when he made his pro debut with the Baltimore Orioles (then of the International League) in 1914. He began his career as a pitcher. During the spring, Ruth squared off against several major-league clubs in exhibitions and fared exceptionally well. Financially strapped, the Orioles sold him to Boston in July for a sum in excess of $25,000. He was worth every penny.

Ruth's rise from a left-handed pitching sensation to a prolific slugger is a story that has captivated millions throughout the years. In his first full season in Boston, he notched an 18–8 record with a 2.44 ERA. He led the club with four homers in just 92 at-bats. In 1916, he won 23 games and tossed nine shutouts—an AL record for left-handers. He also tied a record with homers in three consecutive games. In 1917, his last season as a full-time hurler, he added 24 more victories and hit .325 with 11 extra-base hits. His bat was too valuable to keep out of the lineup, and by 1919, he was pitching only sporadically.

Over portions of six seasons as a moundsman for the Red Sox, Ruth compiled an 89–46 record with an ERA in the low twos. His contributions on the mound and at the plate helped Boston to three World Series titles, in 1915, 1916, and 1918. It was the greatest four-year run of any Red Sox team during the twentieth century. The Babe's departure to New York before the 1920 slate would haunt the Sox for decades as they failed to capture another championship for more than 80 years.

It was tough to get any attention in Boston during the late Deadball Era, with Ruth soaking up most of the glory. But the dominant Red Sox clubs of the 1910s were well-stocked with lesser-known players who had ample talent.

TRIS SPEAKER, OUTFIELD

Born in Hubbard, Texas, Speaker was thrown from a horse twice as a kid. He broke his collarbone and dominant right arm, forcing him to throw left-handed for the rest of his life. He managed to set the all-time record for assists by an outfielder anyway.

It was a hard road to the Red Sox for Speaker. He played in Houston and Little Rock during the 1907 and 1908 campaigns and was called to Boston both years. He failed miserably with the bat, hitting just .215 in 38 games. He worked hard to be of value to the club. "When I was a rookie, Cy Young used to hit me flies to sharpen my abilities to judge in advance the direction and distance of an outfield-hit ball," he remembered in later years. By 1909, he had won the starting center-field job. In his first full season, he collected 35 assists—a record he would tie three years later.

In Boston, fans and teammates took to calling him "Spoke." His more famous nickname, the "Grey Eagle" came later, in reference to his fielding prowess and prematurely grey hair. Speaker said he would likely have spent his entire career in Boston if not for the frugality of Boston management. When Federal League representatives tried to lure Speaker into their fold, the Red Sox gave him a substantial pay increase. After the Feds went out of business, the Boston brass sought to slash Speaker's salary considerably. The marquis outfielder initially balked at an offer from the Indians before the 1916 campaign. "You've not only got a bad ballclub, but you've got a bad baseball town," he told

GM Bob McRoy. Speaker eventually had a change of heart, negotiating a $10,000 signing bonus that made him one of the highest-paid players in the league.

Speaker played a shallow center field and felt the need to justify his strategy. "I know it's easier to come in on a ball than to go back," he once explained. "But so many more balls are hit in front of an outfield-er . . . I still see more games lost by singles that drop just over the infield than triples over the outfielder's head." Hall of Famer Joe Sewell, who played alongside Speaker in Cleveland, marveled at his unusual style. "I played seven years with him right behind me in shallow center field. . . . In all that time, I never did see him turn. He'd be turned and gone with his back to the plate, the ball, the infield, and when he'd turn around again, there would be the ball."

Not just a great defensive center fielder, Speaker was one of the most prolific hitters of the Deadball Era and perhaps of all time. A left-handed batter, he hit to all fields, never generating much home-run power. During his time with Boston, he led the league in doubles twice. He retired with more two-baggers than any player in the history of the game (792). Speaker's finest offensive season with Boston came in 1912, when he gathered 75 extra-base hits and paced the circuit with a .464 on-base percentage. He was named MVP.

Speaker played in Cleveland for 11 seasons and served as player-manager for eight of them. Sportswriter Grantland Rice described Speaker as "not only a great ballplayer, but a magnetic leader who knows how to get 100 percent from the efforts of his men." Speaker's own efforts in 1920 pushed the Indians to the first championship in franchise history.

In 1926, Speaker was accused of throwing a game back in 1919, along with Ty Cobb. Commissioner Kenesaw Mountain Landis investigated the claim and cleared both men. Speaker ended up with the Senators in 1927, and the A's the following year. Finished as a player, he managed for portions of three seasons in the minor leagues. He later worked as a broadcaster in Kansas City. He took an interest in Negro League standout Larry Doby and helped him become one of the top center fielders in the AL.

Speaker's Hall of Fame plaque states that he was the "greatest center fielder of his day." That's quite an accomplishment considering that Ty Cobb was another potential candidate.

HARRY HOOPER, RIGHT FIELD

Hooper's SABR biography states that he "eschewed flamboyance for simplicity, exaggeration for modesty." A contemporary referred to him as "unostentatious, but marvelously efficient." It's true that none of Hooper's statistics leap off the page, but he was an irreplaceable member of three world championship squads.

Born in the Santa Clara Valley, Hooper allegedly honed his throwing skills tossing various objects about on his family's ranch. This included fresh eggs, which allegedly splattered against the side of a barn. Hooper could never have imagined he would be throwing major-league runners out at home plate one day. His first serious baseball experience came at St. Mary's College in Oakland. At the junior varsity level, he switched from pitching to the outfield because he was considered to be a bit undersized. Hooper was a good athlete and a bright student, excelling at math and civil engineering. When he negotiated a contract to play for Sacramento in the California League, he insisted that the owner find him a surveyor's position—a demand that was met.

Hooper fared so well in the minors that he was labeled the "Ty Cobb of the State League." Eventually, the Red Sox offered him a hefty contract that would have eclipsed his earnings as an engineer. He set his aspirations outside of baseball aside. He hit .282 in his 1909 debut and would remain a fixture in the Boston outfield throughout the 1910s.

Right field in Fenway Park is known as a sun field, and Hooper made all the necessary adjustments to master his craft. He has been given credit for inventing the outfield slide that allowed him to snag shallow flies and knock down the ones that were beyond his reach. He made some spectacular catches throughout the years, particularly in the final game of the 1912 World Series, when his barehanded grab of a ball hit by Larry Doyle more or less robbed the Giants of a championship. At an old-timers' luncheon many years later, Doyle was asked if he remembered Hooper. "How the hell could I ever forget him!" Doyle proclaimed. The devoutly religious Hooper attributed the catch to divine intervention.

None of Hooper's single-season offensive statistics are awe-inspiring, but he was a model of consistency for many years. Serving mostly as a leadoff hitter, he finished in double digits for triples on nine occasions. He gathered no fewer than 20 doubles and 75 walks in six straight seasons. A smart baserunner, he averaged 89 runs scored per year between 1910–1924. In the World Series, he was a tough out, reaching base 41 times in 24 games.

In 1913, Hooper led off both games of a doubleheader with a home run—a feat that would go unmatched for 80 years. In the eighth inning of a game against Washington the following year, Hooper and his "Golden Outfield" comrades successfully executed a triple steal with Hooper on the front end.

Disgusted with owner Harry Frazee's roster liquidation, which included the ill-advised sale of Babe Ruth before the 1920 campaign, Hooper held out for more money after the season was over. Frazee dumped him, sending him to the White Sox in exchange for two players. In his three seasons with Chicago, Hooper hit .302—more than 30 points higher than when he was with Boston.

When his major-league career was finished, Hooper was a player-manager in the Pacific Coast League. He later coached at Princeton University but was forced to resign during the Great Depression due to budget cuts at the school. He turned to real estate and became wealthy in his old age. He is a member of the National Baseball Hall of Fame and the St. Mary's College Hall of Fame. He currently ranks second all-time in double plays by a right fielder and fourth in assists.

DUTCH LEONARD, PITCHER

Originally signed by the A's in 1911, the Philly rotation was crowded with established stars, and Leonard never threw a single pitch for them. He ended up in the Western League with the Denver Grizzlies, posting a 22–9 record with 326 strikeouts. He arrived in Boston in 1913, and became a major contributor, although his attitude left much to be desired. Leonard developed a well-deserved reputation as a malcontent during his career. He argued with management about salary everywhere he went, blamed others for shortcomings, and feuded with officials frequently. Umpire Billy Evans once admitted that AL arbiters didn't care for Leonard because "he whined on every pitch called against him." Squandering his vast talents, the volatile southpaw was suspended for more than two seasons after jumping to an independent league during a salary dispute with the Tigers before the 1922 slate.

Leonard wore a Red Sox uniform from 1913–1918. He won at least 14 games in five straight seasons, and his ERA never exceeded 2.39. He threw two no-hitters, one in 1916 against the Browns and another in 1918 versus the Tigers. In 1914, he posted one of the lowest ERAs of any hurler during the twentieth century, with a mind-boggling mark of 0.96. He won 19 games that year and almost certainly would have won more had his season not ended in September due to a wrist injury.

Leonard relied on a fastball–curve combination. He later added a spitball and was allowed to continue using it (thanks to a grandfather clause) even after the pitch was banned. In Boston, Leonard was a frequent victim of poor run support—especially in 1917, when he compiled a 16–17 record despite his spectacular 2.17 ERA. The Sox scored 2 runs or less in half of his starts that year.

Leonard made two World Series appearances for the Red Sox and was impressive. In Game 3 of the 1915 Fall Classic, he outdueled Pete Alexander of the Phillies, allowing just three hits in a 2–1 win. The following October, he gave Boston a 3–1 Series lead with a five-hit victory over the Brooklyn Robins. He undoubtedly would have seen action in the 1918 Series had he not ended his season prematurely in a successful attempt to avoid the World War I draft. He ended up pitching for a shipyard team in Massachusetts.

Before the 1919 slate, Leonard was traded to the Yankees. He bickered with management about his salary and was sold to the Tigers. Relying heavily on the spitball by then, he remained in the majors for portions of five more seasons, posting a pedestrian 49–50 record. After leaving baseball behind, he built a successful career in the wine industry. He died at the moderately young age of 60.

DUFFY LEWIS, LEFT FIELD

Lewis patrolled the left-field perimeter of Fenway Park from 1910–1917, playing alongside Cooperstown-bound teammates Speaker and Hooper. He actually had the most difficult job of the three. Prior to the 1934 slate, there was a steep embankment in front of the left-field fence. Roughly 10 feet high, it was a looming hazard to visiting outfielders. Lewis would arrive at the ballpark early on game days and have coaches hit balls onto the hill so he could practice scrambling up and down. He once commented that the descent was the most difficult part of the process. He grew so adept at navigating the incline, it eventually bore his name ("Duffy's Cliff").

While Lewis was never in the same class as Speaker, numbers show that he was a slightly better player than Hooper in some respects while the two were in Boston. Between 1910–1917, Lewis surpassed Hooper in multiple offensive categories. In the outfield, Lewis and Hooper were equally skilled (although Lewis probably deserves more credit for working around the treacherous hill). During their eight seasons together, both men finished among the league leaders in multiple defensive categories. So why did Hooper get the call to Cooperstown when Lewis was found wanting? Perhaps because Lewis's career was shorter. He joined the U.S. Navy in 1918 and missed the entire season. Traded to the Yankees for the 1919 slate, he ended up competing for playing time and performing below expectations. He was out of the majors by 1922.

As a rookie, Lewis was highly confident, resisting hazing traditions and refusing to back down from a challenge. This strained his relationship with Tris Speaker, who didn't care for Lewis's swagger. Lewis threw his bat at Speaker one day when the veteran center fielder kept teasing him in front of fans. The bat hit Speaker in the shins, and he had to be helped off the field. As the story goes, Speaker kept knocking Lewis's hat off and Lewis had told him, "You do that again and I'll kill you."

In three World Series with the Red Sox, Lewis accrued a creditable .299 batting average. He played in 18 postseason games. As time wore on and Babe Ruth claimed almost every long-distance hitting record in the books, Lewis gained widespread acclaim for being the first man ever to pinch hit for the Babe. It happened during Ruth's rookie season of 1914, before his power was fully realized.

Lewis lost his financial investments in the stock market crash of 1929. He ended up coaching the Boston Bees from 1931–1935. In 1936, he became the team's traveling secretary and kept the job until 1961. He retired to Salem, New Hampshire, and lived to the advanced age of 91.

EVERETT SCOTT, SHORTSTOP

Diminutive in stature at 5-foot-8, 148 pounds, Scott was even smaller during his minor-league days, weighing only 120. This prompted a Senators scout to pass on him. Scott signed with the Red Sox in 1914, despite having received a more lucrative offer from Indianapolis of the FL. He remained in Boston from 1914–1921.

Shortstops in Scott's era were not expected to contribute offensively, and Scott was no exception. But he did polish his craft. Although his batting average hovered in the low .200s during his first five seasons, he exceeded the .260 mark on five occasions between 1919–1926. Primarily a singles hitter, he rarely struck out, averaging just one "K" per 21 at-bats. He was a good bunter, executing 23 or more sacrifices five years in a row and peaking at 41 in 1917.

Beginning on June 20, 1916, Scott played in 1,307 consecutive games, a record that would later be broken by Lou Gehrig. Scott wore padded shoes to escape being cut—an unusual practice for the era. According to columnist Harry Grayson, "Scott came out of plays with his shoes looking like a remnant sale at a ribbon counter." He suffered from periodic attacks of boils and played in pain regularly.

According to numerous contemporaries, Scott was among the smartest players in the majors. He knew where to play opposing hitters. He had an exceptionally quick release and could throw accurately from anywhere on the diamond. He led AL shortstops in fielding percentage each year from 1916 through the 1923 slate.

Scott was friendly and popular among teammates. He was a man of many hobbies off the field, among them poker, fishing, and bowling, which he excelled at. He also enjoyed solving math problems and even wrote a children's book entitled *Third Base Thatcher*, which was published during the 1920s.

When Secretary of War Newton Baker issued a "work or fight" order in 1918, requiring eligible men to enlist or work in war-related industries, Scott and teammate Harry Hooper were the only men to play in every Sox game. In the World Series that year, Scott managed just two hits and a walk in six contests, but he played errorless ball, with 11 putouts and 26 assists. Traded to the Yankees in 1922, he went on to win a fourth World Series the following year.

After his playing days were over, Scott managed various bowling alleys and pool halls in Fort Wayne, Indiana. He competed in numerous pro bowling tournaments, reportedly rolling more than 50 perfect games. He died in 1960, at the age of 67.

CARL MAYS, PITCHER

Mays compiled a 24–8 record with the Providence Grays of the International League in 1914, before arriving in Boston. There wasn't a lot of room for him in the rotation, so he was unofficially designated the team's closer. He finished 27 games, collecting seven saves (tops in the AL) and winning six. Inserted into the rotation the following year, Mays became one of Boston's regular starters. He won 18 games and posted a 2.36 ERA—second on the club to Babe Ruth.

Mays had a submarine delivery that kept hitters off balance. He threw so close to the ground, his knuckles sometimes scraped the dirt. He used various arm angles to make his pitches sink or curve. He was also known to doctor the ball from time to time.

Like most pitchers of his day, Mays was comfortable moving batters off the plate. He led the league in hit batsmen during the 1917 campaign and finished second for two straight seasons after that. His reputation as a headhunter was etched in stone after the 1920 slate, when he hit and killed Indians shortstop Ray Chapman with a pitch. Even before the tragedy, Mays was widely disliked. One contemporary described him as having the temperament of a "man with a permanent toothache." He yelled at his teammates for errors and often griped about poor run support.

The ornery right-hander's finest season with Boston came in 1917. He posted a 22–9 record with a 1.74 ERA. He followed that performance with a 21–13 mark, leading the league with 30 complete games and eight shutouts. In two World Series with the Sox (1916 and 1918), he posted a 2–1 record with an ERA in the low twos. He would appear in two more Fall Classics with the Yankees.

In 1919, Mays pitched well but ended up getting off to a 5–11 start. In July of that year, he was hit in the head by a throw from catcher Wally Schang, who was attempting to gun down Chicago's Eddie Collins at second base. Mays stormed off the mound and refused to finish the game. Later, he hopped on a train bound for Boston and demanded a trade. AL president Ban Johnson wanted Mays to be suspended for his actions, but owner Harry Frazee traded him to the Yankees instead. When Johnson tried to nullify the transaction, he was thwarted by legal means. Frazee would eventually trade most of his best players to New York, stocking the Yankees with all the ingredients necessary for multiple championships.

While numerous opponents clamored for Mays's permanent banishment in the wake of the Chapman incident, the right-hander played on, enjoying some of his best seasons. He was a 20-game winner outside of Boston on three occasions, retiring with 207 career victories. Later in life, he lamented the fact that his entire career was overshadowed by the 1920 mishap. "I won over 200 big-league games," he said. "No one remembers that. When they think of me, I'm the guy that killed Chapman."

LARRY GARDNER, SECOND BASE/THIRD BASE

Gardner stuck around Boston from 1908–1917. While his accomplishments were often eclipsed by the brighter stars around him, the Red Sox would have been hard-pressed to find a more reliable infielder.

Gardner was born in Enosburg Falls, Vermont, and is considered by many to be the greatest player the Green Mountain State has ever produced. He majored in chemistry at the University of Vermont and made the varsity baseball squad in his first year. He blossomed into a star, grabbing the attention of Boston scouts and earning call-ups from the Red Sox in 1908 and 1909. By 1910, he was their regular second baseman.

Gardner was moved to third the following year because manager Patsy Donovan felt he lacked range. He made the transition smoothly, leading the AL in assists and double plays four times apiece. He also finished among the top five in fielding percentage nine times during his career, pacing the circuit in 1920.

Gardner hit .281 or better five times as a full-timer in Boston. His best offensive season with the Red Sox came in 1912, when he compiled a .315 batting average with 18 triples, 86 RBIs, and 232 total bases. Gardner played in three World Series for the BoSox, and although he hit for low averages, he was dependable in the clutch. He collected five RBIs in the 1912 Fall Classic, delivering the Series-clinching run with a sac fly off of Giants ace Christy Mathewson. He added six more ribbies in Boston's five-game win over Brooklyn in 1916.

Gardner remained a respected hitter long after he left Boston. Commenting on his adeptness with a bat, one writer crowed, "Ask any pitcher in the circuit whom they would rather face in a tight hole—Babe Ruth, the socking terror, or Larry Gardner, the famed Clevelander who is like gold bond when there's a panic on Wall Street. They'll answer Larry without even emitting a hiccough."

Gardner had more than one interesting talent. He was an excellent ventriloquist, entertaining teammates by throwing his voice. He also sang tenor in a Red Sox barbershop quartet that toured the vaudeville circuit during the offseason.

Traded to Philadelphia for Stuffy McInnis in 1918, Gardner would end up with the Indians the following year. He made the Red Sox regret trading him by hitting .327 against Boston pitchers through 1924, which was his last season in the majors.

Gardner was a fount of baseball knowledge. In 1922, he wrote a syndicated article about playing his primary defensive post. In it, he offers the following advice to aspiring third basemen: "I consider a study of the batter of the utmost importance. It will enable the third baseman in a great many cases to determine whether the batsman intends to bunt or hit. . . . Another important thing is to learn as soon as possible the field to which a batter is most likely to hit."

Gardner put his wisdom to work, managing Dallas of the Texas League and Asheville of the South Atlantic League. He later became head coach of the baseball team at the University of Vermont, additionally serving as athletic director for several years. He was inducted into the college's athletic hall of fame. He died in Vermont at the age of 89.

BILL CARRIGAN, CATCHER/MANAGER

Carrigan spent his entire 10-year playing career in Boston. When he retired after the 1916 slate, the Red Sox attempted to lure him back almost every season as a manager. He finally acceded in 1927, but by then the team was in a dreadful state, and even Carrigan couldn't save them.

A native of Lewiston, Maine, Carrigan attended the College of the Holy Cross, excelling at both football and baseball. Signed by the Red Sox in 1906, he hit just .211 in 37 games but caught the eye of management with his solid defensive play. He was sent to Toronto of the Eastern League, where he honed his skills sufficiently to rejoin the Sox for good in 1908.

Carrigan played backup to Lou Criger in 1908 but was the club's first-string catcher for the next several seasons after that. Aggressive by nature, Carrigan was not one to back down from an argument or fight. In 1909, he engaged in a vicious brawl with Tigers third baseman George Moriarty after a collision at home. Carrigan was known for stubbornly blocking the plate, one of numerous traits that earned him the nickname "Rough."

In those days, the Red Sox clubhouse was divided into two rival factions. On one side was a Catholic group, led by Carrigan and outfielder Duffy Lewis. On the other side was a Protestant group, fronted by pitcher Joe Wood and outfielder Harry Hooper. There were a few unpleasant clashes, for example, the bat-throwing incident involving Lewis and Tris Speaker, but mostly it remained a war of words. Teammates knew better than to tangle with Carrigan.

The Red Sox had been in the habit of employing player-managers for years, and in July 1913, Carrigan was handed the reins. His reputation as a tough guy earned him the respect of the players, and he became one of the most successful of his kind during the Deadball Era. Under his guidance, the Red Sox captured two world championships in a four-year span. Carrigan stirred up a bit of controversy in the 1915 Fall Classic, when he limited Babe Ruth to one pinch-hitting assignment. Although many believed the move was personal, Carrigan insisted that he simply didn't want to use a left-hander against the predominantly right-handed Philly hitters.

Offensively, Carrigan measured up well against the backstops of his time. Usually hitting out of the seventh or eighth slot, he reached the .250 mark in five of his 10 seasons, peaking at .296 in 1909. He had little power but was fast enough to steal 10 bases in 1910—a career high. Behind the plate, he finished among the top five in fielding percentage five times and runners caught stealing on four occasions. He is on a short list of catchers to participate in three no-hitters during his career.

Carrigan disliked being disconnected from his family, and in September 1916, he announced his retirement. After baseball, he worked in real estate and banking. He owned several theaters and eventually sold them for a huge profit. After a decade of refusals, he returned to Boston in 1927, to manage the Sox. There was scarcely a talented player to be found, and the club finished dead last for three straight years under his watch. He quit baseball for good after the 1929 campaign. He was elected to the College of the Holy Cross Hall of Fame in 1968. He died the following year at 85 years of age.

FAST FACT: Babe Ruth was not the only former Bostonian to have a major impact in New York. When the Yankees clinched their third straight pennant in 1923, they did it with a roster full of Bean Town alumni. Three of the Yankees' top four pitchers that year—"Sad Sam" Jones, "Bullet Joe" Bush, and Herb Pennock—had been property of the Red Sox in 1918. Shortstop Everett Scott and catcher Wally Schang (also members of the pennant-winning 1923 Yankees squad) were significant contributors to Boston's last championship run of the twentieth century.

6

NEW YORK GIANTS
1921–1924

After clashing repeatedly with American League president Ban Johnson, Orioles player-manager John McGraw jumped to the New York Giants in July 1902. He brought several high-profile players with him, including the Hall of Fame battery of Roger Bresnahan and Joe McGinnity. Although the Giants finished last in 1902, they climbed to second place the following season. McGraw remained at the helm in New York for more than 30 years.

The Giants were among the most successful teams of the Deadball Era with six pennants to their credit. McGraw ran a tight ship, earning the nickname "Little Napoleon" for his despotic managerial style. He imposed heavy fines for minor infractions and tolerated no divergence from instructions. "With my team, I am absolute czar," he once said. "My men know it. I order plays, and they follow them. If they don't, I fine them." In addition to fines, McGraw also orchestrated frequent trades of players who didn't measure up to his standards. Casey Stengel, who played in New York from 1921–1923, commented, "McGraw Men were brought up to hustle. He kept you liking the game. If he couldn't, he'd get rid of you so quick you wouldn't have time to notify the post office of your change of address."

McGraw was blessed with a steady stream of talent throughout his career. Nearly two dozen Hall of Famers were under his command at various points in time as the club remained in pennant contention almost every year. But the Giants were habitual postseason losers, dropping four World Series before the 1920s arrived.

In 1919, the club was purchased by Charles Stoneham—a New York City stockbroker. While highly invested in the team's daily affairs, he allowed McGraw to be the front man while he operated behind the scenes. McGraw had a knack for maximizing the potential of players, and by 1921, the Giants had assembled a team for the ages.

A late September call-up in 1917, future Hall of Famer Ross Youngs was the starting right fielder in New York for the better part of 10 seasons. Equipped with a powerful arm, he led National League right fielders in assists five times. Although he didn't have much power offensively, he hit for high averages and reached base safely in nearly 40 percent of his plate appearances. George "High Pockets" Kelly began his path to Cooperstown at the age of 19. When first baseman Hal Chase was banned from baseball after throwing games in 1919, Kelly was installed as a replacement. Tall for the era, at 6-foot-4, he used his lanky frame as an advantage, leading the league in putouts and assists on multiple occasions. He was pretty good with a bat as well, consistently placing among the team leaders in home runs and RBIs.

Acquired from the Phillies in June 1920, future Hall of Famer Dave Bancroft was among the smartest shortstops in the majors. He once remarked that the "business of batting and fielding is a contention between minds." Studying opposing batters carefully, he knew exactly where to position himself on the diamond. Although shortstops were not expected to contribute offensively, Bancroft held his own at the plate. From 1920–1923, he hit .312 for the Giants while averaging 32 doubles per year.

Rounding out one of the most talented infields ever assembled, Frankie Frisch began his Cooperstown journey with the Giants in June 1919. A switch-hitter, he had the peculiar habit of batting cross-handed from the right side of the plate. Ugly as it was, he hit no lower than .314 for six straight seasons, peaking at .348 in 1923, before a trade sent him to St. Louis.

With the Giants poised to dominate the NL for years to come, Colonel Jacob Ruppert's humble Yankees had finally climbed into contention after 18 consecutive seasons without a pennant. In 1912, the Yankees (known then as the Highlanders) had begun jointly occupying the Polo Grounds. After Babe Ruth arrived in 1920, and started using the park as a launching pad for his tape measure home runs, the Yankees began outdrawing the Giants. Ban Johnson, who was harboring a grudge against Ruppert for directly disobeying his orders, tried to persuade Charles Stoneham to evict the Yankees. The Yankees began making arrangements to play their games at Fenway Park (imagine that—the Boston Yankees!), but Stoneham didn't want to lose the revenue and, in the end, renewed their lease.

While McGraw's Giants would capture four straight pennants from 1921–1924, they never really ran away with it. Their highest win total was 95 games in 1923, and their largest margin of victory was a seven-game advantage over the Reds in 1922. For three consecutive seasons, they met the Yankees in the World Series, emerging victorious in the first two meetings. In 1923—the year the Bombers finally moved into their own stadium—Ruth and his Bronx associates had their revenge, beating the Giants in six games to claim the first championship in franchise history.

The 1924 Giants were among the most star-studded clubs of all time. In addition to the aforementioned Frisch, Kelly, and Youngs, a new crop of baseball immortals had arrived. After Dave Bancroft's departure to Boston, 20-year-old Travis Jackson assumed full-time duties at shortstop. Jackson would earn the nickname "Stonewall" for his unparalleled defensive range during a career spent entirely with New York. Freddie Lindstrom, an 18-year-old plucked from the American Association, would slowly assume third-base responsibilities. Like Jackson, his productive bat and reliable glove would ultimately land him in the gallery at Cooperstown.

As if that weren't enough to give the club an edge, McGraw also had future Hall of Famers Hack Wilson and Bill Terry on his bench. Both were late-season call-ups in 1923. Wilson would enjoy his best seasons with the Cubs, but Terry would spend his entire career in New York, accruing a handsome .341 lifetime batting average (among the top 20 marks of all time).

Before the Giants' last homestand in 1924, the team became embroiled in controversy. In the midst of a tight pennant race with Brooklyn, New York outfielder Jimmy O'Connell tried to bribe Phillies shortstop Heinie Sand—an old friend of his—into "taking it easy" on the Giants. Sand declined the offer and reported it to Philly skipper Art Fletcher. Giants coach Cozy Dolan was implicated as well. In the wake of the 1919 World Series scandal, incidents of this nature were taken very seriously. After an investigation by Commissioner Kenesaw Mountain Landis, both O'Connell and Dolan were run out of baseball.

The 1924 Fall Classic ended on a sour note for the Giants. After blowing a 3–2 Series advantage in Game 6 at Washington, the New Yorkers led by a score of 3–1 in the finale. A succession of mishaps in the 12th inning sent the Giants home empty-handed. Catcher Hank Gowdy dropped an easy foul pop. Travis Jackson botched a ground ball at short. With two runners on and one out, Senators leadoff man Earl McNeely rapped a grounder that took a bad hop over the head of Lindstrom at third. The deciding run scored on the play, giving the Senators their first world championship.

The seven-game loss marked the end of an era in New York. Even with a vastly talented cast of characters, the Giants failed to capture another pennant until after McGraw's retirement. Meanwhile, the Yankees became the toast of the town, dominating the sport for decades to come. Although the Giants would show periodic flashes of brilliance throughout the years, they would retain their status as New York's "other team" until 1958, when they moved to San Francisco.

Despite their mixed success in the postseason, the Giants of the 1920s can still be classified as one of the elite teams in baseball history. Since the roster was so cluttered with Hall of Famers, the accomplishments of multiple lesser stars have been largely overshadowed.

ROSS YOUNGS, OUTFIELDER

Born in Shiner, Texas, Youngs's father was a railroad worker who moved the family to San Antonio and became a rancher there. Youngs attended the West Texas Military Institute, and although he excelled at football, he was partial to activities on the diamond. He got started as a pro in the Texas League during the 1914 slate and failed to draw any major attention until the Giants purchased his contract in 1916. Assigned to Rochester the following year, Youngs hit .356, earning a late-season call-up. McGraw had told Rochester manager Mickey Doolan earlier in the season that Youngs was among the most talented players he had ever seen.

Impressed with Youngs's hustle, McGraw gave him the nickname "Pep." In 1918, Youngs took over for right fielder Dave Robertson, who had left the club to manage a local military team. Youngs was known for his hard style of play. He frequently threw full-body blocks on opponents around second base to break up double plays. In the outfield, he was equally assertive. During a spring training game in 1923, he reportedly rifled a throw to the plate that trapped Earl Sheely of the White Sox in a rundown. Not content to watch from right field, Youngs sprinted onto the diamond and became involved in the play. When he eventually tagged Sheely out, he was credited with a putout and an assist—unusual for an outfielder. According to multiple sources, Youngs once climbed several rows deep into the stands to catch a foul ball. The right field foul line at the Polo Grounds in New York was only 258 feet from home plate. Youngs became an expert at playing the wild bounces. "He played that carom as if he'd majored in billiards," said Yankees hurler Waite Hoyt.

In 10 seasons, Youngs compiled a .322 batting average. He spent roughly equal portions of time in the top five positions of the batting order. He was particularly successful in the third slot, hitting .339. Like most batters of the era, he punished the lowly Phillies, raking their pitching at a .352 clip, while running up a .438 on-base percentage against them. An industrious postseason hitter, he carried a .328 batting mark into the 1924 World Series before slumping to .185 in seven games.

In 1926, Youngs fell ill with a kidney disorder known as Bright's disease, for which there was no effective treatment. He played until early August but was instructed by John McGraw to go home. The illness eventually consumed Youngs, as he dropped from 170 pounds to 100 at the time of his death in 1927. He was only 30 years old. Before he died, he had been grooming a young Mel Ott to replace him. Ott would become one of the greatest Giants sluggers of all time.

Shortly after his death, Youngs was honored with a bronze plaque in right field at the Polo Grounds. It was financed by fans who contributed $1 apiece. McGraw had become extremely attached to Youngs and, according to one family member, was like a father to the outfielder. McGraw reportedly kept only two photos on his desk throughout the years—one of pitching great Christy Mathewson and another of Youngs.

Youngs was not elected to the Hall of Fame until 1972. By then, former teammates Bill Terry and Frankie Frisch had joined the Veteran's Committee, serving to champion Youngs's cause. According to some, the selection of Young was questionable since his career was so short. Charges of cronyism eventually surfaced.

FRANKIE FRISCH, SECOND BASE

Perhaps best remembered for his days with the Cardinals, Frisch established himself with the Giants. He attended Fordham University in the Bronx and was a four-sport star, earning his enduring nickname the "Fordham Flash." Frisch's coach at the school was Art Devlin—a former Giants third baseman. Devlin arranged a tryout at the Polo Grounds, and Frisch didn't disappoint. The brainy Frisch was majoring in chemistry, and his father told him he could play with the Giants only during the summer. His contract had a clause stating that, if he didn't prove himself within two seasons, he would receive an unconditional release.

Frisch's first season was mediocre, but in 1920, he raised his batting average to .280 and drove in 77 runs. By 1921, Frisch had become one of the most exciting players in the majors, leading the NL in steals, collecting 100 RBIs, and finishing among the top 10 with a .341 average. McGraw took a liking to Frisch and named him team captain. Frisch emerged as a brilliant postseason performer, gathering 37 hits and scoring 11 runs during the Giants four straight World Series appearances.

Being one of McGraw's favorites was a blessing and a curse. McGraw was not shy about berating players in front of teammates. When the Giants failed to capture pennants in two consecutive seasons, McGraw became increasingly impatient and irritable. In a game against the Cardinals in August 1926, Frisch allegedly missed a sign that cost the Giants a run. McGraw unleashed a brutal stream of verbal abuse after the game, and Frisch hopped a train back to New York. Although he returned to finish the season, he was fined $500 and traded. He continued his Hall of Fame journey in St. Louis (details of which can be found in a later chapter).

GEORGE KELLY, FIRST BASE

Kelly's early years with the Giants were disastrous. He went hitless in his first 23 at-bats, drawing harsh criticism from the New York press. One writer remarked that he would retire if Kelly actually hit safely. Another quipped that Kelly generated some of the prettiest balls that were ever caught. After compiling a .158 batting average in 1915 and 1916, and going 0-for-4 in his first nine appearances the following year, John McGraw had little choice but to cast him adrift. The Pirates selected him off of waivers but abandoned the project in August. McGraw had so much confidence in Kelly's abilities, he reclaimed the young first baseman and allowed him to sit on the bench during the 1917 World Series. Years later, when Kelly was coaching in the Pacific Coast League, a fan asked him how his aunt, Mrs. McGraw, was. "That's how lousy I was when I first got there," Kelly joked. "[Fans] wondered why McGraw would keep me around and figured I must be related to him."

McGraw's instruction and encouragement to Kelly eventually paid off. What had been holding Kelly back was his inability to handle curveballs. He practiced the skill in the minors until 1919, when he finally got the hang of it. Late in the season, he was installed as a replacement for star first baseman Hal Chase. Fans reportedly booed Kelly until it became common knowledge that Chase had been throwing games. Kelly hit .290 in 32 appearances and would remain a fixture in the Giants lineup for the next seven seasons.

From 1920–1926, Kelly topped the .300 mark at the plate six times. He led the league in RBIs twice and homers once. He had a pair of three-homer games—a major-league record that stood until Johnny Mize broke it in 1940. Although his postseason numbers were not particularly awe-inspiring, McGraw insisted that Kelly made more big plays for him than anyone on the team. Fans eventually embraced the slick-fielding, hard-hitting first-sacker, referring to him as "Long George" or "High Pockets." Kelly was quiet and unassuming, rarely drawing undue attention to himself.

At 6-foot-4, Kelly was among the tallest players at his position. One journalist wrote that he could "grab a ball nine feet in the air without taking his feet off the ground." This helped him collect 1,759 putouts in 1920—an all-time record that still stands. Kelly led NL first baseman in putouts and assists three times apiece. His career range factor is fifth on the all-time list.

With Bill Terry waiting in the wings, McGraw ended up trading Kelly to the Reds before the 1927 campaign. Kelly played five more seasons before retiring. He coached for the Reds and later for the Boston Bees under Casey Stengel. Later still, his coaching career continued with Oakland of the PCL. Since Kelly's prime years were somewhat abbreviated, some have argued that he was a poor choice for the Hall of Fame. In particular, historian Bill James has contended that Kelly is among the weakest players enshrined at Cooperstown.

DAVE BANCROFT, SHORTSTOP

Hailing from Sioux City, Iowa, Bancroft logged his minor-league experience between 1909–1914. He spent time in the Northwestern, Pacific Coast, and Minnesota-Wisconsin leagues before the Phillies added him to their roster in 1915. He had an excellent debut, finishing among the league leaders in walks, runs, and homers. Hitting with power from both sides of the plate, he drew comparisons to Honus Wagner. The Phillies went to the World Series that year, and Bancroft's infield hit in the eighth inning of Game 1 ignited a rally that lifted Philly to victory. The rest of the team slumped mightily, as Bancroft hit .294 to the club's collective .182 mark.

Bancroft later feuded with Phillies player-manager Gavvy Cravath and requested a trade to the Reds. That request was denied. Recognizing Bancroft's value, John McGraw was willing to offer two players and $100,000 to acquire his contract. The Phillies accepted, and Bancroft joined the Giants in June 1920. In his first game with New York, catcher Frank Snyder called Bancroft to the mound for a conference. When Snyder offered to review the team's signals, Bancroft said, "Why—have they changed? If not, I already know them."

Defensively, Bancroft was among the most gifted of the era. He was the first shortstop to turn 100 double plays in a season. He was particularly adept at cutting off throws from the outfield and catching runners between bases. Among shortstops, he currently ranks among the all-time leaders in putouts, range factor, and fielding percentage. During his playing days, future Hall of Famer Hughie Jennings remarked,

"Bancroft is one of the greatest shortstops in the history of the game. He can go equally well to his right or left, has a great arm, and is a good hitter. . . . He is more than a great mechanical player. A player like 'Banny' at short means everything to a ballclub."

No one has ever accused Bancroft of being among the elite hitters of his era. But he was very good, finishing among the league leaders in walks eight times, runs scored five times, and doubles on three occasions. His best single-season effort came in 1922, when he hit .321 with 41 doubles and 60 RBIs.

In 1923, Bancroft struggled with leg issues and was hospitalized with pneumonia at one point. He returned for the World Series but hit just .083 against the Yankees that October. Bancroft had expressed a desire to try his hand at managing, and with Travis Jackson groomed as his replacement, McGraw shipped Bancroft to Boston. McGraw was at least partially motivated by the fact that his old friend—Christy Mathewson—had taken over as GM of the Braves. Bancroft became the youngest player-manager in the NL, although he was sidelined with appendicitis for part of the 1924 campaign. The following year, he made some sweeping changes to the Braves roster, and the club climbed from the basement to fifth place. His efforts ultimately proved futile, as the Braves never became a winning team on his watch. He requested a release after the 1927 slate, admitting that the stress of managing was wearing him down.

Bancroft played for the Brooklyn Robins in 1928 and 1929, and then returned to the Giants as an assistant manager and a coach. He made his last appearance as a major-league player in 1930. When Bill Terry took over as manager of the Giants, Bancroft was surprised and somewhat hurt by the decision. He left the organization and piloted several minor-league clubs. In the 1940s, he managed in the All-American Girls Professional Baseball League, which was made famous by the movie *A League of Their Own*. Bancroft made the Hall of Fame via the controversial Veteran's Committee, occupied by former teammates Frankie Frisch and Bill Terry. In subsequent years, the authority of the Veteran's Committee was kept in check.

IRISH MEUSEL, LEFT FIELD

Born Emil Meusel, this California native got his nickname from an associate who thought he looked Irish. He was actually of German descent. Meusel languished in the minors for portions of five seasons before attaining full-time major-league status. He began his career with the Senators but ended up being claimed by the Phillies in the 1917 Rule 5 Draft. Philadelphia was a bottom-dwelling club in those days, and Meusel, despite his obvious talent, was suspended for "indifferent play" in 1921. The Giants jumped at the opportunity to obtain him, acquiring Meusel's services for two players and cash.

The righty-swinging left fielder, who was hitting .353 at the time of the transaction, continued his hot hitting in New York, finishing the year with 201 hits—60 of them for extra bases. Meusel enjoyed his finest seasons with the Giants, collecting no fewer than 102 RBIs between 1922–1925. He led the league in that category during the 1923 slate. Aside from his clutch hitting, he was a reliable defensive performer, finishing among the top five in fielding percentage six times.

Meusel was extremely productive in the postseason. He squared off against his brother Bob—a star outfielder for the Yankees—in three straight World Series. In the battle of the siblings, Irish (who was three years older) emerged with superior numbers as illustrated in the following:

Bob: 19 games/.250 BA/19 hits/6 runs/4 doubles/2 triples/13 RBIs
Irish: 19 games/.297 BA/22 hits/10 runs/3 doubles/2 triples/3 HR/16 RBIs

The Giants won two of three October showdowns as Irish homered in each. Together, the Meusel brothers hit .310 during their careers, cementing their status as one of the top sibling duos in history. From 1921–1928, there was a Meusel in every World Series except for one. The squads they played on won a total of five world championships.

When Irish's numbers dropped off in 1926, he was traded to Brooklyn. He played one season there and finished his career in the Western League. A minor star on the silver screen, Irish appeared in several baseball-themed movies during his lifetime. In *Slide, Kelly, Slide*, released by MGM, Meusel plays himself alongside his brother. The 1927 classic also features cameos from diamond greats Tony Lazzeri and

Mike Donlin. Irish made his last celluloid appearance in a 1932 comedy short entitled *Off His Base*. Meusel wasn't much of an actor, and when talkies replaced silent films for good, he was out of the industry. In later years, he worked at the Santa Anita racetrack in Arcadia, California. He died in 1963, at the age of 69.

HEINIE GROH, THIRD BASE

Groh began his Giants career in 1912, and was promptly packaged in a multiplayer swap to Cincinnati that brought right-hander Art Fromme to New York. Fromme was a bust for the Giants, but Groh played so well for the Reds he was reacquired in December 1921, for two players and a considerable sum of cash.

According to his SABR biography, Groh was among the best third basemen of the Deadball Era. One historian has suggested that Groh would have played on eight All-Star Teams and won half a dozen Gold Glove Awards had those accolades existed in his time. He settled instead for a pair of world championships.

Groh was so short and youthful looking, he was allegedly mistaken for the team's batboy in his first major-league plate appearance. His hands were so small, he petitioned the Spalding Company to fashion a special bat for him. The ones he used resembled a milk bottle with an uncommonly thick barrel and thin handle.

Groh had a habit of positioning himself at the front of the batter's box with his feet facing the pitcher. He would choke up on the handle and slap at the ball. The practice worked marvelously in 1921, when he fashioned a career-best .331 average for the Reds. But his batting mark dropped more than 60 points with the Giants in 1922, inviting the following scornful lines from an International News Service writer: "Harry Knight Groh, otherwise known as Heinie, could place a careless heel upon a banana peel in New York the night before the World Series and quite a few estimable citizens far from chagrined would regard the incident as providential."

Despite that scathing commentary, Groh's oddly shaped bat awoke in the World Series, as he hit in all five games and posted a .474 average—highest on either club. He accrued a handsome .333 mark in three World Series while playing for New York.

Interviewed for Lawrence Ritter's *The Glory of Their Times*, Groh admitted that he had the Yankees' hitting signs figured out in the 1922 Series and was able to make the proper defensive shifts. He also re-counted a Game 3 incident in which Babe Ruth plowed into him at third base. As Groh climbed to his feet, Ruth asserted, "Kid, you know we're both entitled to part of the base path." Groh, who was a much smaller man, shot back, "You take your side and I'll take mine. And if I ever find you on my side, you better watch out!"

Although he never exceeded the .300 mark at the plate after 1921, Groh proved to be irreplaceable with a glove, posting the highest field-ing percentage among players at his position for three straight years (1922–1924). Late in the 1924 campaign, he suffered a knee injury and was replaced by rookie Freddie Lindstrom. One can only speculate what might have happened if the seasoned Groh had been at third base in Game 7 to snare that infamous bad hop. Groh's ailing knee prevent-ed him from appearing regularly again. He ended his career with the Pirates in 1927.

After his playing days were concluded, Groh managed in the minors and served as a scout for many years. He later worked at River Downs race track in Cincinnati. He died in 1968, at the age of 78.

ART NEHF, PITCHER

A left-hander, Nehf won 19 games in the Central League during the 1915 slate, while posting a highly economical 1.38 ERA. This earned him an August call-up from the Braves. He would become ace of the Boston staff in 1917, with a handsome 17–8 record. In August of the following year, he tossed 20 scoreless frames in a marathon game against the Pirates—a record at the time. The Braves were noncontend-ers in 1919, and ended up dealing Nehf to the Giants in the second half for four players and cash. The change of address suited him well, as he won nine straight decisions from August 16 to September 27.

Before aspiring to the majors, Nehf attended the Rose-Hulman In-stitute of Technology in his hometown of Terre Haute, Indiana. He was being used as an outfielder until his coach noticed that he could stand flat-footed in center field and throw the ball effortlessly to the plate. In his first college start, he struck out 13 batters with nothing but a fastball in his repertoire. He later added assorted curves. Nehf was the last player from the school to make it to the majors. The varsity baseball field at the college was named after him.

Between 1920–1925, the diminutive southpaw (standing just 5-foot-9) was one of the most successful members of the Giants staff. He compiled a 98–58 record in that span with a cumulative ERA of 3.59, which was very good for the era. He reached the 20-win threshold in 1920 and 1921.

Nehf was a workhorse for McGraw in the World Series, making nine starts and one relief appearance between 1921–1924. In 1921, he clinched the Series for the Giants with a four-hit shutout over Waite Hoyt and the Yankees. In Game 5 of the 1922 Fall Classic, his complete-game five-hit effort clinched the Series for New York again.

If Nehf had one weakness, it was a lack of durability. After 1922, he never worked 200 innings in any season. Plagued by arm woes in 1926, he was traded to the Reds. He saved his last good effort for 1928, while playing for the Cubs. He went 13–7 with a 2.65 ERA that year.

Nehf spent portions of 15 seasons in the majors and played for four different clubs. His last World Series appearance was a relief outing in 1929. His Cubs held an 8–0 lead and were on the verge of tying the Series at two games apiece when the A's suddenly exploded for 10 runs in the bottom of the seventh—the largest single-inning outburst in postseason history to that point. Nehf was one of four Cubs hurlers who took the mound in the disastrous frame. The Cubs lost, 10–8, eventually dropping the Series in five games.

Nehf died in 1960, at the age of 68, leaving behind a wife and three children (one daughter and two sons). Both of his sons were high-ranking military men.

FAST FACT: The 1921 World Series between the Yankees and Giants was the first of 14 Subway Series in New York. The Yankees were pitted against the Dodgers seven times, the Giants on six occasions, and the Mets once. The Yankees won eleven of those fourteen Series.

7

NEW YORK YANKEES

1926–1928

Many casual fans assume that, because the Yankees have captured so many world championships, they have always been a dominant club. This simply isn't true. They began their existence as the Baltimore Orioles in 1901, moving to New York in 1903, after the roster was picked clean by National League rivals. Playing as the Highlanders from 1903–1912, they finished in the second division six times and lost more than 100 games twice.

A name change in 1913 did nothing to improve the club's standing as the newly christened Yankees placed fourth or lower every year until 1919, when a series of revitalizing transactions with the Red Sox began. Boston owner Harry Frazee, who was juggling multiple business interests, gradually sold off his best players to the Yanks, and by 1926, the conditions in New York were ripe for a dynasty.

In those days, the club was being managed by Miller Huggins. Nick-named "Mighty Mite" for his diminutive stature, he had been a decent player for the Reds and Cardinals during the Deadball years, leading the league in walks four times and on-base percentage once. Taking over a middling Yankees club in 1918, he established a reputation as a disciplinarian. According to various sources, he was not a particularly likable man. He screamed at players regularly and engaged in epic temper tantrums. Although more than one of his pledges would grow to resent him, he guided the team to six pennants and three world championships between 1921–1928.

Because of Huggins, or perhaps in spite of him, half a dozen Yankees players prepped for Cooperstown on his watch. The most famous, of course, was George Herman Ruth. After compiling an 89–46 record in a six-year span as a pitcher for Boston, the Babe began his assault on the record books while patrolling the outfield in the Bronx. Ruth was in a class all by himself. In fact, the term *Ruthian* is still used to describe extraordinary batting feats. When the Bambino retired in 1935, his 714 homers were several hundred more than the closest pursuer. He still holds the all-time mark for slugging percentage. A one-man traveling circus, Ruth lived fast and died relatively young. He signed autographs, promised homers to sick kids, and gave back to the community at large. His daily exploits both on and off the field were chronicled in the papers. There simply has never been another player like him. Even the immortal Lou Gehrig, with all his wondrous talents, seemed somewhat ordinary in comparison.

Gehrig is best known for his incredible streak of 2,130 consecutive games. Inserted into the lineup in early June 1925, as a replacement for regular first baseman Wally Pipp, he played in every Yankees game through May 1, 1939. Nothing could stop him. Hit in the head by an Earl Whitehill pitch in 1933, he stayed in the game. Plunked above the right eye in an exhibition contest the following year, he was knocked unconscious yet returned to the lineup the next day. X-rays taken late in his career revealed that he had sustained multiple fractures throughout the years and kept on going. Before his body was ravaged by amyotrophic lateral sclerosis, he won two MVP Awards, a Triple Crown, and six World Series. Three of the top six single-season RBI totals belong to him. His farewell speech on July 4, 1939, was one of the most iconic moments in U.S. history, and there was hardly a dry eye in the house when he proclaimed that, despite contracting a fatal disease, he felt like the "luckiest man on the face of the earth."

While they deserve a lion's share of the credit, Ruth and Gehrig did not single-handedly lead the Yankees to three consecutive World Series appearances during the late 1920s. A careful examination of the facts reveals that the Yankees roster was inundated with exceptional players, several of whom ended up alongside the aforementioned dynamic duo at Cooperstown.

Unlike the larger-than-life personalities around him, center fielder Earle Combs was content to do his job quietly. The Yankees thought so highly of him at the beginning of his career, they offered him $50,000 to sign—a considerable sum in those days. During Combs's nine years of full-time action, he dropped below .300 at the plate just once, ending up with a .299 mark in 1926 (and that was only because he and several Yankees players were clowning around for fans during a meaningless late-season game against the Browns). He was brilliant in World Series play, fashioning a .350 average in 16 games, with a .451 on-base percentage.

Another highly talented and lesser-known Hall of Famer, Tony Lazzeri was the Yankees' starting second baseman for 12 seasons. He got his nickname, "Poosh 'Em Up Tony," from a restaurant owner in Salt Lake City who took a liking to him during his Pacific Coast League days. The colorful moniker was a reference to the act of hitting the ball hard and moving runners ahead on the bases. Lazzeri was quite adept at that when he played for the Bees, setting a minor-league record with 60 homers and 222 RBIs in 197 games during the 1925 slate. Despite the impressive performance, the Cubs and Reds both passed on him because he suffered from epileptic seizures. The disorder never affected his performance and was never revealed to the public during his career. A lifetime .292 hitter, Lazzeri drove in no fewer than 100 runs seven times in New York and received MVP consideration five times.

Despite the productive bats in the Yankees lineup during the late 1920s, they would never have dominated the majors without pitching. Herb Pennock and Waite Hoyt were the most celebrated members of the staff. Both were generous donations from Harry Frazee. Hoyt arrived in 1921, and Pennock came gift-wrapped two years later. Throwing from opposite sides (Hoyt was a right-hander and Pennock a southpaw), the talented duo kept the Yankees in contention throughout the decade. During portions of 10 seasons together in New York and Boston, they combined for 296 victories and a .621 won–loss percentage. Pennock got the jump on Hoyt at Cooperstown when he was inducted in 1948. Hoyt joined him two decades later via the Veteran's Committee.

With enough great players to fill an All-Star roster, the Yankees subdued their American League rivals each year from 1926–1928. They encountered stiff competition twice—from the Indians in 1926 and the

Athletics in 1928. In 1927, they annihilated everyone who crossed their path. The term *Murderers' Row* had been coined by a sportswriter in 1918, in reference to infielders Frank Baker and Wally Pipp, who propelled the Yankees offense. The moniker eventually fell out of favor but returned more poignantly during the 1927 slate.

The Yankees had lost a heartbreaker to the Cardinals in 1926. The Series ended on a low note when Babe Ruth (who represented the tying run) was caught trying to steal second base with two outs in the ninth inning of Game 7. Attempting to boost morale, Yankees owners offered generous pay increases to virtually every player on the club. It worked like a charm, as the "Murderers' Row" squad proceeded to set multiple AL team records during the 1927 slate, including most wins (110) and largest margin of victory (19 games ahead of the Athletics). After a 21–1 defeat at the hands of the New Yorkers in July, Senators first baseman Joe Judge commented, "These fellows not only beat you, but they tear your heart out. I wish the season was over."

After sweeping the Pirates in the 1927 World Series, the Yankees continued to dominate opponents the following year. They won fewer games but outpaced Connie Mack's powerful Athletics on their way to a second straight Series sweep (the first AL team to turn the trick). This time, it came at the expense of the Cardinals, who had retained several players from their 1926 championship squad.

To date, the Yankees have sent dozens of players to the Hall of Fame, and although they have enjoyed numerous periods of great success, the dynasty of the late 1920s has continued to captivate fans. A simple Google search yields millions of results for Ruth and Gehrig alone. With so much attention being focused on those two men, it stands to reason that the contributions of many others have passed into relative obscurity. Some of those names are resurrected here.

EARLE COMBS, CENTER FIELD

Combs (pronounced "Coombs") was studying to become a teacher at Eastern Kentucky University and playing semipro ball in his spare time when the Louisville Colonels offered him more money than he could ever have made instructing students. After two successful seasons in the American Association, the Yankees acquired his contract. A broken ankle sidelined him for most of the 1924 campaign, but he was a fixture in the Yankees outfield for the next nine seasons.

If Combs had one weakness, it was his throwing arm. Spalding's 1925 guide describes him as the "second best batter in the league and an outfielder of average ability, but not a player of the fast, hard-throwing variety which has made the outfield famous in the major leagues." According to statistician Bill James, Combs compiled the lowest ratio of assists per game of any outfielder born between 1890–1915 with a minimum of 1,000 appearances. Still, he was faster than Babe Ruth in right field and Bob Meusel in left, often coming to their aid. "I was just helping out like a teammate should," said Combs. "I always had a good pair of legs and loved to do it." Combs played hard in center field, and as a result, his career was derailed by numerous injuries—a broken finger late in the 1928 campaign, a fractured skull in 1934, and a career-ending collarbone break in 1935 that prompted the Yankees to bring up Joe DiMaggio as a replacement. He finished among the top five in fielding percentage and putouts six times apiece, leading the league on multiple occasions.

At the plate, Combs's job was to get on base and let the big bats drive him home. "Up here we'll call you 'the waiter,'" manager Miller Huggins once told him. "When you get on base, you just wait there for Ruth or Gehrig or one of the other fellows to send you the rest of the way around." Combs was a tough out at the plate, fashioning a lifetime .325 batting average. He used the deep alleys of Yankee Stadium to his advantage, leading the AL in triples three times. He also collected 30 or more doubles in eight straight seasons. With Combs on base in nearly 40 percent of his lifetime plate appearances, Ruth, Gehrig, and company did their jobs, sending him "around" more than 100 times each year from 1925–1932.

Combs collided with the outfield wall at Sportsman's Park in 1934, fracturing his skull and causing other less serious injuries. He was carried from the field unconscious and spent two months in the hospital. His condition was listed as "critical" for a period of time. While recuperating, he told reporters, "You see? I'm made of tough stuff. They said I was through in 1924 when I broke my ankle. I fooled them once and I'll fool them again." Combs certainly tried, but a subsequent collarbone break compelled the Yankees to promote DiMaggio. It was the end of Combs as a player.

Combs remained in the Yankees organization as a coach for several years. He coached for other clubs as well before retiring to his 400-acre Kentucky ranch. Nicknamed the "Kentucky Colonel," Combs was always grateful for the opportunity to play in the Bronx. In his Cooperstown induction speech, he said humbly, "I thought the Hall of Fame was for superstars, not just average players like me."

TONY LAZZERI, SECOND BASE

Lazzeri was raised in a rough San Francisco neighborhood, the son of Italian immigrants. He got into a lot of fights during his childhood and believed that it helped toughen him up. Lazzeri had early aspirations of becoming a boxer and, bored with school, was expelled at age 15. He went to work with his father as a boilermaker's apprentice. He played ball with various semipro teams before getting a tryout with the Salt Lake City Bees of the PCL.

After a record-setting 60-homer season in 1925, quite a few teams expressed interest in him. But Lazzeri was an epileptic who was prone to seizures, and most of his suitors ended up backing out. After quite a bit of deliberation, the Yankees doled out $50,000 to acquire his contract. It paid huge dividends for the club. Moved from shortstop to second base, Lazzeri hit .275 in his debut season, with 60 extra-base hits and 117 RBIs.

Lazzeri was quiet and modest. When the 1927 Yankees took the league by storm, the hard-hitting second baseman was besieged with interview requests. But he disliked talking about himself. "Interviewing that guy is like mining coal with a nail file," one reporter griped.

Known for his leadership on the diamond, Lazzeri was the first truly great player of Italian descent in New York. Italian Americans came to Yankee Stadium in force, filling the ballpark with shouts of "Poosh 'Em Up Tony!" Lazzeri was once compared to Christopher Columbus by a *New York Times* reporter, who joked that, although Lazzeri was not an explorer, he was superior to Columbus around second base.

In 14 seasons, Lazzeri finished among the top 10 in RBIs six times and triples on four occasions. He set an AL record in May 1936, with 11 RBIs in a game against the A's. He accomplished the feat with a triple and three homers, two of which were grand slams—also an AL first. He finished the month with yet another offensive record—seven homers in a four-game stretch. Most often appearing fifth or sixth in New York's batting order, Lazzeri played in six World Series with the Yankees, helping the team to five world championships.

In 1938, Lazzeri joined the Cubs and faced his former club in the Fall Classic. He made two appearances and went 0-for-2 with a strikeout. After retiring from the majors in 1939, he managed Toronto of the International League. He later played and managed in several minor leagues. In spite of his stellar career achievements, Lazzeri was widely remembered for striking out against Pete Alexander of the Cardinals with two outs and the bases loaded in Game 7 of the 1926 World Series. Making a living as a tavern owner in San Francisco after his baseball days were over, he remarked that his infamous strikeout came up in conversation almost every night.

Lazzeri died young, at the age of 42, in 1946—the victim of a heart attack. He was posthumously elected to the Hall of Fame via the Veteran's Committee.

HERB PENNOCK, PITCHER

Born in Kennett Square, Pennsylvania, the left-handed Pennock went to the Wenonnah Military Academy. He had planned to attend the University of Pennsylvania, but Connie Mack signed him in 1912. Pennock had serious control issues and a below-average fastball in those days. Seldom used until 1914, he notched an 11–4 record on the A's pennant-winning squad that year. Connie Mack got rid of him anyway, later regretting it. "That was my biggest blunder," he said. "I got the impression that he lacked ambition. Pennock made me rue the day."

Mack wasn't alone in his underestimation of Pennock's talents. The easygoing southpaw had a smooth, effortless delivery that made him appear as if he were warming up. He actually became the brunt of jokes. "The only comforting thing about hitting against him is that you don't have to be afraid of getting hurt," said one Tigers player. "Even if he hits you on the head with his fastball, he won't knock your hat off." Later, the joke would be on Pennock's opponents.

Traded to the Red Sox in 1915, Pennock was used mostly out of the bullpen for the better part of three seasons. It was considered a demotion since no one was actually groomed as a reliever in those days. Still struggling with control problems, he spent portions of the 1915 and 1916 campaigns in the minors. After taking a year off for military duty in 1918, he finally had a breakthrough season, going 16–8 with a career-best 2.71 ERA. But the Red Sox were in the early stages of liquidating their roster, and he would eventually be sold to the Yankees.

Pennock was a slow worker. Like Eddie Plank before him, he was always tugging at his cap and belt or walking around the mound. His fluid delivery prompted Yankees catcher Bill Dickey to comment, "You can catch Pennock sitting in a rocking chair." Although he didn't have an overpowering fastball, he studied hitters. "If you were to cut that bird's head open, the weakness of every batter in the league would fall out," manager Miller Huggins once quipped.

Having conquered his control problems, Pennock issued fewer walks per nine innings than any pitcher in the circuit on three occasions between 1925–1931. His WHIP (walks and hits per nine innings) was the lowest in the AL twice in that span. He also proved he was a big-game pitcher. In nine World Series assignments for the Yankees (five of which were starts), he logged a 5–0 record. He was especially effective in Game 5 of the 1926 Series versus the Cardinals, when he outdueled Bill Sherdel for a 3–2 win in 10 innings.

In 1928, the gullible Pennock was talked into trying "bee sting therapy" for a sore arm. It didn't help. "All I got out of it was an arm that was lame *and* sore," he joked. Used less often after that, he still finished in double digits for wins on two occasions. Pennock returned to the Red Sox for his final season of 1934. He later coached in Boston from 1936–1940. In 1944, he took over as GM of the Phillies and was responsible for signing several key players who would lead the club to a World Series berth in 1950. Pennock wouldn't live to see it, however. He died of a cerebral hemorrhage in 1948—the year of his Hall of Fame induction.

WAITE HOYT, PITCHER

Hoyt was precocious. He tossed three no-hitters for Erasmus Hall High School in the Bronx and served as a batting practice pitcher for the Giants. He quickly tired of the subway ride to the ballpark and asked to be paid. At 15 years old, he was the youngest player ever to be offered a contract. It gained him national attention.

Hoyt's pro career started at age sixteen. He joined the Giants in July of 1918 and despite pitching a scoreless inning in his major-league debut, John McGraw didn't feel he was ready. Sent to the minors, Hoyt ended up with the Red Sox in 1919. He went 10–12 in 36 appearances before getting shipped to New York with three other players, among them star catcher Wally Schang.

Hoyt once commented that he did his best not to provoke the ire of Yankees management since he loathed the idea of pitching against them. From 1921–1929, he managed to stay in the good graces of the New York brass, compiling a 155–96 record and becoming a major star. In his finest season of 1927, he compiled a 22–7 record with a 2.63 ERA.

Hoyt was intelligent and well spoken. During an argument with umpire George Moriarty one day, he flustered the arbiter by shouting, "You're out of your element! You should be a traffic cop so you can stand in the middle of the street with a badge on your chest and insult people with impunity!" Aware of his good fortune, Hoyt once proclaimed, "It's great to be young and a Yankee!"

In the offseason, Hoyt—who had a pleasant baritone voice—appeared in vaudeville. He also entered the funeral business. "I'm knocking 'em dead on Seventh Avenue while my partner is laying 'em out up in Westchester," he once said glibly. Referred to by some as the "Merry Mortician," he left the Yankees in 1930, after arguing with manager Bob Shawkey about how to handle A's slugger Al Simmons. Hoyt's skills went into decline outside of New York, and he pitched for five different teams in the next eight seasons. He retired with 237 career wins. Additionally, he picked up six wins in World Series action with a 1.83 postseason ERA.

Finished as a player, Hoyt served as a broadcaster in Cincinnati for 30 years. According to one historian, he became "grouchier" as the years wore on. Even so, he was paid a high compliment by the legendary Mel Allen, who commented that Hoyt was a "highly intelligent, industrious, great storyteller." Ecstatic to be elected to the Hall of Fame, Hoyt reported that he was "shaking all over and crying at the same time" when he got the news. He died in 1984, at the age of 84.

BOB MEUSEL, OUTFIELD

Of all the "Murderers' Row" Yankees not in the Hall of Fame, Bob Meusel was perhaps the most talented. He played for the Bombers from 1920–1929 and was one of the most productive sluggers in the majors during that span. Only three players (Babe Ruth, Rogers Hornsby, and Harry Heilmann) had more RBIs than Meusel during the 1920s. Only four men had more homers. Despite those lofty credentials, Meusel never received more than 5 percent of the Cooperstown vote.

Meusel spent roughly equal amounts of time in right and left field. He was shifted back and forth depending on which field had the most sun. Since he was a better defensive player than Ruth, he drew the tougher assignments. Meusel had developed a strong arm throwing stones long distances as a kid. He led the league in assists twice.

Nicknamed "Long Bob" for his tall, lanky frame (6-foot-3, 190 pounds), he was extremely quiet and displayed a limited range of emotion. Because of these traits, he was labeled "antisocial" by certain teammates and writers. He was also perceived as a "loafer" in the field. One journalist observed,

> In chasing a fly, Meusel gives the impression of one whose interest in the proceedings is most casual. Standing at the plate, he would seem to be a study in suspended animation. On balls hit in front of him, he makes it appear as though the play could have been completed with a little more speed and ambition. Sometimes, he fails to run out infield taps or chase extra-base drives with abandon.

Despite those deficiencies, Meusel was an extremely consistent performer, hitting for both average and power, while demonstrating speed on the bases. A lifetime .309 hitter in 11 seasons, he averaged 13 stolen bases and 56 extra-base hits per year. His finest offensive campaign came in 1925, when Ruth missed more than 50 games. Meusel picked up the slack, leading the league with 33 homers and 134 RBIs. Another major accomplishment, he was the first player of the modern era to hit for the cycle three times.

After the 1921 postseason, Meusel went on a barnstorming tour with teammates Ruth and Bill Piercy—a practice forbidden to World Series participants at the time. The three were warned by Commissioner

Kenesaw Mountain Landis beforehand but went anyway. The result was a lengthy suspension in 1922. Meusel missed more than 30 games that year but still collected 16 homers and 88 RBIs.

The World Series was not always Meusel's finest hour. He played in six of them for the Yanks, gathering 29 hits and 12 walks in 34 games. But from 1926–1928, he managed a paltry .189 batting average. He ended up with a .225 average and three world championships.

Traded to Cincinnati in 1930, he played one season there and then retired. He made several cameo appearances in films during his lifetime—the most famous being *Pride of the Yankees*, released in 1942, and starring Gary Cooper as Lou Gehrig. Meusel's last big-screen appearance was the 1948 feature *The Babe Ruth Story*, in which the Babe was portrayed by actor William Bendix.

After baseball, Meusel worked as a security guard at a former U.S. Navy base in Long Beach, California. He died in 1977, at the age of 81.

MARK KOENIG, SHORTSTOP

Born and raised in San Francisco, Koenig's breakthrough season came in 1925, with St. Paul of the AA, when he hit .308 in 126 games. He was called up to New York that September and played well enough to hang around the Bronx for four full seasons.

Koenig was modest about his abilities, remarking long after his retirement, "I was ordinary, a small cog in a big machine. The Yankees could have carried a midget at shortstop." It's true that Koenig was somewhat "ordinary" at his position. He led the AL in errors twice and the NL once. In three World Series with the Yankees, he added six more miscues. Still, he had enough natural ability to earn glowing praise from umpire and sportswriter Billy Evans in 1927. "He can go to his right or left with equal ease," Evans observed. "[He] has a great arm, which enables him to play a very deep short and thereby cover much more territory, is fast of foot, bats well either right- or left-handed, and is a mighty good baserunner."

The switch-hitting Koenig was among the best offensive shortstops in the majors for a brief spell. From 1926–1929, his batting average ranged from .271 to .319. He most often appeared second in the lineup, sandwiched between Earle Combs and Babe Ruth. With Ruth and

Gehrig backing him in the order, he scored 89 or more runs in three straight campaigns. Koenig rarely struck out and was a skilled bunter, finishing among the leaders in sacrifices more than once.

Koenig played in five World Series, enjoying his finest postseason in 1927, against the Pirates. Surrounded by all-time greats, he still managed to post the highest batting average among New York regulars, going 9-for-18 with five runs scored and a pair of RBIs. He had three hits in Game 2 and Game 4.

When his average dipped to .230 in May 1930, he was traded to Detroit, along with Waite Hoyt. He tried his hand at pitching in the Motor City, appearing in five games and faring poorly. In the spring of 1932, Koenig's contract was sold to the Mission Reds of the PCL. An unfortunate turn of events would land him in another World Series.

In July 1932, Cubs shortstop Billy Jurges was accidentally shot trying to prevent his ex-girlfriend, a lounge singer named Violet Valli, from committing suicide. In his absence, the Cubs acquired Koenig. The former Yankee helped Chicago to a postseason berth with a .353 average in 33 games, but his teammates voted to award him only a half-share of the World Series bonus. A handful of Koenig's former teammates mouthed off about the stinginess of the Cubs, and there was bad blood between the two clubs when they met in the Series that year. Babe Ruth's famous (and widely disputed) "called shot" was the direct result of verbal sparring between the teams. Koenig, himself, wasn't a major factor in the Series, appearing in two games and collecting one hit—a RBI triple off of Red Ruffing in a 12–6 Chicago loss.

Koenig made two more stops before falling from the major-league ranks, playing in Cincinnati and New York (for the Giants). He logged his last professional season in the PCL during the 1937 slate. After his playing days were over, he owned a pair of gas stations in San Francisco and worked in a brewery. He was the last surviving member of the 1927 "Murderers' Row" squad. He died in 1993, at 88 years of age.

JOE DUGAN, THIRD BASE

Dugan acquired the nickname "Jumping Joe" on account of his tendency to leave clubs without permission—a trend that began before he was a professional. While still in high school, he was offered $500 by Connie

Mack to sign with the A's. Mack had intended for Dugan to get a full education first, but Dugan left the College of the Holy Cross after just one season to make good on the deal.

Without any minor-league experience, Dugan's play was substandard. He made more than 100 errors (mostly as a shortstop) in his first three seasons and hit below .200 twice. During a June 1918 contest, the fans jumped all over him for sloppy play. Discouraged by the crowd, he didn't show up for the next game. It became a habit during his days in Philly, and although Mack always took him back, the moody infielder remained tremendously unpopular with A's supporters. Later in life, he commented, "I agree with (W. C.) Fields when he put on his tombstone: 'Better here than Philadelphia.' They had the worst fans in the world down there. They'd boo a wake."

Converted to a third baseman in 1920, Dugan's hitting and defense improved dramatically. He accrued a career-best .322 batting average that year, while fielding his new position above the league average. In 1921, Dugan played solidly again but continued to complain about the conditions in Philly. Mack finally gave him his freedom, arranging a three-team transfer before the 1922 slate. Dugan was sent to the Senators and then shipped out to Boston. He played well enough to capture the attention of the Yankees, who acquired him in late July. He had an immediate impact in New York, hitting .286, while playing sparkling defense. The Yankees won the pennant, and "Jumping Joe" played in all five World Series games, collecting five hits, while scoring four runs. The midseason transaction ruffled the feathers of more than one AL club, and trading restrictions were later imposed.

Dugan remained with the Yankees through the 1928 campaign. His most productive offensive seasons in New York came in 1923 and 1924, when he scored more than 100 runs, clubbed no fewer than 30 doubles, and hit at a cumulative .292 clip. Commenting on the hazards of being surrounded by superstars in the Big Apple, Dugan once comically griped, "It's always the same. Combs walks, Koenig singles, Ruth hits one out of the park, Gehrig doubles, Lazzeri triples. Then Dugan goes in the dirt on his can."

Dugan was a bit superstitious. He refused to throw the ball to the pitcher unless he was recording an assist. During practice, teammates were known to turn their backs on him in an attempt to force him to make the toss, but he would always walk the ball to the mound.

He suffered knee trouble throughout the latter part of his career and played less often as time went on. Despite the malady, he appeared in every World Series for the Yanks between 1926–1928. In the 1926 loss to the Cards, he hit safely in every game but one and fashioned a .333 average. He was a lifetime .267 hitter in 25 postseason contests.

After the 1928 campaign, Dugan was placed on waivers and picked up by the Braves. He griped about having to make the switch to the NL and threatened to hold out. Eventually, he showed up and hit .304 in 60 games. Out of the majors in 1930, he made an unsuccessful comeback attempt with the Tigers the following year.

After his retirement, Dugan ran a beer distributorship and owned a New York bar. He later ran a baseball school and scouted for the Red Sox from 1955–1966. He died in Norwood, Massachusetts, at the age of 85.

FAST FACT: Babe Ruth smashed 60 homers in 1927—a record he believed would stand the test of time. After belting number 60 on September 30, he bragged to reporters after the game, "Sixty—count 'em— sixty! Let's see some son of a bitch match that!" Ruth's personal home- run total in 1927 surpassed the number of long balls generated by all but three major-league teams. Only the Giants, Cardinals, and Cubs outslugged Ruth that year.

8

PHILADELPHIA ATHLETICS

1929–1931

After suffering a humiliating World Series sweep at the hands of the underdog Boston Braves in 1914, disillusioned owner-manager Connie Mack began to dismantle the club that had been the most dominant force in the American League for several years. Second baseman Eddie Collins was dealt to the White Sox. Third baseman Frank "Home Run" Baker temporarily retired on the heels of a bitter salary dispute. Hall of Fame pitchers Eddie Plank and Chief Bender both jumped to the rival Federal League. Completing a mass exodus, shortstop Jack Barry—another vital member of Mack's heralded "$100,000 Infield"—was traded away in the first half of the 1915 campaign, along with pitchers Herb Pennock and Bob Shawkey (both of whom would become superstars with the Yankees).

Justifying his actions to the press, Mack said, "I am not crying out for mercy or making any plea for patronage for the Athletics club, nor do I believe that I have made a mistake in tearing apart the greatest baseball machine of the day. I maintain that I did right and will again say that I will have a greater team in two years than the one I broke up."

That estimate was way off the mark, as the A's languished in the second division for a decade. This included a run of seven straight last-place finishes. But Mack remained dedicated to the cause, toying with the lineup each year, while slowly importing an eclectic mix of young talent and seasoned veterans. By 1929, he was putting the finishing touches on his new "baseball machine," which was fueled by a quartet of Cooperstown greats—pitcher Lefty Grove, catcher Mickey Cochrane, left fielder Al Simmons, and first baseman Jimmie Foxx.

The A's garnered 104 wins in 1929, finishing 18 games in front of the Yankees. They dominated the Bombers all season, prevailing in 14 of 22 head-to-head matchups. Off to a slow start during the early spring, the "Mackmen" rattled off a string of 11 straight victories in May that put them in first place for good. The pennant was clinched by the second week of September.

The 1929 World Series pitted the A's against the Cubs. It lasted five games and is best remembered for two of the most dramatic rallies in postseason history. The Cubs were on the verge of tying the Series at two games apiece, leading 8–0 at Philly, when the A's pulled off the impossible. They sent 15 men to the plate in the bottom of the seventh inning, battering four pitchers for 10 runs and emerging with a rousing Game 4 victory. In the fifth game, the Cubs had regrouped and were sitting on a 2–0 lead in the ninth with their staff ace, Pat Malone, on the mound. Again, the A's pulled off another magic trick, rallying for three runs to clinch the Series.

Two weeks after the A's were crowned champions of baseball, the U.S. stock market crashed and the Great Depression began. Unemployment peaked at almost 25 percent as approximately 9,000 banks failed. Thousands of Americans found themselves standing in breadlines and living in shanty towns. Numerous government reforms eventually provided some relief, but the U.S. economy remained stagnant until the advent of World War II.

Baseball attendance took a sharp dive during this period—dropping roughly 10 percent. The A's were hit especially hard. In 1929, more than 800,000 fans turned out at Shibe Park to see them play. That figure dipped by more than 117,000 in 1930 and continued to decline in the years that followed. The team rattled on nevertheless.

The 1930 campaign saw the A's gather 102 wins, while leaving the second-place Senators eight games behind. In the World Series, they squared off against the Cardinals, who sported a star-studded roster of their own, with future Hall of Famers Jim Bottomley, Frankie Frisch, and Chick Hafey leading the offensive charge. The St. Louis rotation featured Cooperstown-bound hurlers Burleigh Grimes and Jesse Haines, but neither deterred the A's from taking the Series in six games.

In 1931, the A's set a franchise record for wins in a season with 107 (which still stands). They prevailed in 80 percent of their home games and won a total of 31 contests by five or more runs. Favored over the Cardinals in the World Series again, they became embroiled in a nail-biting seven-game affair. Trailing 4–0 in the finale, they were looking for some of the old postseason magic that had propelled them past the Cubs two years earlier. They loaded the bases off of Burleigh Grimes in the ninth and scored a pair of runs on a timely single by Doc Cramer. With two outs and the go-ahead run at the plate, Philly leadoff man Max Bishop flied out to center field. The A's missed becoming the first team to win three straight World Series by a narrow margin.

For Connie Mack, it was the last hurrah. The A's slumped to second place in 1932, and third place the following year. With attendance sagging dramatically, the team fell into debt, and Mack was forced to sell off his best players to stay afloat. The Athletics would not find their way back to the postseason until 1971. By then, the team had moved to Oakland. Although time has served to obscure their accomplishments, the following players are largely responsible for the A's last fruitful period in Philadelphia.

LEFTY GROVE, PITCHER

Born in Lonaconing, Maryland, Grove dominated the sandlots of the Baltimore area during the 1910s. In 1920, he was signed by the Martinsburg Mountaineers of the Class D Blue Ridge League. The club was forced to play its games on the road after a storm destroyed the outfield fence at their stadium. Looking to make necessary repairs, the team owner accepted an offer from Jack Dunn of the Baltimore Orioles to purchase Grove's contract. The money was used to refurbish the ballpark, and Grove later joked that he was the only player in history to be "traded for a fence."

There was no minor league draft in the 1920s, allowing Dunn the luxury of turning down offers from multiple interested parties. Grove had no choice but to wait until his boss was finished with him. He won 108 games for the Orioles before Dunn finally accepted the largest contract bid ever made for a player at $100,600. "When I finally reached the majors I was 25," Grove later complained. "I should have been there three years earlier."

Grove's first season with the A's was subpar. He logged a 10–12 record, while leading the AL in walks. Catcher Mickey Cochrane remarked, "Catching him was like catching bullets from a rifleman with bad aim." Grove worked hard to correct the problem and ended up leading the league with a 2.51 ERA the following year. His walk totals decreased significantly, while his strikeout totals soared to a league-best 194. Grove would win seven strikeout titles consecutively.

Grove had a blazing fastball and a biting curve. He also had a major attitude. Known for brushbacks and epic temper tantrums, he made plenty of enemies throughout the league. Hall of Famer Joe Cronin once said, "Just to see that big guy glaring down at you from the mound was enough to frighten the daylights out of you." It was once comically suggested that Grove "could throw a lamb chop past a wolf." In later years, Grove offered the following explanation for his ferocity: "I was suspicious of everybody. And I guess I was scared of the big cities . . . I figured that if I scared people away, they wouldn't bother me."

During his time in Philly, Grove captured five ERA titles and reached the 20-win threshold in seven straight seasons. He won back-to-back Triple Crowns in 1930 and 1931. In three World Series with the A's, he appeared in eight games, posting a 4–2 record with a 1.75 ERA.

With the Great Depression hurting attendance, Mack sold Grove to the Red Sox before the 1934 campaign. By then, Grove had lost some velocity on his fastball and had begun to spot it better, while using his curve more often. Connie Mack described Grove as a "thrower" who learned to pitch as he got older. Mack also admitted that Grove's "mean disposition" bothered him at times. "I took more from Grove than I would from any man living," he said.

With Boston, Grove was a 15-game winner on four occasions. He hung around the majors long after his prime looking for his 300th career win and retired shortly afterward. Grove became more mild-mannered in his later years, providing uniforms for sandlot teams while coaching youth leagues around Lonaconing. He made multiple appearances at Cooperstown functions throughout the years. He was 75 years old when he died in 1975.

AL SIMMONS, OUTFIELD

Born in Milwaukee, Simmons was a childhood fan of the A's. He had a desire to become a big-league ballplayer from an early age. By some accounts, he was once spanked by his father for voicing those aspirations. Simmons grew tired of people mispronouncing his birth name of "Szymanski" (his parents were Polish immigrants) and changed it after he saw an ad for a popular hardware company.

The right-handed slugger logged his minor-league experience with Milwaukee of the American Association. He also played in the Dakota and Texas leagues. He was a lifetime .359 hitter in minor-league play. Promoted to Philadelphia in 1924, he accrued a .308 average, while driving in 102 runs. He would reach the century mark in RBIs for the next 10 seasons.

Simmons had an unusual stance for the era. He stood with his left foot pointing toward third base. His teammates razzed him about it when he first came up, but Mack promptly instructed them to back off. His odd posture at the plate resulted in the nickname "Bucketfoot Al," which Simmons disliked.

Even as a rookie, Simmons was cocky and defiant. One writer classified him as a "testy character." Overtly aware of his abilities, he could be condescending to less-talented players. He also bullied rookies and questioned Mack's decisions from time to time. Even so, Mack later remarked, "I wish I had nine players named Al Simmons." Simmons later attributed his ornery nature to a difficult childhood.

Simmons was known for his grit and determination on the diamond. He once hit a grand slam after rupturing a major blood vessel in his knee. Shibe Park in Philly had some of the deepest recesses in the majors. Simmons had plenty of power to all fields, although a majority of his homers were hit to the right side. Defensively, he was among the best of the era, leading players at his position in fielding percentage six times. While Mack would have given almost anything to hang onto the greatest outfielder he ever managed, the high salaries and low gate receipts during the Great Depression tore the A's apart. Simmons was dealt to the White Sox with Jimmy Dykes and Mule Haas after the 1932 campaign.

Simmons became a bat for hire, playing for seven different clubs between 1933–1943. He returned to Philadelphia twice in that span. As his numbers crashed back to earth, so did his salary. He retired as a player in 1944, and coached for the A's and Indians. Elected to the Hall of Fame in 1953, he died of a heart attack a few years later. Simmons is actually a member of three different Halls. In addition to the one in Cooperstown, he was inducted into the Wisconsin Athletic Hall of Fame and the National Polish-American Sports Hall of Fame.

MICKEY COCHRANE, CATCHER

Born in Bridgewater, Massachusetts, Cochrane was a football star at Boston University, serving as a quarterback, running back, and punter. He got the nickname "Black Mike" for his competitive nature and foul temper, which he carried throughout his baseball career. A former A's teammate once remarked, "Lose a one-to-nothing game and you didn't want to be in the clubhouse with Grove and Cochrane. You'd be duck-ing stools and gloves and bats and whatever else would fly."

Cochrane turned pro in 1923, with Dover of the Eastern Shore League. He quickly worked his way up the ladder, mostly on the strength of his hitting. When he arrived in Philly, he was rough around the edges. He had served primarily as a shortstop and outfielder in college and didn't really want to catch. "It was thrust upon me," he said. "I was in a fever to get out from behind the plate. Oh boy, was I terrible behind there." Connie Mack tried Cochrane at third base and discov-ered he was even worse in that position. First-string catcher Cy Perkins helped straighten Cochrane out, but Mickey continued to finish among the league leaders in passed balls and stolen bases allowed year after year.

On Opening Day in 1925, Mack was looking to pinch hit for Perkins in the eighth inning of a tight game. Cochrane volunteered to face Rudy Kallio, a sidearmer he had fared well against in the Pacific Coast League. When he delivered a game-winning hit, Perkins said from the bench, "There goes Cy Perkins's job."

In nine seasons with the A's, Cochrane hit .321 and averaged 46 extra-base hits per year. Being a catcher himself, he had an excellent feel for the strike zone, finishing among the league leaders in on-base percentage each year from 1929–1935. He received two MVP Awards—the first one coming with the Athletics in 1928. The A's couldn't afford to keep Cochrane around after the 1933 slate. He was named player-manager in Detroit, leading the club to two consecutive pennants. Although he was adored by fans, he disliked being in the spotlight. "As a player, I worried only about myself," he groused. "Now I have to worry about everybody. . . . If one of them eats something that makes them sick, I get sick too."

Cochrane was hailed as a revitalizing figure in Detroit. A *Time* magazine writer pointed out that his arrival coincided with a boom in the Detroit auto industry. After the Tigers won the World Series in 1935, "Black Mike" was elevated to GM in addition to his player-manager role. He suffered a breakdown the following year, playing in just 44 games and hitting well below his lifetime mark. He recovered and had boosted his average to .306 in 1937, but ended up being struck in the head by a pitch from Bump Hadley of the Yankees. He was unconscious for 10 days and never played again.

Cochrane returned to baseball as a bench manager in 1938, but he was ineffective in his job and was let go. A Hall of Fame inductee in 1947, he coached for the A's in 1955, and then scouted for the Yankees and Tigers. Decades after his passing, statistical wizard Bill James evaluated him as the number-four catcher of all time, behind Yogi Berra, Johnny Bench, and Roy Campanella.

JIMMIE FOXX, FIRST BASEMAN

Like so many players of the early twentieth century, Foxx developed his muscles working on his father's farm. His arms were massive for the era. Yankees hurler Lefty Gomez once noted, "[H]e was the only hitter I ever saw who could hit balls on his fist and still get them out of the park. He had muscles on his muscles."

Foxx got started as a catcher. He was noticed in high school by Frank "Home Run" Baker, who was managing in the Eastern Shore League. Baker invited Foxx to a tryout and, sufficiently impressed with what he saw, notified Connie Mack. Foxx didn't even finish his senior year of high school, joining the A's at the age of 17. The youngest player in the AL, he spent most of his time on the bench that year.

The A's were in the process of grooming Mickey Cochrane, and Foxx was willing to try out other positions to help the team. He spent some time at third base before finding a home at first. Foxx's offensive accomplishments often overshadowed his defensive abilities. His lifetime .992 fielding percentage is two points above the league average for the time period. He led AL first basemen in assists and fielding percentage three times apiece.

Foxx earned the fearsome nicknames "Beast" and "Double-X" on account of his raw power. When he retired, only Babe Ruth had surpassed his lifetime total of 534 homers. He currently ranks among the top 10 in RBIs and slugging percentage. In 1932—arguably his best season—he hit 58 long balls and drove in 169 runs, capturing a MVP Award. The following year, he won a Triple Crown with 48 circuit blasts, 163 ribbies, and a .356 batting average. Like Babe Ruth, he swung for the fences and put up high strikeout totals, leading the league seven times during his prime slugging years. According to multiple sources, he lost several home runs at Sportsman's Park in St. Louis due to a screen in right field that increased the height of the fence by more than 70 feet. During his 58-homer campaign, he supposedly hit two more shots at Shibe Park that were discounted.

What especially impressed fans and peers was the length of Foxx's homers. He once cleared the roof of the left-field grandstand at Comiskey Park—a feat matched only by Babe Ruth before him. He has been given credit for the longest homer in Shibe Park history, which was estimated to be more than 500 feet. He also drove a ball out of Cleveland's cavernous League Park.

A reliable postseason performer for the A's, Foxx hit .344 in World Series play with a .609 slugging percentage. His 500th career homer came at the age of 32. He seemed destined to challenge the Babe's record, but during a barnstorming tour in Winnipeg, he was hit in the head with a pitch. He wasn't quite the same afterward, suffering from sinus pain and vision problems.

Traded to Boston before the 1936 slate, Foxx had several productive seasons before going into decline. When he was done playing, he managed several teams in the minors and at the college level (with the University of Miami). He tried his hand at broadcasting in 1946. In 1952, he managed the Fort Wayne club of the All-American Girls Professional Baseball League. The character of Jimmy Dugan in the film *A League of Their Own* is loosely based on Foxx. The slugger died in 1967, from what was initially believed to be a heart attack. It was later discovered that he had died of asphyxiation from choking on a piece of meat. Coincidentally, his wife had died of asphyxiation just months before.

MAX BISHOP, SECOND BASE

Nicknamed "Camera Eye" for his masterful sense of the strike zone, Bishop would have fit nicely into Billy Beane's "Moneyball" scheme. While he didn't always hit for a high average, Bishop wore pitchers down with his infinite patience at the plate. In nine of his 12 major-league seasons, he posted an on-base percentage in excess of .400. He still holds multiple records for bases on balls.

Bishop came of age in Baltimore and got his start with the Orioles of the International League. Signed by the A's in 1923, he made his big-league debut the following year. In Baltimore, Bishop had been a slugger, leading the league in homers once. It was Connie Mack who encouraged him to be more selective and develop a leadoff hitter's mentality.

Bishop's family was never terribly supportive of his baseball career. He once told a reporter that "they think I might make better use of my time." This may have contributed to his somewhat businesslike attitude toward the game. One sportswriter referred to him as "bland, blond, phlegmatic, and no more responsive to the glamour of his game than a dead man to an indictment." Even Connie Mack once griped, "He hasn't any heart for the game. He plays for the first and the 15th of the month. If it weren't for pay days, I don't think he would ever take a ball in his hands."

Although he may have lacked passion for the sport, he was cool and efficient on the field. Hall of Famer Lefty Gomez was baffled by Bishop's ability to draw walks, commenting that he didn't really do anything special at the plate to make him a tougher out than the average batter. Teammate Jimmy Dykes explained, "If he didn't swing at a pitch, the umpires just assumed that it didn't catch the plate and called it a ball." From 1926–1933, Bishop drew at least 100 walks each year. In May 1930, he became the first man to walk eight times in a doubleheader (a record he would tie four years later). He drew five walks in a game twice during his career—the only player in history to accomplish the feat.

When he did decide to swing the bat, he had little power. More than 70 percent of his hits were singles. He reached the .300 mark at the plate just once—in 1928, when he posted a .316 average. But he found a way to get on base to the very end. In his final major-league season, he posted a highly respectable .377 on-base percentage. His career mark of .423 is among the top 20 totals of all time.

Bishop was so good at getting on base, his defense was often overlooked. In three World Series with the A's, he handled 69 chances at second base without an error. During the regular season, he posted the highest fielding percentage in the AL three times and finished among the top five in assists on six occasions. Sabermetric scores compare Bishop favorably to Eddie Stanky, another exceptional player who ended up just shy of Cooperstown.

Traded to the Red Sox in another one of Mack's fire sales, Bishop was finished in the majors by the end of the 1935 campaign. He played one season in the minors after that. In 1938, he took a job as U.S. Naval Academy baseball coach. He occupied the position for 24 years and retired after leading the team to a 24–2 record in 1961. It was his most successful season ever. He died in 1962, from heart complications.

GEORGE EARNSHAW, PITCHER

Aside from Lefty Grove, Earnshaw was Connie Mack's most successful hurler during the late 1920s and early 1930s. The right-handed flame-thrower recorded 127 lifetime victories and packed nearly 70 percent of them into a four-year span from 1929–1932.

Earnshaw was born into a wealthy family and didn't put much stock in baseball. He was a holdout before his pro career even began. He demanded $600 to sign with Baltimore of the IL and simply walked away when owner Jack Dunn refused to pay it. An agreement was eventually reached in 1924. With the departure of Lefty Grove, Earnshaw became the Orioles' staff ace. He was 28 years old by the time he reached the majors.

Nicknamed "Moose" for his sizable 6-foot-4, 210-pound frame, Earnshaw relied heavily on his fastball. "I didn't fool around with those junk pitches," he once told a reporter. "I didn't need them." That wasn't entirely true. Earnshaw did employ a curve and changeup at times, along with a flamboyant windup and high leg kick. He finished among the top 10 in strikeouts each year from 1928–1932.

Earnshaw led the league with 24 wins in 1929, and fashioned a 3.29 ERA, despite averaging more than four walks per nine innings. After three consecutive 20-win campaigns from 1929–1931, he collected 19 victories the following year.

In the World Series, Earnshaw was Connie Mack's "go-to guy." He played in every Fall Classic during the Athletics' glory years of 1929–1931, and retired with a 4–3 record. In 62.2 postseason innings, he yielded just 39 hits, while striking out 56 batters. He was masterful in the 1930 Series against the Cardinals, making three starts and getting a pair of wins. Future Hall of Famer Frankie Frisch said of Earnshaw's performance, "The critics say that we weren't hitting in the Series. True enough. But I'd like to see some of them jump into monkey suits, go to that plate, and try to watch that stuff of Earnshaw's shoot and snake and wiggle and then buzz right past you. He is matchless." Earnshaw retired with a miserly 1.58 postseason ERA in eight appearances.

Among his many talents, Earnshaw was an excellent hitter for a moundsman. He batted .263 with a pair of homers and 13 RBIs during the 1931 slate and followed up the performance with a .286 mark in 1932. In 770 plate appearances, he clubbed 36 extra-base hits, scored 61 runs, and gathered 70 RBIs.

With the Great Depression gripping the United States, Earnshaw took a dramatic pay cut before the 1933 campaign. His work ethic suffered terribly, and he was suspended twice for being out of shape. He was eventually sent home in August after recording a 5–10 record with an inflated 5.97 ERA. Earnshaw seemed to be in denial about his horrific performance. "I haven't any fault to find with Mr. Mack," he told the press. "I don't know why he doesn't want me to pitch, but I guess he has his reasons."

Earnshaw played for three teams during the next three seasons. He ran up a 6.40 ERA in 20 games during the 1936 slate and fell from the major-league ranks for good. After his retirement, he ran his own insurance business and played some semipro ball. He later served in the U.S. Navy, coaching baseball at the Jacksonville Naval Air Station.

Eventually rising to the rank of lieutenant commander, he received a Bronze Star for his service aboard the *Yorktown* during World War II.

Earnshaw remained in the navy until 1947, and then became a Phillies scout and pitching coach from 1949–1951. He died in 1976, at the age of 76.

MULE HAAS, OUTFIELD

From 1923–1925, Haas spent time in four different minor leagues. He was in the Southern Association when the Pirates called him up in mid-August 1925. He appeared in just four games, primarily as a defensive replacement. While playing for the Atlanta Crackers in 1926 and 1927, he caught the attention of the A's. His contract was purchased for a reported sum of $16,000.

Had there been a Rookie of the Year Award in 1928, Haas would have received some consideration. In 75 games as a starter, he hit .292 with 21 doubles and six homers. For the next three seasons, he would be among the Athletics' starting nine more often than not.

Haas could not have asked for a better teacher, as future Hall of Famer Tris Speaker personally tutored him on the finer points of playing center field. Haas adopted Speaker's strategy of playing shallow and going back on the ball. It worked well for him, as he finished among the top defensive players several times during his career.

Haas received the nickname "Mule" from a sportswriter who believed his bat had the "kick of a mule." During the Athletics' three-year period of dominance, he fashioned a .311 batting mark, while averaging 34 doubles and 69 RBIs per year. One of his most fruitful seasons came in 1929, when he scored 115 runs and pounded 66 extra-base hits. During the Athletics' miraculous Game 4 rally against the Cubs that year, Haas's three-run inside-the-park homer was the turning point of the contest. In Game 5, his two-run shot in the bottom of the ninth tied the score and set the stage for a Series-clinching victory.

Haas most often hit out of the second slot. He was called upon quite often to sacrifice leadoff man Max Bishop into scoring position. He executed 40 sacrifices in 1929, and then led the league in that category for five years in a row. His career total of 227 is among the top figures of all time.

Haas was tall and slender, at 6-foot-1, 175 pounds. He was described by one writer as a "fun-loving type of fellow who knows how to be serious when it counts." His departure from Philadelphia in September 1932 represented the beginning of the end for the A's, as Connie Mack shipped him to Chicago, along with Jimmy Dykes and Al Simmons, for $100,000. Several other blockbuster trades would doom the A's to the second division.

Haas spent several seasons in Chicago, playing competently in all but one. In 1938, Mack brought him back to Philly for a curtain call. Upon retiring, he coached the White Sox for seven years and managed in the minors for four. He died in 1974, at the age of 70.

RUBE WALBERG, PITCHER

According to multiple sources, Walberg was "discovered" throwing chunks of coal at fence posts in his brother's Seattle coal yard. He ascended to the big leagues within a year of turning professional. Athletically built at 6-foot-1, 190 pounds, he got his start with Portland of the PCL in 1922. He was purchased by the Giants in September of that year but failed to impress manager John McGraw. The A's signed him in May 1923, and sent him to Milwaukee of the AA when he compiled a bloated 5.75 ERA in 32 scattered appearances.

Walberg would spend 11 seasons in Philadelphia, hitting his stride between 1926–1932, when he averaged 16 wins per year. He was often summoned to bail out his teammates, making 48 closing appearances during that span and finishing among the top 10 in saves on four occasions (a statistic that did not exist then). Against New York, the left-handed Walberg was sometimes called upon to face Ruth and Gehrig in tight spots. Although he frequently got the best of them, Ruth victimized him for 17 home runs—more than any other hurler.

Walberg had a good fastball and was crafty about changing speeds. He suffered from bouts of wildness and lacked the intensity of his Hall of Fame staffmate Lefty Grove. On one particular afternoon, ultracompetitive catcher Mickey Cochrane literally kicked Walberg in the rear end during a mound conference to wake him up. Walberg continued to require periodic reminders from batterymates about his concentration on the mound.

An article in the *Milwaukee Journal* paints Walberg as a nervous sort who had trouble sleeping on the nights before his starts. Later in his career, when he pitched for Boston, manager Joe Cronin would avoid telling him he was scheduled to pitch until the day of the game. Walberg at least took comfort in playing alongside Grove in Philadelphia. After the 1930 World Series, he told a reporter, "It was a great mental satisfaction to know that if I faltered I would be replaced by the greatest pitcher in the game. I could put everything I had in every pitch knowing that if my endurance gave out, Grove would come in and set them down."

Walberg appeared in every World Series for the A's between 1929–1931. He was used somewhat sparingly, making five appearances. He lost his only start in Game 3 of the 1930 Fall Classic against the Cardinals but was effective overall, compiling a 1.93 ERA in 14 innings of work.

When his record fell to 9–13 in 1933, Walberg was included in a trade that sent Lefty Grove and Max Bishop to the Red Sox. He served mostly as a reliever in Boston and retired after the 1937 campaign. He owned a bar in a suburb of Philly for several years and reportedly enjoyed reminiscing with patrons about his glory years on the mound. He did some scouting for the A's but eventually left the game behind. In 1963, he appeared at a celebrity golf tournament and told a reporter, "I haven't seen a game in eight years. After all, why should I hang around the fringes trying to capitalize on a name? The game owes me nothing." He passed away in Tempe, Arizona, at the age of 82.

JIMMY DYKES, INFIELD

The career of Dykes straddled six decades and included 16 years as a player, six as a player-manager, and 16 at the helm of several different clubs. As a manager, he compiled a sub-.500 record and never finished higher than third. His most successful years by far were spent as a player in Philadelphia.

Dykes was invited to Connie Mack's home after his first big-league tryout went poorly. The kindly manager assigned Dykes to the Blue Ridge League in 1917, and encouraged him to keep honing his skills. Mack would later hand-pick Dykes to succeed him as manager when he finally retired after the 1950 slate. "Mr. Mack was my tutor, mentor, my friend, and my personal hero through the years," Dykes writes in his autobiography, *You Can't Steal First Base*.

Dykes was one of the most colorful characters in baseball history. His *New York Times* obituary describes him as a "little round man who usually could be found enveloped in the smoke of a big cigar . . . sometimes his remarks evoked laughter, in others they carried barbs." Dykes, himself, would have agreed with that assessment. "My tongue was as busy at 35 as when I broke in at Gettysburg, fresh and 21," he once remarked. "I got my digs, my wisecracks, my chatter every day."

Although only 5-foot-9, Dykes was solidly built at 185 pounds. He played hard and was not easily intimidated. After being picked off at second base by Eddie Rommel, Ty Cobb threatened Dykes (who had taken Rommel's throw and applied the tag).

"You want to go to the hospital?" Cobb growled.

"You cut me and you'll go, too," Dykes barked back.

It was not the last time the two would clash. Cobb had a superstition of touching second base on his way in from center field, and when Dykes rushed out to his own defensive post to block the bag several times one afternoon, Cobb butted him with his hip. Dykes butted him back, and Cobb suddenly burst out laughing. "I guess I don't need any help to beat this lousy club of yours," he said before jogging away.

Dykes was extremely versatile, appearing at every position except catcher. He was even handed a pair of pitching assignments in 1927, working two innings and giving up just one run. Appearing most often at second and third base, he was a reliable fielder—particularly at third, where he led the league in assists twice and fielding percentage once.

Dykes was used in various batting order positions, typically hitting out of the seventh spot. During his 15 seasons in Philly, he finished in double digits for sacrifices in 11 straight seasons. From 1924–1931, his batting average never dropped below .273. He compiled an on-base percentage in excess of .390 four times in that span.

An indispensable member of the club, Dykes played in every World Series between 1929–1931. He enjoyed his most productive October against the Cubs in 1929, posting the highest batting average among Philly regulars, at .421. During the Athletics' remarkable 10-run rally in Game 4, Dykes got overexcited and accidentally knocked Connie Mack to the ground. After being helped to his feet, the 66-year-old Mack patted Dykes on the arm and said, "Anything goes at a time like this. It's wonderful, isn't it?" In 18 postseason games, Dykes performed admirably, reaching base 28 times by walk or base hit.

With the Great Depression putting the squeeze on Mack, Dykes was sold to the White Sox in September 1932, along with Al Simmons and Mule Haas. He assumed the position of player-manager in Chicago before the 1934 slate, and closed out his playing career there in 1939. In 1960, he was included in an extremely rare trade of managers, as Cleveland GM Frank Lane shipped Joe Gordon to Detroit and got Dykes in return. Dykes remained with the Indians through the 1961 slate and retired as a skipper. He coached through the 1964 campaign. Born and bred in Philly, he died in his beloved city at the age of 79.

BING MILLER, OUTFIELD

Miller started in the minors as a teenager and had a long road to the big leagues. Mistakenly sold to both the Senators and the Pirates, Commissioner Kenesaw Mountain Landis presided over a dispute of ownership. By the time Miller made his debut with Washington, he was 26 years old.

The Senators were a team on the rise in 1921, with Walter Johnson anchoring the pitching corps and future Hall of Famer Sam Rice patrolling the outfield. Miller was one of several promising young players on the club, hitting .288 with 71 RBIs in 114 games. Despite his auspicious debut, the Senators traded him to the A's before the 1922 slate.

Miller was a reliable offensive presence wherever he went. In 16 seasons (portions of 12 spent with Philly), he fashioned a highly credible .311 batting average. During his prime years (1922–1931), he hit .322 or higher six times. While he didn't have a lot of home-run power, he gathered 30 or more doubles in six straight seasons. In 1929, he finished third in the AL with 16 triples.

Connie Mack made a major miscalculation in June 1926, when he dealt Miller to the Browns for outfielder "Baby Doll" Jacobson. Jacobson was used as trade bait to acquire pitcher Howard Ehmke. Miller hit .328 for St. Louis in portions of two seasons. Realizing the error of his ways, Mack brought Miller back to Philadelphia for the 1928 campaign.

Miller played in all three World Series from 1929–1931. His finest performance came in 1929, versus the Cubs, when he hit .368 with four RBIs. His Series-clinching double in Game 5 was witnessed by President Herbert Hoover and his wife. Miller later thanked Cubs manager Joe McCarthy for leaving the right-handed Pat Malone on the mound to face him in the bottom of the ninth. Miller admitted that he had always disliked facing lefties. "I'm about the rottenest right-handed batter against southpaws in this league," he said, although statistics don't back up that claim. He actually hit .375 against left-handed starters in 1929.

The affable Miller was nicknamed after a comic strip character, "George Washington Bings." His 1933 Goudey baseball card states, "He is well-named. Any time he hits a ball it goes places." As he began to age, he continued to swing a potent bat, leading the league in pinch hits for two straight years (1934 and 1935). During the 1936 slate, he was the oldest player in the majors. He retired at season's end.

Miller coached for several AL teams between 1936–1953. He remained an avid Philly supporter to the end. On May 7, 1966, he was returning from a ballgame at his old stomping ground (renamed Connie Mack Stadium by then) between the Phillies and Pirates. He got into a serious car accident and died at the hospital of a heart attack. The medical staff noted that he was wearing a diamond tie clasp with the inscription "1930 World Champions."

FAST FACT: Although it's hard to believe, the A's of 1928 were even more star-studded than the club that won the World Series the following year. Including Connie Mack, the 1928 squad had eight future Hall of Famers on their roster, among them aging superstars Eddie Collins, Tris Speaker, and Ty Cobb. Even so, they finished second to the Yankees, who were carrying a total of 10 eventual Cooperstown inductees (manager Miller Huggins included). Ten is the major-league record for any one team.

9

ST. LOUIS CARDINALS
1930–1934

At the heart of any successful club is a competent group of executives. Through the 1920s and 1930s, the Cardinals had some of the brightest baseball minds of the era in their front office. Owner Sam Breadon rose to prominence as an auto dealer in St. Louis. In 1917, he purchased a minority stake in the Cardinals, and within a few years, he ascended to the role of majority owner. Prior to his arrival, the club had placed no higher than third after joining the National League as the St. Louis Browns in 1892.

Breadon was noted for being rather frugal and demanding. At the same time, he was not afraid to make bold moves for the benefit of his club. To overcome the debt he had inherited, he struck a deal with Browns owner Phil Ball to allow the Cardinals to jointly occupy Sportsman's Park. He later sold the team's crumbling edifice (Robison Field) to the city. Securing a future for the franchise, he placed dynamic manager Branch Rickey in charge of developing a farm system. There could not have been a more capable man fronting the project.

A law school graduate and former major-league catcher, Rickey had served as manager of the Browns from 1913–1915. He demonstrated a keen eye for talent and was among the first to use statistical analysis to evaluate players. When Phil Ball purchased the Browns in 1916, he objected to Rickey's deeply religious nature and intellectual approach to the game. Rickey was released as manager and assigned exclusively to player development. Unhappy in the role, he defected to the Cardinals organization.

Rickey's farm system (the first of its kind) was born in the early 1920s, when a new agreement allowed major-league franchises to own minor-league clubs. Among the first teams to align themselves with the Cardinals were the Houston Buffaloes of the Texas League, the Fort Smith Twins of the Western Association, and Syracuse Stars of the International League. Dozens of others would follow. The Cardinals were contractually tied to their junior affiliates. This prevented them from losing players in bidding wars to richer, more successful clubs.

Commissioner Kenesaw Mountain Landis was highly opposed to the new system, believing that it transformed minor-league pennant races into virtually meaningless exhibitions. On two separate occasions, Landis compelled the Cardinals to release dozens of players he believed were deliberately being kept hidden from other teams. Despite his best efforts, the St. Louis farm system survived, becoming a blueprint for other franchises to follow.

When the Cards got off to a poor start in 1925, it became evident that Rickey could no longer balance his responsibilities as both manager and executive. Despite his objections, he was moved into the front office full time. Rogers Hornsby took the reins, and the club finished strong, winning 15 of the last 20 games. Owing much to Rickey's tireless efforts, the Cardinals had finally arrived.

After knocking off the powerful Yankees in the 1926 World Series, the Redbirds returned for an encore in 1928. They proved to be no match for one of the greatest Yankees teams of all time, getting swept by a combined score of 27–10. But better Octobers lay just ahead.

The 1930 squad was a gifted aggregation of seasoned veterans and budding stars. Signed during an open tryout before the 1920 campaign, Jim Bottomley became one of the finest first basemen in Cardinals history. Nicknamed "Sunny Jim" for his cheerful disposition, he can be seen smiling and clowning around in numerous photos. He was all business at the plate, fashioning a lifetime .310 batting average on the road to Cooperstown.

The Cardinals outfield featured the immensely talented yet physically impaired Chick Hafey. Hafey battled serious sinus problems throughout his career and also suffered from extremely poor eyesight. He once reported that his vision changed daily, forcing him to keep multiple pairs of glasses with diverse prescription strengths. Despite various handicaps, he established himself as one of the NL's most gifted hitters, ultimately ending up in the Hall of Fame.

Acquired from the Giants before the 1927 slate, infielder Frankie Frisch completed the second leg of his storied career with St. Louis. Having been traded for Rogers Hornsby, there was intense pressure on him to perform when he arrived. He was up to the task, providing plenty of punch out of the third slot in the batting order with a .337 average and league-high 48 stolen bases. Frisch had been team captain in New York, and recognizing his leadership abilities, the St. Louis brass promoted him to player-manager in 1933. He remained in charge for portions of six seasons.

There was no shortage of gifted pitchers in the St. Louis rotation. Hall of Famer Jesse "Pop" Haines spent his entire career with the Cardinals, enjoying his most fruitful seasons during the 1920s. Although he was 36 years old and fading by the time the 1930s arrived, he could still dispose of hitters with precision on a good day. Another aging right-hander, Burleigh Grimes, donated his last two effective seasons to the St. Louis cause. Enshrined at Cooperstown in 1964, Grimes was the last legal spitball pitcher. Joining the Cards in June 1930, he won 10 of his last 13 decisions. He followed with an outstanding 17–9 effort the following year.

In 1930, the Cardinals captured their third pennant in a five-year span. It wasn't easy, as they spent a majority of the season in fourth place. A strong 21–4 run in September sent them to the World Series against the powerful Athletics. After dropping the first two games on the road, they bounced back with a pair of wins at St. Louis. Game 5 remained scoreless until a towering ninth-inning homer by Jimmie Foxx sank the Cardinals. The Series ended anticlimactically with a 7–1 Philly romp in Game 6.

The 1931 pennant was a runaway affair, as St. Louis finished 13 games ahead of the Giants. Using the same cast of characters with a few useful upgrades, they won a World Series rematch over the A's in seven games. George Earnshaw and Lefty Grove did most of the pitching for Philly, as only one St. Louis hitter (outfielder Pepper Martin) reached the .300 mark at the plate. Cardinals hurlers were even better, holding Philly opponents to a collective .220 batting average.

The 1932 campaign was a disaster. After capturing a batting title the previous year, Chick Hafey held out for more money in training camp and ended up being dealt to the Reds. Jim Bottomley slumped throughout the spring, sitting out more than 50 games. Frankie Frisch was limited to 115 appearances, and the 38-year-old Jesse Haines was largely ineffective on the mound. While the Cardinals slumped to sixth place that year, there was reason to be hopeful, as a pair of bright, young rookies joined the club.

In his 1930 major-league debut, Dizzy Dean had tossed a three-hitter. Unfortunately, the St. Louis staff was cluttered with talent, and he was sent back to the farm. After a 26-win effort for the Houston Buffaloes in 1931, the Cardinals decided it was time for another promotion. Dean was the NL's most dominant right-hander for five seasons. Notoriously arrogant, the trash-talking moundsman would often boast of the various feats he was going to accomplish on the field. He followed through more often than not and justified his conceit with the statement, "It ain't bragging if you can back it up."

Another irrepressible prospect, slugger Joe Medwick led the Texas League in homers during the 1931 campaign. He was vying for a batting title when the Cardinals summoned him to St. Louis in September 1932. The rough-and-tumble Medwick quickly emerged as one of the most productive hitters of the era. According to one contemporary, Medwick "stood up there and whaled everything within reach. Doubles, triples, home runs—he sprayed 'em all over the park."

In 1933, Gabby Street was dismissed as manager when the Cards got off to a mediocre 46–45 start. The team played slightly better under his replacement, Frankie Frisch, finishing 11 games over .500. Sportswriters recognized the Cardinals' vast potential, but opinions were mixed as to how the team would fare in the coming season.

The 1934 Cardinals were one of the most colorful squads of all time. As the story goes, the term *Gashouse Gang* was coined by shortstop Leo Durocher, who joked to a reporter that the Cardinals would never be allowed in the American League. "They think we're just a bunch of gashousers," he quipped. When the team was on a winning streak, players refused to wash their uniforms. "We looked horrible, we knew it, and we gloried in it," Durocher later boasted. Their grit and determination endeared them to millions of Depression-Era Americans, who saw them as blue-collar heroes.

With much pomp and swagger, the "Gashouse Gang" captured the NL pennant despite stiff competition from the defending world champion New York Giants. The World Series went the distance, but the Cardinals came out on top. Game 7 is best remembered for a near riot in Detroit, touched off by an altercation between Joe Medwick and Marv Owen. The Cardinals were cruising to an easy win, leading 7–0 in the top of the sixth. With a runner on second and two out, Medwick hammered a ball to the right-field wall. Despite his team's considerable lead, the ultracompetitive slugger opted to try for a triple. Owen spiked him on the leg at third base, and Medwick responded by kicking Owen in the stomach. Disgruntled fans showered Medwick with garbage when he assumed his left-field post in the bottom of the frame. He was eventually pulled from the lineup for his own safety. His refusal to lay up, even with the game well in hand, captured the spirit of the 1934 Cardinals: bold, ornery, and irrepressible.

After the glory of the 1934 campaign, the Cardinals began a slow descent into mediocrity. They finished second in 1935 and 1936, and then slumped to fourth place the following year. By 1938, Frisch and Haines had retired. Durocher and Dean had left for other clubs. Medwick joined the mass departure from St. Louis in 1940, bringing the "Gashouse" years to an unceremonious end.

While numerous Cardinals players of the early 1930s have received their just rewards from the Hall of Fame electorate, the names of many have gradually faded into obscurity through the years. Some of those names are resurrected on the pages that follow.

JIM BOTTOMLEY, FIRST BASE

Bottomley was a cheerful character, earning the nickname "Sunny Jim." A reassuring presence on the Cardinals bench, he was known to offer comfort and advice to rookies. Infielder Les Bell told a story about how he threw two balls over the first baseman's head in one of his earliest major-league appearances with the Cards. Bottomley put his arm around Bell in the dugout afterward and offered words of encouragement. "That made me feel better," Bell said. "What a fine gentleman he was." According to his *New York Times* obituary, the gentlemanly Bottomley was quite popular with female fans on Ladies Day as well.

Bottomley grew up in rural Illinois. At age 16, he became a blacksmith's apprentice. He was among the first major stars to be plucked from the newly established Cardinals farm system. Called to St. Louis in August 1922, he would spend the next 15 seasons in major-league service.

According to teammate Frankie Frisch, Bottomley was one of the best clutch hitters in the majors. "It was a standing joke with us on the Cardinals bench whenever the fellow in front of Jim was given a walk," Frisch said. "Imagine walking a guy to get at Bottomley! And Jim loved it. He'd just grin wider and strut up to the plate. Pow!"

Bottomley topped the .300 mark nine times between 1922–1931. He narrowly missed in 1926, finishing at .299. He led the NL in doubles and RBIs twice, and won a homer crown in 1928—the same year he was named NL MVP. In September 1924, he had one of the finest days ever assembled by a big-league hitter. Facing the Brooklyn Robins at Ebbets Field, he hit three singles, a double, and a pair of homers, collecting a record 12 RBIs. He added another six-hit game to his resume in 1932.

Bottomley was not always successful in World Series play, but he was facing some of the greatest pitchers of all time, among them Waite Hoyt, Herb Pennock, and Lefty Grove. A lifetime .200 hitter in four Fall Classics with the Cardinals, his greatest postseason performance came against the Yankees in 1926, when he logged a .345 average with three doubles and five RBIs.

Limited to 91 games in 1932, Bottomley was traded to the Reds in the offseason. He spent three years in Cincinnati, putting up ordinary numbers. In 1936, he had a resurgence with the Browns, hitting .298 with 95 RBIs. He took over as player-manager the following year when Rogers Hornsby was let go. He slumped at the plate as the Browns lost 108 games. Bottomley had been playing with arthritis and bone spurs in his back. After the 1937 campaign, he was finished in the majors.

He was out of baseball after that until 1955, when the Cubs offered him a job as a scout. He was promoted to manager in the Appalachian League that year, but suffered a heart attack and was forced to quit. He died in 1959 due to ongoing heart issues. He was elected to the Hall in 1974.

CHICK HAFEY, LEFT FIELD

In addition to sinus problems and poor eyesight, Hafey had other assorted illnesses that kept him on the bench for periods of time. Cardinals executive Branch Rickey commented, "I always thought that if Hafey had been blessed with normal eyesight and good health, he might have been the greatest right-handed batter baseball had ever known." Despite that ringing endorsement, Rickey argued with Hafey about his salary almost every season. One year, Hafey got so frustrated, he left spring training abruptly and traveled thousands of miles by car to his home. He remembered tearing through the desert at 90 miles per hour.

Hafey developed a reputation as a slugger. He used a long-handled bat and generated scorching line drives with his wiry arms and powerful wrists. Teammate Jim Bottomley remarked that Hafey could hit the ball harder than Rogers Hornsby. "When he leaned on the ball, you could hear the seams crack," Bottomley said of Hafey.

Among the cavalcade of stars to arrive in St. Louis during the 1920s, Hafey didn't appear in more than 100 games until his fourth season. Hit twice by pitches during a game in 1926, he was examined by the team doctor, who discovered that Hafey couldn't see his hand when it was raised above a certain height. The outfielder was instructed to wear glasses on the field after that. He was among the first major leaguers to do so. Hafey's vision changed constantly, and he was forced to keep multiple pairs of spectacles around with varying prescription strengths.

Infielders had a tendency to play deep when Hafey was at bat. In one amusing anecdote, Hafey beat out a bunt one afternoon when he noticed that third baseman Fresco Thompson of the Dodgers was stationed near the outfield grass. Thompson arranged to have an ice cream bar delivered to Hafey in the dugout, instructing the vendor to pass on the following message: "If you'll bunt again next time, Mr. Hafey, he said he'll send you another."

Described as being quiet and shy, Hafey was a lion at the plate. In his prime years of 1927–1932, his batting averages ranged from .329 to .349. The latter mark earned him a batting crown. He appeared in four World Series with the Cards, managing a somewhat feeble .205 average. But he slammed five doubles in six games against the A's in the 1930 Fall Classic.

In the spring of 1932, Rickey and Hafey had one of their epic salary disputes. Although Hafey had won a batting crown the previous year, Rickey refused to meet his demands, shipping the marquis outfielder off to Cincinnati. Hafey ended up having two sinus operations that year and was also out with the flu for a spell. Still, he hit .344 in 83 games. He appeared in baseball's first All-Star Game in 1933, going 1-for-4. His hit was a bloop single off of Yankees great Lefty Gomez.

Hafey's sinus condition worsened, and he retired in 1935, at the age of 32. He made a comeback attempt in 1937, but his numbers were pedestrian. Leaving baseball behind, he returned to his California ranch to raise sheep and cattle. In declining health, he was elected to the Hall of Fame in 1971, via the controversial Veteran's Committee, which ended up being accused of cronyism. Hafey was pleased to be there regardless, commenting that it was the "greatest thing that had ever happened to [him] in baseball."

JESSE HAINES, PITCHER

Haines developed a knuckleball when it became apparent that his other pitches were ordinary. He used the knuckleball until his fingers literally bled. He also added a changeup later on. "I threw a hard knuckler, a lot harder than they throw today," Haines commented in his later years. "It broke sharper, too."

Haines may have been a soft choice for the Hall of Fame. He posted a won–loss record below .500 in four seasons, hit his peak rather late, and lumped his best efforts into a short span. He was 43 years old during his last campaign, and his nickname, "Pop," originated from his advanced playing age. Through it all, he worked hard and expected a lot from himself. Teammate Terry Moore remarked, "When I saw how hard a nice old man like 'Pop' took losing a game, I realized why he'd been a consistent winner."

The right-handed Haines was a fast worker, partly because umpires demanded it, but also by choice. He once likened himself to Bob Gibson, who was all business on the mound. "He doesn't fool around out there, and I didn't either," the hurler remarked. Ironically, Haines's best single-game effort—a no-hitter against the Braves in July 1924—coincided with the worst season of his career. He was 8–19 that year with a 4.41 ERA. Three years later, he had his greatest season, winning 24 games and leading the league with six shutouts.

Haines was a big-game pitcher, fashioning a 3–1 record in four World Series with a 1.67 ERA. In the 1926 October Classic versus the Yankees, he allowed just two earned runs in more than 16 innings of work. Had the Cardinals not committed a slew of errors in his only start during the 1928 Series, Haines might have remained undefeated. He is one of only two pitchers to homer in his own World Series shutout.

During the Cardinals' back-to-back pennant-winning efforts in 1930 and 1931, Haines went 25–11 with a 3.78 ERA. As a 40-year-old member of the "Gashouse Gang" in 1934, he entered 37 regular-season games and averaged less than a run per appearance. He retired in 1937, and moved on to coach for the Dodgers the following year. He was elected to Cooperstown in 1970.

BURLEIGH GRIMES, PITCHER

By the time Grimes joined the Cardinals in June 1930, he was in his 15th major-league season. Legends of his fierce competitiveness abounded. Traded from the Pirates early in his career after a bloody fistfight with the team's manager, he once knocked down five batters in a row and threw at a player in the on-deck circle. He was even accused of smacking a 12-year-old autograph seeker after a particularly tough loss one afternoon.

Grimes had five effective pitches in his arsenal—among them a fastball, curve, and spitter. The latter offering made him famous. The last legal spitball pitcher in the majors, Grimes moistened the ball by chewing slippery elm bark. Since the resin irritated his skin, he avoided shaving on the days of his starts. He ended up with the nickname "Ol' Stubblebeard." Grimes had a hatred of batters, which he explained as follows: "There was only one man standing between me and more money, and that was the guy with the bat. I knew I'd always have to fight the man with the bat as if he were trying to rob me in a dark alley."

Since Grimes was such an overpowering pitcher in his prime, his batting is often overlooked. A lifetime .248 hitter, he collected 75 extra-base hits and drove in 168 runs—excellent numbers for a moundsman. He enjoyed his best offensive year at the plate in 1928, running up a

.321 batting average in 48 games. He was especially adept against the Pirates during his career, hitting .273 in 77 appearances. Comfortable on the October stage, Grimes had a pair of multihit efforts for the Cardinals in World Series play.

A Game 1 loser against the A's in the 1930 Series, Grimes allowed just five hits and two runs when he returned to the mound in Game 5. He was saddled with a second loss when the Cardinals failed to push any runs across. Against the same opponents in 1931, Grimes won both of his starts as St. Louis hitters spotted him nine runs. He lasted 8.2 innings in the second outing, dislocating one of his vertebrae while trying to retire the last hitter. According to multiple sources, he could barely make it back to the dugout. Traded to the Cubs the following year, the 38-year-old spitballer got shelled by the Yankees in two World Series appearances. He was 3–4 with a 4.29 ERA overall in postseason play.

Grimes lasted 19 seasons in the majors, averaging 14 wins per year. He managed in the minors before succeeding Casey Stengel as Brooklyn skipper. He spent two seasons at the Dodger helm, guiding the club to a sub-.500 record. He worked with a handful of aging Hall of Famers, but aside from that, the talent was rather thin. He later scouted for several teams. He was a member of the 1964 Hall of Fame class.

DIZZY DEAN, PITCHER

Every now and then, a player comes along who transcends the sport. Dean was one of those exceptional men. In an era when many Americans were down and out, Dean showed them that folks from humble beginnings could overcome major obstacles and make it big.

The son of a poor sharecropper, Dean more or less raised himself. His formal education ended in fourth grade, and he joined the U.S. Army at the age of 16. Tiring quickly of the military lifestyle, he begged his brother to come rescue him. Paul Dean secured his brother's discharge for a reported sum of $120—an enormous chunk of cash for a farmer.

Dean won 51 games in two minor-league seasons, but the Cardinals were a pitching-rich club and they waited until 1932 to promote him full-time. In 1932, he proved what he could do, leading the league in shutouts and strikeouts, while winning 18 games for a team that finished sixth. For the next four seasons, Dean was the hottest property in baseball, gathering no fewer than 20 victories per year. In 1934, when he captured a MVP Award, he was 30–7 with a 2.66 ERA.

Dean's value to the club went far beyond his stats. While he portrayed a hillbilly image to the public, he was much brighter than he let on. A shameless self-promoter and Cardinals ambassador, he was loud, boastful, and flamboyant. His memorable quotes and outrageous behavior filled the columns of newspapers and magazines. In 1934, when the Cardinals won the World Series, there was a tremendous increase in attendance at Sportsman's Park. While many teams were losing money, the Cardinals were doing okay.

Dean was brilliant in his only World Series with St. Louis. A hard-luck loser in Game 5, he won both of his other starts. His masterpiece came in Game 7, when the Cardinals polished off the Tigers in dramatic fashion with an 11–0 drubbing. Facing four of the games' best hitters—Gehringer, Greenberg, Goslin, and Cochrane—Dean allowed just six hits and retired eight straight batters at one point. His second victory fulfilled a boast that he and his brother would win two games apiece. In the fourth inning of Game 4, he was inserted as a pinch-runner for Spud Davis. While breaking up a double play, he was hit in the head with the ball and ended up in the hospital. After being released he told reporters with tongue in cheek, "The doctors X-rayed my head and found nothing."

After going 52–25 in 1935 and 1936, Dean's downfall came rapidly. Chosen for the All-Star team in 1937, he didn't want to go. He had hoped to get some fishing in with the extra days off, but his wife insisted he attend. In the third inning, future Hall of Famer Earl Averill lined a ball off of Dean's toe. Informed that it was fractured, he allegedly said, "Fractured! Hell, the damn thing's broken!" Shortly afterward, he was back on the mound with a splint and special shoe. He was favoring his other foot and using an altered follow-through motion. After a few pitches, Dean reported, "[T]here was a loud crack in my shoulder, and my arm went numb down to my fingers."

Traded to the Cubs in 1938, he managed a 16–8 record in portions of four seasons. He retired in 1941. Dean became a broadcaster for the St. Louis Browns after that, frequently disregarding standard rules of grammar and syntax. When the St. Louis Board of Education demanded that he be taken off the air, he admonished, "Let the teachers teach English, and I will teach baseball. As for this use of 'ain't,' there is a lot of people in the United States who say 'isn't' and they ain't eatin'." During his Hall of Fame speech in 1953, Dean remarked memorably, "The good Lord was good to me. He gave me a strong body, a good right arm, and a weak mind."

FRANKIE FRISCH, SECOND BASE

When Frisch served as captain of the Giants under John McGraw, the team's signs were relayed through him. McGraw would sometimes leave the park early, putting Frisch in charge. It was apparent that he was being groomed for the manager's job. But during the 1926 pennant race, the Giants faltered, and the ever petulant McGraw became increasingly contentious. Hall of Famer Freddie Lindstrom remembered, "[T]here was a constant squabbling between them, and they became terrible enemies." Frisch grew tired of taking the brunt of losses and ended up leaving the team briefly. In December of that year, he was traded to the Cardinals with pitcher Jimmy Ring for Rogers Hornsby.

Frisch quickly established himself as one of the best players on the club, hitting .337 in his St. Louis debut. He played the game hard and fast, stealing 24 or more bases for the Cardinals four times during an era when the stolen base had fallen out of fashion. He developed an ongoing feud with headhunter and future teammate Burleigh Grimes, who would knock Frisch down every time the two squared off. "That Frisch was a sassy kid," said Grimes. "But he had a lot of guts . . . I'd try to drive him back, but he'd lean in there and try to hit me to left field."

Frisch replaced Gabby Street as manager late in the 1933 campaign. He had difficulty controlling the type-A personalities in St. Louis, especially Dizzy Dean. During a spring training game against the Giants, Dean was touched up for seven runs in one inning. After stomping around the mound angrily, he proceeded to deliberately hit several Giants players in a row. Finally, Frisch screamed at the umpire to get the "maniac" off the mound. "They drove me nuts," Frisch later said of the unruly "Gashouse Gang." "But if I could have a bunch of guys like that every year, I'd be quite content to stay nuts."

During Frisch's prime years with the Cardinals, which lasted from 1927–1934, his batting averages ranged from .292 to .346. In 1931, he was named NL MVP. Defensively, he finished first or second in fielding percentage on seven occasions. Some of Frisch's fondest memories were tied to the 1934 World Series. He described it as the "roughest, toughest, saltiest in which [he] ever played." In the third inning of Game 7, the Tigers walked Jack Rothrock to load the bases for Frisch. Rising to the challenge, Frisch slammed a bases-clearing double. By his own admission he could have ended up on third but got so excited he sort of froze. "If one of my guys had stopped at second base the way I did, I would have fined him," he later said. In four World Series with the Cardinals, Frisch gathered 21 hits (five for extra bases) and scored five runs, while driving in six.

When the Cardinals slid in the standings, Frisch was replaced at the St. Louis helm. He later managed for the Pirates and Cubs. Known as an umpire baiter, Frisch pretended to pass out while arguing with Bill Klem one day. Klem shouted at him as he lay on the ground, "Frisch, if you ain't dead, you're out of the game!" On another occasion, Frisch came to the plate with an open umbrella to argue in favor of a rainout. That scene inspired a famous painting by Norman Rockwell.

Frisch made it to Cooperstown in 1947. During the 1950s, he worked as a play-by-play announcer for the Giants. A heart attack in 1956 forced him to step aside. As a member of the Hall of Fame Veteran's Committee, he presided over some of the most controversial selections in history—including former Cardinals teammates Jesse Haines and Chick Hafey. Frisch died in March 1973, from injuries sustained in a car crash a month earlier. The *Sporting News* selected him as one of the top 100 players of all time.

JOE MEDWICK, LEFT FIELD

Medwick was born to Austro-Hungarian immigrants in Carteret, New Jersey. Solidly built at 5-foot-10, 187 pounds, he became a multisport star in high school, excelling at football and basketball, in addition to baseball. He was signed by the Cardinals off the New Jersey sandlots while still a teenager, rapidly working his way up through their farm system. In two seasons with the Houston Buffaloes, he punished opposing pitchers. By 1933, he was a regular in the Cardinals outfield, where he would stay until June 1940.

Medwick preferred the nickname "Muscles," but a female fan saddled him with the facetious moniker "Ducky." A free-swinger who loathed walks, he gathered 76 extra-base hits (including a league-leading 18 triples), along with 106 RBIs, during the Cardinals' championship run of 1934. He would reach his peak in 1937, leading the NL in a dozen major offensive categories, while capturing a Triple Crown and a MVP Award. At the start of the 2016 campaign, he remained the last NL player to have won a Triple Crown.

Medwick was combative and somewhat unpopular among certain teammates. Frankie Frisch once groused about Medwick's tendency to roughhouse with other players. "I'd walk into the clubhouse and Medwick or Pepper Martin would be wrestling on the cement floor with Dizzy Dean. A million dollars' worth of talent wrestling on the cement!" Medwick got into real scrapes with Ripper Collins, Ed Heusser, and Tex Carleton. He exchanged angry barbs with both of the Dean brothers as well. Describing Medwick's character, Leo Durocher said he was the "meanest, roughest guy you could imagine." His scrape with Marv Owen in the 1934 World Series (described earlier in this chapter) solidified that reputation.

When it came to negotiating contracts, the self-confident Medwick refused to back down. He once commented that baseball was all about "base hits and buckerinos." During one particular dispute, Cardinals owner Sam Breadon allegedly told Medwick he would rather throw $2,000 out the window than include it in the slugger's paycheck. "Mr. Breadon," Medwick replied sardonically, "If you threw $2,000 out the window, you'd still be holding it when it hit the ground." St. Louis management eventually tired of Medwick's attitude and traded him to the Dodgers in June 1940. He left St. Louis with a cumulative .336 regular-season batting average and a .379 mark in World Series play.

Medwick stirred up trouble for himself in Brooklyn as well. One week after his trade, he got into a bitter argument with Cardinals pitcher Bob Bowman in a hotel elevator. Bowman, who was slated to pitch against the Dodgers that day, became angry, threatening to "take care of" Medwick and Leo Durocher. Bowman ended up hitting Medwick in the head with a pitch, sending him to the hospital. Dodgers owner Larry MacPhail successfully lobbied for an investigation of the incident, but Bowman went without punishment. He claimed that the pitch had slipped out of his hand and that his threat had not been literal.

While he still posted highly respectable batting averages, Medwick's power numbers tapered off after the beaning. Signing with the Cardinals again in 1947, he closed out his career in the city that had made him a household name. Upon falling from the major-league ranks, he managed in the Florida International League and Carolina League. He would take a job as a Cardinals minor-league batting instructor in 1966. At some point after his retirement, Medwick traveled to Italy and met the pope. Asked to state his occupation, he reportedly said, "Your holiness, I'm Joe Medwick. I, too, used to be a Cardinal."

PEPPER MARTIN, OUTFIELD/THIRD BASE

Many colorful phrases have been used to describe Pepper Martin. Historian Lee Allen referred to him as a "chunky, unshaven hobo who ran the bases like a berserk locomotive." Associated Press writer Edward J. Neil characterizes him as a "good-natured wild wahoo." Few players in baseball history have demonstrated more hustle and grit.

Born in Temple, Oklahoma, Martin participated in multiple sports while growing up. A local scribe who saw him play football labeled him the "Wild Horse of the Osage." The nickname stuck. He received his first big-league call-up in April 1928. He hit .308 in 39 games but failed to find a regular spot in the Cardinals lineup. That day would finally come in 1931.

In his first season as a full-timer, Martin impressed sportswriters and fans with his no-holds-barred style of play. He tore around the bases with reckless abandon, taking advantage of every hesitation or miscue by opponents. He became famous for his headfirst "belly slides." Even his own teammates were a bit intimidated by him. Ripper Collins commented, "Sometimes, he could scare you as bad playing with him as against him. I played some outfield alongside him, and I hated to hear him coming."

After hitting an even .300 during the 1931 regular season, Martin turned in one of the greatest performances in World Series history. He gathered 12 hits (five of them for extra bases) and stole five bags off of rifle-armed Athletics catcher Mickey Cochrane. In a syndicated article penned after Game 2 of the Series, Cochrane griped about Martin, "Folks, we've tried to fool the Cardinals' young center fielder with everything in the book. . . . To date, he doesn't have a weakness."

While hunting in the offseason, Martin received a nasty insect bite that became badly infected. The condition plagued him into the 1932 campaign. He broke a finger at some point during the year and kept the injury hidden until his bandage unraveled as he was throwing to first base, leaving a trail across the infield. Asked about the finger, Martin said, "It was just a small bone." Limited to 85 games, he slumped to .238 at the plate.

In 1933, Martin was moved from the outfield to third base to make room for Joe Medwick. He was slow in adjusting to the position, making numerous wild throws, while regularly allowing balls to carom off his chest. According to one teammate, Martin hated it when batters bunted on him, and he would deliberately aim for the runner instead of first base. He finished second among NL third basemen in errors that year but reached a career-high mark of .316 at the plate.

Off the field, Martin was a notorious practical joker who was known to drop water balloons on sportswriters and release sneezing powder in hotel lobbies. He also played guitar in the Cardinals' hillbilly band, known as the "Mississippi Mudcats." Teammate Frankie Frisch described Martin as a "fighter, but a happy-go-lucky, fun guy."

Martin's numbers in the 1934 World Series were outstanding, as he rapped 11 hits and scored eight runs. He was a lifetime .418 hitter in postseason play. Although his hard-nosed style of play frequently kept him on the bench with injuries, he led the league in stolen bases three times and was named to four All-Star Teams. Demoted to the farm in 1941, he returned to St. Louis for a curtain call in 1944.

Martin kept busy after his playing days were over, managing various clubs in several different minor leagues during a 14-year span. He was equally aggressive as a manager, getting suspended and fined for choking an umpire on one occasion. He also served a suspension for hitting a fan. Outside of baseball, Martin served as a deputy sheriff and director of a state penitentiary. He owned a 970-acre ranch that was used to raise beef cattle. He died moderately young at the age of 61.

RIPPER COLLINS, FIRST BASE

Born James Anthony Collins, "Ripper" received his nickname playing ball as a boy, when one of his line drives reportedly got stuck on a nail in the outfield fence. He worked as a coal miner in Altoona, Pennsylvania, before a strike prompted him to put down his shovel and pick up a bat professionally. Living up to his moniker, he won a Triple Crown in the Three-I League during the 1928 slate. The following year, he led the IL with 38 homers and 134 RBIs, while guiding the Rochester Red Wings to a pennant. His record-setting 180 ribbies in 1930 prompted the Cardinals to finally promote him.

The first-base job in St. Louis belonged to Jim Bottomley, and Collins served as an understudy, hitting .301 with 59 RBIs during his rookie year of 1931. To keep his bat in the lineup, manager Gabby Street planted Collins in the outfield 60 times in 1932. Bottomley's offensive numbers began to taper off, and Collins was gradually phased in. By 1933, "Sunny Jim" was gone and "Ripper" was St. Louis's full-time first baseman.

Collins was small compared to other players at his position. He stood just 5-foot-9 and weighed 165 pounds. He swung a potent bat from both sides of the plate, enjoying his most productive offensive span from 1932–1935. He exceeded the .300 mark at the plate three times in that stretch. He reached the century mark in RBIs and runs scored twice. The 1934 season was his signature offensive campaign, as he collected 200 hits and led the league with 35 homers. His 369 total bases that year were a record for NL switch-hitters.

In the 1934 World Series, Collins played in all seven games and accrued a .367 batting average with 11 base hits. He went 4-for-5 in the Cardinals' 11–0 Game 7 romp. He would return to the postseason with the Cubs in 1938, hitting just .133 against Yankees hurlers. He played in 13 postseason games overall, compiling a .277 average.

Collins was a fun-loving guy, described by multiple sources as a "ringleader" of the rowdy "Gashouse Gang." He was a member of the club's "Mississippi Mudcat" band and dabbled in songwriting in his spare time. On the field, he was all business. Typically batting out of the third or fourth slot, he broke up four no-hitters during his career.

Collins's production lagged a bit in 1936. He had trouble hitting lefties, managing a meager .214 average against them. In October of that year, the Cardinals used him as trade bait to lure Cubs right-hander Lon Warneke away from Chicago. Warneke (known colorfully as the "Arkansas Hummingbird" for the movement on his pitches) had several excellent seasons in St. Louis. Collins never attained his previous level of success, although he remained popular with fans in Chicago. After his 1939 release, one columnist wrote, "He had a spirited, joyous disposition and brought the color and aggressiveness of the Gashouse Gang into Chicago. What he didn't bring, though, was his potent bat. He wasn't the same hitter."

Out of the majors in 1939 and 1940, the Pirates gave him one last try the following year. He hit just .210 in 49 games. He continued in the Pacific Coast and Eastern leagues through 1947, serving as a player-manager. In 1944, he was named Minor League Player of the Year—one of the oldest men ever to claim the award, at the age of 40. After his playing days were over, he managed numerous clubs in various minor-league circuits. He was elected to the International League Hall of Fame in 1951. He served as a broadcaster for a spell before returning to major-league service as a Cubs coach from 1961–1963.

Collins also worked for the Wilson Sporting Goods Company. His autograph appeared on Wilson first baseman mitts for some time. He maintained his passion for the game in later years, assembling a massive collection of memorabilia. His home in New Haven, New York, was surrounded by a fence made of baseball bats. He died in 1970, at age 66.

FAST FACT: In 1935, a fading Babe Ruth—then with the Braves—faced Dizzy Dean in his prime. After walking Ruth twice, Dean, beaming from ear to ear, dramatically waved his outfielders back toward the outfield fence and whistled a fastball straight down the pipe. The 40-year-old slugger swung and missed. In a 1948 promotional appearance at Sportsman's Park, Dizzy faced the Babe again. This time, Ruth was in declining health, and the bat slipped off his shoulder. Dean playfully strolled to the plate and gestured toward the right-field bleachers in an imitation of Ruth's mythical "called shot." Fans voiced their approval of the gesture.

10

NEW YORK YANKEES

1936–1939

While the Yankees squads of the 1920s were undoubtedly among the greatest ever assembled, the Bombers of the late 1930s took greatness to another level. Before then, no club had ever won three consecutive world championships—let alone four. And while the Babe Ruth era continues to captivate generations of fans, the Yankees attained their highest level of success after Ruth was gone.

When manager Miller Huggins died unexpectedly in September 1929, the Bombers were a team without a rudder. Art Fletcher, who had piloted the dreadful Phillies for four unsuccessful campaigns, was recruited to finish the season. The following year, former Yankees pitching great Bob Shawkey guided the club to a lukewarm third-place finish. In 1931, GM Ed Barrow hired Joe McCarthy to turn things around.

During his tenure, "Marse Joe" would guide the Yankees to eight pennants and seven world championships. Having steered the Cubs to the 1929 Fall Classic, he became the first manager to capture pennants in both leagues. Described as "self-effacing and relentlessly confident," McCarthy had his share of detractors. Rival manager Jimmy Dykes once referred to the Yankees pilot as a "push-button manager" who got by solely on the vast talents of his players. Proving a point, McCarthy sat out all of his Yankees All-Stars during the 1943 Midsummer Classic. The American League won anyway, 5–3.

After capturing the fourth championship in franchise history during the 1932 slate, the Yankees became rooted in second place for three straight seasons. Ruth's skills were in decline, pitcher Herb Pennock was no longer effective, and outfielder Earle Combs suffered a pair of serious injuries, the latter of which ended his career. There was no shortage of talent in New York, however, and the club wouldn't stay down for long.

The most productive Yankee during the 1930s was first baseman Lou Gehrig. The durable slugger recorded 13 straight seasons with at least 100 RBIs. He led the league in on-base percentage five times, runs scored four times, and walks on three occasions. To date, several of his records still stand, including most consecutive years with 100 runs scored (13) and most RBIs in a season by an American Leaguer (184 in 1931).

Making his Yankees debut in 1936, Joe DiMaggio finished among the league leaders in nearly a dozen major offensive categories. Had there been a Rookie of the Year Award back then, he undoubtedly would have won it. "Joltin' Joe" would spend his entire career in the Bronx, getting three MVP nods, while establishing one of the most airtight records of all time—a 56-game hitting streak (in 1941).

Although he was beginning to slow down a bit by the late 1930s, Tony Lazzeri was still among the better infielders in the majors. The 1936 campaign was a banner one for the veteran second baseman, as he set an AL record with 11 RBIs in a game on May 24. He finished the season with 109—his highest total in several years. When Lazzeri's regular-season batting average dropped to .244 in 1937, he was released. Fortunately for the Yankees, they had one of the most bountiful farm systems in the majors. Called up from Newark in 1938, Joe "Flash" Gordon began his own road to Cooperstown. Gordon played second base with more pizzazz—gaining widespread acclaim for his diving stops. He had more power at the plate than his predecessor as well, enjoying multiple 20-homer campaigns in the Bronx.

Rounding out a fine assortment of Hall of Fame regulars, Bill Dickey was the Yankees' number-one catcher from 1929–1943. Dickey was a notorious bad-ball hitter who collected 80 or more RBIs seven times while hitting out of the middle to lower half of the batting order. There were few who could match him defensively.

Dickey called pitches for a host of talented hurlers throughout the years. Two of the best, Lefty Gomez and Red Ruffing, were largely responsible for the team's success in the late 1930s. Ruffing broke in with the dreadful Red Sox squads of the 1920s and almost certainly would have won 300 games had he been traded to the Yankees sooner. Gomez was not only among the most successful Yankees hurlers for more than a decade, but he was also the most amusing. While capturing a pair of Triple Crowns, he provided some of the most memorable quotes in baseball history.

The Yankees began their second era of dominance in 1936, gathering 102 wins and finishing 19 1/2 games ahead of the Tigers. More than 30 percent of their victories were by a margin of five or more runs. In the World Series, they faced the crosstown rival Giants. After dropping the opener at the Polo Grounds, the Bombers lived up to their reputation by administering one of the nastiest beatdowns in Series history. Even the notoriously weak-hitting Lefty Gomez had a pair of RBIs as the Yankees touched up five different hurlers for 18 runs on 17 hits. One headline read, "Pitching Will Win—Giants Don't Have It." That statement rang true in Game 6 as the Giants emptied out their bullpen again in a 13–5 Series-ending loss.

It was more of the same in 1937, as the Yankees rattled off 102 victories again and spent a total of 148 days in first place. The Tigers, despite Hank Greenberg's Herculean 183-RBI effort, lagged 13 games behind. Again, the Yankees squared off against the Giants in the World Series, and, again, it wasn't much of a contest, as the Bronx inhabitants won the first three games by a combined score of 21–3. Giants staff ace Carl Hubbell hardly knew what hit him, emerging with an ERA nearly .80 above his career average. The Yankees captured the Series in five games.

In 1938, the Bombers had trouble shaking the Red Sox, who were helped tremendously by Jimmie Foxx's banner year (50 HR/175 RBI/ .349 BA). Even after a 20–5 run in July, the Yanks were nursing a slender two-game lead at the beginning of August. They extended it to 14 by the end of the month and hung on despite losing eight of nine games in late September. The World Series was a laugher, as the Yankees rolled to a sweep over Chicago. The Cubs scored just nine runs and managed a collective .243 batting average. One reporter referred to their performance as "pitiable."

Tragedy struck the Yankees in 1939. Through 10 exhibition games, Lou Gehrig was hitting a decidedly un-Gehrig-like .100 with no extra-base hits. During the winter, he had been misdiagnosed with a gallbladder problem and encouraged to follow a special diet. It clearly wasn't helping. During one batting-practice session, Joe DiMaggio noted that the "Iron Horse" swung and missed more than a dozen fastballs. Still, no one was alarmed until he fell over backward in the clubhouse one afternoon while putting on his uniform. Pitcher Wes Ferrell remarked that Gehrig just lay there on the floor frowning "like he couldn't understand what was going on." After eight regular-season games, Gehrig removed himself from the lineup for the good of the team.

Although the move was expected to be temporary, Gehrig's condition worsened throughout the next month. He traveled with the club but was too weak to play. Finally, he underwent testing at the Mayo Clinic. The results were devastating, as he was diagnosed with amyotrophic lateral sclerosis—a crippling disease that ravages the body while leaving the mind intact. On July 4, he gave his famous farewell speech in front of 62,000 fans at Yankee Stadium. Scrambling for a replacement, the Yankees settled on Babe Dahlgren, a journeyman who would play for eight teams in 12 major-league seasons. With unimaginable pressure on him, he managed a weak .235 batting average.

Saddened but inspired by the tragedy, the Yankees collected 106 wins and ran away with the pennant. In the World Series, they vanquished the Reds in four games, becoming the first team in major-league history to capture four consecutive championships. They finished their remarkable four-year run with a 16–3 postseason record.

The Yankees roster was so cluttered with Hall of Famers during the late 1930s, it was difficult to get any recognition. If the hitting exploits of Gehrig and DiMaggio failed to grab headlines, the performances of Lazzeri, Dickey, Gomez, Ruffing, and Gordon provided plenty of fodder for beat writers. Unbeknownst to many outside the Bronx, the Yankees had enough minor standouts on their roster to assemble a second AL All-Star squad. The accomplishments of some are chronicled on the pages that follow.

JOE DIMAGGIO, CENTER FIELD

Although DiMaggio became a cultural icon, his numbers were not as stellar as other mythical Yankees figures, for example, Ruth, Gehrig, and Mantle. There are at least two reasons for this. First and foremost, DiMaggio missed three full seasons in his prime to military service during World War II. Second, he lasted just 13 years in the majors due to injuries that seriously began to slow him down during the 1948 campaign.

Often referred to as the "greatest living ballplayer" in his twilight years, the so-called "Yankee Clipper" was an intensely private and vain man who could be prickly with teammates, journalists, and fans. DiMaggio had an enormous ego and a sense of entitlement to go with it. After his retirement, appearances at Yankee Stadium were carefully choreographed to accommodate his needs. Whenever he showed up at the Hall of Fame in Cooperstown for a new exhibit, museum staff were instructed to close whatever area he was in to the general public—a relatively uncommon practice among former ballplayers.

In spite of his personal flaws, he was indisputably among the greatest players ever to don pinstripes. After his 56-game hitting streak was stopped almost single-handedly by a diving, sprawling Ken Keltner (Indians third baseman), DiMaggio hit in 16 more games. Remarkably, the 1941 skein was not the longest of his career. As a 19-year-old unknown in the Pacific Coast League, he had hit safely in 61 consecutive games.

Baseball ran in the DiMaggio blood. Two of Joe's brothers—Vince and Dominic—had successful careers of their own. While playing for the Red Sox, Dom was one of the best leadoff men in the AL for a full decade. Vince spent several seasons as a reliable run producer with the Braves, Pirates, and Phillies. Joe was light years ahead of both siblings.

When Earle Combs suffered a series of career-shortening injuries, DiMaggio replaced him in center field. "Joe D." hit .398 in the PCL in 1935. He set a rookie record during his first month in the majors with 48 hits. The hits would keep coming throughout his career. During the Yankees' record-setting four-year championship run from 1936–1939, DiMaggio's regular-season average never dropped below .323. In the postseason, he hit .304 with 3 homers and 12 RBIs. When he retired in 1951, due to a bad heel, he had nine World Series rings in his collection—a record that stood until Yogi Berra broke it.

DiMaggio's famous marriage to the sultry Marilyn Monroe in 1954 ended in ruin months later. She sought a divorce on the grounds of "mental cruelty." At Monroe's funeral, Joe saw to it that many of her friends, whom he believed had taken advantage of her in various ways, were excluded. DiMaggio worked in the front office of the A's in 1968 and 1969, also serving as a coach. He was a *Mr. Coffee* spokesman for years and appeared at many Old-Timers' Games. He died in 1999—the year the Yankees won the second of three straight championships.

JOE GORDON, SECOND BASE

Had Gordon not found his way into the Hall of Fame, he would still be remembered as the first manager in major-league history to be traded for another manager. It happened in 1960, while he was at the helm in Cleveland. The Tigers decided that Gordon would be an improvement over Jimmy Dykes and agreed to the transaction. Neither team fared well in the standings that year, as the Indians finished fourth and the Tigers placed sixth.

In his playing days, Gordon was remembered as a wide-ranging, clutch-hitting second baseman with home-run power. He enjoyed the defensive end of the game best, commenting, "Hitting—what is there to it? You swing and if you hit the ball, there it goes. Ah, but the fielding. There's rhythm, finesse, teamwork, and balance."

A majority of the men who reach the majors excel at multiple sports on their way up. Gordon participated in an interesting array of competitive activities at the University of Oregon. In addition to baseball, he was a gymnast, long jumper, and soccer player. He also played the violin. He would later demonstrate his gymnastic ability around second base for the Yankees and Indians. Former teammate Bob Feller was sufficiently impressed with Gordon's range, commenting in later years, "He was an acrobat around the bag. He was all over the place in the field."

In 1937, Gordon cracked 26 home runs for the Newark Bears, earning himself a promotion. He was brilliant in his Yankees debut, going deep 25 times, while driving in 97 runs. He also posted the highest range factor among his AL peers (although the statistic didn't exist then). The Yankees went to the World Series that year, and Gordon was up to the challenge, hitting .400 with a homer and six RBIs versus the Cubs. The Yankees swept the Series.

During the next five seasons, Gordon would establish himself as one of the top second basemen in the AL, making the All-Star Team every year, while generating consistent power. He reached the century mark in RBIs three times between 1939–1943. He was named AL MVP in 1942.

When Pearl Harbor was attacked, scores of ballplayers joined the war cause. Gordon was a licensed pilot and owned his own airplane. He entered the U.S. Air Force in March 1944. Stationed mostly in San Diego and Hawaii, he played for the 7th Air Force Team—one of the best military squads of the era. When he returned to the majors in 1946, he had his worst season ever. Co-owner Larry MacPhail accused Gordon of being out of shape and ordered player-manager Bill Dickey to bench the All-Star second baseman. Dickey refused and ended up re-signing as manager that September. In the offseason, Gordon was traded to Cleveland.

The trade rejuvenated Gordon's career. In 1947, he hit 29 homers and drove in 93 runs. The following year, he drilled 32 long balls and collected a career-high 124 RBIs as the Indians won the World Series over the Braves. Gordon had two more decent seasons before retiring as a player.

He later managed in the PCL and served as a Tigers scout before taking over the Indians in 1958. In portions of three seasons, he kept the team above .500. After the famous managerial swap in 1960, Gordon managed the A's for part of the 1961 campaign and the Royals in 1969. He entered the real estate business after leaving baseball behind. He died in 1978, of a heart attack, and was posthumously elected to the Hall of Fame.

BILL DICKEY, CATCHER

In high school and college, Dickey served as a pitcher and second baseman. He subbed for a friend behind the plate one day in a semipro game and impressed the team's manager with his strong, accurate throwing arm. When Dickey signed with the Yankees in 1928, New York scout Johnny Nee staked his reputation on the young backstop's success, vowing that he would quit if Dickey didn't make it. In the early years, Dickey swung for the fences, until manager Miller Huggins explained, "We pay one player here for hitting home runs and that's Babe Ruth." The Yankees skipper advised Dickey to "choke up on the bat and drill the ball," assuring him that it would lengthen his career.

From 1929–1934, Dickey reached the .300 mark at the plate each year, peaking at .339. Although he never led the league in any offensive category, he blossomed into the finest defensive catcher of the era. Hall of Famer Bob Feller once remarked that he could have won 35 games in a season if he had worked with Dickey. "A catcher must want to catch," Dickey said. "He must make up his mind that it isn't the terrible job it is painted." With a positive mindset, Dickey led the AL in putouts and range factor six times apiece. He also posted the highest fielding percentage during four seasons. According to batterymate Charlie Bevens, Dickey "was always one pitch ahead of batters." Said Bevens, "He not only called a great game, but had the best arm I've ever seen." A reliable target behind the plate, Dickey went the entire 1931 season without a passed ball.

During the Yankees' four-year championship run, Dickey fizzled offensively in both Series against the Giants. Facing the Cubs in the 1938 Fall Classic, he raked Chicago pitching at a .400 clip. His finest moment on the October stage came in Game 5 of the 1943 Series, when his homer off of Mort Cooper broke a scoreless tie and lifted the Yanks to a championship over the Cardinals.

Dickey served in the U.S. Navy for two years during World War II. Upon returning in 1946, he replaced Joe McCarthy as manager. The team played somewhat poorly under him, and he squabbled with Yankees owner Larry MacPhail. Unable to handle the conflict, he resigned in September. His All-Star selection that year was the 11th and final of his career, as he retired at season's end.

Dickey later scouted and coached for the Yankees. He was among the first to sing Mickey Mantle's praises. He also helped mold Yogi Berra into a major star. His number "8" was retired by the New York Yankees. He shared the number with Yogi Berra, and both men were honored with plaques in Yankee Stadium's Monument Park.

In 1942, Dickey played himself in *The Pride of the Yankees*—a biopic about Lou Gehrig. He also portrayed himself in *The Stratton Story*, which was released in 1949. The latter script called for Dickey to take a called third strike from actor Jimmy Stewart. Dickey objected, telling director Sam Wood that he had never taken a called third strike in his life. But when the cameras rolled, the Yankees backstop stuck to the script. After several takes, he joked, "I've struck out more times this morning than I did throughout my baseball career."

RED RUFFING, PITCHER

Ruffing's father worked in the Illinois coal mines until a mishap left him with a broken back. He aspired to the position of superintendent and later served multiple terms as mayor of Coalton. Red was being groomed for a life in the mines before his left foot was crushed between two coal cars. He ended up losing several toes. The accident forced him to switch to pitching full time. "The foot bothered me the rest of my career," Ruffing said. "I had to land on the side of my left foot follow-through."

Ruffing polished his craft sufficiently to enter the Red Sox farm system. After Harry Frazee's fire sale, the Sox were starving for talent, and Ruffing was promoted before he was ready. While he became Boston's top pitcher, the team played poorly, and his won–loss record suffered. He led the league in defeats for two straight seasons.

Traded to the Yankees at the age of 25, Ruffing's career took off. Yankees manager Bob Shawkey noticed that Ruffing was putting too much stress on his arm and helped alter the right-hander's delivery. His stamina increased dramatically. Ruffing's most fruitful period came between 1934–1941, when he gathered no fewer than 15 victories per year, while reaching the 20-win threshold four times (in consecutive seasons). He kept his ERA below the 4.00 mark in all but two of his 15 years with the Yankees.

A six-time All-Star, Ruffing appeared in seven World Series and was often a Game 1 starter. He posted a 5–1 record in that role. He enjoyed his finest postseason start in the 1939 opener versus the Reds, holding Cincinnati hitters to just one run on four hits. In Game 1 of the 1942 Series, Ruffing issued several walks but held the Cardinals hitless into the eighth. The soft-spoken hurler grew tired of being ignored by teammates who were trying not to jinx him and said, "You guys don't have to be so damned quiet. I know I've got a no-hitter, and if I get through the eighth, I'll keep it." He didn't, getting chased from the game in the ninth after giving up four runs. Still, he ended up with a win.

Ruffing was an excellent hitter with some power. He collected 34 home runs as a pitcher—fourth on the all-time list. He compiled a .269 lifetime batting average. Opponents occasionally walked him to get at weaker hitters, like shortstop Frank Crosetti.

Catcher Bill Dickey marveled at how Ruffing continued to make adjustments throughout his career. In 1936, when Ruffing was 31 years old, he developed a sharper curve. "Until then, he had just a slight ripple in his snap," said Dickey. "The way the guy suddenly developed was a revelation."

Ruffing ended his career with the White Sox and stuck around as a scout for a while afterward. He also managed and scouted for the Indians. Ruffing had a stroke that paralyzed him at the age of 68 but still managed to make it to Cooperstown for induction ceremonies each year. He died of heart failure in 1986. In 2004, a plaque was installed in Yankee Stadium's Monument Park honoring his accomplishments. His Hall of Fame induction occurred in 1967.

LEFTY GOMEZ, PITCHER

Renowned for his comical anecdotes and colorful quotes, Gomez became an extremely popular dinner speaker after he retired. During his playing days, he exasperated the sober Joe McCarthy with his offbeat behavior. Gomez once held up a World Series game to watch a plane fly overhead. Carrying the nickname "Goofy," he left behind a legacy of memorable utterances, among them the following:

> "I was the worst hitter ever. I never even broke a bat until last year when I was backing out of the garage."
> "I talked to the ball a lot of times in my career. I said, 'Go foul! Go foul!'"

Gomez was born in Rodeo, California. His grandfather was Spanish and his grandmother Portuguese. A standout on the sandlots of Oakland, he was signed by the San Francisco Seals of the PCL. Upon reaching the majors, he was a bit frail, at 6-foot-2, 155 pounds. The Yankees gave him an unlimited meal allowance and encouraged him to drink mass quantities of milk.

After a somewhat rocky debut in 1930, the slender southpaw won no fewer than 21 games in three of the next four seasons. He is among an elite group of hurlers to capture a pair of Triple Crowns. He did it in 1934 and 1937. His 1934 effort was the better of the two. He was 26–5 that year with a 2.33 ERA. Additionally, he led the league in winning percentage, complete games, and shutouts.

Gomez made a living off of his fastball. Known for his use of brush-backs, he was asked by a reporter one day if he would throw at his own mother. "You're damn right I would," he said. "She's a good hitter." Gomez had trouble moving slugger Jimmie Foxx off the plate and was in awe of his raw power. While facing Foxx one day, Gomez shook off all of catcher Bill Dickey's signs, prompting a mound conference. When Dickey asked Gomez what he wanted to throw, the ace replied, "Noth-ing—let's just stall around and see if maybe he'll go away." Gomez was equally intimidated by pitcher Bob Feller. Batting against Feller after a light fog had settled on the field one day, he brought a cigarette lighter to the plate and lit it. When the umpire asked if he could see Feller okay, he responded, "I can see him just fine. I want to make sure that wild man out there can see me." (Numerous versions of the tale exist.) A notoriously poor hitter, Gomez once smashed himself in the ankle while trying to knock mud out of his spikes. He ended up in the hospi-tal.

Gomez fared exceptionally well in high-profile games. He made five All-Star starts and was credited with three wins. In World Series play, he was undefeated, posting an immaculate 6–0 record. In the 1937 Fall Classic against the Giants, he allowed just three earned runs in 18 innings of work.

In 1939, Gomez suffered a string of injuries that curtailed his effec-tiveness. Most notably, he hurt his back while covering first base on a ground ball. He inadvertently altered his pitching motion and suffered arm trouble for the rest of his career. His last good season came in 1941, when he posted a 15–5 record. He appeared in 13 more regular-season games for the Yankees before being sold to the Braves. His stay in Boston was brief. Manager Casey Stengel was prone to waxing poetic about the accomplishments of iconic Giants manager John McGraw. Gomez grew impatient one day and snapped at Stengel, "Case, the problem with this National League is that McGraw's been dead for 10 years and you fellows don't know it." Gomez was let go a few days later. The Senators picked him up, but he fared poorly. He retired after the 1943 slate.

Gomez managed the Binghamton Triplets of the Eastern League in 1946 and 1947, inserting himself into a couple of games. They were his last appearances. Elected to the Hall of Fame in 1972, the pithy moundsman quipped, "It's only fair. After all, I helped a lot of hitters get in." He died in 1989, of heart complications.

JOHNNY MURPHY, PITCHER

Murphy played for the Yankees from 1932–1946, losing two years to military service. He spent his first full season as a swingman, going 14–10 with a 3.12 ERA in 40 games. There was no absence of reliable starters in New York, and Murphy eventually became the club's number-one closer. From 1937–1943, he placed among the top three in games finished each year. In that same span, he led the league in saves four times.

Born in the Bronx, Murphy was noticed by Yankees scout Paul Krichell while playing for Fordham Prep School. Krichell kept an eye on Murphy as he moved on to Fordham University, signing him on the eve of his last college game. In Murphy's era, the concept of a relief specialist was relatively new. The "save" wasn't even an official statistic yet. Many managers used a bullpen-by-committee format, while others enlisted pitchers that were either over the hill or lacking the stamina to start. Although Murphy landed in neither category, he became Joe McCarthy's go-to guy in tight spots. Often summoning Murphy with the bases loaded and dangerous hitters at the plate, McCarthy once commented, "Johnny is the one man I can always count on."

Murphy was at his best in the postseason. During the Yankees' World Series run of 1936–1939, he closed four games and allowed just two runs in 8 1/3 innings. He would later appear in the 1941 and 1943 Fall Classics, retiring with a 1.10 ERA in eight games. His 107 lifetime saves were remarkable for the era. Asked by a reporter how many games he would win one year, the pithy Lefty Gomez answered, "Ask Murphy."

Murphy carried multiple nicknames, among them "Fireman" (an obvious one) and "Grandma." He received the latter handle from a teammate, who objected to Murphy's endless complaining about food and lodging. Apparently, Murphy was fond of fancy cuisine and fine wine. The Yankees started grooming Joe Page for the closer's job in 1946, and Murphy was released in April of the following year. He played his last season with the Red Sox, accruing an efficient ERA of 2.80.

When his playing days were over, Murphy worked as a scout for the Red Sox. He later became director of the club's minor-league operations. He also served as GM for the Mets and was responsible for signing several of the players who would contribute heavily to New York's surprising 1969 World Series victory. He died of a heart attack in 1970, at the age of 61.

RED ROLFE, THIRD BASE

Born in Penacook, New Hampshire, Rolfe attended high school in Exeter before moving on to Dartmouth College. He played for the Big Green and graduated in 1931. He began his minor-league career with Albany of the Eastern League, working his way up to the Double-A level at Newark. Several of his teammates would join him in New York, including George Selkirk, Johnny Murphy, and Dixie Walker, who would later win a batting title and become a fan favorite in Brooklyn.

Rolfe began his career as a shortstop and was later converted to a third baseman. He found the hot corner a more suitable working environment. "Third base is easier than shortstop," he once said. "For one thing, you don't have to hurry your throws. You can boot one a little at third and still recover in time to get your man at first or on a force play."

Rolfe played backup to Jack Saltzgaver (another Newark teammate) in 1934, and became the Yankees starting third baseman the following year. His value to the club was multidimensional. He was a slick fielder, winning back-to-back defensive titles in 1935 and 1936. Hitting out of the second spot, he demonstrated excellent bat control, adeptly hitting behind runners, laying down bunts, and spraying the ball to all fields. He reached the .300 mark in four of five seasons between 1935–1939, scoring 100 runs each year. His best offensive effort came in 1939, when he hit .329 and led the league in runs (139), hits (213), and doubles (46). He made the third of four consecutive All-Star appearances that year.

In the postseason, Rolfe was a consistent performer. He played in six World Series and posted a .300 average in four of them. He had a highly productive October 1936, raking Giants pitching for 10 hits. In 28 postseason games, he reached base by hit or walk 42 times.

In 1942, Rolfe was out of action for most of April, May, and June. He got into just 69 games that year, slumping to .219 at the plate. He had been plagued by stomach ulcers and various other ailments throughout his 10-year run with the Yankees. Retiring as a player after the 1942 campaign, his athletic career continued into the 1960s.

Rolfe coached baseball and basketball at Yale University from 1943–1946. He was a Yankees bench coach for a brief spell and served as farm director for the Tigers in 1948. While managing the Tigers for portions of four seasons, he compiled volumes of notes that were posthumously published in a book entitled *The View from the Dugout: The Journals of Red Rolfe*. Things were not always blissful in Detroit, as player dissension led to some ugly flare-ups in 1952. After breaking up a clubhouse scuffle that year, Rolfe commented, "I wish my players would confine their fighting to other American League teams."

Rolfe was replaced as manger by Fred Hutchinson in July 1952, after the Tigers got off to a poor start. He moved on to a much quieter job as athletic director at his old alma mater. Although Rolfe didn't hang around the majors long enough to get any serious Hall of Fame consideration, one of the Ivy League divisions is named after him, along with a playing field at Dartmouth College. He died moderately young, at the age of 60, in 1969.

FRANK CROSETTI, SHORTSTOP

Crosetti was nicknamed "Crow," not only because it was an abbreviation of his last name, but also for his high-pitched, shrill voice, which could often be heard echoing across the diamond. At one time, he held a record for years of service to the club. He played from 1932–1948, and then worked as a third-base coach from 1949–1968. He won 17

World Series altogether. According to one source, the club started giving him engraved shotguns in place of rings.

Born in San Francisco, Crosetti spent four seasons with the PCL Seals. The Yankees purchased him for a sum of $75,000—a sizeable figure in the Depression Era. He was the last surviving Yankee in uniform on the day of Ruth's disputed "called shot" in the 1932 World Series. He insisted that it never happened.

Crosetti was a gifted fielder. He led the league in putouts and double plays twice apiece. He also paced the loop in assists and fielding percentage once each. He was never much of a hitter. His averages ranged from .288 to .194 during his prime years, and he retired with a lifetime .245 mark. But he had a good eye and moderate power, finishing in double digits for homers four times. He also had decent speed, leading the league in steals during the 1938 campaign with 27. He was not afraid to take one for the team, getting hit by more pitches than any of his AL peers in five consecutive seasons from 1936–1940. He paced the circuit eight times in that category.

Crosetti appeared in every World Series from 1936–1939. In the 1938 Fall Classic, he played superb defense, making three game-saving stops in the first contest. His home run off of Dizzy Dean in Game 2 earned him ringing endorsements from numerous writers, who unofficially declared him the "hero" of the Series. Dean liked to spin a tall tale about the encounter. According to Diz, whose career was in decline due to a serious injury sustained in the 1937 All-Star Game, he shouted to Crosetti as he was rounding the bases, "You wouldn't-a got a loud foul off-a me a year ago!" "I know, Diz," Crosetti allegedly shouted back. Asked about Dean's colorful anecdote years later, Crosetti disputed its validity, just as he had with Ruth's alleged "called shot."

In 1941, the Yankees began to groom Phil Rizzuto for the starting job. Crosetti was gradually phased out. Rizzuto fondly remembered Crosetti working diligently to show him the ropes at shortstop during his rookie year while other veteran players were literally shoving him out of the batting cage during practice. With Rizzuto in the armed forces during the 1945 campaign, Crosetti returned to full-time duty. He hit just .238.

As a coach, Crosetti polished the art of sign-stealing, helping the Yankees cause until 1968. After that, he coached the Seattle Pilots and

Minnesota Twins. His baseball career ended in the early 1970s. He lived to be 91 years old.

FAST FACT: Babe Dahlgren was one of the unluckiest players in Yankees history. Faced with the daunting task of replacing Lou Gehrig at first base in 1939, he hit just .235. Although he fared better the following season, raising his average by nearly 30 points and leading the league in putouts, manager Joe McCarthy needed someone to blame for the club's third-place finish. McCarthy endorsed the sale of Dahlgren to the Braves, making the preposterous claim that Dahlgren's arms were "too short."

11

NEW YORK YANKEES

1949–1953

After a three-year drought, the Yankees captured a pennant and won the World Series over the Dodgers in 1947. Some sweeping changes had taken place in the Bronx during the war era. Third baseman Red Rolfe and pitcher Lefty Gomez bid farewell to New York after the 1942 slate. Manager Joe McCarthy resigned in May 1946. He was replaced at the helm by catcher Bill Dickey, who quit that September after clashing with new owner Larry MacPhail. It was a banner year for departures, as veteran right-hander Red Ruffing was released with several games still remaining in the season. Second baseman Joe Gordon joined the exodus a few weeks later, finishing his career with the Cleveland Indians. Any fan returning to the sport after an absence of five years or longer would hardly have recognized the 1947 championship squad.

The illustrious Joe DiMaggio was still going strong of course (although injuries would soon begin to slow him down). And a pair of new Hall of Famers had arrived. Taking over for Frank Crosetti in 1941, Phil Rizzuto missed three full seasons while serving in the U.S. Navy. By 1947, he was entering his prime. Nicknamed "Scooter" for the way he ran the bases, the diminutive shortstop (5-foot-6, 150 pounds) was among the top defensive players of the era. He was also known for his leadership qualities, earning praise from opponents and teammates alike. Ted Williams once remarked that Rizzuto made the difference in the tight Yankee–Red Sox pennant races. Vic Raschi told writers that his best pitch was anything an opponent hit in Rizzuto's direction. A steady postseason performer, "Scooter" added seven World Series rings to his collection before he retired.

Making his Yankees debut in September 1946, Yogi Berra would share catching responsibilities with Aaron Robinson and Gus Niarhos until 1949. Aside from his 15 All-Star selections and three MVP Awards, he would gain lasting fame for his unintentionally funny remarks (which became known as "Yogi-isms"). Commenting on his short, stout, and somewhat homely appearance one day, Berra quipped, "So I'm ugly. So What? I never saw anyone hit with his face." Berra's looks certainly didn't stop him from collecting 358 homers during his career—among the top totals for players at his position.

The Yankees followed their 1947 championship with a near miss in 1948, coming out on the short end of a three-way dogfight. Cleveland and Boston finished the regular season tied for first place, with the Yankees sitting just two and a half games out. A one-game playoff was necessary to decide the pennant. It took place at Fenway Park and resulted in an 8–3 Red Sox loss. The Indians, helped tremendously by Bronx refugee Joe Gordon (who posted the highest single-season homer total of his career), went on to capture the second world championship in franchise history.

Looking to find their way back to the postseason, Yankees owners Dan Topping and Del Webb (who had bought out MacPhail before the 1948 campaign) dismissed manager Bucky Harris and replaced him with Casey Stengel. A new era of dominance immediately followed.

The decision to bring Stengel to the Bronx was held in question by many. He had managed in Brooklyn and Boston for nine seasons, finishing above .500 just once. His antics on the field had earned him a reputation as a clown. And he had a knack for fracturing standard rules of grammar and semantics when speaking to reporters. His confusing dialog became known as "Stengelese." Despite his numerous quirks, the "Old Perfessor" (as he came to be known) had an encyclopedic knowledge of the game. His skillful juggling of the Yankees lineup led to the invention of the phrase "platooning." Although he didn't originate the practice, he employed it successfully for many seasons in New York, piloting the club to 10 pennants and seven World Series titles.

The Stengel dynasty began in 1949, when the team won 97 contests and finished one game ahead of the Red Sox. Hampered by a heel injury in 1948, DiMaggio missed the first three months of the 1949 campaign. The Yankees soldiered on without him, beginning the season in first place and building a modest four-and-a-half game lead by the time their prized slugger returned to action. The BoSox came on strong in the second half, posting a 54–22 record. Seeking to hold them at bay, the Yankees acquired Hall of Fame slugger Johnny Mize from the Giants in late August. While the 36-year-old Mize had seen better days, he still had plenty of power and was known for delivering in the clutch. Trailing Boston by a single game with two remaining, the Yankees squared off against the Sox at home. They won both meetings, clinching the pennant on the last day of the season.

The Fall Classic wasn't much of a "classic." After splitting a pair of tight pitching duels at Yankee Stadium, the Dodgers dropped three in a row at Ebbets Field. They trailed by at least three runs in each of those losses and never held a lead. On the heels of a crushing 10–6 defeat in Game 5, Brooklyn manager Burt Shotton commented, "They had just a little bit more all the way around than we did." For the next four seasons, the Bombers had more than any team in baseball.

The 1950 season was a coming-out year for several high-profile Yankees players. Phil Rizzuto had his most productive season at the plate, hitting .324 and capturing MVP honors. Yogi Berra enjoyed his first sensational offensive campaign, with 28 homers and 124 RBIs. He also paced the circuit in multiple defensive categories, including putouts and assists. While Yogi and "Scooter" were endearing themselves to Yankees fans, a 21-year-old left-hander by the name of Edward "Whitey" Ford made a promising debut.

Summoned from Kansas City of the American Association in July, Ford posted a 9–1 record in the second half, with a 2.81 ERA. It was the beginning of a fruitful career, as he would eventually become the most successful Yankees hurler of all time, with 236 wins. He added 10 more in the postseason, earning the nickname "Chairman of the Board" for the way he controlled a game and the players around him. Casey Stengel once said of the crafty southpaw, "If you had one game to win and your life depended on it, you'd want him to pitch it."

With a stellar cast of characters, the Yankees finished three games ahead of the Tigers in 1950, and squared off against Philadelphia in the World Series. Nicknamed the "Whiz Kids" for their youth and spirit, the Phillies hadn't seen postseason action in more than 30 years. They proved to be no match for Stengel's mighty Bombers, bowing in four games—all of which were low-scoring affairs. The Phillies would wait another 30 years for an encore on the October stage. For the Yankees, it was a matter of months.

The showdown between the Yankees and Giants in 1951 marked the sixth chapter of the storied rivalry. Managed by the fiery Leo Durocher, the Giants jumped out to a 2–1 Series advantage before losing three consecutive meetings. Outscored by a 19–3 margin in Game 4 and Game 5, Durocher's squad staged a valiant ninth-inning rally in the finale that ended prematurely with the go-ahead run at the plate. It was the swan song for Joe DiMaggio, who retired at season's end.

As "Joltin' Joe" was making an exit, another Yankees icon was making a grand entrance. Mickey Mantle was just 19 years old when he made his major-league debut in April 1951. Scouting reports had him pegged as a five-tool player, and although he got off to a decent start in the spring, his numbers began to slide in July. Demoted to Kansas City, Mantle called his father and told him, "I don't think I can play baseball anymore." The next day, Mutt Mantle made the drive from Commerce, Oklahoma. He explained to his son that the alternative to baseball was a life of drudgery in Commerce's lead mines. Mickey broke down crying and agreed to give it one more shot.

After elevating his average to .361 at Kansas City, Mantle was re-called by the Yankees. He hit safely in 20 of his last 27 games, with six homers and 20 RBIs. In Game 2 of the World Series, he suffered an injury that would plague him on and off for the rest of his career. In the fifth inning, Willie Mays hit a ball toward the center-field gap. Mantle had been advised by Casey Stengel before the game that DiMaggio's range was limited. Stationed in right field, Mantle sprinted toward the ball, only to find DiMaggio already there, poised to make the catch. Looking to avoid a collision, he stopped dead and caught his spikes on the cover of a drain pipe, tearing his knee apart.

Mantle moved on to a storied career nevertheless, blasting some of the longest homers in history, while receiving three MVP Awards. His finest offensive season came in 1956, when he captured a Triple Crown with 52 homers, 130 RBIs, and a .353 batting average. He finished with 536 long balls—a number that placed him at third on the all-time list when he retired. At the time of this writing, he held a rank of number 17.

On October 5, 1953, the Yankees set a record that still stands with their fifth consecutive World Series title. It came at the expense of the Dodgers, who dropped four Fall Classics to the Bombers in a seven-year span. Interviewed after their theatrical Game 6 victory (which was decided in the final at-bat), several Yankees players predicted that the team would capture eight straight pennants. "I don't see any reason why this ballclub shouldn't keep winning pennants indefinitely," said Rizzuto. "After all, we're loaded with young players. I'm the only old guy on the club." Despite their confidence, the Yankees finished second to the Indians in 1954. They continued to dominate the American League for another decade but never came close to matching the incredible five-year championship run that began in 1949.

When tales of that dynasty are told, the names of DiMaggio, Rizzuto, Berra, Mantle, and Ford inevitably come to the forefront. Although the contributions of those five core players were significant indeed, there are numerous other players whose efforts are worth mentioning.

GIL MCDOUGALD, INFIELD

Born and raised in San Francisco, McDougald attended college there as well. He signed with the Yankees prior to the 1948 campaign and spent three seasons in the minors, hitting well everywhere he went. He was promoted to the big leagues in 1951.

McDougald was known for his versatility, logging more than 500 games at second and third base, while also making close to 300 appearances at shortstop. He consistently finished among the top five in various defensive categories, and his lifetime fielding percentages were above average at each position. He was stellar in his 1951 debut, hitting .306 with 63 RBIs. Baseball writers acknowledged his efforts by naming him Rookie of the Year. He captured the honor by a narrow margin over Minnie Minoso of the White Sox.

McDougald had an odd batting stance that was described by an Associated Press writer as follows: "He stands spraddle-legged, splay-footed, almost facing the pitcher with his knees bent and the bat held loosely below his right hip." While he rarely hit for high average, his numbers were steady, ranging from .250 to .311. He was equally consistent at rounding the bases, scoring 65 or more runs each year from

1951–1958. Although he was by no means a slugger, he did have moderate power, launching 10 or more homers in eight straight seasons.

A five-time All-Star, McDougald wasn't always stellar at the plate during the postseason. He played in eight World Series for the Yankees and hit below .200 twice. But he almost always had a major impact. Between 1951–1953, he gathered 15 hits, drilled 4 homers, and drove in 14 runs. In Game 5 of the 1951 Fall Classic, his grand slam off of Larry Jansen of the Giants helped the Yankees breeze to a 13–1 victory. He had seven postseason homers in all, including a game-winner in 1958.

McDougald is perhaps best remembered for an unfortunate mishap that occurred during the 1957 campaign. Facing Herb Score of the Indians, he slammed a line drive back through the box that struck the promising young hurler in the eye. Score never got back on track after leading the AL in strikeouts in 1955 and 1956. The regrettable incident haunted McDougald for the remainder of his career, and some say he became a different player afterward. He suffered a major injury of his own when he was struck in the ear by a line drive off the bat of Bob Cerv during batting practice one day. He later went completely deaf and underwent surgery to restore his hearing.

McDougald had another respectable season in 1960, and hit .278 in the World Series that year. When the campaign was over, he surprised everyone by retiring at the age of 32. He ran a successful company called Yankee Corporate Maintenance after his playing days and also coached at Fordham University for several years. He died in 2010, at the age of 82.

BILLY MARTIN, SECOND BASE

Martin's name is associated with a host of negative anecdotes—his violent altercations both on and off the field, his tempestuous relationship with Yankees owner George Steinbrenner, and his well-publicized struggle with alcoholism, to name a few. But before his reputation was irrevocably blemished, he was the indispensable sparkplug of four world championship squads.

Martin had played for Casey Stengel in the minors at Oakland. Their relationship had a father–son dynamic to it. Martin was a fine defensive second baseman, but he rarely hit for average. Asked why he held Martin is such high regard, Stengel replied, "If liking a kid who never let you down in the clutch is favoritism, then I plead guilty." Martin's connection with Stengel led to his 1950 promotion to the Yankees. He played in 34 games and hit just .250 but made an impact with his hustle and competitive spirit.

Martin would spend portions of seven seasons with the Yankees, sometimes as a regular and other times as a reserve. He lost the entire 1954 campaign and most of 1955 to military duty. He enjoyed his finest all-around season in 1953, gathering 15 homers and 24 doubles, while driving in 75 runs. Additionally, he led AL second basemen in double plays and finished second with a sparkling .985 fielding percentage. It was the only year he received MVP consideration.

Martin always seemed to raise his game to another level during the postseason. A lifetime .333 hitter in World Series play, he had an epic October 1953, hammering 12 hits and driving in eight runs in six games. The previous year, he had single-handedly saved the Series for the Yanks. With the Bombers leading 4–2 in the seventh inning of Game 7, the Dodgers staged a two-out rally, loading the bases against right-hander Vic Raschi. Jackie Robinson hit a high popup that was apparently lost in the sun by first baseman Joe Collins. With the runners in motion, Martin alertly took charge of the play, racing in from second to make a spectacular shoe-top catch, ending the Brooklyn threat. The Yanks held on for a Series-clinching 4–2 win.

Martin became fast friends with Mickey Mantle and Whitey Ford. In 1957, he and several teammates were involved in an ugly brawl at the Copacabana night club in New York City. Upon hearing of the incident, the Yankees brass traded Martin to the Kansas City A's—citing him as a bad influence on Whitey and Mickey. The pugilistic infielder played for five teams between 1958–1961. He retired after the latter campaign.

Martin moved on to a successful managerial career that was marred by various unsavory episodes. Known for his fiery temperament, he clashed with players, umpires, and bosses wherever he went. But he had a penchant for making decent clubs even better. He led the Twins, Tigers, and A's to playoff appearances. Fired and rehired numerous times by George Steinbrenner, he captured two pennants and a World Series title in New York. He died in a car accident on Christmas Day 1989. He was only 61 years old.

ALLIE REYNOLDS, PITCHER

Reynolds grew up in Oklahoma and attended college there. His grand-mother was a Creek Indian, and like many other Native Americans who played in the majors, Reynolds was strapped with a racially based nick-name. He was referred to as "Super Chief," in deference to his heritage and commanding presence on the mound.

Reynolds attended college on a track scholarship and wasn't even interested in baseball until a knee injury prevented him from participating in his sport of choice. Signed by Cleveland in 1939, he was sent to Springfield of the Class C Middle Atlantic League. By 1943, he was pitching for the Indians. He had an overpowering fastball but battled control issues throughout his career, issuing 90 or more walks in 10 consecutive seasons. Additionally, he led the AL in hit batsmen and wild pitches once apiece.

Traded to the Yankees for Joe Gordon in 1946, Reynolds developed into a major star, earning five All-Star selections. From 1947–1952, he won at least 16 games each year. His crowning achievement came in 1951, when he tossed no-hitters against the Indians and Red Sox. During the latter game, Yogi Berra misplayed a popup hit by Ted Williams, prolonging the at-bat. Williams ended up popping out anyway, ending the game. Reynolds downplayed the significance of his accomplishment, commenting, "A no-hitter is not the best standard by which to judge a pitcher. That's just luck." He added that he had pitched four games better than his no-hitters, losing three of them.

In the postseason, Reynolds was a dominant force. He played in every Fall Classic from 1949–1953, compiling a 6–2 record and a 2.45 ERA. His World Series resume included two complete-game shutouts against the Dodgers. In Game 1 of the 1949 October showcase, he tossed a two-hitter, striking out nine Brooklyn batters. He played on six championship squads.

Reynolds hit fairly well for a pitcher, finishing with double-digit RBI totals three times, while compiling a .268 average with runners in scoring position. He was also extremely versatile on the mound, appearing as both a starter and reliever. Casey Stengel once commented that Reynolds was "two pitchers rolled into one." During his eight seasons in the Bronx, Reynolds closed 70 regular-season games, earning 40 saves. He picked up four more saves in postseason play.

After a solid effort in 1954, Reynolds opted for retirement. He is recognized by many as one of the best hurlers not in the Hall of Fame. In 1969, he served as head of the American Association. That league's top pitching award was named after him. The ball field at Oklahoma State University is also named in Reynolds's honor. At the time of Reynolds's death in 1994, he was serving as president of the National Hall of Fame for Famous American Indians in Anadarko, Oklahoma.

EDDIE LOPAT, PITCHER

Originally a first baseman in the minors, Lopat was converted to a pitcher when he failed to hit consistently. He was extremely high strung early in his career, worrying excessively about his performance and occasionally resorting to tantrums when things went poorly. With the help of doctors and family members, he learned to control his anxiety. Broadcaster Mel Allen later referred to him as "Steady Eddie."

Lopat began his major-league career with the lowly White Sox, and although he performed rather well for them, he ended up with a 34–36 record in his first three seasons. Traded to the Yankees in February 1948, he became one of the most successful pitchers in the majors.

Lopat was among New York's core starters from 1948–1954. He was nicknamed the "Junkman," in reference to the assortment of curves, sliders, screwballs, and knuckleballs he used to retire hitters. Casey Stengel once commented hilariously, "Lopat looks like he's throwing wads of tissue paper. Every time he wins a game, fans come out of the stands asking for contracts." The crafty southpaw expertly mixed speed and location to keep opponents on their heels. He had decent control, never walking more than 73 batters in a season. He was an exceptional fielder as well, enjoying two errorless campaigns.

Between 1948–1954, Lopat won no fewer than 15 games on five occasions. He put forth his finest effort in 1953, accruing an .800 winning percentage and a 2.42 ERA (both tops in the league). Additionally, he posted the lowest WHIP (walks and hits per nine innings) in the circuit that year. His highest single-season win total came in 1951, when he prevailed in 21 decisions.

During his 12 years in the majors, Lopat appeared in five World Series, posting a 4–1 record. He was virtually unhittable against the

Giants in 1951, winning both of his starts while yielding just one earned run in 18 innings of work. He might have added a fifth victory to his career totals had Stengel not replaced him with a pinch-hitter in Game 3 of the 1950 Fall Classic. The Yankees were trailing 2–1 when Lopat was pulled in the bottom of the eighth. They rallied for a 3–2 win.

Beset by arm trouble late in his career, Lopat was traded to Baltimore in July 1955. He went 3–4 for the O's in 10 games and was released. He pitched one more season in the minors and then announced his retirement.

Finished as a player, he managed the Richmond Virginians of the International League for three seasons. He scouted for the Yankees in 1959, and then coached for three different major-league clubs before managing the A's in 1963 and 1964. He later ran his own baseball clinic in Florida. He also scouted for the Expos. He died in 1992, of pancreatic cancer.

HANK BAUER, RIGHT FIELD

Prior to his major-league career, Bauer served in the U.S. Marines during World War II, missing several seasons. He was wounded on Okinawa and received four commendations, including a pair of Purple Hearts. Before enlisting, he had spent one season in the Class D Wisconsin State League.

Upon returning from the war, Bauer honed his skills in the minors for three more years, breaking the .300 mark at the plate each season. Making his Yankees debut in September 1948, he accrued an anemic .180 batting average in 19 games. Casey Stengel liked what he saw anyway, handing Bauer a full-time roster spot the following year.

Solidly built at six feet, 192 pounds, Bauer was described by one writer as having a face like a clenched fist. He was a key ingredient to the Yankees' success from 1949–1953, playing in more than 100 games each year and hitting .293 or better in four straight seasons. He assembled one of his finest offensive campaigns in 1950, amassing 13 homers and 70 RBIs with a career-best .320 batting average.

Bauer was among Stengel's favorites. He played to win and was intensely focused. He would reportedly snarl "Don't screw with my money!" to any teammate who failed to hustle. A lukewarm World

Series performer early in his career, he would later compile a 17-game hitting streak in the Fall Classic. His three-run triple in the final game of the 1951 Series lifted the Yanks to a 4–3 win over the Giants. He also made a nifty sliding catch in that game to end a rally as the tying run was racing home. He retired with seven long balls and 24 RBIs in 53 World Series games.

A three-time All-Star, Bauer was used primarily in right field. He had excellent range, finishing among the top five in putouts on seven occasions. He posted the highest fielding percentage among players at his position twice. Traded to the Kansas City A's in 1960, he would serve as a player-manager the following year before retiring.

In 1964, he assumed managerial responsibilities in Baltimore. He spent portions of five seasons with the club, leading the O's to a world championship in 1966. Under his guidance, the team won no fewer than 94 games in three straight seasons. Future Hall of Famer Jim Palmer described Bauer as a "players' manager," adding that "he didn't overcomplicate things." Bauer finished his career as a skipper in Oakland during the 1969 slate, retiring with a won–loss percentage well above .500. He was 84 years old when he died in 2007.

VIC RASCHI, PITCHER

Raschi was scouted by the Yankees as a teenager. Although the club initially intended for him to finish college, the young hurler was persuaded by team representatives to leave the College of William and Mary in Virginia to get some minor-league experience.

Raschi went pro with the Amsterdam Rugmakers of the Canadian-American League in 1941. He was promoted to Class B in 1942, and then missed three full seasons while serving as a physical trainer in the U.S. Air Force. By the time he made his major-league debut in 1946, he was 27 years old. Roster spots weren't easy to come by in the Bronx, and Raschi started the 1947 slate in the Pacific Coast League. He went 8–2 and was recalled by the Yanks in July. He won his first six decisions before dropping a pair of quality starts in August—one of them an 11-inning complete-game effort.

From 1948–1953, Raschi was a top-shelf hurler for New York, winning 16 or more games in five consecutive seasons. His most productive span occurred between 1949–1951, when he led the Yankees staff with 21 wins each year. In 1949, he was on the mound for the winner-take-all regular-season finale against the Red Sox. He scattered five hits in nine innings, emerging victorious. His .724 winning percentage in 1950 was tops in the AL. He paced the circuit with 164 strikeouts the following year.

Primarily a fastball pitcher, Raschi had an effective slider and changeup as well. He used all three to win five of eight World Series decisions during his career. His most impressive October performance was in Game 1 of the 1950 Fall Classic. He tossed a two-hitter, winning a tight 1–0 pitching duel over Jim Konstanty of the Phillies. Raschi posted a lifetime 2.24 ERA in 11 World Series games. He helped the Bombers to six world championships.

In 1953, Raschi won 13 games and balked at a salary cut. He ended up with the Cardinals in 1954, posting an 8–9 record. He split the 1955 campaign with the Cardinals and A's, closing out his major-league career with a 132–66 record. Raschi lived in Groveland, New York, after his retirement, coaching baseball and basketball at Geneseo State Teacher's College. He also operated a liquor store. He died in 1988, at the age of 69.

PHIL RIZZUTO, SHORTSTOP

Rizzuto was one of those Yankees figures who gained lasting fame after his retirement. Serving as a Yankees broadcaster from 1957–1996, he endeared himself to multiple generations of fans. He became renowned for his use of the phrase "Holy Cow!" when something interesting happened on the field. He was also fond of jokingly referring to people as "Huckleberries."

Rizzuto was a native New Yorker, born in Brooklyn to Italian parents. He had his first tryout at the age of 16. Noticing his diminutive size, Giants manager Bill Terry advised him to "get a soap box" and start shining shoes. But size proved deceptive when Rizzuto was named Minor League Player of the Year in 1940. He was used to being underestimated, remarking that he was often the last one chosen during neighborhood pickup games as a kid.

Targeted as a replacement for veteran shortstop Frank Crosetti, Rizzuto hit .300 at each minor-league stop. He was sparkling in his 1941 major league debut, posting a .307 batting average, while finishing among the league's top defensive players. The Yankees faced the Dodgers in the World Series that year, and Rizzuto fizzled at the plate, managing just two hits in five games. He did make 12 putouts and 18 assists, while turning six double plays, however.

After an excellent follow-up effort, Rizzuto entered the U.S. Navy and missed three full seasons. When he returned in 1946, he was hit by a pitch from Nels Potter of the Browns. He suffered dizzy spells on and off for the rest of his career. But it didn't slow him down. In the 1947 World Series against the Dodgers, he compiled a .308 batting average. He hit .316 against the same opponents in 1953. Rizzuto's finest regular-season showing came in 1950, when he crafted a .324 batting mark with 200 hits and 66 RBIs. Defensively, he led the league in putouts and fielding percentage. While his numbers were not as eye-popping as some of the other contenders, Rizzuto's intangible qualities earned him MVP honors.

Rizzuto received glowing praise from his Yankees peers throughout the course of his career. Joe DiMaggio remarked that Rizzuto "[held] the team together." Casey Stengel considered him one of the greatest shortstops he had ever seen, although he had an odd way of expressing it. "[Rizzuto] can't hit with Honus Wagner," said Casey one day. "But I've seen him make plays the Dutchman couldn't."

Rizzuto's numbers tapered off during the early 1950s. In 1954, he failed to raise his batting average above .200. In 1955 and 1956, he split time at short with Billy Hunter and Gil McDougald. "Scooter" appeared in his last Yankees game during the 1956 slate. His number "10" was later retired. A sign in Yankee Stadium's Monument Park reads, "The 'Scooter' was the Yankees catalyst, leading them to nine World Series. His outstanding talents and enthusiasm made him the best shortstop the Yankees ever had."

YOGI BERRA, CATCHER

In his 1989 autobiography *Yogi . . . It Ain't Over,* Berra devotes an entire chapter to discrediting some of the popular sayings that have been attributed to him throughout the years. He admits that his image as a clueless bumpkin bothered him to an extent. "I am asked a lot if it hurt to be bashed for all those years," Berra writes. "The serious answer to that question is this: It did hurt, but it did motivate me."

Berra was born in an Italian neighborhood known to some as "Dago Hill." His parents had emigrated from Italy in the early 1900s and settled in St. Louis. Berra grew up in the same neighborhood as future major leaguer and broadcaster Joe Garagiola. The two became fast friends. Yogi's first experience in organized ball came in the American Legion leagues. Originally known as "Larry," he got his nickname from boyhood pal Bobby Hofman, who allegedly saw a movie about an Indian snake charmer and felt that the character bore a resemblance to Berra.

The Yankees signed Yogi in 1943 and assigned him to the Piedmont League. He excelled there, driving in 23 runs in one particular doubleheader. During World War II, Yogi served as a machine gunner aboard the USS *Bayfield* and participated in the D-Day invasion of France. Upon returning to the United States, he played for the Newark Bears. He was called to the Bronx in September 1946, entering seven games and hitting .364. He served as backup to catcher Aaron Robinson the following year. But Robinson lacked the offensive punch of Berra and soon lost his first-string status.

During the course of his storied career, Berra appeared on 14 pennant-winning squads. He would later find success as a manager, leading both the Mets and Yankees to World Series appearances. During his playing days, he won three MVP Awards and was named to 15 All-Star Teams consecutively. Because he was short, paunchy, and somewhat awkward on the field, the press often had unflattering things to say about him. Although it was meant as a term of endearment, Yogi could not have been happy with the nickname "Little Squat Man" that was bestowed upon him. Regardless of what anyone thought of him, Yogi knew how to win. When he earned his 10th World Series ring as a player in 1962, he broke the previous record set by Joe DiMaggio.

Berra was a spokesman and coowner of the Yoo-hoo Company until 1981. He helped popularize the chocolate beverage and reportedly visited the bottling plant in New Jersey regularly. Due to a long-standing feud with George Steinbrenner, Yogi was conspicuously absent from Old-Timers' Games for more than a decade. Shortly before the "Boss's" death, the two reconciled, and Berra made a triumphant return to Yankee Stadium. His number has been retired by the club, and a plaque honoring him stands in Monument Park.

Berra authored several books throughout the years. He received a honorary Ph.D. from Montclair State University in New Jersey. The city is home to the Yogi Berra Museum and Learning Center, as well as a baseball stadium bearing his name. Berra died in 2015, at the age of 90.

WHITEY FORD, PITCHER

With a dream team behind him throughout most of his career, Ford compiled the highest won–loss percentage among players with at least 200 victories during the twentieth century. When he pitched 33 consecutive scoreless innings in the World Series, it broke a record previously held by another Yankees great—Babe Ruth. "I don't care what the situation was," said Mickey Mantle. "The bases could be loaded and the pennant riding on every pitch, it never bothered Whitey Ford. He pitched his game. Cool. Craft. Nerves of steel."

Ford was born in Manhattan and came of age in Queens. His father and two of his uncles had played semipro ball, so Whitey became interested at an early age. He got his first taste of the game playing stickball on the sandlots next to the Madison Square Garden Bowl.

Ford was fond of the night life during his career and, according to one account, received the nickname "Slick" after being caught out on the town past curfew with teammates. Casey Stengel called a meeting afterward and accused several players of becoming "whiskey slick." The term allegedly stuck to Ford. The hurler was also known as the "Chairman of the Board" for his coolness under fire and his ability to control a game.

As Ford's career was fading, he was accused of tampering with baseballs. Although he readily admitted to this, he insisted that he had never cheated until the end of his career. He claimed to have used a ring with a sharpened edge to slice the rawhide surface of game balls. It made his pitches sink more dramatically. Ford was caught red-handed by rival manager Al Dark and reprimanded by umpire Hank Soar.

Prior to that, Ford didn't need much help on the mound. He had a wide assortment of pitches, among them a curve, slider, and changeup.

The crafty left-hander used his sizeable repertoire to lead the league in wins three times between 1955–1963. During the Yankees' five-year championship run, he lost a season and a half to minor-league service and two full years to army duty during the Korean conflict. He posted a collective 27–7 regular-season record for the Yankees in that span. He was 1–1 in three World Series appearances, with a 2.16 ERA. In later years, he became Stengel's official Game 1 starter, serving in that capacity eight times during his career.

Circulatory problems and bone spurs eventually slowed him down. After his retirement, he served as a Yankees pitching coach until health problems forced him to step aside. He stayed on as a spring training instructor for years. In 1987, a plaque was dedicated to him in Yankee Stadium's Monument Park. Ford has continued to make annual appearances at Old-Timers' Games.

MICKEY MANTLE, CENTER FIELD

With his speed, power, and movie-star good looks, Mickey Mantle became the living embodiment of the Yankees during the 1950s and 1960s. A favorite of the rabid New York press, Mantle knew how to fend off the sharks and protect his teammates when the club was slumping or there was controversy afoot. He was universally popular among people inside and outside the baseball establishment.

An eminent home-run threat, Mantle not only hit them in bunches, but he also propelled them into the great beyond. At least 10 of his homers were measured in excess of 500 feet. Mantle claimed the "hardest ball" he ever hit was at Yankee Stadium in the 11th inning of a 1963 game against the A's. With the score tied at seven, Bill Fischer tried to slip a fastball by Mantle. The switch-hitting slugger drove the pitch into the right-field facade just below a light tower. The ball struck the facade with such force, it bounced all the way back to the infield. Estimates vary widely, but multiple sources suggest that the blast would have traveled more than 700 feet. In a 1951 spring training game at USC's Bovard Field, one of Mantle's clouts allegedly sailed 656 feet. He has also been given credit for the longest homer ever hit at Griffith Stadium in Washington. The 565-foot bomb off of left-hander Chuck Stobbs hit a beer sign and ricocheted into the backyard of a neighboring house on

Oakdale Street. Former teammate Billy Martin once said, "No man in the history of the game had as much power as Mickey Mantle. No man. You're not talking about ordinary power. . . . It's an altogether different level."

Like Ruth before him and Reggie Jackson after him, Mantle was a reliable October performer. In 12 World Series, he slugged 18 homers—an all-time record. Additionally, he is the lifetime Fall Classic leader in total bases, runs scored, and RBIs. While Mantle could easily have been the biggest hot dog in baseball history, there was a surprising humility about him. "After I hit a home run, I had a habit of running the bases with my head down," he said. "I figured the pitcher already felt bad enough without me showing him up around the bases."

Mantle actually began his career as a shortstop. He committed 55 errors in the minors one year and, despite that performance, would make sporadic appearances for the Yankees at his original position. Although he never gained lasting acclaim for his defense, he covered a lot of ground in center field and had good instincts. He led AL center fielders in double plays three times and fielding percentage twice, but also placed first or second in errors on six occasions. It hardly mattered, as Mantle was among the top sluggers in the majors for more than a decade. He captured three MVP Awards and finished second in two other seasons. The ultimate clutch hitter, he accrued a .325 batting average with the bases loaded and a .321 mark from the seventh inning on in games that were close.

Mantle was fond of the New York club scene and developed a chronic drinking problem, which remained hidden from the public for most of his career. His good friend Whitey Ford once quipped, "Everybody who roomed with Mickey said he took five years off of their career." Poor health ran in Mantle's family, and he always believed he would die young. In later years, he said, "If I knew I was going to live this long, I'd have taken better care of myself."

When Mantle hit his early 30s, injuries began to take their toll. His knee bothered him constantly, and he was stricken with osteomyelitis, which weakens the structure of the bones. On some days, Mantle could hardly grip a bat. He soldiered on until the age of 36, when he realized he was little more than a sentimental favorite in New York. He retired after the 1968 campaign and was inducted to the Hall of Fame, along with Whitey Ford, in 1974.

Near the end of his life, Mantle's liver began to fail, and he underwent a transplant. He appeared on numerous TV shows to warn kids about the dangers of drugs and alcohol. Ultimately, it was cancer that took him at the age of 63.

FAST FACT: During the 1950s, there was no Monument Park at Yankee Stadium. The three existing monuments dedicated to Miller Huggins, Lou Gehrig, and Babe Ruth were located in fair territory in deep center field. It was a challenging target, as the distance from home plate to the center-field wall was 461 feet.

12

BROOKLYN DODGERS
1952–1956

The Dodgers have carried numerous monikers during their long history, including the Atlantics, Grays, Bridegrooms, Superbas, and Robins. During the nineteenth century, an intricate network of trolley routes crisscrossed the borough of Brooklyn, and folks hailing from the area were sometimes referred to as "trolley dodgers." The antiquated slang was shortened to become the team's permanent name in 1932.

Whatever identity they assumed, the Dodgers had a knack for building up the hopes of fans and then letting them down. After more than a decade of mediocrity, manager Wilbert Robinson guided the club to a pair of World Series berths in 1916 and 1920. Both were losing causes. During the "Roaring Twenties," the team fell on hard times again, earning the nickname "Daffiness Boys" for their overtly sloppy play.

No one embodied the spirit of the club in the late 1920s more than outfielder Babe Herman. Herman compiled a .324 lifetime batting average and hit for the cycle three times during his career. But he earned a reputation as a bungling clown with his misadventures on the field. In addition to passing teammates on the base paths and sliding into occupied bags, he was reportedly hit on the head while trying to catch a popup one afternoon.

In the 1930s, the "Daffiness Boys" handle was laid to rest (more or less) by artist Willard Mullin when he created the image of the "Brooklyn Bum" to represent the Dodgers in his *New York World-Telegram* sports cartoons. Mullin's caricature was based on famous circus clown Emmett Kelly. The image caught on, and the Dodgers would be known to many as "Dem Bums" from that point onward.

During the 1940s, the Dodgers continued to torment their fans with a series of humbling defeats. In 1941, they were one pitch away from tying the World Series at two games apiece when a dropped third strike by catcher Mickey Owen led to an improbable Yankees victory. In 1947, the Dodgers jumped out to a 2–0 second-inning lead over the Bombers in Game 7 but failed to get a runner past first base from that point on. The result was a crushing 5–2 loss. Two Octobers later, the "Bums" were back in business against the Yankees, dropping the Series in five games. Dating back to the nineteenth century, it was the sixth October failure in franchise history.

As the Dodgers continued to disappoint year after year, there were legions of fans who kept the faith. In his critically acclaimed work *The Boys of Summer*, Roger Kahn explains, "You may glory in a team triumphant, but you fall in love with a team in defeat." Pulitzer Prize–winning author Doris Kearns Goodwin echoes that belief in her touching memoir *Wait 'Til Next Year*, contending that "for every tale of woe there was a tale of joy." There is no ignoring the fact that the Dodgers of the 1950s were among the most powerful teams in baseball history. The only thing preventing them from building a dynasty was the New York Yankees.

A total of three men took the helm in Brooklyn during that golden decade. Burt Shotton logged 14 years of experience as a player before taking over the odorous Phillies in 1928. During his six seasons in Philadelphia, the team never finished higher than fourth. After a brief layover in Cincinnati and a long minor-league stint, he won two pennants with Brooklyn, in 1947 and 1949. Described by a New York columnist as "one of those strong, silent men," he was replaced by Chuck Dressen after the Dodgers ended up two games behind the Phillies in 1950.

Dressen had been a multisport star, spending eight years at third base for the Reds and Giants. Additionally, he had played in the American Professional Football Association (precursor to the NFL) as a quarterback. Before taking the reins in Brooklyn, he had managed the Reds to several lackluster finishes. During Game 3 of the 1951 National League tiebreaker against the Giants, it was Dressen's decision to bring in pitcher Ralph Branca to face Bobby Thomson in the bottom of the ninth. It remains one of the most criticized moves in baseball history (details to follow). Dressen stayed on for two more pennant-winning seasons before ending up on the short end of a contract dispute with owner Walter O'Malley after the 1953 campaign.

Dressen's replacement, Walter Alston, would remain in charge for more than two decades, guiding the club to a total of seven pennants and four World Series titles. Prior to his arrival in Flatbush, he had logged just one major-league at-bat (a strikeout) with the Cardinals in 1936, and had never managed a major-league club. A popular question among New York reporters during spring training of 1954 was, "Who's he?" But by the time Alston stepped aside in the 1970s, he had piloted seven All-Star Teams to victory (a record) and won six NL Manager of the Year Awards. He would later be enshrined at Cooperstown.

It has been argued by some that the wealth of talent in Brooklyn would have bolstered the reputation of any manager, and perhaps that's true to some extent. The Dodgers owed much of their success in the 1940s and 1950s to a quartet of Cooperstown legends. The brightest star of all was Jackie Robinson. Whenever Robinson's tale is told, the narrative invariably focuses on the breaking of baseball's color barrier in 1946. Although Robinson's statistics seem immaterial compared to his monumental contribution to the civil rights movement, the numbers are remarkable nonetheless. With unimaginable pressure on him to perform and only 124 games of minor-league experience under his belt, Robinson bravely endured death threats, intentional beanings, and humiliating ethnic slurs on his way to capturing Rookie of the Year honors in 1947. During the next several campaigns, he would establish himself as one of the most gifted infielders in the majors.

With the color barrier officially removed, the Dodgers promoted Roy Campanella in 1948. Often cited as one of the top five catchers in baseball history, "Campy" captured three MVP Awards in a career shortened by a tragic car accident that left him paralyzed after the 1957 slate. The short, somewhat portly backstop was once compared by Roger Kahn to a sumo wrestler. Battling injuries throughout his career, he still managed to make eight consecutive All-Star appearances. A positive clubhouse presence, he was described by one researcher as a "cheerleader, almost childlike in his enthusiasm."

Another clubhouse leader, Pee Wee Reese, is best remembered for helping resolve the internal strife that arose with the arrival of Jackie

Robinson. When teammates circulated a petition protesting Robinson's presence, Reese openly defied them by refusing to sign. At several points during Robinson's debut season, Reese offered encouraging words to the beleaguered rookie. These gestures defined Reese's character—a noble, compassionate man who would more than once be referred to as the "heart and soul" of the Dodgers.

At the heart of the Dodgers offense was a fearsome slugger with a regal nickname. Referred to by one sportswriter as a "graceful center fielder with a picture-perfect swing," Duke Snider collected more homers and RBIs than any player in the game during the 1950s. Among the most industrious performers in postseason history, he went deep four times in two different World Series (1952 and 1955)—the only player to do so. His 11 Fall Classic homers are the most by any NL player.

Beginning in 1947, the Dodgers captured six pennants in a 10-year span. They came remarkably close on two other occasions. In 1950, they spent most of June in first place, ultimately finishing two games behind the Phillies. The following year, they remained on top for a total of 147 days but couldn't hold off the rampaging Giants. On the final day of the season, the two teams were locked in a first-place tie. A rare three-game playoff format was employed to determine the pennant winner.

The Giants took the first game at Brooklyn thanks to a pair of solo homers by Monte Irvin and Bobby Thomson. But the Dodgers came storming back in Game 2 at the Polo Grounds, battering three different New York hurlers for a 10–0 victory. The third contest contained one of the most epic moments in baseball history. Brooklyn led, 4–1, in the ninth inning of Game 3, when starter Don Newcombe ran out of gas. With one out, two men on, and a run already in, manager Chuck Dressen made a fateful decision, bringing in right-hander Ralph Branca to face Bobby Thomson. Branca had given up a homer to Thomson in Game 1, but Dressen apparently figured that lightning couldn't strike twice. He was wrong. Thomson hit his famous "Shot Heard 'Round the World," as radio announcer Russ Hodges immortalized the moment by manicly repeating the phrase, "The Giants win the pennant!" In some newspapers, the Giants' victory took up more space than a Russian atomic bomb test. Years later, several Giants players admitted that manager Leo Durocher had set up a sign-stealing operation at the Polo Grounds to inform New York hitters what pitch was coming.

The Dodgers recovered from the trauma, capturing back-to-back pennants in 1952 and 1953. Again, the Yankees robbed them of glory both times. The 1953 Series was the seventh consecutive postseason loss for Brooklyn. After the final pitch had been thrown, Campanella (the eternal optimist) commented disconsolately, "It was a wonderful season, but it ended in a heap of nothing." Asked by reporters what the Dodgers needed to do to beat the Yankees, Pee Wee Reese admitted, "I don't know what the answer is. I've been trying to find it for 12 years now."

The solution finally arrived in 1955, when the Dodgers ran away with the pennant and met the Bombers for the sixth time in World Series play. After dropping the first two games at Yankee Stadium, Alston's resilient crew bounced back with three straight wins at home. But the Yankees would not go quietly. A five-run explosion in the first inning of Game 6 was all they would need with staff ace Whitey Ford on the mound. Ford scattered four hits and struck out eight in a 5–1 victory. Southpaw Johnny Podres, who had posted a substandard 9–10 record during the regular season, became the unlikely Series hero for Brooklyn in Game 7, picking up his second win with a complete-game shutout. "Just give me one run," he had asked his teammates before clinching the Series for Brooklyn.

It was their first World Series title of the twentieth century, and although the game was played at Yankee Stadium, a large throng of fans swarmed onto the field to celebrate. An Associated Press writer describes the scene in the Brooklyn locker room as follows: "There was shouting and back pounding, cheering and embracing, and it was spontaneous, genuine, and totally unabashed." In Flatbush, church bells rang, factory whistles blew, and thousands of people danced in the streets. Banners and bunting flew from windows, and effigies of Yankees players hung from lampposts. The Dodgers held a celebration dinner at the Bossert Hotel. Jackie Robinson offered the following words to the cheering crowd outside: "The whole team knows it was the fans that made it for us. It was your support that made this great day possible. We thank you from the bottom of our hearts."

The Dodgers' championship reign would be brief, as the Yankees beat them (yet again) in the 1956 Fall Classic. For many Brooklyn stars who played in that Series, it was the beginning of the end. Robinson opted for retirement in the offseason at the age of 38. After his ordeal in the majors, he looked 10 years older. Lacking the defensive range of his prime years, Reese was moved to third base in 1957. He served a utility role the following season. In late January 1958, Campanella's rented car hit a patch of ice and skidded into a telephone pole, breaking the All-Star catcher's neck. "Campy" would regain use of his arms and hands but never play ball again.

As if Campanella's accident wasn't devastating enough, Brooklynites were still trying to cope with the harsh reality of the club's impending move to Los Angeles. When the announcement was made in the summer of 1957, owner Walter O'Malley became one of the most vilified figures in sports history. A popular joke later surfaced.

Q: "If you were sitting in a room with Josef Stalin, Adolf Hitler, and Walter O'Malley, armed with a gun that contained just two bullets, who would you shoot?"

A: "O'Malley, twice!"

In February 1960, a demolition crew began destroying the beloved Brooklyn cathedral that had been the site of so many moments of heartbreak and joy. The wrecking ball was painted white with stitches to represent a baseball. Although the stadium itself was reduced to rubble, the memories have been preserved in hundreds of subsequent writings. While Robinson, Reese, Campanella, and Snider have been elevated to folk-hero status, there were many lesser stars who deserve a lion's share of the credit for Brooklyn's successful run during the 1950s.

GIL HODGES, FIRST BASE

Although Hodges has yet to gain entry into the Hall of Fame as of this writing, he received plenty of support during his first 15 years on the ballot. Between 1969–1983, he captured at least 50 percent of the vote 11 times, peaking at 63 percent in his final year. His name has appeared on Veteran's Committee ballots several times. To some, the decisions of that committee have been erratic and unjust—especially in the case of Hodges.

Hailing from Indiana, Hodges was a multisport athlete in high school, participating in track, baseball, basketball, and football. He declined a contract from the Tigers to attend St. Joseph's College near Indianapolis. When the Dodgers approached him in his sophomore year, the offer was too good to pass up. He made his major-league debut in 1943, and then lost two full seasons to military duty in the U.S. Marines. He served as a gunner in a South Pacific antiaircraft battalion and rose to the rank of sergeant. He also won a Bronze Star.

Throughout the years, teammates and sportswriters had many flattering things to say about Hodges. Pee Wee Reese once remarked, "If you had a son it would be a great thing to have him grow up like Gil Hodges." Journalist Arthur Daley referred to him as a "noble character" and stated that he was one of the "finest men" in or out of sports. A soft-spoken man, Hodges could be quite intense, intimidating opponents and pressmen with a hostile glare.

Serving as the Dodgers' regular first baseman from 1948–1959, he won three Gold Gloves, earned eight All-Star selections, and finished among the top 10 in MVP voting three times. A powerful hitter and reliable RBI man, he clubbed 27 or more homers in eight consecutive seasons, while reaching the century mark in ribbies seven times. He most often hit fifth or sixth in the lineup, and pitchers worked carefully when he was at the plate. He averaged 74 walks per year from 1949–1959. Aside from one abysmal October in which he fell into an 0-for-21 slump, he was a consistent World Series performer, hitting .318 in six other Fall Classics with 15 runs scored and 21 driven in. Several of those RBIs were game-winners.

When his numbers began to taper off in the early 1960s, the Dodgers traded him to the fledgling Mets. He hit the Mets' first-ever home run but was hampered by knee problems. Even so, Casey Stengel remarked, "(Hodges) fields better on one leg than anybody else I got on two." Finished as a player after 1963, he went on to manage the "Miracle Mets" to a World Series victory in 1969. Hall of Famer Tom Seaver once asserted," "No one had more impact on my career than Gil Hodges." Hodges had just finished a round of golf before spring training in 1972, when he died unexpectedly of a massive heart attack.

DON NEWCOMBE, PITCHER

At 6-foot-4, 220 pounds, Newcombe was an imposing presence on the mound. Before joining the Dodgers, he pitched for the Newark Eagles of the Negro National League. He was signed by Brooklyn before the

1946 campaign and assigned to Nashua of the New England League. He worked his way up from Class B to the Triple A level at Montreal before his promotion to the Dodgers in 1949.

Although Newcombe fared poorly in his first major-league appearance (a relief stint), manager Burt Shotton had faith in the young hurler, handing him a starting assignment two days later. Newcombe rose to the challenge, tossing a complete-game shutout over the Reds. He added four more shutouts for the league lead and posted the highest win total on the Dodgers staff, with 17. In the World Series, he was saddled with a pair of losses, despite pitching moderately well. In Game 1, he held the Yankees scoreless for eight innings before yielding the deciding run in the bottom of the ninth. In Game 4, he was pulled in the fourth inning with two outs and three runs in. Despite those setbacks, it was a sensational debut for "Newk," and he was acknowledged by baseball writers as Rookie of the Year.

The big right-hander won 19 games in 1950 and 20 in 1951, becoming the first African American to reach that milestone. Considered one of the most dominant pitchers in the majors, he lost two seasons in his prime to military duty. The 1953 Dodgers won 105 games without him, and one can only imagine how they might have fared if he had played.

After a long layoff, Newcombe returned to action in 1954, but had an off year. He came back strong the following season, jumping out to an 18–1 record before faltering a bit down the stretch. In 1956, Newcombe reached the peak of his career, winning 27 games, while posting a personal-best 3.06 ERA. His efforts were rewarded, as he became the first hurler to win a Cy Young and MVP in the same season.

A fact that is sometimes overlooked, Newcombe was one of the finest hitting pitchers in history, breaking the .300 mark four times. While he threw right-handed, he batted from the left side. In 1955, he set a single-season record for NL hurlers with seven homers. To date, that mark has been tied but never broken. Newcombe was so reliable with a bat, he was used as a pinch-hitter more than 100 times during his career. He gathered 20 hits and 17 walks in that role.

Traded to the Reds in June 1958, "Newk" had one good season left in him, going 13–8 with a 3.16 ERA for Cincinnati the following year. He was ineffective after that. He pitched for the Spokane Indians in 1961, and migrated to Japan in 1962, where he played first base and outfield. Showing off his power, he drilled 12 homers in 279 at-bats.

Finished as a player, Newcombe worked in the Dodgers front office. He struggled with alcoholism for years and pawned his World Series ring at one point to pay off his mounting debts. In a candid interview, he indirectly blamed Walter Alston for encouraging players to drink beer. He stated that excessive alcohol use was a problem among numerous Dodgers players in his time. Newcombe eventually got clean through Alcoholics Anonymous and has maintained his sobriety for decades.

Many sportswriters believe that "Newk" would have received more Hall of Fame consideration had the game been integrated when he started in 1944. He certainly had the talent. With two years lost to segregation and two more to the military, his career was simply too brief for enshrinement at Cooperstown.

CARL FURILLO, OUTFIELD

Born near Reading, Pennsylvania, Furillo was nicknamed the "Reading Rifle" on account of his exceptional arm in the outfield. In 13 seasons as a full-time player, he averaged 12 assists per year. He once threw Pirates hurler Mel Queen out at first base on what should have been a single to right field. Furillo gained widespread acclaim for the way he played the unpredictable caroms of the right-field wall at Ebbets Field. It has been noted by one historian that there were literally hundreds of trajectories a ball could take off of the wall's odd facets, which included a towering screen that was considered in play. Summing up his right-field experience in Brooklyn, Furillo commented, "[T]he angles were crazy."

Furillo dropped out of school after eighth grade to help support his family. He played baseball throughout his childhood years and went pro in 1940, in the Eastern Shore League. He honed his skills in the minors until 1943, when he joined the U.S. Army. He saw combat in the Pacific Theater and was wounded. He earned three battle stars.

Upon joining the Dodgers in 1946, he clashed with manager Leo Durocher over salary and personal issues. He was known to make off-color comments from time to time and ended up being labeled a hothead and a malcontent. Sensitive about his lack of schooling, he refused to socialize with various players who were more educated. It hardly affected his value to the club.

From 1947–1958, Furillo collected 83 or more RBIs nine times, reaching the century mark twice. In that same span, he hit .290 or better on 10 occasions. This included a batting title in 1953, which he won during an injury-shortened season. On September 6 of that year, he was hit on the wrist by Ruben Gomez of the Giants. There had always been bad blood between the two clubs. "We hated the Giants," Furillo admitted in later years. "We just hated the uniform." Furillo believed that Leo Durocher, who had taken over as manager in New York midway through the 1948 campaign, had ordered the beaning, and he charged toward the Giants dugout. In the ensuing melee, his hand was stepped on and broken, keeping him out of action until the World Series. His .344 average in 132 games was sufficient to claim the batting crown.

Furillo played in seven World Series for the Dodgers. An offensive no-show in 1949 and 1952, he hit .299 with seven doubles, two homers, and 13 RBIs in five other postseason appearances. He was named to two All-Star Teams but never logged an at-bat. He received moderate MVP consideration in 1949 and 1953.

After experiencing chronic leg pain, he was released by the Dodgers in May 1960. He later sued the club, contending that he should not have been let go on account of a baseball-related injury. He was awarded back pay but ended up being blacklisted from the game. He ran a delicatessen/restaurant in Queens, New York, and later moved back to Reading to join the construction trade. He died in 1989, at the age of 66.

CARL ERSKINE, PITCHER

Of Scottish ancestry, Erskine was known to Brooklyn fans as "Oisk." In a comical (and possibly apocryphal) moment from Erskine's childhood, his father accidentally threw a ball across the family's living room while teaching young Carl how to grip a curve. The ball smashed a glass cupboard, prompting the elder Erskine to joke that it was the best break he ever got on a pitch.

Carl made his major-league debut with Danville of the Three-I League in 1946. He had a breakthrough season in 1947, going 19–9 with a 2.94 ERA. From 1948–1950, he would spend portions of each season in both the majors and the minors. In August 1948, he injured his shoulder and was instructed to keep playing (sports medicine was not terribly advanced in those days). The injury would hamper him on and off for years, and he pitched in pain constantly. He fared quite well in the previously mentioned span nevertheless, accruing a 35–17 record on the farm, while going 21–10 for the Dodgers.

Erskine spent the entire 1951 slate in Brooklyn and would remain a fixture in the rotation for six seasons. Using the curveball his father had taught him with some modifications, he posted double-digit win totals from 1951–1956. In 1953, he paced the NL with a .769 winning percentage. He compiled a 15–2 record during the last three months of the season and finished at 20–6. During the World Series that year, he struck out a record 14 Yankees during Game 3 and emerged with a 3–2 victory. The mark would stand until Sandy Koufax fanned 15 batters in Game 1 of the 1963 Fall Classic.

Erskine is among a handful of pitchers to toss multiple no-hitters. The first one came in 1952, versus the Cubs, and the second one in 1956, against the Giants. He was known to lose the plate at times, averaging more than three bases on balls per nine frames during his career, but he emerged with a favorable strikeout-to-walk ratio in all but two of his 12 seasons.

The Yankees could be hard on opponents, and Erskine had some rough moments on the October stage. In his Game 5 start during the 1952 Series, he got hammered for five runs in the fifth inning. Chuck Dressen considered pulling him with two outs but thought better of it. Erskine retired the next 19 batters he faced for an awkward 6–5 win. In 11 postseason appearances, he notched a 2–2 record with a suspect 5.83 ERA.

Erskine got hit hard during the 1959 slate and opted for retirement. After his career ended, he worked in the insurance and banking industries. He also coached baseball at Anderson College, leading the team to four conference championships. He received two honorary college degrees.

JIM GILLIAM, SECOND BASE

Born in Nashville, Tennessee, Gilliam played in the Negro Leagues from 1946–1950, spending each of those seasons with the Baltimore Elite Giants—a club that produced Hall of Famers Biz Mackey, Leon Day, and Roy Campanella.

Gilliam was a low-key figure who always seemed to leave the spotlight to the higher-profile players around him. Teammates called him "Devil," in reference to his activities as a pool hustler during spring training. Gilliam was well-liked by teammates. He often took young infielders under his wing, showing them the ropes. He was also known for his dark sense of humor. Catcher John Roseboro recounted an incident in which an opponent was knocked unconscious by a throw during a double-play attempt. As players huddled around the fallen runner, Gilliam grabbed the ball and applied the tag. "First time I ever tagged out a dead man," he joked.

Gilliam logged his minor-league experience in the International League at Montreal. His breakthrough season came in 1952, when he reached the century mark in walks, runs scored, and RBIs, while hitting .301. In 1953, he was Brooklyn's regular second baseman, displacing Jackie Robinson. He captured Rookie of the Year honors on the strength of his 125 runs scored and league-leading 17 triples. Additionally, he finished near the top of the NL leaderboards in various defensive categories. Gilliam played every station except shortstop, pitcher, and catcher for the Dodgers throughout the years and was competent at all of them. Walter Alston once proclaimed, "(Gilliam) did the little things to win ballgames. He never griped or complained. He was one of the most unselfish ballplayers I know."

Gilliam's career stretched well into the 1960s, and he played in a total of seven World Series, winning four. In 39 postseason games, he rapped 31 hits and drew 23 walks. His finest Series was in 1953, against the Yankees, when he hit .296 with a pair of homers.

An extremely patient hitter, Gilliam had a masterful feel for the strike zone. He spent a majority of his career as a leadoff man, accruing a .369 on-base percentage in that capacity. He scored no fewer than 81 runs each year from 1953–1960, including four straight seasons of more than 100. He was relatively swift on the bases, finishing among the top five in steals six times.

Gilliam played his last season in 1966, and worked as a Dodgers coach for a decade. In 1978, with the Dodgers cruising to a division title, he drove manager Tom Lasorda to the ballpark and went home to catch a quick nap. He never awoke, falling into a coma after suffering a cerebral hemorrhage. He was only 49 years old. Dodgers players wore black arm bands to honor him during the World Series.

JOHNNY PODRES, PITCHER

Born in northern New York, Podres's father was an iron miner in the Adirondacks. Johnny grew up following the Dodgers and was ecstatic when they showed interest in him before the 1951 slate. Signed by a part-time scout and restaurant owner from Amsterdam, New York, Podres worked his way up through the lower ranks quickly, reaching the Triple A level in his second professional season. In 1952, the Indians reportedly offered the Dodgers $250,000 to sign Podres, but GM Buzzie Bavasi balked at the deal. By the age of 20, Podres was wearing a Brooklyn uniform.

Podres appeared in 33 games during his rookie season. There was plenty of room for improvement, as he allowed more hits than innings pitched, while averaging five walks per nine frames. Teammate Clem Labine hinted that Podres lacked maturity in his debut, commenting, "Nothing concerned him except having a good time." Still, the left-hander posted a 9–4 record and made the postseason roster. His first World Series start was forgettable. In Game 5, he coughed up a first-inning homer to Gene Woodling and got into trouble in the top of the third, issuing two walks and a hit-by-pitch. His relief, Russ Meyer, promptly yielded a grand slam to Mickey Mantle as the Yankees romped to an 11–7 win. It was the only Series loss Podres would ever be charged with.

Podres had three effective pitches in his arsenal—a fastball, change, and curve. He combined them successfully to win 148 games in 15 seasons. He played four years in Brooklyn, missing the 1956 slate while serving in the military, and moved with the club to Los Angeles. While playing on the West Coast, he posted double-digit win totals in six straight campaigns and guided the Dodgers to world championships in 1959 and 1963. But the season Dodgers fans cherish the most is 1955.

Podres had an erratic year, winning seven of his first 10 decisions before slumping in the second half. From August through September, he was 1–4, with four no decisions. But Walter Alston had confidence in the cool southpaw, handing him the ball in Game 3 of the Fall Classic. He didn't disappoint, pitching nine strong innings and earning an 8–3 win. Game 7 was Podres's personal masterpiece. With more than 62,000 fans on hand, he stymied the Yankees offense, scattering eight hits in a 2–0 Series-clinching victory. Yogi Berra once famously quipped that "it gets late early" at Yankee Stadium. Podres conserved his energy, and as shadows began to fall in the fifth inning, he used his fastball and hard curve more often. He retired the side in order in the fifth and ninth but got into trouble in the bottom of the sixth. With Billy Martin and Gil McDougald aboard, Berra hit a ball toward the left-field corner, setting the stage for a spectacular catch by reserve outfielder Sandy Amoros. "When Yogi hit that ball, I thought it was out," Podres told *Baseball Digest*. "I don't know if Junior [Gilliam] would have caught it, being that he was a right-handed thrower. . . . All I know is we won the game." Podres received the first World Series MVP Award in history.

The left-hander had several excellent seasons afterward, winning an ERA title in 1957, and pacing the NL in winning percentage during the 1961 slate with a stellar 18–5 record. Still, nothing came close to the euphoria of the Dodgers' first world championship. As time passed, Podres had trouble recalling the elation he felt. "I can't remember the feeling I had," he once said. "There was too much hysteria going on." Teammate Don Zimmer remembered the celebration vividly. "We partied all night, and Johnny was right in the middle of it," he said.

Podres began to lose his effectiveness in the late 1960s. He played for the Tigers in 1967 and Padres in 1969, which was his last season in the majors. When his playing days were over, he served as a pitching coach for the Twins and Phillies. Cy Young Award winner Curt Schilling wrote after Podres's 2008 passing, "Johnny made me realize that being a man wasn't about the macho cool stuff we think men are supposed to be, but rather compassion, care, commitment, loyalty, integrity, and drive." Podres was 75 years old when he died.

CLEM LABINE, PITCHER

Labine's parents were Canadian immigrants who settled in Woonsocket, Rhode Island. Until the age of seven, Clem spoke only French. Signed as an amateur free agent in 1944, he was originally scheduled to try out for the Braves at Braves Field. As the story goes, he couldn't get into the dressing room to change and ran into Dodgers coach Chuck Dressen by chance. Dressen invited him to audition for Brooklyn instead.

Labine had an excellent sinker and curve, inducing a lot of ground-ball outs. While he was extremely durable, he once told teammate Carl Erskine that he had no designs on becoming a starter since he enjoyed the pressure of entering a game with so much at stake.

During his rookie season of 1951, Labine shut out the Giants in Game 2 of the NL playoff. He posted a 5–1 record and 2.20 ERA in 14 appearances that year, finishing third in Rookie of the Year voting. He developed arm problems in 1952, and spent a portion of the season with the Triple A St. Paul Saints. By 1953, he had become the ace of the Dodgers bullpen.

From 1953–1959, Labine closed more than 200 games, winning 57 and saving 80. He led the league twice in saves, once in overall appearances, and once in games finished. He posted a highly respectable 3.54 ERA in that stretch, while earning two All-Star nods. His only appearance in the Midsummer Classic was a disaster. With the American League nursing a 3–2 lead in 1957, Labine took the mound in the ninth. The highlight of the inning was his strikeout of Mickey Mantle. The lowlight was the potential double-play ball that was booted by Hall of Famer Red Schoendienst, which put two men on with nobody out. A single to Al Kaline and a double by Minnie Minoso brought three runs in—only one of which was earned. The AL hung on for a 6–5 win.

Labine enjoyed far better afternoons with the Dodgers in the Fall Classic. In 1955, he made four appearances as a closer, picking up a win and a save. The following year, he made a rare start in Game 6, winning a 10-inning pitching duel over Bob Turley of the Yanks. His clutch performance evened the Series at three games apiece. Traded to Pittsburgh in 1960, Labine played in his final World Series (against the Yankees yet again), getting hammered in four innings of work. He posted a 2–2 record with a 1.65 ERA in the postseason while wearing a Dodgers uniform.

Labine finished his career with the pathetic Mets in 1962. After his retirement, he moved back to Woonsocket, where he became an executive of a company that manufactured sports team jackets. Labine created many of the designs himself. Broadcaster Vin Scully once paid him a high compliment, remarking, "He had the heart of a lion and the intelligence of a wily fox, and he was a nice guy too."

PEE WEE REESE, SHORTSTOP

Hailing from Kentucky, Reese played in only five games during his senior year of high school because the coach felt he was too small. Born Harold Henry Reese, he was given the nickname "Pee Wee" during his days as a championship marble shooter. Although he had put on a little weight by the time he reached the majors (he was listed at 160 pounds), he still looked like a teenager. Reese admitted to being scared to death when he first arrived in Brooklyn. But his warm personality won over the veterans on the club. "Wherever they went, they took me with them," he remembered fondly. "Why did they do it? Beats the hell out of me."

Reese picked up a second nickname during his minor-league days— the "Little Colonel." Named captain of the Dodgers, he developed a reputation as a team leader and amateur psychologist. "Reese was the force that kept the Dodgers together in the clubhouse," said owner Walter O'Malley. "Any player who had a personal problem would always make his way to Reese's cubicle, as he took them under his wing and offered friendly advice."

Reese had difficulty accepting acclaim for holding the team together during the turbulent days of Jackie Robinson's rookie campaign. "I got a lot of credit and I appreciate it, but after a while, I thought of [Jackie] as I would Duke Snider or Gil Hodges or anyone else," he told one writer. "We were just playing ball and having fun."

A fine defensive shortstop, Reese finished among the top five in fielding percentage for 11 straight seasons. Typically appearing second in the batting order, he was a patient hitter, drawing 80 or more walks during nine campaigns. He ended up with a highly respectable lifetime on-base percentage of .366. In later years, he told a journalist, "If I had my career to play over, one thing I'd do differently is swing more. Those 1,200 walks I got—nobody remembers them." Opposing teams found them rather difficult to ignore, as Reese consistently made a nuisance of himself on the base paths, averaging 15 steals and 84 runs scored per season during his 16-year major-league career.

Reese was a major postseason contributor, gathering 46 hits and 16 RBIs in seven World Series with the Dodgers. Ten of those hits came in 1952, against the Yankees. He reached base safely in six of seven meetings on his way to accruing a handsome .345 average—tied with Duke Snider for highest on the club.

Reese lost his shortstop job to Charlie Neal in 1957. He moved with the club to Los Angeles and retired before the 1959 campaign. After serving as a Dodgers coach briefly, he teamed with Dizzy Dean to call games on NBC. He later held an executive position with the Louisville Slugger company. He gained entry to the Hall of Fame in 1984. In 2001, Bill James ranked him among the top 10 shortstops of all time.

JACKIE ROBINSON, INFIELD

Prejudice was not the only reason for the exclusion of black players from the major leagues. It was presumed by many that the integration of the majors would lead to the end of the Negro Leagues (a prophecy that was eventually fulfilled) and the loss of revenue for black owners and players. Dodgers GM Branch Rickey had more than one motive for bringing an African American player to Brooklyn. First and foremost, he wanted the Dodgers to win pennants and saw the Negro Leagues as a vast, untapped talent pool. Second, he saw segregation as a largely unChristian practice. Rickey was aware that the first black player would be subjected to all sorts of unpleasantness and was discerning in his decision.

To scout the Negro Leagues without drawing suspicion, Rickey announced that he was forming a six-team black baseball league with a franchise in Brooklyn that would be known as the Brown Dodgers. He referred to this fictional league as the United States Baseball League. Potential candidates participated in role-playing exercises with Rickey to gauge their reactions to discriminatory scenarios. Jackie Robinson was chosen partly because he was from California, where the racial climate was somewhat milder. Robinson had also participated in integrated sports at UCLA, where he was a standout in track, football, and swimming. Another factor in Rickey's decision to bring Robinson to the majors was Robinson's interest in civil rights. Robinson left UCLA a few credits short of graduation to join the U.S. Army. With the help of boxer Joe Louis, he successfully opened an officer's candidate school for African American soldiers. Robinson himself rose to the rank of second lieutenant.

After leaving the armed forces in 1944, Robinson joined the Kansas City Monarchs. When he was summoned to the Dodgers front office, he assumed he would be asked to play for Rickey's illusory Brown Dodgers. When Rickey told him he intended to integrate the major leagues, Robinson was quite surprised and more than a little reluctant. In the end, Rickey was very persuasive, and Robinson signed a contract to play for the Montreal Royals—the Dodgers' top minor-league affiliate.

Rickey officially announced his plan in an article for *Look* magazine. Journalist Wendell Smith helped spread the word in his *Pittsburgh Courier* features. Smith would serve as Robinson's personal assistant during Robinson's first season in Brooklyn. In 1946, Robinson played in 124 games with the Royals, hitting .349 on his way to capturing league MVP honors.

When Rickey announced that Robinson would be promoted to the Dodgers in 1947, several Brooklyn players objected. A petition was circulated and presented to manager Leo Durocher while the team was playing a series of exhibition games in Panama. Durocher rousted his players out of bed for an early morning team meeting. He explained what a great player Robinson was and how everyone would benefit in the long run. "I'll play an elephant if he can do the job, and to make room for him, I'll send his own brother home," the fiery Durocher allegedly said.

Durocher ended up getting suspended for associating with gamblers before the season began, and Robinson made his Brooklyn debut under interim manager Clyde Sukeforth. The treatment he received throughout the league was as bad or perhaps even worse than expected. He endured death threats and hostile remarks from numerous sources. Opposing pitchers deliberately threw at him when he came to bat, and runners tried to hurt him on the base paths with their spikes. Robinson stood tall, taking the abuse without retaliation. Arthur Daley of the *New York Times* notes, "[T]he muscular Negro minds his own business and shrewdly makes no effort to push himself. He speaks quietly and intelligently when spoken to and has already made a strong impression."

During the next several campaigns, Robinson would establish himself as a marquee infielder. Used most often as a second baseman, he was equally adept at several other positions. He led the NL in double plays four times and won three fielding titles at his primary station. He was a tough out at the plate, never accruing an on-base percentage below .367 in any of his 10 seasons. He retired with a .409 mark, which is among the top totals of all time. On the base paths, he created havoc, swiping 20 or more bags five times and leading the league twice in that category. One of the most iconic World Series moments of all time occurred in Game 1 of the 1955 Fall Classic, when Robinson brazenly stole home against Yankees ace Whitey Ford. Asked about the play many times throughout the years, Ford's batterymate, Yogi Berra, insisted that Robinson was out. A careful review of the game footage strongly suggests that Yogi was mistaken.

Robinson had started his career late, and by 1956, he was wearing down. Although he announced his intention of retiring to a writer from *Look* magazine near season's end, he failed to officially notify the Dodgers. Traded to the Giants in the offseason, he was reportedly offered $60,000 to keep playing. As he was considering the deal, Dodger GM Buzzie Bavasi accused Robinson of using deception to land a bigger contract. Robinson proved Bavasi wrong by retiring.

After baseball, Robinson grew progressively ill with diabetes. He suffered two heart attacks, succumbing to the second one at his Connecticut home in 1972. He was a member of the Hall of Fame class of 1962. His life story has been the subject of multiple books and movies. His number "42" has been retired by Major League Baseball.

ROY CAMPANELLA, CATCHER

Campanella was born to a mixed-race couple in Philadelphia. Though his father was Italian, he was still subject to the color barrier. Campanella was only fifteen years old when he joined the Negro National

League. Competing against older, established veterans, he emerged as a smooth-fielding, power-hitting star. While playing for the Baltimore Elite Giants, he received instruction from legendary backstop Biz Mackey, who passed on various bits of baseball wisdom.

In 1942, Campanella was suspended for appearing in an exhibition game with the Cincinnati Buckeyes without receiving permission. Hit with a $250 fine, he jumped the Baltimore club and was expelled from the circuit. He appeared in multiple Hispanic leagues, becoming fluent in Spanish—a skill that would later help him communicate with his Latino teammates in Brooklyn.

Campanella loved the position of catcher, feeling that it kept him continuously in the flow of the game. "I never had to be lonely behind the plate, where I could talk to hitters," he once said. "I also learned that by engaging them in conversation, I could sometimes distract them."

In 1945, Campanella impressed Brooklyn coach Charlie Dressen while on a barnstorming tour against a major-league squad. After Jackie Robinson was signed, Campanella took a significant pay cut to enter the Dodgers farm system. He played at Nashua, Montreal, and St. Paul before becoming the first African American catcher in the majors. In his 1948 debut season, he played well enough to displace incumbent catcher Bruce Edwards as a first stringer.

During his 10 seasons in the majors, "Campy" (as he came to be known) drilled 30 or more homers four times. In 1953, he set a record for RBIs by a catcher with 142. He was equally productive in postseason play, scoring or driving in a total of 26 runs in 32 games. His eighth-inning homer off of Vic Raschi in Game 3 of the 1953 World Series was the game winner. A perennial All-Star, he was known for his good humor and enthusiasm for the game. "I never want to quit playing ball," he once said. "They'll have to cut this uniform off of me to get me out of it."

In the end, it was a tragic accident that forced him out. A series of injuries in the mid-1950s forced him to think about life after baseball. He purchased a liquor store in Harlem and was driving home in January 1958, when his rented Chevy sedan hit a telephone pole and flipped over. While he would later regain use of his arms, he would never walk again.

In 1959, the Dodgers honored their beloved catcher on "Roy Campanella Night" at the LA Coliseum. A record crowd of more than 93,000 turned out to celebrate Campy's birthday with the proceeds going toward his health-care costs. After a brief speech by Campanella, the lights went out and fans lit matches. "The Coliseum burst into a mass of twinkling stars," Campy recalled. "I've never seen anything like it."

Inducted into the Hall of Fame in 1969, Campanella attended activities in Cooperstown regularly after that. He continued operating his liquor store for a while and also hosted a radio show known as "Campy's Corner." He stayed busy with the Dodgers as well, serving as a scout, a coach, and later a public relations assistant. He died of a heart attack in 1993.

DUKE SNIDER, CENTER FIELD

Snider's career coincided with those of two of the greatest center fielders in history—Mickey Mantle and Willie Mays. The three were immortalized in the chorus of the song *Talkin' Baseball* by Terry Cashman in 1981. Although Snider didn't always get as much attention as Willie or the Mick, he held his own statistically.

Snider grew up in Compton, California, and signed with the Dodgers in 1944. A preview of things to come, he led the Piedmont League in home runs before losing part of two seasons to service in the U.S. Navy. Snider's big-league debut was overshadowed by the arrival of Jackie Robinson in 1947. He played in his first game the same week but failed to grab many headlines that season with his .241 average.

Demoted to Montreal in 1948, GM Branch Rickey subjected Snider to a crash course in strike zone-ology. Under the watchful eye of Hall of Famer George Sisler, the young slugger was forced to allow pitch after pitch go by while his bat remained inactive. The instruction paid off, as he hit .292 with 23 homers and 92 RBIs for the Dodgers in 1949.

Snider lived in Flatbush and became a folk hero to fans who considered him one of their own. But his moody nature failed to endear him to sportswriters. His temper tantrums over hotel accommodations and failures at the plate became legendary. In 1955, he declared that the fans in Brooklyn didn't deserve a pennant. During an interview for

Collier's magazine, he insinuated that he was only in the game for the money. Despite his blustery nature, he later remarked, "When they tore down Ebbets Field, they tore down a little piece of me." And fans in Brooklyn almost always forgave him for his transgressions.

Snider succeeded Pete Reiser—a popular and promising young star who kept running into outfield fences. Snider's 326 homers and 1,031 RBIs were the most by any slugger during the 1950s. He was also an exceptional defensive player, leading his NL peers in fielding percentage three times. One day, left fielder Gene Hermanski missed a shoestring catch and the ball rolled into the corner. Sprinting all the way over from his center-field post, Snider nailed the runner at third with a laser throw. He would lead the league in assists during the 1949 slate, while placing third on three other occasions.

Snider moved with the club to LA but began to suffer from knee trouble. He was removed from Games 1 and 2 of the 1959 World Series for defensive purposes. His third-inning homer in the sixth contest helped the Dodgers to a championship over the White Sox. In 1961, Snider broke his elbow and split time with 22-year-old Ron Fairly.

The Mets purchased Snider's contract in 1963, hoping he might draw fans to the ballpark. He was the lone Mets representative in the All-Star Game that year but hit just .243 with 14 homers. He appeared in his last game with the Giants the following year.

After his retirement, Snider worked as a scout and minor-league manager. He later joined the Expos' broadcasting team. It took him more than a decade to get into the Hall of Fame. His autobiography, *The Duke of Flatbush*, was released in the 1980s. He passed away in 2011, at the age of 84.

FAST FACT: From 1952–1956, the Dodgers compiled a .630 winning percentage during the regular season. They were far less successful in postseason play, winning just 44 percent of their games in that span.

13

LOS ANGELES DODGERS

1963–1966

While Brooklynites were mourning the loss of their beloved Dodgers in 1958, West Coast fans were busy embracing them as their own. Even with a lackluster 71–83 record, the fledgling LA squad ranked second in attendance, drawing nearly 2 million fans. A National League pennant and World Series victory over the White Sox kept the turnstiles in motion the following year.

After a series of legal battles, construction finally began on a new ballpark in Chavez Ravine, a hillside area overlooking Los Angeles. In the meantime, the Dodgers played their games at the LA Coliseum, home of the USC Trojans and Los Angeles Rams. Since the stadium was designed for football, the field was just barely large enough to accommodate a baseball diamond. The left-field fence was only 250 feet from home plate. The Dodgers were ordered to install a 40-foot screen to keep balls inside the park. A subsequent rule change required all ballparks built after 1958 to have 325-foot foul lines.

Dodger Stadium took four years to complete at a cost of $23 million (quite a sum in those days). It opened in 1962, with a puzzling irregularity. The foul poles had been placed entirely in foul territory, and the club was compelled to seek a special dispensation from NL officials to host games there. The problem was corrected before the 1963 campaign.

By the time the colorful new stadium opened, the Dodger roster had undergone a major facelift. Jim Gilliam and Johnny Podres were still productive, but Gil Hodges had been lost to the expansion draft and Duke Snider was in serious decline. The most prominent members of the "new" club were Don Drysdale and Sandy Koufax.

Koufax had actually been kicking around since the championship season of 1955; however, he had toiled in relative anonymity due to his extreme wildness. Manager Walter Alston later recalled getting a first glimpse of Koufax during spring training in 1955. The 19-year-old southpaw was playing catch with a teammate on the sidelines, and according to Alston, roughly half of his throws were sailing over the other man's head.

A Brooklyn native, Koufax had been signed that year as a "bonus baby." Under existing "bonus rules," Brooklyn was required to keep him on the roster for two years. The future Hall of Famer was extremely slow in developing, averaging more than five walks per nine frames in his first six seasons, while posting a cumbersome 36–40 record. At some point during spring training of 1961, catcher Norm Sherry reportedly noticed that Koufax was gripping the ball too tightly when he threw. A simple adjustment was all that was necessary to turn his career around.

From 1961–1966, Koufax won three Triple Crowns, while posting the lowest ERA in the majors for five straight years. He earned six consecutive All-Star selections and became the first pitcher in history to toss four no-hitters. This included a perfect game on September 9, 1965—the only game of its kind by a Dodger. Teammate Don Sutton remarked that a "foul ball was a moral victory" for opposing batsmen. Forced into retirement after the 1966 campaign due to an arthritic elbow, Koufax ended up with fewer victories than most of the starting pitchers in the Hall of Fame.

Completing one of the greatest tandems in pitching history, Don Drysdale was among the fiercest competitors of the era. He once stated that he had a "two-for-one" rule. Whenever one of his teammates got knocked down with a pitch, he knocked down two opponents. "I hate all hitters," he once said. "I start a game mad and stay that way until it's over." Infielder Dick Groat commiserated that "batting against Don Drysdale is like making a date with a dentist."

Tall and broad-shouldered at 6-foot-5, Drysdale was nicknamed "Big D." He finished with double-digit hit-by-pitch totals in nine straight seasons, and his career sum of 154 is among the top 20 marks of all time. His period of dominance lasted longer than Koufax's, as he gathered 14 or more victories on eight occasions between 1957–1968. An eight-time All-Star, he captured a Cy Young Award in 1962, with a 25–9 record and a 2.83 ERA. His crowning achievement came in 1968, when he tossed a record six consecutive shutouts. His streak of 58 scoreless innings that year was a record that stood until Orel Hershiser (another Dodger) broke it in 1988.

With Drysdale and Koufax dominating the opposition, the Dodgers narrowly missed a World Series berth in 1962. They ended up tied with the Giants on the last day of the season. In a scenario eerily reminiscent of the 1951 campaign, a three-game playoff was arranged to decide the pennant. The Dodgers split the first two games and carried a 4–2 lead into the ninth inning of the finale. LA reliever Ed Roebuck, who came on in relief of southpaw Johnny Podres in the sixth, couldn't hold off the Giants. He walked the bases full and gave up a RBI single to Willie Mays. Stan Williams and Ron Perranoski were both summoned from the Dodgers bullpen to squelch the rally but couldn't get the job done. The Giants moved on to the World Series with a 6–4 win.

The Dodgers regrouped in 1963, posting 99 victories and finishing six games ahead of the Cardinals. In the World Series, they pulled off an astonishing sweep of the Yankees. All four games were tightly pitched contests, with neither club putting up more than five runs. Dodgers hurlers collectively held the Bombers to a .171 team batting average. After watching Koufax shut down the Yankees, Yogi Berra commented, "I can see how he won 25 games. What I don't understand is how he lost five."

After a disappointing sixth-place finish in 1964, the Dodgers climbed back on top the following year. While they finished near the bottom of the pack offensively, ranking eighth in runs per game and last in homers, crisp pitching and aggressive baserunning allowed them to sneak past the Giants. The Dodgers assembled an incredible late-season run, winning 15 of their last 16 contests and finishing two games ahead of their oldest nemeses. To this day, the Giants–Dodgers rivalry is one of the most intense in all of sports.

The 1965 World Series pitted the Dodgers against the Twins, who were making their first postseason appearance since leaving Washington and changing their identity. Led offensively by Harmon Killebrew,

Tony Oliva, and Zoilo Versalles (who captured American League MVP honors that year), the Twins overwhelmed the Dodgers at Metropolitan Stadium in Minnesota, winning the first two games by a combined score of 13–3. The big story was Sandy Koufax, who was scheduled to pitch the opener but refused because it fell on Yom Kippur—the Hebrew "Day of Atonement." Although he was not the first ballplayer to sit out on the holy day, he made the biggest impact. In his biography, *Sandy Koufax: A Lefty's Legacy*, author Jane Leavy writes, "By refusing to pitch that day, Koufax became inextricably linked with the Jewish experience. He was the New Patriarch: Abraham, Isaac, Jacob, and Sandy." Forced to pitch in Koufax's spot, Drysdale was chased from the mound in the third inning. When the so-called "Left Arm of God" returned to action the following day, he was largely ineffective, putting LA in a 2–0 hole. But the Twins' offense sputtered on the road as the Dodgers won the next three meetings. A Minnesota victory in the sixth contest set the stage for Koufax's redemption, which came in the form of a brilliant three-hit shutout in the finale. For the second time in three years, the Dodgers were world champions.

In 1966, LA bolstered its pitching staff with the promotion of Don Sutton. Although his prime years would come a bit later, the 21-year-old right-hander made a promising debut. Used as a fourth starter behind Koufax, Drysdale, and Claude Osteen, Sutton worked more than 200 innings and posted a respectable 2.99 ERA as the Dodgers won another tight pennant race over the Giants. When Sutton's turn in the rotation arrived during the World Series, the Orioles were leading three games to none and Alston opted for Drysdale instead. Sutton would appear in three Fall Classics with the Dodgers during the 1970s and end up in the Hall of Fame.

The 1966 Series sweep at the hands of the Orioles was the end of an era, as the Dodgers failed to capture another pennant until 1974. By then, Koufax and Drysdale were gone, along with most of the other members of the old guard. Unlike many dominant teams of the expansion era, there was a conspicuous absence of Hall of Famers in LA during the 1960s. The club relied heavily on lesser stars to carry them to October glory. The contributions of the following players were crucial to the team's success.

WILLIE DAVIS, CENTER FIELD

Davis grew up in Los Angeles and was a three-sport star in high school, playing baseball and basketball, while also running track. He was signed by the Dodgers upon graduating in 1958. Demonstrating tremendous speed, he reportedly scored from first base on singles numerous times while playing at Reno in 1959. By September 1960, he was wearing a Dodgers uniform.

Davis was nicknamed "3-Dog" for his ability to stretch doubles into triples. He led the league twice in that category and finished among the top 10 regularly. Hitting primarily out of the third slot in the batting order, he finished in double digits for homers on 11 occasions, with a high of 21 in 1962. A lifetime .279 hitter, he broke the .300 mark four times during his career. Additionally, he stole 20 or more bases in 11 straight seasons.

A bit error prone in the outfield, he finished first among NL center fielders in miscues several times but also managed to win three Gold Gloves. During the 1966 World Series, he experienced the ultimate defensive nightmare. In the fifth inning of Game 2, he committed three errors—a Series record. Bombarded by reporters after the game, he said, "It's not my life, it's not my wife, it's just a game." He redeemed himself to an extent in Game 3, making a spectacular leaping catch to rob Orioles slugger Boog Powell of a home run. Davis played in three World Series for the Dodgers during his career, managing a feeble .167 batting average. He wasn't alone. Never known for their abundant offense, the Dodgers hit .214 as a team in the 1963 Fall Classic and .142 in the 1966 postseason.

Late in his career, Davis became a member of a Buddhist sect and could be found chanting with prayer beads before games. The practice may or may not have helped him secure a place among the franchise leaders in hits (2,091), runs scored (1,004), and triples (110). Additionally, his 31-game hitting streak in 1969 is the longest by a Dodger.

Davis had a buoyant personality. He once told a reporter that nothing on the field could get him down. "If we win, I am happy for myself," he said. "If we lose, I am happy because of the happiness it has brought the other guy." Aside from his baseball pursuits, he had several acting roles, appearing on such TV comedies as *Mr. Ed* and *The Flying Nun*.

He also had a sizeable part in the Jerry Lewis film *Which Way to the Front?* Davis died in 2010, at the age of 69.

CLAUDE OSTEEN, PITCHER

Osteen spent portions of 18 seasons in the majors, packaging his best efforts into a 10-year span from 1964–1973. During that remarkable stretch, he won no fewer than 15 games eight times, reaching the 20-win threshold twice.

Osteen came of age in Reading, Ohio, where he guided his high school to a state championship in 1957. Signed by Cincinnati at the age of 17, he would have multiple trials with the Reds and Senators before attaining full-time major-league status in 1962. On a miserable Washington squad that lost 100 games each year from 1962–1964, Osteen managed to accumulate 32 victories. He was dealt to Los Angeles in a seven-player swap before the 1965 slate. The transaction sent slugging outfielder Frank Howard to Washington, where he would earn the nickname the "Capital Punisher" for his prodigious home-run power. Dodgers fans were initially upset with the trade, but Osteen pitched brilliantly in LA, softening the blow.

The Dodgers had a somewhat anemic offense in those days, and Osteen was supported by two runs or less in 28 of his regular-season outings between 1965–1966. He won 32 games anyway, posting a handsome 2.82 ERA. The reliable left-hander would appear in two World Series with the Dodgers and lose two of three decisions, despite averaging less than a run per nine frames. Osteen's defining postseason moment came in 1965. Sandy Koufax refused to pitch on Yom Kippur, and his replacement, Don Drysdale, didn't have his best stuff, as the Dodgers lost, 8–2. Koufax followed with a poor start. With the Dodgers in a precarious situation, Osteen was slated to pitch the third contest. By his own admission, he was a nervous wreck, but he rose to the occasion with a five-hit shutout victory. It was just what LA needed to turn the Series around.

Osteen remained with the Dodgers until December 1973, when he was traded to the Astros in a blockbuster deal that landed slugger Jim Wynn in LA. During his nine seasons on the West Coast, Osteen posted a 147–126 record with an ERA of 3.09. Extremely durable, he averaged

37 starts and 266 innings per year. Traded to the Cardinals in August 1974, he finished his major-league career with the White Sox the following season. He moved on to a career as a pitching coach for several major-league teams.

MAURY WILLS, SHORTSTOP

Wills grew up in Washington, DC, and to date is the only player from Cardozo High School to reach the majors. He waited a long time to get there. With Hall of Famer Pee Wee Reese at shortstop, Wills languished in the Dodgers farm system for nearly a decade. He finally received a call-up in June 1959. He hit .260 in 83 games and maintained a regular spot in the lineup for the next seven years.

Wills had two stints in Los Angeles during his career, spending 12 seasons with the club. A five-time All-Star, he led the league in stolen bases each year from 1960–1965. In 1962, he set a record for steals in a season (since broken) with 104. Additionally, he led the league in triples, earning a MVP Award. His body became so horribly bruised that year, doctors were prescribing enzymes to stop the internal bleeding. Two months after the season was over, Wills was depressed and still limping noticeably. He visited renowned Las Vegas hypnotist Arthur Ellen, who allegedly "cured" him of a "mental block" that had been hindering his recovery. The fleet-footed infielder returned to action in 1963, leading the league in steals on three more occasions. When he retired in 1972, his total of 586 placed him at number 10 on the all-time list—the most by any player since the 1920s.

Wills had virtually no power at the plate, never collecting more than six homers and 19 doubles in any season. But he maintained a steady batting average during the regular season, compiling a lifetime mark of .281. The postseason was an entirely different story. Wills appeared in four Fall Classics, winning three rings, but he was not successful in all of them. In the 1963 sweep of the Yankees, he went 2-for-15 at the plate. In the four-game loss to Baltimore in 1966, he put forth a pathetic 1-for-13 effort. He proved quite valuable in 1965, against the Twins, tagging Minnesota pitchers for 11 hits. He ended up with a middling .244 World Series batting average.

Following his departure from the majors, Wills had highly publicized alcohol and drug problems. In December 1983, he was arrested for cocaine possession, although the charges were dismissed. The Dodgers paid for him to attend rehab, but he walked out to continue his drug use. In 1989, he got clean. His book *On the Run: The Never Dull and Often Shocking Life of Maury Wills* was somewhat controversial. In it, Wills cites a love affair with Doris Day that is refuted by the actress in her own autobiography. Wills's book also led to a falling out with his son Bump, who played for the Rangers and Cubs in a six-year major-league career. Bump was unhappy about being included in a particular anecdote, which he claimed was both inaccurate and scandalous. The two later reconciled.

Wills remained in the game for several years after his playing days were over, serving as a base-running instructor for several teams. In 1980, he replaced Mariners manager Darrell Johnson, guiding the club to a lackluster 20–38 record down the stretch. When the team got off to a 6–18 start the following year, Wills was fired. As a manager, he once called for a relief pitcher when there was no one warming up in the bullpen. He also held up a game for 10 minutes picking out a pinch-hitter. On another occasion, he left a spring training game still in progress to catch a flight elsewhere. In one of his most infamous gaffes, he ordered Mariners groundskeepers to make the batter's box longer than regulation. The alteration was discovered by A's manager Billy Martin (who rarely missed a trick). Wills admitted he was trying to give his players an advantage and was suspended and fined.

In 2012, Wills insinuated to journalist Craig Calcaterra of NBC Sports that he belongs in the Hall of Fame. "Maybe they're waiting to do me like they did Ron Santo," Wills said. "He dies and they put him in the next year. Isn't that ridiculous?" According to sabermetric measurements, Wills compares favorably to Dave Bancroft and Johnny Evers, both of whom have plaques hanging at Cooperstown.

RON PERRANOSKI, PITCHER

Born and raised in New Jersey, Perranoski attended Fairlawn High School and later Michigan State University. He spent three years at the college before embarking on a pro baseball career. The left-hander got his start in the Cubs farm system during the 1958 campaign. In April 1960, he was traded with two players and cash to the Dodgers for Don Zimmer. He had an excellent year in the minors and joined the parent club in 1961.

For 10 major-league seasons, Perranoski was a durable reliever for the Dodgers and Twins, leading the league in appearances three times and games finished twice. His finest campaign came in 1963, with LA, when he won 16 games and recorded 21 saves, while accruing a stingy 1.67 ERA. Credited with just three losses, he posted the highest winning percentage in the league. In the World Series that year, he picked up another save in Game 2.

During the Dodgers' run of dominance from 1963–1966, Perranoski entered no fewer than 55 games per year, compiling a record of 33–23, while collecting 59 saves. He posted a cumulative ERA of 2.49 in that span. He made five World Series appearances for the Dodgers, allowing no earned runs in three of them. Traded to the Twins in 1967, with John Roseboro, he would lead the league in saves during the 1969 and 1970 campaigns. He retired with 178, which was among the top marks at the time. He is featured in John Thorn's 1979 book *The Relief Pitcher: Baseball's New Hero*. In it, he is listed with Hall of Famers Hoyt Wilhelm and Rollie Fingers as one of the top 10 relievers in history.

Perranoski was known for his wide-breaking curve and composure on the mound. Walter Alston once commented, "He's got the right temperature for a relief pitcher. It's like ice water." In Perranoski's day, relief pitching was not considered a glamorous job—a fact that didn't sit well with the talented closer. "Relief pitchers are just as important as starters," he told an Associated Press reporter after being overlooked for the All-Star Team in 1970. "Teams that win the pennant win it with their bullpens. I don't see why we should be shunned just because we don't start." Perranoski never made an All-Star appearance despite his overwhelming success.

After his retirement, Perranoski worked as a minor-league pitching coach. He joined the Dodgers staff in 1981, and remained with them through 1994. In 1997, he was hired by the Giants as a coach. He eventually moved to the front office.

TOMMY DAVIS, OUTFIELD/THIRD BASE

Davis came of age in Brooklyn and attended high school there. Before signing with the Dodgers in 1956, he received a personal phone call from Jackie Robinson, who encouraged him to join the franchise. Davis had a stellar minor-league career, capturing two batting titles, in 1957 and 1959. He broke in with the Dodgers full-time in 1960, hitting .276 with 11 homers in 110 games. He finished fifth in Rookie of the Year voting.

Although Davis had played outfield throughout his professional career, the Dodgers tried to convert him to a third baseman in 1961. He had never been taught how to throw from that station, and his relays kept sailing over first base. The experiment was abandoned after the 1963 slate; however, he still made an occasional appearance. He was far more competent as a left fielder, posting the highest fielding percentage among players at his position twice.

Davis's major league career spanned eighteen seasons and included imore than 2,000 base hits. He had a banner year with the Dodgers in 1962, leading the league with 230 hits, 153 RBIs, and a .346 batting average. Still, he finished as a runner-up for MVP. Davis followed with another batting title in 1963. His .400 World Series batting average that year was tops on either club. He would appear in one more Series with the Dodgers, managing a far less proficient .250 mark.

The turning point in Davis's career occurred on May 1, 1965. Facing the Giants at home, he slid awkwardly into second and twisted his ankle. He ended up with a break and dislocation that laid him up in the hospital for a while. Davis's replacement, Lou Johnson, hit a game-winning homer in Game 7 of the World Series that year. Returning in 1966, Davis's power stroke was gone. He managed just 15 extra-base hits but led the team with a .313 average. The Dodgers traded him to the Mets in the offseason.

Davis had several solid seasons elsewhere, breaking the .300 mark with the Mets, A's, and Orioles. He ended up playing for nine different teams after leaving LA, serving mostly as a designated hitter. He became somewhat bitter about his frequent changes of address. "Why do I keep getting released? Don't ask me no reason why," he once groused. One sportswriter asserted, "When Tommy left for an evening at the ballpark, his wife never knew whether to pack him a lunch or a suitcase."

Davis had a laid-back approach to the game. While playing for the Orioles, he was known to leave the dugout between at-bats to read or shave. "The lazier I felt, the better I hit," he later boasted. There was some truth to that statement, as Davis accrued one of the highest batting averages of all time by a pinch-hitter with a minimum of 150 at-bats.

After his playing days, he worked as a minor-league instructor for the Dodgers and served as batting coach for the Mariners. He also started his own company, selling promotional items to large corporations. He coauthored a book with sportswriter Paul Gutierrez entitled *Tommy Davis's Tales from the Dodger Dugout*. A resident of Rancho Cucamonga, an affluent community roughly one hour southeast of LA, he was recognized by the city council in 2013 for his community service. Davis has been an active promoter of the Rancho Cucamonga Quakes—a minor-league ballclub. He has also been an active participant in various youth baseball camps.

JOHN ROSEBORO, CATCHER

Among the most stable presences in the Dodgers lineup, Roseboro was the starting catcher in Los Angeles from 1958–1967. In that span, he made three All-Star appearances, while helping the club to four World Series berths. While his offensive numbers don't exactly leap off the page, he is generally considered one of the greatest backstops in franchise history.

Born and raised in Ashland, Ohio, Roseboro signed as an amateur free agent with the Dodgers in 1952. He hit .365 in his first pro season and missed the entire 1954 campaign while serving in the military. Called to the majors in 1957, he played backup to Roy Campanella. When "Campy" was paralyzed in a tragic car accident during the offseason, Roseboro took over first-string duties. For the next 10 seasons, he performed the job admirably.

An exceptional defensive catcher, Roseboro led the league in putouts four times, double plays three times, and caught stealing percentage twice. Additionally, he posted the highest range factor among NL backstops for five straight seasons (1958–1962). He worked especially well with Sandy Koufax, catching two of the southpaw's no-hitters. A fiery competitor, Roseboro is perhaps best remembered for his altercation with Giants pitcher Juan Marichal during a game on August 22, 1965. The two teams were engaged in a tight pennant race, and Marichal had issued brushback pitches to multiple Dodgers hitters. Since the gentlemanly Koufax was too ethical to retaliate, Roseboro took matters into his own hands, grazing Marichal's ear with a carefully placed return throw to the mound. Marichal went ballistic, clubbing Roseboro over the head with his bat and opening up a gash that required stitches. A bench-clearing brawl ensued. Roseboro returned to the lineup shortly afterward and hit .286 in the World Series that year.

After posting a .272 batting average in 1967, Roseboro was included in a five-player trade that landed him in Minnesota. He spent two seasons as the Twins number-one catcher, making a final postseason appearance in the 1969 playoffs. He finished his career with the Senators in 1970.

From 1972–1974, Roseboro served as a bullpen coach for the Angels. He ran into extreme financial difficulty after that. "I considered sticking someone or someplace up," he later admitted. "I was an honest man, but I was desperate." He eventually entered the insurance business and landed back on his feet. His autobiography, *Glory Days with the Dodgers and Other Days with Others*, was later released. During his prime years, he appeared in the TV pilot of *Dragnet*, playing Sergeant Dave Bradford. He made a handful of appearances on various other TV dramas. He died in 2002, at the age of 69.

FAST FACT: During their three World Series appearances between 1963–1966, Dodgers pitchers held opponents to a collective .190 batting average. But LA batters weren't exactly breaking down fences themselves. In those three October showdowns, they compiled a lowly .225 team batting mark. During the 1966 Fall Classic, they were shut out in three straight games.

14

ST. LOUIS CARDINALS

1964–1968

The Cardinals are among the most successful clubs in the majors, having captured 11 world championships through the 2015 campaign. That total is second only to the Yankees. After knocking off the Red Sox in seven games during the 1946 World Series, the club experienced a long drought, failing to make another postseason appearance until 1964.

The most heralded members of the 1964 squad were future Hall of Famers Lou Brock and Bob Gibson. Traded by the Cubs in June of that year, Brock had an immediate impact in St. Louis, raising his batting average by more than 60 points, while stealing 33 bases. He collected nine hits in the World Series against the Yankees, including a towering Game 7 homer that staked the Cardinals to a 4–0 lead.

Had the Cubs known how Brock's career would turn out, they almost certainly would have hung on to him. The lefty-hitting outfielder enjoyed more than a dozen productive seasons in St. Louis, resetting the all-time mark for stolen bases with 938. Although the record was broken in 1991, by Rickey Henderson, the annual award given to National League stolen-base leaders is named after Brock.

A ferocious competitor, Gibson was among the most dominant pitchers of his era. "You've got to have an attitude if you're going to go far in this game," he once remarked. Carrying those words to an extreme, he inspired fear in the hearts of opponents by frequently throwing at them. He hit more than 100 batters during his career and was just naturally wild enough to prevent anyone from getting too comfortable at the plate. Describing the right-hander's intensity, batterymate Joe Torre remarked, "Bob wasn't just unfriendly when he pitched. I'd say it was more like hateful."

Using his menacing persona to an advantage, Gibson struck out more than 200 batters in nine seasons and led the league in shutouts four times. He enjoyed his most successful campaign in 1968, the so-called "year of the pitcher." With offense on the rise in the majors, Commissioner Ford Frick in 1963 opted to expand the strike zone. The effects were felt dramatically in both leagues, as more than 339 shutouts were thrown that season (almost double the amount recorded in 1962). Gibson accumulated 22 victories and posted the lowest ERA since the Deadball Era, at 1.12. His streak of 47 consecutive scoreless innings was the second longest in NL history at the time.

Gibson was a dominant force during the 1964 championship run, collecting a total of 21 victories (including the postseason). The Cardinals had two reliable run producers that year—corner infielders Bill White and Ken Boyer. For White, it was his third consecutive season with 100 or more RBIs. Boyer drove in a league-high 119 runs, while finishing among the top 10 in hits, total bases, and homers. He was named MVP on the strength of that performance.

The 1964 NL pennant race was a four-way shootout between the Cardinals, Giants, Phillies, and Reds. The Giants were in the hunt early on but slumped in July and August, ultimately ending up on the fringe. The Phillies took over first place shortly after the All-Star break and built a healthy lead before a 10-game losing streak in September dashed their pennant hopes. Cincinnati manager Fred Hutchinson announced before spring training that he would continue his duties, despite being diagnosed with multiple cancerous tumors. The travel eventually wore him down, and he was forced to step aside in August. His replacement, Dick Sisler, presided over a valiant late-season surge that fell just short. In the end, the Cardinals barely hung on, finishing one game ahead of the Phillies and Reds.

The World Series pitted the aging Yankees against a rejuvenated St. Louis squad with something to prove. Playing in his last Fall Classic, Mickey Mantle belted three homers, bringing his Series career total to 18—a record that still stands. Among the most successful hurlers in World Series history, Whitey Ford went out with a whimper, getting hammered in his only start. The Cardinals averaged more than four runs per game, capturing their first world championship in nearly two decades.

In August 1964, St. Louis owner "Gussie" Busch made a sweeping series of front-office changes. Manager Johnny Keane's job was spared, although rumors circulated widely that Leo Durocher would take over in 1965. Keane drafted a resignation letter in September and, despite the favorable postseason outcome, presented it to Busch and new GM Bob Howsam. Future Hall of Famer Red Schoendienst, one of Keane's coaches, was assigned to the vacant position.

Schoendienst had spent more than two decades as a professional player. Used primarily at second base, he posted the highest fielding percentage among NL peers on six occasions. Stan Musial once remarked that Schoendienst had the "greatest pair of hands" he had ever seen. The switch-hitting infielder was named to 10 All-Star Teams and played on two world championship squads, one of them in St. Louis.

Schoendienst had a laid-back approach to managing. In 1968, his entire spring training speech was comprised of the following words: "Run everything out and be in by 12." *Sports Illustrated* writer William Leggett remarked, "[Schoendienst's] ways on the field are not flamboyant, but he makes moves during a game that are far more daring than his personality would seem to promise, and he has stolen more than one pennant with a team whose abilities are questionable."

Schoendienst got off to a rocky start in 1965, as offensive production in St. Louis dropped off sharply. The club plummeted to seventh place and fared only slightly better the following year with an 83–79 record. By 1967, the Cardinals lineup had undergone a major overhaul. White and Boyer were gone, along with former MVP shortstop Dick Groat. The pitching rotation was retooled as well. Aside from Gibson, only one starter from the 1964 championship club remained.

Two of the available roster slots were filled with future Cooperstown inductees. Among the first in a long line of successful Puerto Rican players, Orlando Cepeda began his career with the Giants in 1958, capturing Rookie of the Year honors. Traded to the Cardinals in May 1966, he proved to be a major asset with his reliable bat and cheerful personality. He picked up the nickname "Cha Cha" for the Latin music he played in the clubhouse. "We were one of the loosest teams ever," he later recalled. "We'd play around until about five minutes before the game." When the games were over, he would lead his teammates in a cheer of sorts that always began with the question, "All right, El Birdos—who's the best team in the league?!" Cepeda's signature performance came in 1967, when he led the league in RBIs, while finishing among the top 10 in more than a dozen other offensive categories. He was a unanimous choice for MVP that year.

Bolstering the pitching corps, the Cardinals promoted Steve Carlton, a 22-year-old southpaw who had spent a majority of the 1966 campaign in the Pacific Coast League. A big man, at 6-foot-4, 210 pounds, Carlton had a hard-breaking slider and explosive fastball. He was known for his intense concentration on the mound. Teammate Tim McCarver once explained, "Carlton does not pitch to the hitter, he pitches through him. The batter hardly exists for him. He's playing an elevated game of catch."

Off the field, Carlton was aloof, often alienating teammates, reporters, and fans. He could be abrupt and egotistical. But that didn't stop him from assembling an impressive Hall of Fame resume that included more than 300 wins and 4,000 strikeouts. He added four Cy Young Awards to his collection along the way. While he would not hit his peak until he was traded to the Phillies in 1972, he was a reliable member of the St. Louis rotation during the pennant-winning seasons of the late 1960s.

Led by a multitude of all-time greats, the Cardinals accumulated 101 victories in 1967, and finished 10 1/2 games ahead of the Giants. They accomplished this despite the loss of Bob Gibson in mid-July. The St. Louis ace was struck by a hard liner off the bat of Roberto Clemente. He faced three more hitters before his fibula bone snapped. When Gibson returned to action in September, the Cardinals were still in possession of first place.

With career-defining performances from Carl Yastrzemski and Jim Lonborg, the Red Sox made their first postseason appearance in more than 20 years. Lonborg, a hard-throwing right-hander, paced the American League with 246 strikeouts and 22 wins. Yastrzemski captured a Triple Crown with 44 homers, 121 RBIs, and a .326 batting average. Both performed remarkably well in the 1967 Fall Classic, but not well enough to avoid a seven-game defeat at the hands of the Cardinals. Gibson was the star of the show for St. Louis, winning all three of his starts, while fanning 26 Bostonians in 27 innings of work.

During the "year of the pitcher," the Cardinals managed a pedestrian .249 team batting average. Lou Brock led the league with 46 doubles and 14 triples, but not a single St. Louis regular reached the 20-homer threshold. Only one position player (Curt Flood) hit .300. Despite their listless attack, the Cards won 97 games and ran way with the NL pennant.

Again, the Fall Classic dragged on for seven games, but this time the Cardinals came away empty-handed. Borrowing a page from Bob Gibson's postseason playbook, Tigers southpaw Mickey Lolich derailed the St. Louis offense in each of his starts, emerging with three complete-game victories and World Series MVP honors. The Cardinals slumped to fourth place the following year and would not return to the October stage until 1982.

Outside of Gibson, Carlton, Brock, and Cepeda, the Cardinals squads of the 1960s generate little discussion nowadays. A thorough examination of the lineups reveals a sizeable list of lesser-known stars whose contributions have avoided detection in recent years.

ROGER MARIS, OUTFIELD

While much attention has been paid to Maris's days with the Yankees, little is mentioned about his successful twilight years with the Cardinals. Maris made a name for himself in 1961, when he broke Babe Ruth's single-season mark for homers. The pressure of chasing such a coveted record made him a nervous wreck, and as his hair began to fall out in clumps, he was frequently misrepresented by members of the hostile press corps. After drilling homer number 61 on the last day of the season, controversy continued to swirl. Since Ruth had established the record in a 154-game season, Commissioner Ford Frick, an old friend of the Babe's, suggested that an asterisk be placed next to Maris's accomplishment in the record books. Commenting on his stressful experience, Maris said, "As a ballplayer, I would be delighted to do it again. As an individual, I doubt if I could possibly go through it again."

Maris got his professional start in the Cleveland organization, working his way up to the Double A level in 1955. Sensitive and temperamental, he changed the spelling of his birth name from Maras to Maris when fans began referring to him as "Mare-Ass." Although he was considered a "can't-miss" prospect, manager Dutch Meyer kicked him off the team at Tulsa after he hit just .233 in 25 games. At Indianapolis in 1956, he raised his average considerably and earned a 1957 call-up to Cleveland. Failing to live up to expectations, he was traded to the Kansas City A's in June 1958. The A's were little more than a farm club for the Yankees in those days and ended up shipping Maris to New York for the 1960 campaign.

Maris assembled back-to-back MVP seasons and followed his historic 1961 effort with another solid run (33 HR/100 RBIs). Over the next several seasons, Maris was hampered by injuries, which the Yankees claimed were fabricated. Unfairly painted as a lackadaisical whiner by the New York press, the Bombers traded him to the Cardinals in December 1966. It was later discovered that he had been playing with a broken bone in his hand.

While it was far from a career revival, Maris performed well in St. Louis. Several teammates credited him as being instrumental in turning the team around. During the 1967 and 1968 campaigns, Maris played in more than 200 regular-season games, hitting .258 with 59 extra-base hits and 100 RBIs. Serving primarily as a right fielder, he posted the highest fielding percentage among players at his position in 1967.

Maris had a major impact in the 1967 World Series, accruing an on-base percentage of .433, while gathering seven RBIs. His two ribbies in Game 1 accounted for all the St. Louis scoring in a 2–1 victory. Only Lou Brock had more hits and a higher batting average. Maris returned to action in the 1968 Fall Classic and reached base eight times in six games, while scoring five runs. When the season was over, he officially put an end to his trying ordeal in the majors.

"Gussie" Busch granted Maris a lucrative beer distributorship after he retired. In later years, Maris remained bitter about his home-run record. "They acted as though I was doing something wrong, poisoning the record books or something," he griped to one writer. "Do you know what I have to show for 61 home runs? Nothing. Exactly nothing." The controversial slugger died of lymphatic cancer at age 51.

BILL WHITE, FIRST BASE

Born in Lakewood, Florida, White's family moved to Ohio when he was quite young. In high school, he demonstrated the leadership abilities that would help him later on, getting elected class president in his junior and senior years. White had aspirations of becoming a doctor and attended prestigious Hiram College briefly. He set his studies aside after the Giants offered him a lucrative contract in 1952.

In Danville of the Carolina League, White was the only black player on the team. Although the color barrier had been broken several years earlier, prejudice was still rampant among Southern fans, and White had an uncomfortable minor-league experience. He spent portions of four seasons on the farm before getting a May call-up to New York in 1956. In his rookie year, he clubbed 52 extra-base hits and drove in 59 runs.

White spent all of 1957 and a good portion of the 1958 campaign in the U.S. Army. Stationed at Fort Knox, Kentucky, he quit playing baseball for his post team after an ugly racial incident surfaced. When he rejoined the Giants in 1958, he discovered that the club had found a more than capable replacement at first base—rookie Orlando Cepeda. White was traded to St. Louis in 1959, and assigned to the outfield until an alternate arrangement for Stan Musial could be made. The two switched positions the following year. White would blossom into one of the finest fielding first basemen in the NL, capturing seven straight Gold Gloves.

In addition to his defensive aptitude, White was pretty handy with a bat. From 1959–1965, his average never dropped below .283. He reached the 20-homer mark seven times during his career and drove in 100 runs in four campaigns. He also had decent speed, swiping more than 100 bags during his tour of the majors and finishing among the top five in triples on three occasions. He was named to five All-Star Teams.

After the 1965 slate, White was traded to the Phillies. He would return for one last season with the Cardinals in 1969. Many fans remember White as a longtime broadcaster in the Bronx, calling Yankees games alongside Phil Rizzuto. In 1989, the former Cardinals standout was named president of the NL—the first black man to achieve the position. White served for five years, and in 1993, he supervised the expansion of the NL. In 2011, he released his autobiography, *Uppity:*

My Untold Story about the Games People Play. In it, he writes at length about the racial tensions that existed in the major leagues while he was playing.

KEN BOYER, THIRD BASE

Boyer was among the top third basemen in the majors during the late 1950s and early 1960s. Incredibly, he had six siblings who played professionally. Cloyd, a pitcher, spent portions of five seasons with the Cardinals and A's. Clete played third base for the Yankees and won two World Series rings. Ken was undisputedly the most talented of the bunch, winning five Gold Glove Awards and earning seven All-Star selections.

Boyer began his career as a pitcher, but his hitting prowess overshadowed his abilities on the mound. He served as captain of the Cardinals from 1959–1965. Although he captured MVP honors in 1964, he actually had a better year offensively in 1961, scoring more runs, collecting more hits, and hitting 34 points higher. Boyer had moderate speed, stealing more than 100 bases during his career. He also hit for power, launching no fewer than 23 homers in seven straight campaigns. He collected 90 or more RBIs each year during that period. He was a major contributor in the 1964 World Series. His grand slam off of Al Downing in Game 4 lifted the Cardinals to a 4–3 win over the Yankees. He scored three runs on three hits in the Series finale.

In 1965, Boyer began to suffer from back trouble, and his power numbers declined. He was traded to the Mets before the 1966 slate. After his playing days, he managed in the St. Louis farm system. He took over the Cardinals after Vern Rapp was fired shortly into the 1978 campaign. While the 1979 squad finished in third place, Boyer guided the club to a sub-.500 record in portions of three seasons. He was dismissed before the All-Star break in 1980. After his departure, Keith Hernandez told the Associated Press that Boyer would probably be happier away from the game. "He liked to go out and hang around with the guys, and as a manager he couldn't do that," said Hernandez. "So in that respect he wasn't cut out for managing."

After the '81 slate, Boyer learned that he had inoperable cancer in both lungs. He hung on until September of the following year. Former

Cardinals GM Bing Devine commented, "He never complained about his illness or sat around wondering 'why me?' That's the kind of ballplayer he was. He went about his business and never complained." Boyer has received modest support from Hall of Fame voters throughout the years, peaking at 25 percent in 1988.

CURT FLOOD, OUTFIELD

Flood attended McClymonds High School in Oakland, California—the same school that had sent Hall of Famers Ernie Lombardi and Frank Robinson to the majors. Signed by the Reds in 1956, Flood honed his skills in the minors for two full seasons, getting brief call-ups with the Reds in 1956 and 1957. Traded to the Cardinals before the 1958 campaign, he would remain a regular in the St. Louis lineup for more than a decade.

Among the finest defensive center fielders of the era, Flood did not commit a single error in 1966, and went without a miscue for 223 consecutive games. He captured a Gold Glove each year from 1963–1969, while leading the league in putouts four times.

During the course of his career, Flood typically occupied the top three spots in the batting order. He had several fine seasons at the plate, pacing the NL with 211 hits in 1964. In 1967, his batting average reached a career-high .335. Even in the "year of the pitcher," he fashioned a .301 mark (fifth best in the league). Flood was primarily a singles hitter, although he finished in double digits for homers four times. He liked to put the ball in play, never drawing more than 51 walks in any season. The righty-swinging outfielder played in three World Series with the Cardinals, reaching base by hit or walk 27 times in 21 games. He scored 11 runs.

In 1969, Flood was dealt to the Phillies, along with Tim McCarver and Joe Hoerner. He found out about the trade from a reporter who was looking for a reaction. This infuriated Flood, who expected more after 12 years of service in St. Louis. Causing a major stir, Flood raised several objections to playing for the Phillies, including the club's dilapidated stadium and poor record. He also felt that fans in Philadelphia were racist.

Believing he had the makings of a successful lawsuit, he consulted with Marvin Miller—executive director of the Major League Baseball Players Association. Flood's challenge to the reserve clause was taken to U.S. District Court in New York, and while he lost that case, the Supreme Court agreed to listen to the appeal. The justices ruled against Flood in the end, but his legal struggles led to modification of existing reserve rules and the establishment of free agency.

Flood sat out the entire 1970 campaign and eventually ended up with the Senators the following year. The long layoff did him no good. Hitting just .200 at the end of April, he was finished in the majors. His autobiography, *The Way It Is*, was released in 1971. In it, he details his struggles as a black player and rails against baseball's power structure.

After his playing days, Flood was a radio broadcaster for the A's. He also owned a bar in Majorca, a Spanish island in the Mediterranean Sea. From 1989–1990, he was commissioner of the short-lived Senior Professional Baseball Association. Diagnosed with throat cancer in 1995, he was operated on and lost the ability to speak. He died in 1997, of pneumonia. In 1998, the Curt Flood Act was introduced into the Senate and was enacted into law a year later. It established antitrust law protection for major leaguers.

TIM MCCARVER, CATCHER

The son of a policeman, McCarver was born and raised in Memphis, Tennessee. He was the most successful of several Christian Brothers High School alumni to reach the majors. He signed with the Cards in 1959, and spent four years in the minors before becoming a full-time player in St. Louis. Although he led the league twice in passed balls, he also posted the highest fielding percentage among NL catchers the same number of times.

McCarver had good speed for a catcher, gathering 13 triples in 1966 (a major-league record). He was successful in 55 percent of his lifetime stolen-base attempts. A contact hitter, he averaged only one strikeout per 13 at-bats during his career. He had little power at the plate; however, he did collect no fewer than 11 homers in three straight seasons (1965–1967). Appearing most often in the lower third of the batting order, he launched six career grand slams and compiled a handsome

.326 batting average with the bases loaded. His overall average was .280 or better during six campaigns.

McCarver played in three World Series with the Cardinals and was a prominent offensive presence in two of them. In the 1964 Fall Classic, his .478 batting average was tops among St. Louis regulars. His three-run homer in the 10th inning of Game 5 lifted the Cards to a 5–2 win. In the 1968 Fall Classic, he hit safely in six of seven games. Again, he blasted a three-run homer that helped St. Louis to a Game 3 victory.

In 1969, the veteran receiver was traded to the Phillies in the infamous Curt Flood transaction. The Cardinals sent Willie Montanez when Flood failed to report. McCarver would return to St. Louis for a brief stint in 1973 and 1974. His major-league career lasted 21 seasons.

After his playing days, McCarver became a distinguished broadcaster, calling games for all four of the major U.S. television networks. During the 1992 National League Championship Series, he inadvertently provoked a bit of drama when he criticized multisport star Deion Sanders for playing baseball and football on the same day. After Sanders's Braves had won the pennant, Deion dumped water on McCarver during a clubhouse celebration. "You're a real man, Deion!" McCarver shouted at him. In 2013, McCarver served as a member of the Fox World Series crew and hosted his own syndicated TV show—a 30-minute sports interview program. The previous year, he was inducted into the broadcaster's wing at the Hall of Fame. To date, he has won three Emmy Awards.

BOB GIBSON, PITCHER

Gibson was among the most ferocious competitors in history. Ron Smith of the *Sporting News* painted an accurate picture of Gibson's delivery from a batter's perspective. He described it as follows: "Gibson, cap pulled down low over a glowering face, sets his powerful jaw and stares at his newest worst enemy. Everything about him looks mean as he begins a three-quarters delivery that will propel the ball homeward." Commenting on Gibson's fiery nature, manager Red Schoendienst remarked, "As long as I've been with him, I've never seen him smile on a day he's pitching. Whether he's winning or losing 1–0 or 12–0, he's all business."

Putting batters even further off guard, Gibson had a tendency to lose the plate. In his first four seasons, he averaged more than four walks per nine innings. He finished with double-digit hit-by-pitch totals in four campaigns. Speaking colorfully about his on-field persona, Gibson said to a reporter,

> Have you ever thrown a ball 100 miles per hour? Everything hurts. Even your ass hurts. I see pictures of my face and say "holy shit!" but that's the strain you feel when you throw. I had one of those faces you look at it and say, "Man, he's an asshole." Could be—depends on if you pissed me off or not.

Whatever his temperament on a given day, Gibson was among the most dominant pitchers of the 1960s and perhaps all time. In 17 seasons, he averaged 15 wins per year, while striking out more than 3,000 batters. His best season by far came in 1968, when he tossed 13 shutouts and posted the lowest ERA of the modern era.

On the October stage, Gibson was masterful, winning seven of nine decisions, while limiting opponents to less than two runs per nine innings. From October 4, 1967, through October 6 of the following year, he yielded just four earned runs in 45 innings of postseason work. He was MVP of the 1967 World Series with a 3–0 record and 1.00 ERA. He had moderate power at the plate, hitting homers in two consecutive Fall Classics. During the regular season, Gibson went deep 24 times in his career, seventh among hurlers.

Gibson was so tough, he once faced three batters with a broken leg. On July 15, 1967, Roberto Clemente hit a hard liner back through the box, fracturing Gibson's fibula. The resilient hurler stayed in the game, walking Willie Stargell and inducing a fly ball off the bat of Bill Mazeroski. After issuing a free pass to Donn Clendenon, he literally collapsed on the mound. He was out until Labor Day but returned to vanquish the Red Sox in the World Series.

Gibson finally lost his effectiveness in 1975, posting a 3–10 record with a 5.04 ERA. He never threw another pitch in the majors. Elected to the Hall of Fame in 1981, he coached for the Mets, Braves, and Cardinals. In 2004, he joined the Baseball Assistance Team, a group of former major leaguers who pool their efforts to provide financial, medical, and psychological support to players in need.

LOU BROCK, LEFT FIELD

Brock grew up in a poor community in rural Louisiana. The school he attended had only one teacher and no running water. Brock was sensitive about his skin color and socioeconomic status, reportedly lying awake in bed worrying about how his life might turn out. As the story goes, he was sent to the library one day after misbehaving in class. While conducting research, he discovered how much money he could make playing baseball.

Lou kept up with his studies while polishing his skills on the diamond. He earned an academic scholarship to all-black Southern University, where he chose math as a major. He failed to maintain an acceptable GPA, however, and lost the scholarship. Determined to stay in school, he tried out for the university's baseball team and made it.

Scouted by the Chicago clubs, Brock had a tryout with each. He signed with the Cubs and entered their farm system in 1961. While he obviously had potential, he was rough around the edges, striking out too much, while making mistakes on the bases regularly. During trials with the Cubs in 1961 and 1962, his shaky defense inspired Bob Smith of the *Chicago Daily News* to remark that he had a long way to go to prove he wasn't the "worst outfielder in baseball history." Brock pressed too hard at times, and his intensity level was noticed by teammates. Pitcher Larry Jackson commented, "He'd break out in a big sweat just putting on his uniform." When Brock failed to develop by June 1964, the Cubs packaged him in a six-player deal and shipped him off to St. Louis. It was there that his career really took off.

During the Cardinals' stretch of dominance from 1964–1968, Brock hit .293, while averaging 59 stolen bases per year. Although he had power—peaking at 21 homers in 1967—he stopped swinging for the fences and became the NL's premier leadoff man. Brock liked to swing the bat, never drawing more than 76 walks in any season. He led the NL in steals eight times during his career and was the all-time leader in that category until 1991.

Commenting on his drive to succeed in the majors, Brock once said, "Show me a guy who's afraid to look bad and I'll show you a guy who can beat you every time." A six-time All-Star, some of Brock's finest moments came in the World Series. In three Fall Classics with the Cardinals, he compiled a .391 batting average. His finest performance came against the Tigers in 1968. He collected 13 hits (six for extra bases) and swiped seven bags. Had Detroit's pitcher, Mickey Lolich, not stolen Brock's thunder with three wins and a 1.67 ERA, the Cardinals might have taken the Series. Brock would likely have been named MVP.

The speedy outfielder finally began to slow down in the late 1970s. He went out with a bang, hitting .304 in his last season. He was elected to the Hall in his first year of eligibility. His number "20" was retired by the Cardinals. The *Sporting News* listed Brock as one of the top 100 players of all time. Since his retirement, he has engaged in a number of successful business endeavors. He is also an ordained minister.

ORLANDO CEPEDA, FIRST BASE

In his 2001 *Historical Baseball Abstract*, baseball authority Bill James evaluated Cepeda as follows: "He was a poor defensive first baseman, and Alvin Dark, who managed him in the early '60s, thought that his fundamentals were appalling. But he did play with great enthusiasm. He made baseball fun to watch, and he did improve as an all-around player later in his career."

Cepeda's father, Pedro, was a famous player in Puerto Rico. This put immense pressure on Orlando at an early age. "I started playing ball when I was five," Cepeda recalled. "It was fun at first, but then it became a burden. They wanted impossible things. They expected Perucho's boy to hit a home run every time up, and when I didn't, they were disappointed."

As a teenager, Cepeda hurt his right knee and underwent surgery to repair it. It would hamper him significantly later in his career. After tearing up the Northern League, he joined the Giants and captured Rookie of the Year honors in 1958. Six consecutive All-Star selections would follow. Cepeda peaked at 46 homers and 142 RBIs in 1961, but finished second in MVP voting to Frank Robinson. In 1963, he hurt his knee again while lifting weights to get back into shape during the winter. He was afraid to tell manager Alvin Dark what had happened and played the next two seasons in pain. In May 1965, he opted for surgery. Accused of being a malingerer, he was traded to the Cardinals early in the 1966 campaign.

Initially, Cepeda was hurt by the transaction. But his transition was made easier by the warm welcome he received from established players in St. Louis. "My attitude changed immediately," he said. "I thought the Giants may have actually done me a favor. I was walking into a great situation."

He certainly was.

Rejuvenated by Cepeda's enthusiasm, the Cardinals captured back-to-back pennants in 1967 and 1968. In the former campaign, Cepeda finally captured an elusive MVP Award, leading the league in RBIs—more than 20 of which were of the game-winning variety. In portions of three seasons with the Cards, Cepeda hit .290, while averaging 19 homers and 81 RBIs per year. He generated a low batting average in World Series play, but it was an era dominated by pitching.

Traded to Atlanta in 1969, Cepeda's numbers began to dwindle. He had a resurgence with the Red Sox in 1973, driving in 86 runs, but was more or less finished after that. He ended his major-league career with the Royals in 1974. The following year, Cepeda landed himself in hot water when federal agents found 160 pounds of marijuana in the trunk of his car at the San Juan airport. He was imprisoned for 10 months. "The isolation, the disgrace, the feelings of numbness, they were horrible," he recalled. He returned to baseball eventually, working for the White Sox in 1980. He later served as a Giants community representative. The Veteran's Committee voted him into the Hall of Fame in 1999.

STEVE CARLTON, PITCHER

Born and raised in Miami, Carlton played Little League and American Legion ball as a youngster. He later attended Miami-Dade College and signed with the Cardinals for a $5,000 bonus. He made his major-league debut at the age of 20. Tall and sturdily built, at 6-foot-4, 210 pounds, he had a lively fastball and sharp-breaking slider. Carlton developed a contempt for the media early on, explaining in later years, "I got slammed quite a bit. To pick up a paper and read about yourself getting slammed, that doesn't start your day off right." Eventually, he refused to speak to reporters altogether. In 1981, one journalist quipped, "The two best pitchers in the National League don't speak English—Fernando Valenzuela and Steve Carlton."

In Carlton's opinion, he was almost always the smartest guy in the room. He dabbled at Far Eastern philosophy and pseudo-metaphysics. As part of his training routine, he would immerse himself in dry rice and spend 20 minutes or so jogging in it. He once remarked conceitedly that he was probably the best-conditioned athlete of his time.

Carlton felt no need to connect with teammates. He tuned out all distractions. When he considered teammates to be a distraction, he either ignored them or directed contemptuous stares in their direction. In his book *The Spirit of St. Louis*, sportswriter Peter Golenbock observes, "Carlton was not your normal guy. Communicating with him was not always easy." The erratic hurler became a bit of a recluse, avoiding autograph seekers and alienating peers with his arrogance.

Despite his quirky, abrasive personality, Carlton was among the most overpowering left-handers ever to take the mound. Willie Stargell once griped that hitting Carlton was like "trying to drink coffee with a fork." Richie Ashburn referred to him as an "artist." Although Carlton had some mediocre seasons, leading the league in losses twice while posting ERAs in the high threes on multiple occasions, he balanced it out with 10 All-Star selections, four Cy Young Awards, and a Triple Crown performance in 1972. His 329 career wins are second among left-handers. His 4,136 strikeouts are fourth on the all-time list, behind Nolan Ryan, Randy Johnson, and Roger Clemens.

Carlton was used sparingly in the 1967 and 1968 World Series. He made three appearances and recorded only one decision—a loss in a quality start against the Red Sox. In 10 innings, he posted a serviceable 2.70 ERA. In 1969, Carlton struck out 19 Mets in a game, establishing a new record (since broken). The following year, he was a no-show at spring training due to a salary dispute. He was later traded to the Phillies. Although a no-hitter eluded him during his career, he authored six one-hitters. He made it to the Hall of Fame in his first try. His number "32" was retired by the Phillies, and a statue honoring him stands outside Citizens Bank Park.

FAST FACT: Despite the Cardinals' success in the postseason, the club has suffered through numerous dry spells, failing to capture pennants in five different decades: 1900–1909, 1910–1919, 1950–1959, 1970–1979, and 1990–1999.

15

BALTIMORE ORIOLES
1966–1971

When the Orioles arrived in Baltimore for the 1954 season, they were a star-crossed franchise. In the previous five decades, they had played as the St. Louis Browns, finishing in the second division more than 40 times. This included 10 last-place showings.

Owner Bill Veeck tried to boost attendance during the early 1950s with such zany promotional stunts as sending a three-foot, seven-inch circus performer named Eddie Gaedel to the plate and allowing fans to act as managers for a day. Nothing proved to be a permanent fix, and the team eventually left St. Louis.

When the Browns expressed their desire to relocate to Baltimore, Senators representatives objected to having a competitor so close to their own market. Jerold Hoffberger, president of the National Brewing Company, helped defuse the situation by becoming a Senators sponsor. Hoffberger assembled a syndicate to buy the Browns for $2.5 million, establishing a new home and identity for the club. He assumed majority ownership in 1965, and maintained that status into the late 1970s.

The newly christened Orioles continued the old tradition of losing, placing fifth or lower in each of their first six seasons. Things began to turn around in the early 1960s with the addition of several high-profile players. Making his Baltimore debut in 1955, Brooks Robinson was perhaps the greatest defensive third baseman in the history of the game. Nicknamed the "Human Vacuum Cleaner," he frustrated opponents at the hot corner for portions of 23 seasons. Hall of Fame manager Sparky Anderson once griped, "[Robinson] can throw his glove out there and it will start 10 double plays by itself." Only one player surpassed Robinson's total of 16 Gold Gloves (pitcher Greg Maddux). Commenting on Robinson's tremendous popularity with fans, Associated Press writer Gordon Beard quipped, "Brooks never asked anyone to name a candy bar after him. In Baltimore, people named their children after him."

While he failed to attain the level of adulation enjoyed by Robinson, relief specialist Hoyt Wilhelm was indisputably a master of his craft. Acquired off of waivers late in the 1958 campaign, the Orioles used him primarily as a starter the following year. He adjusted well to the new role, winning 15 games and leading the American League with a 2.19 ERA. Shifted back to the bullpen for good partway through the 1960 slate, the veteran right-hander used his signature knuckleball to gather 40 saves for the O's in a three-year span. Wilhelm pitched until he was 49 years old, becoming the third-oldest hurler to work in the majors. More than just a novelty act, he appeared in 16 games during his final campaign. "It takes no effort at all to pitch a knuckleball," he once said. "It's so simple that very little warm-up in the bullpen is required. That's why I can pitch so often without being overworked." Wilhelm retired with 143 wins and 228 saves—numbers good enough for the Hall of Fame.

A mainstay in the Baltimore rotation for eight seasons, Milt Pappas landed on a short list of post–Deadball Era hurlers to collect 150 wins before the age of 30. From 1959–1965, he was one of the club's most reliable starters, averaging 14 victories per year. But the O's had a promising crop of young pitchers, and Pappas was deemed expendable. Before the 1966 slate, he was shipped to Cincinnati, along with two low-impact players, in exchange for Frank Robinson. It was one of the wisest decisions the Orioles ever made.

Robinson had made a big splash in his major-league debut, slamming 38 homers at the age of 20. During his first 10 seasons, he was among the National League's most productive hitters, collecting 30 or more long balls seven times, while regularly exceeding the .300 mark at the plate. Cincinnati GM Bill DeWitt made a colossal miscalculation prior to the 1966 campaign when he surmised that Robinson was an "old thirty." Proving just how wrong DeWitt was, the hard-hitting outfielder captured a Triple Crown and a MVP Award in his Orioles debut with 49 homers, 122 RBIs, and a .316 batting average. On Mother's Day, he drove a ball out of Memorial Stadium—the only player ever to do so. The transfer of Robinson to Baltimore was so notoriously ill-advised that it was referenced more than two decades later in the popular baseball film *Bull Durham*.

By 1966, the Orioles were carrying four eventual Hall of Famers on their roster. Acquired in 1963 from the White Sox, Luis Aparicio completed a nine-year reign as the AL stolen-base king. He was also one of the smoothest-fielding shortstops in the majors, capturing nine Gold Gloves during his career—two of them while playing in Baltimore. Rounding out an impressive cast of characters, 19-year-old Jim Palmer began his journey to Cooperstown in April 1965. Impressing manager Hank Bauer with his poise and fluid delivery, the precocious right-hander won a spot in the starting rotation the following year. He led the staff with 15 wins as the O's captured their first pennant.

In the 1966 World Series, Baltimore trampled the Dodgers in four games, outscoring the men in blue by a collective margin of 13–2. LA batters set a dubious postseason record by failing to score a run in 33 consecutive innings. Asked if he thought the Dodgers could have won the Series, manager Walter Alston fixed his questioner with a sour look and said curtly, "If I didn't think so, we would have stayed back at the hotel."

There would be no encore for Baltimore the following year. The pitching staff was beset by injuries—most notably Palmer, who was sent to the minors with shoulder and back problems. Robinson sat out most of July after sustaining a concussion in a collision at second base. Aparicio slumped to .233 at the plate. He wasn't alone, as only two Orioles regulars posted a batting average in excess of .290. The defending world champions compiled a lackluster 76–85 record, sliding into the second division.

Mired in third place at the All-Star break in 1968, the Orioles fired manager Hank Bauer and replaced him with Earl Weaver. It was the beginning of a beautiful friendship, as Weaver would spend portions of 17 seasons at the helm, guiding the club to six division titles, four pennants, and a world championship. Weaver was known for his use of statistics in evaluating matchups between pitchers and hitters. His recipe for success was "pitching and three-run homers." He was not a players' manager, rarely socializing with his pledges unless he felt they needed instruction or discipline. "You're the person who decides all the worst things in their lives . . . you can't help loving them, but you can't afford to," he once said. Weaver was not an imposing physical presence, at 5-foot-7, but he kept challenges to his authority in check with his volcanic temper and acidic tongue. His 94 ejections are among the top totals of all time. The Orioles finished strong in Weaver's debut, ending up with a 91–71 record. It wasn't good enough, as the Tigers squeezed 48 wins out of starters Denny McLain and Mickey Lolich, capturing a pennant and a World Series title.

In 1969, the Orioles found their way back to the top. After struggling with physical problems and falling to the Class A level in 1968, Palmer finally regained his form and returned to Baltimore. He prevailed in 16 of 20 decisions, posting the highest winning percentage in the league. The two Robinsons combined for 55 homers and 184 RBIs as the O's assembled the best record in baseball at 109–53. After sweeping the Twins in the American League Championship Series, Weaver's crew squared off against Gil Hodges's so-called "Miracle Mets." A 4–1 win over Tom Seaver in the opener was the high point of the affair, as Baltimore hitters managed just five runs the rest of way, dropping four straight games. One writer referred to the Birds as a "sham of a super team."

The Orioles breezed to another pennant in 1970, winning 108 games and leaving the second-place Yankees 15 games behind. Again, the Twins put up little resistance in the ALCS, losing all three meetings by at least four runs. In the Fall Classic, the O's were on the verge of a sweep when an eighth-inning homer by Cincinnati's Lee May eradicated a 5–3 Baltimore lead. It was the only game the Reds would win as the Birds romped to a 9–3 victory the following day. Brooks Robinson put on a stupendous fielding display throughout the Series and raked Cincinnati pitching at a .429 clip, capturing MVP honors. The award came with a new car from Toyota, prompting Reds catcher Johnny Bench to jibe, "If we had known he wanted a car that badly, we'd all have chipped in and bought him one."

In 1971, the Orioles reached the century mark in victories for the third straight season. It was the "year of the pitcher" all over again in Baltimore, as each member of the starting four posted at least 20 wins—a feat that had not been accomplished in more than 50 years.

After spending the entire month of May in second place, the O's posted a 20–9 record in June, opening up a three-and-a-half-game lead over the Red Sox. By season's end, they were sitting on top by a wide margin. Only three other AL clubs (the Tigers, Yankees, and A's) had ever captured three consecutive pennants.

A sweep of the A's in the ALCS sent Baltimore to the World Series against Pittsburgh. After winning the first two games at home, the Orioles lost four of the next five meetings, handing the Pirates their first championship in more than a decade. On the streets of Pittsburgh, riot squads were dispatched to break up a crowd of approximately 100,000 merrymakers, some of whom had resorted to looting and vandalism. In Baltimore, Earl Weaver interrupted a postgame interview to assert that the Orioles were still the best team in baseball. "We'll prove it by winning a hundred games next year to become the only team ever to do that four seasons in a row," he boldly proclaimed.

Weaver's estimate was way off the mark, as the O's slumped to third place in 1972. Although Palmer was still in the early stages of his career, the Robinsons were aging out. Realizing that Frank was approaching his twilight years, the Orioles traded him to the Dodgers in December 1971. He would have one more excellent season with the Angels in 1973, before moving on to become the first black manager in major league history. Brooks began a gradual decline that reduced him to part-time playing status in 1976. He remains one of the most highly regarded figures in Orioles history. Baltimore would make one more World Series appearance under Weaver in 1979, losing to the Pirates (again) in seven games.

Many accounts of the Orioles' dominant run in the late 1960s and early 1970s are monopolized by references to the Hall of Famers who helped elevate the club to near-dynastic status. But as everyone knows, it takes more than a small group of luminaries to win a world championship. During the aforementioned period, the Orioles had one of the most talented aggregations of minor stars in history.

BOOG POWELL, OUTFIELD/FIRST BASE

Born in Lakeland, Florida, Powell was a mischievous kid, earning the nickname "Boog" (a colloquialism for "bugger"). His family later relocated to Key West, where he completed high school. Powell was signed by the Orioles in 1959, immediately following his graduation. Just 17 years old in his pro debut, he hit .351 in 56 games at the Class D level. He continued to swing a potent bat wherever he was assigned, leading the Fox Cities Foxes of the Three-I League and Rochester Red Wings of the International League in homers. Promoted to the Orioles in 1961, he became a full-time player the following year.

At 6-foot-4, 240 pounds, Powell fit the role of a slugger. During his 17 years in the majors, he smashed no fewer than 21 homers nine times, collecting 30 or more on four occasions. Appearing primarily in the heart of the order, he compiled a .282 batting average with runners in scoring position during the course of his career. This included seven grand slams. A four-time All-Star, his best offensive season came in 1969, when he hit .304 with 37 homers and 121 RBIs, finishing second to Harmon Killebrew of the Twins in MVP voting. Powell came back strong the following year and claimed the honor for himself. He had 35 long balls and 114 RBIs that season.

Powell was tremendously popular in Baltimore, and chants of "Boooooog!!" would often fill Memorial Stadium. A productive postseason performer, the lefty slugger fashioned a .306 lifetime average in ALCS play. In 21 World Series games, he reached base by hit or walk 25 times. He was a major offensive presence in both of the Orioles' championship seasons.

Powell began his career as a left fielder but was shifted to first base permanently in 1966. Never known for his fielding prowess, he led the league in putouts in 1968, and fielding percentage during the 1975 campaign. After two down seasons in 1973 and 1974, Powell was traded to Cleveland. Playing under newly appointed manager Frank Robinson, he returned to form with 27 homers and 86 RBIs. Derailed by a leg injury in 1976, he ended with Los Angeles for the 1977 slate. The Dodgers released Powell in August, robbing him of a final World Series appearance.

After baseball, Powell owned a marina in Key West and resurfaced in Miller Lite Beer commercials during the early 1980s. In 1985, he competed against Frank Robinson in a pregame home-run derby at Memorial Stadium. By then, Powell weighed more than 300 pounds and couldn't fit into an Orioles uniform. The 44-year-old Powell bested the 50-year-old Robinson, prompting the elder participant to crack, "It just goes to show, it ain't how you look." After taking a great deal of clubhouse ribbing, Powell joked, "Don't let anyone fool you. I never was pretty."

At the time of this writing, Powell was the proprietor of "Boog's Corner," a popular barbecue stand with two locations, one at Camden Yards.

DAVE MCNALLY, PITCHER

Born in Billings, Montana, left-hander Dave McNally lived his entire life there, becoming a revered member of the community. McNally's father was killed while fighting in Okinawa during World War II. He was raised by his mother, who worked in social services. As a teenager, McNally's team went to the Legion World Series. He was a dominant force on the mound, striking out 27 batters in one game.

McNally was signed out of high school by the Orioles and sent to the minors, where he fared rather poorly in his first year. At the Class A level in 1962, he pitched well enough to earn a call to Baltimore. He would remain with the club for 12 full seasons.

Using a fastball, curve, and changeup combination, McNally gradually became a core member of the starting rotation. In 1965 and 1966, he posted a 24–12 record with an ERA in the low threes. He developed a sore elbow the following year and lost some velocity on his fastball. According to one source, he could hardly even comb his hair with his left arm after the season was over. In the spring of 1968, he added a slider to his arsenal, which he hadn't used since his minor-league days. It ended up being the missing link, as he went on to compile four consecutive 20-win campaigns. In 1969, he began the season with 15 straight victories.

McNally appeared in four World Series with the Orioles, making nine appearances and winning four games. In 1966, he clinched the Series for the O's with a four-hit shutout over the Dodgers. Facing the Pirates in the 1971 opener, he allowed just three hits and no earned runs. His most brilliant postseason performance came in Game 2 of the 1969 ALCS against the Twins. He lasted through 11 innings, striking out 11 batters and scattering three hits in a grueling 1–0 victory.

Earl Weaver liked his starters to work quickly and stay on the mound for as long as possible. McNally met those expectations year after year, completing 11 or more starts in seven straight seasons, while averaging 261 innings per year during that span. Weaver could be notoriously hard on pitchers, and McNally kept him moderately satisfied.

After the 1974 campaign, McNally was the most successful Orioles pitcher in history, with 181 regular-season victories. Although he went 16–10 that year, he wasn't entirely pleased with his performance and felt that a change of scenery might "wake [him] up." Behind the scenes, he was at odds with Baltimore management over salary issues. Frank Cashen later referred to McNally as "intractable" when it came to negotiations. Traded to the Expos in 1975, McNally became embroiled in a famous challenge to baseball's reserve clause. Feeling that the Expos had not delivered on several promises they had made to him, he teamed with Dodgers pitcher Andy Messersmith to buck the system. In November 1975, a hearing was held, and arbitrator Peter Seitz granted both men free agency. Commissioner Bowie Kuhn labeled the landmark decision "destructive to baseball." McNally could have signed with a different team but chose retirement instead.

After baseball, McNally entered the car business with his brother. He was inducted into the Orioles Hall of Fame in 1978. In 1999, he was named Montana's athlete of the century by *Sports Illustrated*. He was also included on the Orioles All-Century Team. A heavy smoker, McNally lost his battle with cancer in 2002.

MARK BELANGER, SHORTSTOP

Belanger was the premier defensive shortstop of his era, holding down the starting job in Baltimore for 13 full seasons. He worked with two undersized black gloves each year and loosened them up using saliva and coffee. "When I first managed Mark at Bluefield in the Rookie League, I could see he was a natural," said manager Billy Hunter. "At 18, there wasn't much anyone could teach him about playing shortstop." Belanger had a smooth, effortless style of fielding, never leaving his feet and always using a classic overhand throwing motion. Many who watched him commented that he made extremely difficult plays look easy.

Belanger was born in Pittsfield, Massachusetts. He was an All-American basketball star in high school. He also excelled at baseball, earning an invitation to spring training with the Orioles in 1963. He joined the Air National Guard before the season began and didn't play. He got his first major-league call-up in 1965, and replaced Luis Aparicio three years later.

Belanger was a student of the game, studying pitch counts and the habits of batters. This helped him tremendously in positioning himself for the high hops. He sprinted toward grounders and used his glove to redirect the ball to his throwing hand. During the course of his career, Belanger was awarded eight Gold Gloves. He led AL shortstops in assists and fielding percentage three times apiece. He was masterful around second base, finishing among the top five in double plays five times (he led the league in 1975).

Belanger played in an era when shortstops weren't expected to hit. He was definitely a lightweight with a bat, managing a paltry .228 lifetime average. The Orioles typically buried him at the bottom of the batting order. Still, he had a few decent seasons at the plate, reaching career-high marks in hits (152), RBIs (50), and batting average (.287) during the 1969 slate. He hit .266 in 1971, and .270 in 1976. Belanger had ample speed when he did reach base, swiping 15 or more bags in four straight seasons, with a high of 27. He was also a skilled bunter, leading the league twice in sacrifices.

Belanger appeared in four World Series with the Orioles (including the 1979 affair) and wasn't much of an offensive presence. On defense, he handled 46 chances in 1969 and 1970, registering 18 putouts and 28 assists with just one error. He had an uncharacteristic postseason in 1971, committing three errors in seven games.

After his 1982 retirement, Belanger continued his work with the Major League Baseball Players Association as a union representative and later as an assistant to President Donald Fehr. He had begun his association with the organization in 1971. A heavy smoker, he died of cancer at age 54 in 1998. After his death, Fehr commented, "Players owe a debt of gratitude to [Belanger]. I personally miss the wisdom and insight he provided on virtually every important decision the MLBPA has made over the last three decades."

MIKE CUELLAR, PITCHER

Born in Las Villas, Cuba, Cuellar pitched in the army of dictator Fulgencio Batista. He tossed a no-hitter one day, grabbing the attention of scouts. Signed by the Reds, he played for the Havana Sugar Kings for four years, earning a call to the majors in the spring of 1959. He fared poorly in two appearances. The Reds let him go and he would play for several minor-league affiliates before earning another summons to the Show from the Cardinals in 1964. Again, he didn't quite make the grade, going 5–5, mostly in relief, with a mediocre 4.50 ERA. The Astros offered him a trial in 1965 and liked what they saw. Cuellar's first successful seasons took place in Houston, as he compiled a 36–32 record between 1966–1968.

Before the 1969 campaign, Cuellar was included in a five-player transaction that landed him in Baltimore. For the next six years, he was one of the premier pitchers in the AL, reaching the 20-win threshold four times and gathering no fewer than 18 victories. He led the AL in 1970, when he prevailed in 24 decisions. In 1969, he shared Cy Young honors with Tigers ace Denny McLain, becoming the first Latin-born recipient of the award.

Jim Palmer once referred to Cuellar as an "artist," commenting that he could "paint a different picture every time he went out there." At six feet, 165 pounds, Cuellar wasn't a very intimidating physical presence. He didn't have much speed on his fastball either, prompting one sportswriter to quip that his "swiftest offering could be caught barehanded." The crafty left-hander relied instead on an assortment of slow junk pitches, which he threw at various speeds and angles. Earl Weaver remembered Cuellar "making fools" of baseball's best hitters with his screwball, which was arguably his most effective offering.

Cuellar appeared in all three World Series between 1969–1971, winning two of four decisions, while posting a highly respectable 2.61 ERA. He averaged six strikeouts per nine frames. His finest Series start came in the 1969 opener versus the Mets. He scattered six hits and struck out eight in a 4–1 triumph. It was the O's only win of the Series.

In 1976, Cuellar was 39 years old and virtually washed up. He slumped to 4–13 with a bloated ERA. Weaver commented after the season was over that he had granted Cuellar more chances than his first wife. Released by the Orioles, the aging hurler had two rocky outings with the Angels the following year. Gone from the majors, he continued playing in the Mexican League and the short-lived Inter-American League. At age 52, he pitched for the Winter Haven Super Sox of the Senior Professional Baseball Association. He died of stomach cancer in 2010.

PAUL BLAIR, OUTFIELD

Blair grew up in Los Angeles and was a three-sport star in high school. He had a tryout with the Dodgers at age 17 but wasn't signed. In July 1961, the Mets picked him up to fill the position of shortstop. He was quickly reassigned to center field. When the Mets left him unprotected in the 1962 first-year draft, the Orioles took advantage of their oversight. Blair was a September call-up in 1964, and a full-time center fielder with Baltimore the following year.

Although he hit just .234 in his first full season, Blair posted the highest fielding percentage among players at his position. In 1966, he raised his batting average to .277 and hit a game-winning homer in the World Series. Blair had moderate power, peaking at 26 long balls in 1969. He led the league in triples during the 1967 slate. In 12 full seasons with the O's, his batting averages ranged from .293 to .197. He had a tendency to strike out, averaging one whiff per seven at-bats during his career.

Blair was renowned for his superb defense, capturing seven straight Gold Glove Awards from 1969–1975. He played extremely shallow and encouraged corner outfielders to position themselves toward the lines to give him plenty of room. It was a rare occasion when a ball landed over his head or in one of the gaps. Teammate Don Buford once remarked, "When you talk about the greatest defensive center fielder, [Blair] was right in the mix." Blair explained that the "Oriole way" was to rely on pitching and defense, while avoiding the small mistakes that negatively impact games.

Blair's finest single-game offensive performance came in April 1970, when he hit three homers and drove in six runs against the White Sox. A month later, he was beaned by Angels pitcher Ken Tatum, sustaining a broken nose and serious facial injuries. Although Blair insisted it didn't affect him, he never came close to matching the power numbers he had put up in 1969.

In the 1970 World Series, Blair set a record with nine hits in five games. He batted .474—the highest mark on either club. When his regular-season average plummeted to .197 in 1976, the Orioles traded him to the Yankees. In Game 1 of the 1977 Fall Classic, he drove in the winning run with a 12th-inning single. He would spend portions of four seasons in the Bronx before retiring in 1980.

In 1989, Blair played for the Gold Coast Suns of the Senior Professional Baseball Association. He coached college ball at Fordham University and Coppin State University. He survived a heart attack in 2009, but died in December 2013, after collapsing during a charity bowling event.

BROOKS ROBINSON, THIRD BASE

Bill James pays Robinson an interesting compliment in his *Historical Baseball Abstract*, remarking that "defense is, by its nature, a selfless, team-oriented skill, while hitting is a glamour job. Thus, it is perhaps natural that defensive positions [such as third base] would attract and develop players whose focus extends beyond their self-interest."

Undoubtedly the greatest defensive third baseman of all time, Robinson was groomed as a replacement for fading Hall of Famer George Kell, who spent his last two seasons in Baltimore. Born in Little Rock, Arkansas, Robinson's father taught him to play with a broom handle and rubber ball at an early age. A high school standout, Robinson's parents were skeptical about Brooks signing with Baltimore since the O's were such a poor club. But a scout explained that Robinson would have a chance to move up quickly. He did—making his major-league debut at the age of 18.

Robinson was a stand-up guy, drawing admiration from multiple generations of fans. His SABR biography contends, "Success did not compromise the integrity or upstanding character of Brooks Calbert Robinson. . . . He conducted himself with class throughout his 23 seasons in a major-league uniform and fulfilled extraneous obligations with joy and enthusiasm."

Robinson was a bit slow in developing. In sporadic appearances from 1955–1957, he never raised his batting average above .239. But by the time the 1960s arrived, he had established himself as a marquee player. Robinson's career accomplishments include 15 All-Star selections, 16 Gold Gloves (won consecutively), and an AL MVP Award. He was also MVP of the 1966 All-Star Game and 1970 World Series. His performance in that Series is considered to be among the greatest of all time. After he almost single-handedly shut down the Reds offense with a string of stupendous defensive plays, players took to calling him "Hoover," in reference to the vacuum cleaner. Manager Sparky Anderson joked to a reporter, "If I dropped this paper plate, he'd pick it up on one hop and throw me out at first."

While his defense invariably dominates any discussion of his career, Robinson was a more than competent batsman, generating 2,892 hits (831 for extra bases), including the postseason. Most often hitting fifth or sixth in the order, he drove in 80 or more runs eight times. The only thing that seemed to be lacking from his game was speed on the bases. Former Red Sox great Johnny Pesky once remarked, "If Robinson could run, he would be the perfect ballplayer."

After baseball, Robinson worked as an Orioles broadcaster. He was elected to the Hall of Fame in 1983. In 2012, a statue was dedicated to him outside Orioles Park at Camden Yards. He was still alive as of this writing.

FRANK ROBINSON, OUTFIELD

Robinson had enough siblings to organize a baseball team. He was one of 10 children. He grew up in West Oakland as a sports enthusiast, playing baseball, football, and basketball. While starring for the McClymonds High School baseball team, he got noticed and signed by a Reds scout. He was only 17 years old when he turned pro. Called to Cincinnati in 1956, he blasted 38 homers and led the league in runs scored. He was a unanimous choice for Rookie of the Year.

After two decades of mediocrity, the Reds finally put together a pennant-winning team in 1961. This was due largely to Robinson's monster season. He hit .323, drove in 124 runs, and led the league with a .611 slugging percentage on his way to claiming the first of two MVP

Awards. The Reds were shut down by the Yankees in the World Series, and Robinson was limited to three hits in five games—although all of them went for extra bases.

In 1966, GM Bill DeWitt made an infamous blunder when he traded Robinson to the Orioles, commenting that he was an "old 30." Robinson was not too old to capture a Triple Crown with 49 homers (a career-high), 122 RBIs, and a .316 batting average. In the World Series versus the Dodgers, he made his hits count, cracking a two-run homer off of Don Drysdale in Game 1 and a solo shot that was the series-clincher in Game 4. Again, the clout came off of Drysdale.

Robinson gained a reputation as a feisty player and a tough out at the plate. "Pitchers did me a favor when they knocked me down," the slugger once said. "It made me more determined. I wouldn't let that pitcher get me out." Many pitchers chose to avoid him altogether. From 1956–1965, he led the NL in hit-by-pitch six times and intentional walks on four occasions. In that same span, he drilled more than 300 homers. Yankees hurler Jim Bouton was once asked by a fan how he pitched to Robinson. "Reluctantly," the pithy hurler replied.

Robinson was injured for an extended period in 1967, and again the following year. Healthy again in 1969, he rebounded with 32 homers and 100 RBIs. That season, Robinson organized a clubhouse court in which he acted as judge (inspired by the popular television comedy *Laugh-In*). He imposed fines for such infractions as missing the team bus or throwing inaccurately to a cutoff man. Robinson stayed productive in 1970 and 1971, but ended up being traded to the Dodgers. He would play for the Angels and Indians before retiring.

When Robinson became player-manager of the Indians in 1975, he was the first African American to manage in the majors. He would spend 16 seasons at the helm of five different clubs. His last stint came in 2006, with the Washington Nationals. In 2012, he was hired by MLB as executive vice president of player development. Before then, he had served on Commissioner Bud Selig's special committee for on-field matters. When Selig was replaced in 2015, Robinson accepted a position as special advisor to the new commissioner, Rob Manfred. He was also named honorary president of the AL. His plaque was installed in the gallery at Cooperstown in 1982.

JIM PALMER, PITCHER

The handsome Palmer was smart, well-spoken, and prone to pouting when he didn't get what he wanted. He griped about not winning awards and argued with Earl Weaver constantly. When a teammate's defense wasn't up to snuff, he made his disapproval obvious. Even so, the men who played alongside him had flattering things to say about him. Shortstop Cal Ripken Jr. remarked, "He kept us in every game he pitched. He always had so much energy." Batterymate Elrod Hendricks said, "If he got to the sixth or seventh, you could just mail the game in. He was the best finisher I ever saw." Even Weaver, who engaged in a long-standing public feud with Palmer, had kind words. "He certainly helped me keep my job all those years in Baltimore," said Weaver. "His work habits were excellent, and he was a leader."

At the dawn of the twenty-first century, Palmer was one of only three AL pitchers to have won 20 games eight times. He did it in a nine-year span from 1970–1978, capturing three Cy Young Awards in the process. Palmer was fairly tall, at 6-foot-3, and his delivery was effortlessly smooth. Former pitching coach Ray Miller compared it to "watching ballet." Palmer himself was a bit put off by his own mechanics. "Looking at films of myself, I felt like maybe I ought to put more into this," he once said. He used a fastball, slider, and changeup combination, later adding a curve to his selection.

Palmer was adopted by wealthy parents shortly after he was born. During his childhood, he lived on Park Avenue in New York City and also spent a brief period of time in Beverly Hills. He came of age in an affluent area of Scottsdale, Arizona, where he honed his baseball skills.

The right-handed Palmer had control issues early in his career. The Orioles were in the habit of starting rookies in a reliever's role, and Palmer served in that capacity during his 1965 debut. He won five of nine decisions but averaged five walks per nine innings. By 1966, he was ready for the starting rotation. He led the staff with 15 wins, while improving his control dramatically. In his first career World Series start, he outpitched Dodger great Sandy Koufax, coming away with a four-hit shutout. He also ended up with a sore arm and would not return to full-time action with the O's until 1969.

Between 1966–1971, Palmer compiled a 74–34 record with a cumulative 2.80 ERA. He was 6–1 in postseason play during that span. He would continue to dominate the opposition for years to come, retiring with 268 wins. He never gave up a grand slam.

Palmer was enshrined at Cooperstown in 1990. Near the end of his playing days, he gained notoriety as a spokesman for Jockey underwear. Former staffmate Mike Flanagan joked, "[Palmer] has won 240 games, but it took a picture of him standing in his underwear to get nationally known." In 2012, a statue of Palmer was installed outside of Oriole Park at Camden Yards. It stands in proximity to a statue of Earl Weaver. Palmer had once said of his old adversary, "The only thing Earl knows about big-league pitching is that he couldn't hit it."

FAST FACT: The Baltimore player development scheme of the 1950s came to be known as the "Oriole Way." Created by GM Paul Richards and farm director Jim McLaughlin, the philosophy was condensed into a manual used by minor-league instructors. It emphasized such funda-mentals as how to execute cutoffs and prevent double steals. When Earl Weaver took over as manager in 1968, he felt that the "Oriole Way" was being neglected and brought it back to the forefront. The philosophy was not always embraced warmly by players. Hall of Famer Jim Palmer once griped, "I hate the cursed Oriole fundamentals. I've been doing them since 1964. I do them in my sleep. I hate spring training."

16

OAKLAND ATHLETICS

1972–1974

Various words have been used to describe A's owner Charles Finley—
not all of them terribly positive. To some he was a visionary and to
others a tyrant. By the time he sold the club during the 1980 campaign,
he was universally disliked by those inside the baseball establishment.
But he left behind a legacy of colorful innovations and entertaining
anecdotes.

Finley got rich selling insurance during the 1940s and was initially
outbid when he attempted to purchase the Kansas City Athletics. He
obtained a majority of the club's stock after owner Arnold Johnson
passed away. Although the A's were a weak team, Finley did his best to
establish a fan base. Fostering a carnival-like atmosphere, he dressed
his players in tacky green and yellow uniforms. He placed sheep with
dyed wool (tended by a shepherd) in a pasture beyond the outfield
fence and also installed a children's zoo. He mounted a mechanical
rabbit named "Harvey" behind home plate. With the press of a button,
"Harvey" popped up and supplied umpires with fresh balls. A mule
named "Charlie O" was designated team mascot. The animal appeared
at numerous opening-game ceremonies and was even allowed inside
the team's hotel. On one particular occasion, "Charlie O" was deliberately paraded through the press room after a generous feeding to irri-
tate reporters.

There was virtually no end to Finley's wild ideas. He even released helium balloons containing A's tickets into the countryside one day. In one of his more innovative promotions, he arranged to have shortstop Bert Campaneris change positions every inning. This included stints as pitcher and catcher. Despite numerous schemes, attendance remained lackluster throughout the decade. In 1968, Finley angered many when he moved the club to Oakland. It was there that he built a championship squad.

During their final season in Kansas City, the A's had finished dead last with a dismal 62–99 record. A change of scenery worked wonders for Finley's beleaguered troops, as the club finished above .500 for the first time in more than a decade. While the 82–80 mark was only good enough for sixth place, it was a sign of better things to come.

The A's carried a trio of future Hall of Famers on their 1970s roster. A durable right-hander with impeccable control, Jim Hunter joined the club in 1965. He accepted the nickname of "Catfish" given to him by the PR-conscious Finley. Between 1971–1975, Hunter won at least 21 games each year and finished among the top five in Cy Young voting on four occasions. He captured the honor in 1974, with 25 victories and a league-leading 2.49 ERA. His Hall of Fame plaque would later read, "The bigger the game, the better he pitched." Born and raised in rural North Carolina, Hunter was a country boy at heart. He was good-natured with reporters and had a unique sense of humor. He became known for the adage, "The sun don't shine on the same dog's ass all the time."

Chosen in the first round of the 1966 amateur draft, slugger Reggie Jackson quickly ascended through the minor-league ranks. In desperate need of some offensive punch, the A's promoted him in 1967, at the age of 21. He hit just .178 in 35 games but came back strong the following year. Jackson was one of the most exciting players of the era. Contentious, animated, and articulate, he is best remembered for his World Series heroics with the Yankees, which earned him the nickname "Mr. October." But he enjoyed some of his best seasons while wearing an A's uniform. In 1973, he led the league in runs scored (99), homers (32), RBIs (117), and slugging percentage (.531). He was a unanimous choice for American League MVP.

Jackson may very well have been the most arrogant player in baseball history. Imminently aware of his postseason accomplishments, he once boasted, "The only reason I don't like playing in the World Series is I can't watch myself play." Teammate Darold Knowles aptly commented about Reggie's monster ego, "There isn't enough mustard in the whole world to cover that hotdog." By the time he retired after the 1987 campaign, Jackson had attained a rank of number six on the all-time home run list with 563 clouts. He had also set a career record for strikeouts. That's what made him such an exhilarating player. He connected and whiffed with equal gusto.

When Jackson showed up for spring training in 1972 with a full beard, several teammates were not pleased since it violated the league's long-standing facial hair policy. Relief ace Rollie Fingers was among the dissenters. He and several others stopped shaving in the hope that Finley would mandate a no-hair policy. Instead, Finley offered cash incentives to the players who could grow the best tresses. A throwback to an earlier era, Fingers began wearing his famous handlebar moustache.

Aside from making one of the most unique fashion statements in baseball history, Fingers is also remembered for his excellence on the mound. Called to Oakland from the South Atlantic League in 1968, the right-hander would use his trademark slider to establish himself as the most dominant relief pitcher of the 1970s. He was a seven-time All-Star and four-time Rolaids Relief Award recipient. He led the league in saves three times, while capturing Cy Young and AL MVP honors. He was also named MVP of the World Series in 1974.

Oakland's climb to the top was gradual. After finishing second in the AL West during the 1969 and 1970 campaigns, the club enjoyed a breakout year in 1971, posting a 101–60 record and capturing a division title. Victimized by the Orioles in the American League Championship Series, they returned to the postseason the following year. The battle for the 1972 AL pennant between the A's and Tigers was a classic, going the full five games. In a seldom mentioned but shining moment from Reggie Jackson's storied career, the flashy slugger stole home in the second inning of the finale, tying the score at one apiece. He tore a hamstring on the play and was out for the rest of the year. The A's clinched the pennant without him, moving on to a hard-fought seven-game victory over the Reds in the World Series. It was the club's first championship in more than 40 years.

The A's got off to a sluggish start in 1973. At the end of May, they were sitting in fifth place with a middling 24–24 record. By late June, they had gained momentum, taking over the AL West. A 15–3 run in mid-August gave them a lead they would not relinquish. After taking out Baltimore in the ALCS, the A's squared off against the Mets, who were led by the brilliant pitching trio of Tom Seaver, Jerry Koosman, and Jon Matlack. Two of the first three contests were decided in extra innings. The New Yorkers jumped out to a 3–2 Series advantage before dropping the last two games at Oakland. A pair of two-run homers by Campaneris and Jackson in the third inning of Game 7 sealed the Mets' fate.

Despite the on-field success, the A's became known for their clubhouse drama. With so many colorful personalities sharing the spotlight, clashes between players were inevitable. In 1974, a highly publicized fight between outfielders Bill North and Reggie Jackson took place. Pitchers Blue Moon Odom and Rollie Fingers went at it later that year. Charlie Finley fueled the fire as well. When second baseman Mike Andrews committed a pair of 12th-inning errors in Game 2 of the 1973 Fall Classic, Finley forced him to sign an affidavit fraudulently stating that he was injured. Realizing that something was amiss, A's players taped Andrews's number "17" to their uniforms in a gesture of support. When Commissioner Bowie Kuhn found out what was going on, he forced Finley to reactivate Andrews. Tired of all the backbiting in Oakland, manager Dick Williams resigned shortly after the A's clinched the 1973 Series. He was replaced by Alvin Dark, who guided the club to a third consecutive world championship. Only one other team duplicated the feat during the twentieth century—the New York Yankees.

During the 1974 slate, Finley violated the terms of Catfish Hunter's contract. An arbitrator made Hunter a free agent, and he defected to the Yankees. Without his services, the A's were swept by the Red Sox in the 1975 ALCS. Finley fired Alvin Dark and began trimming costs, virtually eliminating promotions. With free agency threatening the solvency of his club, he attempted to sell of his stars, but was blocked by the commissioner. The team slumped in the standings, and attendance dropped off sharply. When Finley sold the franchise in August 1980, his name was in ill-repute.

Few dynasties in baseball history were as colorful and controversial as the A's of the 1970s. Despite a five-year span of excellence, only three members of the squad have been deemed Hall of Fame worthy. For all he did to turn the team around, even Charlie Finley remains an outsider. And a majority of the stars who led the A's to a three-peat championship run have faded into relative obscurity throughout the years.

REGGIE JACKSON, RIGHT FIELD

Jackson made such a name for himself with the Yankees, his early years in Oakland are often overlooked. Reggie was born and raised in Pennsylvania. During his junior year of high school, he sustained a serious knee injury and was cautioned by doctors to quit playing football. Ignoring their advice, he returned for the final game of the season and fractured five cervical vertebrae. He spent six weeks in the hospital and several more in a neck cast. He was told he might never walk again but defied the odds.

Jackson attended Arizona State University and was drafted by the A's when they were still in Kansas City. His breakthrough season came in 1969, when he collected 37 homers before the All-Star break—a record that stood until 2001. Two years later, he hit a memorable clout off of Dock Ellis in the All-Star Game. The blast might have cleared the roof of the right-field grandstand at Tiger Stadium had it not struck a light tower. Broadcaster Ernie Harwell said that it was the hardest-hit ball he had ever seen. "I didn't think it would ever land anywhere," he remarked.

Reggie's statistics contain some stark contrasts. While his lifetime totals for homers and RBIs are among the top marks in baseball history, he raised the bar for strikeouts with a staggering total of 2,597. He was also a defensive liability throughout his career, leading players at his position in errors on numerous occasions. Aware of his ineptitude, he once joked, "The only way I'm going to win a Gold Glove is with a can of spray paint."

Despite his shortcomings, Jackson was one of the most exciting players of the 1970s. During Oakland's three-peat championship run of 1972–1974, Reggie averaged 29 homers and 95 RBIs per season. In addition to capturing AL MVP honors in 1973, he was named MVP of the World Series. His five extra-base hits and six RBIs propelled the A's to a seven-game win over the Mets. In later years, Jackson would carry postseason heroics to an even higher level.

With free agency in full swing, Charles Finley dealt his prized slugger to the Orioles in 1976. Jackson had a productive regular season but ended up missing out on October festivities when the Orioles finished more than 10 games behind the Yankees. He was invited to join Howard Cosell and Keith Jackson during ABC's broadcast of the ALCS. During the fifth game, there was an interesting exchange between Cosell and Jackson. When Cosell announced that Yankee outfielder Mickey Rivers had received a reprimand from George Steinbrenner, Reggie sniped, "Always amazes me how somebody that's never played the game can tell somebody how to play it."

"Don't be bitter," Cosell replied.

"I'll keep it in," Reggie chuckled.

"Gonna have to," said Cosell.

"Don't come down to the Oakland clubhouse or the Baltimore clubhouse and tell me what to do," Reggie countered ominously.

His adventures in the Bronx are chronicled in another chapter.

ROLLIE FINGERS, RELIEF PITCHER

In Fingers's day, relief pitchers were expected to work several innings at a time. The right-hander was well-equipped, having begun his career as a starter. His pitch selection included a hard-sinking fastball and an elusive slider. Had Fingers not been assigned to the bullpen, his career would likely have ended prematurely. "He was one of those kids that was just so nervous," said teammate Joe Rudi. "If he knew he was going to start, by the time the game started, he had worked himself into such a frenzy that he would almost throw up." By 1972, he found himself pitching exclusively out of the bullpen.

Born in Ohio, Fingers went to high school in California. He got started in American Legion ball. Signed as an amateur free agent in 1964, he spent four seasons in the minors before finding a permanent roster spot in Oakland.

Fingers was never entirely comfortable in the spotlight. He once said, "I don't want to get into autobiographies. I don't want to talk about myself." But after he started shutting down AL opponents, the interview requests kept right on coming. From 1972–1976, Fingers finished among the top five in saves each year. He won 50 games for Oakland in that span, while keeping his ERA below the 3.00 mark each season. "When he came in, you took a deep sigh of relief," said third baseman Sal Bando. "You knew the game was in control." In later years, fellow reliever Dan Quisenberry would refer to him as the "master."

In the World Series, Fingers was indeed masterful. He closed 10 games for the A's during their three-year championship run, allowing just five earned runs in more than 33 innings of work. He picked up six saves. In 1974, he entered four games and came away with Series MVP honors.

Although that could easily have been the high point of Fingers's career, it wasn't. Signed by the Padres before the 1977 slate, he went on to become a league leader in saves on three occasions. He helped the Brewers to a playoff appearance in 1981, and a World Series berth the following year. His finest season came in 1981, when he appeared in 47 games and posted a microscopic 1.04 ERA. He cleaned up in every award category that year, claiming a Cy Young, MVP, and Rolaids Relief Award, along with an All-Star selection. Fingers retired with 341 saves—a record at the time. He was inducted into Cooperstown in 1992. After his playing days, he kept a low profile, commenting, "When I got out of baseball, I got all the way out."

CATFISH HUNTER, PITCHER

In his autobiography *Nobody's Perfect*, pitcher Denny McLain has the following words to say about Hunter: "I used to wonder how the hell he ever won a game. His fastball is ordinary and his breaking stuff isn't all that good. But he knows what he's doing out there." That was no understatement. Hunter was adept at avoiding batters' strengths. He had excellent control and rarely got behind hitters. He didn't make waves with umpires or anyone else for that matter. As a result, he ended up in the Hall of Fame.

Born to a poor sharecropping family in North Carolina, Hunter remembered playing baseball constantly while growing up. "Even when it rained, we'd go in the barn and break up corn cobs and hit them with a stick," he said. "We didn't have much money, but we always had baseball." Hunter was being scouted by several teams in high school when he was involved in a hunting mishap. His brother's shotgun accidentally discharged, filling his foot with buckshot. Remarkably, he made a full recovery. By then, some of the scouts had backed off, and he ended up signing with the lowly A's in June 1964. They sent him to their Florida instructional league.

Existing rules required the A's to keep Hunter on their roster in 1965. He rode the bench until mid-May, when he began to draw some middle-relief assignments. By July, he was starting regularly. In May 1968, he tossed a perfect game against the Twins. Charlie Finley called him on the phone afterward, informing him that he had just cost the club $5,000.

"I'm sorry," Hunter said politely, "Who got it?"

"You did," said Finley. "It'll be in your next contract."

As the A's improved in the standings, so did Hunter in the win column. From 1970–1974, he gathered no fewer than 18 victories, reaching the 20-win plateau in four straight seasons. He was a reliable postseason performer throughout, prevailing in seven of nine decisions against five different opponents. Teammate Reggie Jackson said that winning came easily to Hunter. "If he's got a big lead in the eighth, he'll just lay it in there and make them hit it. He doesn't care if he beats you 11–10, as long as he beats you."

Before the 1975 campaign, Finley violated terms of Hunter's contract and ended up losing him to the Yankees. It came as a blow to Jackson, who predicted, "With Catfish, we were champions. Without him, we have to struggle to win the division." That wasn't entirely true, as the A's remained atop the AL West for most of the 1975 campaign. But without Hunter to pitch in the big games, the A's were swept by the Red Sox in the ALCS. The rest of the A's staff compiled a collective 4.32 ERA against the BoSox.

Hunter spent five seasons with the Yankees, making fewer appearances as arm trouble set in. He posted a mediocre 63–53 record in pinstripes. In three trips to the postseason with New York, he was 2–4 with an inflated 4.70 ERA. After his retirement, he authored two cookbooks. Since he was partial to both clubs he played for, his plaque at Cooperstown has no logo on the cap—a rare example of this. Hunter died in 1999, of Lou Gehrig's disease. He was only 53 years old.

VIDA BLUE, PITCHER

Blue was asked by Charlie Finley to change his first name to "True." Unlike "Catfish" Hunter, who accepted a new moniker, Blue openly refused. He explained that the word meant "life" in Spanish and had belonged to his father. By some accounts, he challenged the brash owner with the statement, "How about if you change your name to True Finley?"

Born in Mansfield, Louisiana, Blue was a football star in high school. He threw 35 touchdown passes and was offered multiple scholarships. In need of some quick cash to help out his family, he accepted a huge bonus to sign with Oakland instead.

In portions of three minor-league seasons, Blue won 30 games and posted a 2.57 ERA. He was given a brief trial with the A's in 1969, but wasn't quite ready. Called up in September of the following year, he tossed a no-hitter against the Twins, virtually assuring himself a permanent roster spot. He took the league by storm in 1971, going 24–8 with a 1.82 ERA. He also topped the circuit with eight shutouts. He was the youngest player ever to win the AL Cy Young Award, at 22. The accolades didn't end there, as he was named MVP as well.

Looking to squeeze a few more dollars out of the tightfisted Finley, Blue held out in spring training of 1972. Even President Richard Nixon (a self-proclaimed baseball fan) weighed in on the topic, advising Finley to pay the hurler. Blue finally agreed to terms in May but struggled on the mound, accruing a 6–10 record.

During the next four seasons, the left-hander won no fewer than 17 games and finished among the league leaders in strikeouts each year. An erratic postseason performer, he notched a 1–5 record in 17 appearances with a mediocre 4.31 ERA. His best October outing came in the 1974 ALCS, when he threw a two-hit shutout over the Orioles. He added two quality starts in the World Series that year, although he was saddled with a Game 2 loss.

Blue tried to remain humble after attaining stardom. "I keep telling myself don't get cocky," he once said, "give your services to the press and the media, be nice to the kids, throw a baseball into the stands once in a while." Despite that sentiment, he could never resist the allure of money. After the infamous 1972 holdout, he considered quitting baseball to play quarterback in the newly formed World Football League in

1974. It was just idle chatter, as he resumed his duties with the A's that year.

In 1977, when Blue led the AL with 19 losses, Finley tried to sell him to the Yankees and later to the Reds. Commissioner Bowie Kuhn voided both deals, believing that Finley's fire sale was detrimental to Major League Baseball. Blue ended up with the Giants in 1978, starting in the All-Star Game and being named National League Pitcher of the Year by the *Sporting News*.

While playing for the Royals in 1983, Blue was the subject of a federal drug investigation. He ended up serving time in jail for cocaine use. With his reputation irrevocably blemished, he returned to San Francisco for two mediocre seasons. He was in the process of rejoining the A's for 1987, when he unexpectedly retired. Rumors circulated that he had failed a drug test.

BERT CAMPANERIS, SHORTSTOP

A cousin of major-league standout José Cardenal, Campaneris was born in Pueblo Nuevo, Cuba. He was signed for $500 by the A's in 1961. Originally a catcher, he eventually developed into a fine-fielding short-stop. He was called to Kansas City in July 1964, and homered off of the first pitch he saw in the majors. He added another long ball later in the game to become the second rookie to have a multihomer effort in his major-league debut.

A full-timer in 1965, Campy led the majors with 12 triples and 51 stolen bases. He earned the nickname "Road Runner" for his blazing speed, pacing the AL in steals six times during his career and retiring with 649—among the top 20 totals of all time. Typically appearing at the top of the A's batting order, he averaged 82 runs per year between 1965–1974. He rarely hit for average but was capable of generating some power, as illustrated in 1970, when he suddenly hit 22 homers after putting up single-digit totals each year before then.

A highly competent fielder, Campy finished among the top five in fielding percentage five times. He led the AL three times in putouts. While he never won a Gold Glove, his range factor of 4.99 places him among the top 20 players at his position.

The versatile infielder is perhaps best remembered for playing all nine positions in a game on September 8, 1965. He accomplished the feat during one of Finley's wild promotions. While completing his pitching assignment that day, he worked ambidextrously, throwing lefty to left-handed batters and vice versa. During his catching stint, he was bowled over at the plate by Angels right fielder Ed Kirkpatrick. Precautionary x-rays taken after the game showed no signs of serious injury.

Campaneris became a free agent after the 1976 slate and joined the parade out of Oakland. He played for the Rangers, Angels, and Yankees before retiring after the 1983 campaign. He went on to coach for Japan's Seibu Lions in 1987 and 1988. The team won the Japan Series both years. After that, he spent two seasons with the Gold Coast Suns of the Senior Professional Baseball Association.

KEN HOLTZMAN, PITCHER

Holtzman was born in St. Louis and raised as a Jew. When he signed a bonus contract with the Cubs in 1965, he was hailed as the next Sandy Koufax. He ascended quickly through the lower ranks, getting called to the majors in his first professional season. In a highly publicized showdown, Holtzman faced Sandy Koufax the day after Yom Kippur in 1966. Both men had recognized the holy day by attending synagogue. Holtzman got the best of the encounter, winning a 2–1 nail-biter. Holtzman later dismissed all comparisons to the iconic Dodgers ace. "There is nobody as great as Koufax," he said. "The way some of the Chicago writers wrote about me and my career, I wouldn't even read it. It wasn't only poor writing, but poor reporting."

Holtzman spent five full seasons in Chicago, missing a large portion of the 1967 campaign while serving in the National Guard. He finished with double-digit win totals four times, while tossing a pair of no-hitters. After posting a 9–15 record in 1971, he requested a trade, believing that manager Leo Durocher was hindering his development as a player. The Cubs shipped him to Oakland in exchange for center fielder Rick Monday.

Holtzman enjoyed his most productive campaigns with Oakland, averaging 19 wins per year between 1972–1975. His best season came in 1973, when he compiled a 21–13 record and a 2.97 ERA. He finished among the top five in starts and shutouts. Putting an exclamation point on a stellar campaign, he won three postseason games—one of them an 11-inning three-hitter in the ALCS against Baltimore. Holtzman was a clutch performer in the World Series. He appeared in eight games for the A's and accrued a 4–1 record with a handsome 2.55 ERA. His homer in the 1974 Series was the last by a pitcher in a Fall Classic until Joe Blanton went deep for the Phillies in 2008.

The left-handed Holtzman hung around Oakland through the 1975 campaign, when he won 18 games. He was included in the trade of Reggie Jackson to Baltimore but didn't last a full season there. In June, he was dealt to the Yankees in a 10-player swap. He lost his effectiveness after 1976, and finished his career in 1979.

After his playing days, Holtzman made the most of his college education, working as a stockbroker and in the commercial insurance business. Although he never attained the level of fame enjoyed by Koufax, he won more games during his career.

JOE RUDI, OUTFIELD/FIRST BASE

Born in Modesto, California, Rudi attended two different high schools and starred in three sports—baseball, wrestling, and football. His father wanted him to stop devoting so much time to athletic pursuits and find a "real career." An injury in Rudi's senior year nearly derailed his path to stardom, but an A's scout took a chance on him, offering a marginal bonus.

Rudi spent portions of six seasons in the minors before becoming a full-timer in Oakland. Between 1970–1976, his batting averages ranged from .267 to .309. He led the league in hits (181) and triples (9) during the 1972 campaign. He put forth his best offensive effort in 1974, collecting a league-best 39 doubles, while also pacing the circuit in total bases. Named to three All-Star Teams, he was a runner-up for MVP twice.

Defensively, Rudi was one of the best in the business, placing among the top five in fielding percentage as a left fielder six times (he led the league twice). For years, he was considered an underrated player. In 1974, he commented, "Sometimes all I get is ink about not getting ink. I wish people would just concentrate on the job I do on the field." Rudi gave a lot of credit to Joe DiMaggio for teaching him how to track fly balls. DiMaggio served as an A's coach in 1968 and 1969. The advice paid off, as Rudi won three consecutive Gold Gloves from 1974–1976.

Rudi enjoyed a few moments in the spotlight during Game 2 of the 1972 World Series. His solo homer in the third inning ended up being the winning run. He saved the game himself with a spectacular ninth-inning catch on a long drive that would have scored the tying run. In three Fall Classics, Rudi assembled a .300 batting average with a pair of homers and nine ribbies.

In 1975, the A's shifted Rudi to first base to make room for Claudell Washington. Things began to grow tense between Rudi and Finley when his salary request for the 1976 slate was ignored. Because Finley didn't negotiate and Rudi hadn't signed by the time the season began, the frugal owner slashed Rudi's salary by 20 percent. Finley then tried to sell Rudi and Rollie Fingers to the Red Sox, but the Sox weren't willing to compensate for Rudi's salary cut and Commissioner Bowie Kuhn voided the transaction anyway. Rudi, by his own account, had officially lost his enthusiasm for playing in Oakland at that point. He eventually ended up with the Angels, putting up decent numbers for four seasons. After a stop in Boston during the 1981 slate, he closed out his career in Oakland the following year (Finley was gone by then).

During the mid-1980s, manager Tony La Russa brought Rudi back as a batting/outfield coach. The three-time world champion eventually grew tired of being away from his family and left the game. He was active in real estate for many years and also served as an instructor at a local baseball academy in his hometown.

GENE TENACE, CATCHER/FIRST BASE

Virtually no one had even heard of Gene Tenace before the 1972 World Series. Chosen in a late round of the 1965 amateur draft, Tenace lingered in the A's minor-league system for the better part of six seasons. He had a breakout year with Birmingham of the Southern League in 1969, hitting .319 with 20 homers. He put up similar stats the following year. Called to the A's in September 1969, he failed to secure a roster spot when he managed a frail .158 average in 16 games. Returning to Oakland in July 1970, he topped the .300 mark in limited duty. By 1971, he had earned a job as backup catcher behind first-stringer Dave Duncan.

Tenace spent roughly equal amounts of time as a catcher and first baseman during his career. He had a strong arm behind the plate, finishing among the top five in caught stealing percentage three times. He also topped the circuit in fielding percentage as a backstop in 1979. He earned wider acclaim for his postseason heroics.

During the 1972 campaign, he hit just .225 in 82 games with little power. He fizzled in the ALCS against the Orioles, managing just one hit in 17 at-bats. Once the World Series was underway, he went off on a tear. In Game 1, he homered twice and drove in all three Oakland runs. In the fourth contest, his fifth-inning shot off of Don Gullett put the A's up, 1–0. Later in the game, he singled and scored the winning run. His coming-out party continued in Game 5, as he blasted a three-run homer to give the A's a 3–1 second-inning lead. It wasn't enough, as Cincinnati rallied for a 5–4 win. In the Series finale, Tenace came through in the clutch again, driving home two more runs in a Series-clinching win. He was an overwhelming choice for Series MVP. One sportswriter referred to him as the "Terrible Ten-achi." A 1973 Topps World Series baseball card labeled him "Tenace the Menace." "I don't feel like I'm a hero," he humbly told reporters. "It took 25 men to win this World Series."

Tenace put up his best regular-season numbers between 1973–1976, clubbing no fewer than 22 homers each year. Demonstrating patience at the plate, he drew more than 100 walks six times in a seven-year span. He led both leagues in that category. Tenace's ability to get on base carried over into the postseason, as he compiled a lifetime .405 on-base percentage in World Series play.

Tenace became a free agent before the 1977 slate and joined Rollie Fingers in San Diego. Even with Dave Winfield and Ozzie Smith in the lineup, the Padres were noncontenders in those days. From San Diego, Tenace moved on to St. Louis. He made it to the World Series with the Cards in 1982, but logged just seven plate appearances as a designated hitter and pinch-hitter. Tenace played one more season with the Pirates and then retired.

Throughout the years, Tenace served in various capacities for several different major-league clubs. He had a brief stint as manager of the Blue Jays, taking over the club when Cito Gaston fell ill in 1991. Tenace guided the Jays to a 19–14 record during his tenure. He announced his retirement from the game in 2009.

SAL BANDO, THIRD BASE

Bando was a college standout at Arizona State University, playing alongside future All-Star Rick Monday. Both were chosen in the 1965 amateur draft by the A's. Bando bounced up and down from the majors to the minors in 1966 and 1967, before winning the third-base job in Oakland.

From 1969–1976, Bando was the one of the Athletics' most productive hitters. He smashed 20 or more homers six times in that span, while gathering no fewer than 75 RBIs. In 1969, he put up career-high numbers in runs (106), hits (171), homers (31), and RBIs (113), helping Oakland to a respectable 88–74 record. The solidly built slugger (six feet/200 pounds) had an excellent batting eye and really wore pitchers down. He averaged 82 walks per season as a full-time player.

A four-time All-Star, Bando had a strong arm at third base, placing among the top five in assists six times. He led the league in putouts twice and double plays once. His fielding percentage was third best in the circuit on four occasions.

A clutch October performer, Bando cracked a pair of homers in Game 2 of the 1973 ALCS against the Orioles. His homer in Game 3 of the 1974 ALCS was the game-winner. He played in 39 postseason contests for the A's, reaching base by hit or walk more than 50 times. He went deep five times, while driving in 12 runs.

Before the 1975 slate, Bando got into a salary dispute with the tight-fisted Finley. His numbers dropped off that year. He became a free agent after the 1976 campaign and joined the Brewers. Commenting on his experience in Oakland, he said, "The first few years, Charlie Finley was outstanding. Then he changed. I don't know what the reason was, but he didn't respect the players."

Bando had a handful of good seasons in Milwaukee and was still around when the Brewers squared off against the Yankees in the 1981 American League Division Series. Bando hit .294 with three doubles in the five-game loss to the Bombers. He retired during the offseason. An interesting sidelight from his days with the Brewers: He pitched three innings of a blowout loss to the Royals in 1979. He gave up two runs on three hits and later admitted to throwing several spitballs. Catcher Charlie Moore commented, "The ball was shining when it got to the plate."

When his playing days were finished, Bando served as special assistant to Brewers GM Harry Dalton for a decade. He ascended to the position of GM in 1991, and remained at the post until 1999. The Brewers fielded just one winning team during his tenure. In 1992, he waited too long to offer Hall of Famer Paul Molitor salary arbitration, and Molitor ended up signing with the Blue Jays. Bando apparently did not feel that Molitor was a top priority since he was (quote) "only a DH." The following year, Molitor was named MVP of the Fall Classic. Bando claims that his words were taken out of context; however, many writers have cited it as being among the most glaring PR gaffes in Milwaukee history.

FAST FACT: Maverick A's owner Charlie Finley was always looking to change the game. In 1973, he introduced bright orange baseballs in the hope of generating more offense. Although the balls were easier for umpires and fans to see, pitchers complained that they were slippery, and batters noted that the red seams were indistinguishable, making it difficult to pick up the spin of the pitch. A new prototype with white seams was created, but the experiment was quickly abandoned.

17

CINCINNATI REDS

1972–1976

The Cincinnati Red Stockings were among the first all-professional teams in baseball history. Founded in the 1860s, the club compiled an 89-game winning streak before dissolving in 1870. A new incarnation was formed several years later but ended up being expelled from the National League for playing on Sundays (a capital offense in those days). Reestablished as an American Association entry during the 1880s, the franchise shifted to the NL for good in 1890, and shortened its nickname to the current form.

A host of gifted players led the Reds to sporadic postseason appearances throughout the years. The first championship, in 1919, can hardly be taken seriously since several members of the White Sox conspired with gamblers to throw the World Series. The Reds became legitimate champions in 1940, when they defeated the Tigers in seven games. After two decades of futility, the club returned to the Fall Classic in 1961, falling to the powerful Yankees. Despite their extensive history, the Reds remained one of the least successful teams in the majors at the dawn of the 1970s.

When the "Disco Decade" arrived, the franchise was owned by Francis L. Dale. Dale had earned a law degree from the University of Virginia and become a partner in a Cincinnati-based law firm. While serving as publisher of the *Cincinnati Enquirer*, he fronted a syndicate that purchased the Reds in 1967. Acting as team president for several years, Dale was instrumental in the construction of Riverfront Stadium, which opened in 1970. He typically separated himself from the team's daily affairs, leaving practical matters in the capable hands of GM Bob Howsam, who presided over the assembly of the "Big Red Machine."

The aforementioned term was introduced in a 1969 article penned by *Cincinnati Enquirer* sportswriter Bob Hertzel. It became more relevant in subsequent years when the club rose to prominence. Beginning in the early 1960s, the Reds took several steps toward greatness when they signed a trio of superstars—Pete Rose, Tony Perez, and Johnny Bench. There was plenty of talent in Cincinnati, but the team seemed to be lacking a rudder. Three different managers took the helm between 1965–1968, as the Reds finished in fourth place or lower each year during that span. Help arrived soon afterward with the addition of Sparky Anderson.

A player of meager abilities, Anderson had spent the entire 1959 campaign at second base for the Phillies, struggling to keep his batting average above .200. He finished the year at .218. "I didn't have a lot of talent," he later said, "so I tried to make up for it with spit and vinegar." Anderson received the nickname "Sparky" because of his feisty nature—a trait that got him into trouble early in his career. Unable to control his emotions at times, he was fired from his first managerial position with Toronto of the International League. He spent five seasons as a minor-league skipper, changing teams each year.

In 1969, Anderson landed a coaching job with the Padres. At season's end, he agreed to coach for the Angels but changed his mind when Howsam offered him the managerial position in Cincinnati. He had mellowed considerably by then. While he ran a tight ship, he allowed players to question his decisions and even welcomed their input. "I know there are managers who would never allow themselves to be put on this level with their own ballplayers," he once commented, "but as far as I'm concerned, it's a form of communication." Anderson's interactive style of management produced dramatic results, as the Reds won 5 NL West titles, 4 NL pennants, and 2 world championships between 1970–1976.

After losing to the Orioles in the 1970 Fall Classic, the club suffered through growing pains the following year, slumping to fourth place. During the offseason, the Reds made one of the most important acquisitions in team history, obtaining future Cooperstown inductee Joe

Morgan from the Astros. With Morgan aboard, the "Big Red Machine" began firing on all cylinders, compiling a 95–59 record in 1972, and eliminating the Pirates in the National League Championship Series. Trailing three games to one against the A's in the World Series that year, the Reds rallied to force a Game 7 at Riverfront Stadium. In the end, it was a misplayed fly ball by center fielder Bobby Tolan that proved to be the difference in the finale, as the resulting unearned run helped the A's to a 3–2 win.

The Reds took the West again in 1973, but failed to dispose of the Mets in the NLCS. The showdown between the two clubs was marred by an ugly brawl at Shea Stadium. The Series was tied at one game apiece, and the Mets had just handed the Reds a humbling 5–0 loss in the second meeting. Before Game 3, New York's light-hitting shortstop Bud Harrelson joked that Cincinnati batters resembled him at the plate. Joe Morgan was offended by the comment and confronted Harrelson. The two resolved their differences, but Morgan warned him that Pete Rose was holding a grudge and would be looking for a way to get at Harrelson on the base paths. After the Mets had jumped out to a comfortable 9–2 lead, Rose followed through, knocking the pint-size infielder flat while breaking up a double play. Rose outweighed Harrelson by roughly 40 pounds. The two went at it, and a full-scale brawl erupted at Shea Stadium.

The benches emptied, and Cincinnati reliever Pedro Borbon sucker punched Mets hurler Buzz Capra. Fans went ballistic—especially in the left-field stands, where someone threw a whiskey bottle that narrowly missed Rose's head. An announcement over the PA system cautioned fans to stop or risk a forfeit. NL president Chub Feeney, who was sitting near the Mets dugout, asked manager Yogi Berra to address the crowd. Accompanied by several players, Yogi honored the request. The game eventually resumed, and the Mets won, later advancing to the World Series against the A's.

The Reds came up empty-handed again in 1974. Despite winning 98 games, they couldn't catch up with the Dodgers. A late September surge brought them within two and a half games of the division lead, but LA—led by the one–two punch of pitchers Andy Messersmith and Don Sutton—made their first postseason appearance in nearly a decade. Things would finally fall into place for Cincinnati the following year.

The 1975 Reds won 108 games—the highest total in franchise history. They carried five All-Stars on their roster and spent a total of 124 days in first place. After eliminating the Pirates in the NLCS by a collective margin of 19–7, they met their match in the World Series. The Red Sox had assembled a team for the ages, led by future Hall of Famers Carl Yastrzemski, Carlton Fisk, and Jim Rice, along with Rookie of the Year and MVP winner Fred Lynn. The Series was a classic—best remembered for Fisk's dramatic walk-off homer in Game 6, which happened exactly four hours and one minute after the opening pitch. The Reds silenced a rabid throng of Bostonians at Fenway Park the following evening when they rallied from an early 3–0 deficit to clinch the Series. The so-called "Big Red Machine" had finally won it all. "I've felt for the last four years that we've had the best team in baseball," an elated Joe Morgan told a throng of reporters. "What has been most frustrating for me is not being able to say we were the best."

The 1976 campaign was almost anticlimactic. Cincinnati won 102 games and breezed to a Western title over the Dodgers. After making quick work of the Phillies in the NL playoff, they squared off against the rejuvenated Yankees, who were returning to the postseason after a 12-year absence. The meeting was billed as a showdown between baseball's best catchers: Johnny Bench versus Thurman Munson. The only real drama was inadvertently created by manager Sparky Anderson when he was asked to rate the rival backstops. Anderson remarked that it wasn't fair to "embarrass" any catcher by comparing him to Johnny Bench. Munson commented that he felt "belittled" by Anderson's statement. Sparky later issued a letter of apology to the Yankees captain. By then, the Reds had swept the Bombers, and Bench had captured Series MVP honors, hitting .533 with two homers and six RBIs. Munson wasn't far behind, with a .529 batting average.

After the 1976 campaign, team executives began dismantling the "Machine" piece by piece. Tony Perez was traded to the Expos. Pete Rose signed with the Phillies. Sparky Anderson was fired after a second-place finish in 1978. He didn't even see it coming, as the Reds had just completed a tour of Japan. Unhappy with the direction the team was headed in, Joe Morgan returned to the Astros in 1980. Although Johnny Bench remained a lifer in Cincinnati, the club had slumped to sixth place by the time he retired.

When tales of championship squads in Cincinnati are told, the focus invariably shifts to the heyday of the 1970s. Had the Reds not collided with two of the best teams in American League history, they might have captured four world championships during that decade. While the club came up empty in two World Series, numerous members of the "Big Red Machine" are considered to be among the greatest of any generation.

PETE ROSE, INFIELD/OUTFIELD

Assembly of the so-called "Machine" began in 1963, when the Reds promoted Pete Rose from the South Atlantic League. Rose received the nickname "Charlie Hustle" from Yankees pitching great Whitey Ford, who resented the way Rose sprinted to first base after receiving a walk during a spring training game. A dynamic jack-of-all-trades, Rose played the game hard and fast, bowling over anyone in his path. He became famous for his diving, headfirst slides. Few players have matched his drive for success and enthusiasm for the game. He once remarked that he would "walk through Hell in a gasoline suit to play baseball."

Rose's fiery temperament earned him a reputation as a bit of a bully. His fight with Bud Harrelson in the 1973 NL playoffs (previously mentioned in this chapter) cemented that status. Before then, he had been criticized for bowling over Ray Fosse at home plate while delivering the winning run during the 1970 All-Star Game. Today, the winners of the annual All-Star Game are awarded home-field advantage in the World Series. In those days, there was nothing at stake except bragging rights. Fosse was knocked senseless in the collision, and his career went downhill immediately afterward. Rose commented years later that, if it weren't for him, no one would even know who Fosse was.

Undoubtedly the greatest ballplayer outside the Hall of Fame, Rose collected more hits than anyone in the history of the game and set more than 20 statistical records, including most times on base and most runs scored by a switch-hitter. Banned from Cooperstown for gambling on baseball, Rose has been one of the sport's most active ambassadors during the last two decades. His drive for reinstatement has yet to yield results. Rose lampooned himself in a commercial that aired during the

2015 Super Bowl. In the ad, which promoted Skechers sneakers, Rose was seen walking through a hallway in his house. His wife appeared suddenly, scolding him: "Pete—you're not supposed to be in the hall!" Rose responded dejectedly, "I can't catch a break." In an alternate version of the commercial, he remarked, "Even at home?"

During his 19 seasons in Cincinnati, Rose led the NL in hits six times. He also paced the circuit in doubles on four occasions. He was a three-time batting champion. He reached the summit of his career in 1973, when he captured MVP honors on the strength of his 230 base hits and league-best .338 batting average. Among the most gifted all-around players in history, he remains the only man to log at least 500 games at five different defensive stations.

Rose was the last player-manager in major-league history. While serving in that capacity, he placed numerous bets on the Reds, violating Major League Baseball's Rule 21. After getting caught, he insisted that he only bet on the team to win. Baseball authorities considered the point irrelevant. Rose formally admitted his indiscretions in his auto-biography *My Prison without Bars*, which was released in 2004. Named to baseball's All-Century Team, he was allowed to take the field for a pregame ceremony. Similarly, he was honored at Cincinnati's Great American Ballpark in 2010, on the 25th anniversary of his establishment of the all-time hits record. In an almost comical lapse of judgment, Rose attended an event at a local casino afterward.

TONY PEREZ, FIRST BASE

Surrounded by glitzier teammates, Perez was sometimes lost in the mix. Teammate Pat Corrales remarked, "Tony would get shoved into the background driving in 100 runs every year. You'd see it in the notes at the end of the stories in the paper—oh, by the way, Perez hit a three-run homer to win the game." Although he may not have always occupied a lot of space in newspapers, he commanded respect from team-mates and opponents. Manager Sparky Anderson said that there was no one he would rather have at the plate in a tight spot. Hall of Fame first baseman Willie Stargell remarked, "[W]ith men in scoring position and the game on the line, Tony was the last guy an opponent wanted to see."

Born in Cuba, Perez developed his muscles lifting heavy sacks of sugar in a mill. He reportedly despised the job. In 1960, he had a successful tryout with the Reds, receiving a paltry $2.50 signing bonus—just enough to cover his visa. Perez was only 17 when he arrived in the United States and was not fluent in English. By his own account, he learned a lot by attending movies regularly.

Perez spent portions of five seasons in the minors. He was eventually called up in 1964. While he managed just two hits for the Reds in 25 at-bats, he returned the following year to form a highly effective first-base tandem with Gordy Coleman. Perez was shifted to third base in 1967, to make room for slugger Lee May. He would remain at the hot corner until 1972, when he moved back to his primary station for good. Although Perez led the league in errors several times, he regularly finished among the top five in putouts, assists, and double plays.

Among the most abundant run producers of the 1970s, Perez collected 90 or more ribbies in 11 straight seasons from 1967–1977. He received the nickname "Big Doggie" for his reliability in the clutch. He was a positive clubhouse presence overall; however, he was known for riding teammates he felt weren't living up to their potential. According to Anderson, he managed to do this without offending anyone.

Traded to Montreal after the 1976 slate, his absence was felt dramatically. "Losing Tony took so much chemistry away," said GM Bob Howsam. Anderson echoed that sentiment in one of his autobiographies. "[Tony] was the glue that kept it stuck together," Anderson declared. "I never realized until we traded him after the 1976 World Series."

Perez's best season outside of Cincinnati came in 1980, when he launched 25 homers and gathered 105 RBIs with Boston. He returned to Cincinnati in 1984, to complete the final leg of his Hall of Fame journey. He was the oldest player to hit a walk-off pinch homer, at 42, and the oldest to hit a grand slam, at the age of 44. The latter record was broken by Julio Franco in 2004.

A member of the 2000 Cooperstown class, Perez had a pair of brief managerial stints after his playing days were over. In 1993, he started the season at the helm of the Reds but was replaced by Davey Johnson when the club got off to a 20–24 start. In 2001, he took over for John Boles in Florida, leading the Marlins to a fourth-place finish. Remarkably, Perez was never on the disabled list during his playing career.

JOHNNY BENCH, CATCHER

A writer from the *Sporting News* once commented, "It might not seem fair, but Johnny Bench is the standard by which catchers will be judged forever." A straight-A student and valedictorian of his high school class in Binger, Oklahoma, Bench professed that failure was the only thing he ever feared. Selected by the Reds in the second round of the 1965 amateur draft, he was the Carolina League's Player of the Year during the 1966 slate. By 1968, he had assumed full-time catching responsibilities in Cincinnati. He captured Rookie of the Year honors.

Emminently aware of his abilities, Bench once boasted, "I can throw out any man alive." He backed up the claim by finishing among the top five in caught stealing percentage for 11 straight seasons. He had unusually large hands and was among the first to use a hinged catcher's mitt. He employed a one-handed style, keeping his throwing hand tucked behind his back to protect it from foul tips. Bench was in complete control behind the plate, and his pitchers knew it. Teammate Jim Maloney once remarked, "He'll come out on the mound and treat me like a two-year-old, but so help me, I like it." Bench was nicknamed the "Little General" for his leadership on the diamond. Off the diamond, he maintained a low profile. "Cincinnati is a quiet city—as American as apple pie. I think the club and the fans prefer that I have a wholesome image," he told a reporter.

Offensively, Bench had exceptional power, leading the league twice in homers and extra-base hits. His finest year at the plate came in 1970, when he slammed 45 long balls and drove in 148 runs. He received the first of two NL MVP Awards that year. A productive October performer, Bench compiled a .527 slugging percentage in 10 postseason series. Although many of his career highlights took place during the World Series, there was at least one moment he would have liked to forget.

In Game 3 of the 1972 Fall Classic, he was facing Hall of Fame reliever Rollie Fingers with runners on second and third. He had worked the count full when A's manager Dick Williams pulled a fast one on him. Williams ordered catcher Gene Tenace to set up for an intentional walk but advised Fingers to throw a strike instead. Fingers was reportedly aggravated by Williams's scheme, commenting, "Is this Little League or what?" But the play went off without a hitch, as Tenace crouched behind the plate at the last second and Bench watched strike three sail past him. Bench later asserted that it was one of the most "embarrassing" experiences of his career.

By the time he retired, Bench had little to be embarrassed about, having played on 14 All-Star Teams and captured 10 Gold Gloves. He was elected to the Hall of Fame in 1989. For several years, he was host of a Saturday morning kids show called *The Baseball Bunch*, which costarred the San Diego Chicken and Hall of Fame manager Tom Lasorda. Additionally, Bench served as a Reds broadcaster from 1987–1990.

JOE MORGAN, SECOND BASE

Morgan has been referred to as the "generator" of the "Big Red Machine." At 5-foot-7, 160 pounds, he was deceptively powerful, clubbing 22 or more homers in four seasons. He became widely known for his odd (yet highly entertaining) habit of flapping his left arm at the plate. A consummate team player, Morgan remarked during his Hall of Fame acceptance speech, "I take my vote as a salute to the little guy. . . . I'm proud of my stats, but I don't think I ever got one for Joe Morgan. If I stole a base, it was to help us win a game, and I'd like to think that's what makes me a little special."

Morgan stole plenty of bases during his career—689 to be exact, a number that currently places him at number 11 on the all-time list. Frequently occupying the third spot in the Reds batting order, he wore opposing pitchers down. Between 1969–1977, he drew no fewer than 102 walks eight times. His on-base percentage exceeded the .400 mark in nine of his 22 seasons. He led the league in that category on four occasions.

Scouts ignored Morgan during his high school years in Oakland. He ended up attending Oakland City College and Cal State Hayward. At the latter school, Houston scout Bill Wight saw vast potential in him, commenting that, despite his size, he was "self-assured without being cocky." While playing in the minors, Morgan's boyhood idol, Nellie Fox, suggested he flap his arm to help with his timing at the plate and to remind him to keep his left shoulder up. It became Morgan's trademark.

Morgan came up with the Astros in 1963. In his first full season, he finished second in Rookie of the Year voting. Before the 1972 campaign, he was included in an eight-player trade that saw the Reds give up two of their best players—Lee May and Tommy Helms. Morgan became the only second baseman in history to win back-to-back MVP Awards in 1975 and 1976. Using an undersized mitt that looked a bit like a Little League model, he claimed a Gold Glove each year from 1973–1977.

Gene Mauch, who spent 26 years as a big-league manager with four different clubs, considered Morgan to be one of the smartest players in baseball history. Esteemed statistician Bill James rates "Little Joe" as the number-one second baseman of all time. Even in later years, when Morgan's skills were in decline, he was a stabilizing presence on the clubs he played for. Outside of Cincinnati, he helped the Astros to the NLCS in 1980, and the Phillies to a World Series berth in 1983.

Elected to the Hall of Fame in 1990, Morgan moved on to a long career in broadcasting, calling Sunday night games for ESPN. From 1994–2000, he provided commentary for three World Series, four All-Star Games, and three championship series in both leagues. In 2010, he returned to the Reds as "special advisor to baseball operations."

DAVE CONCEPCION, SHORTSTOP

Concepcion learned the basics of the game in his native Venezuela. As a kid, he idolized fellow countryman Luis Aparicio (a Hall of Fame shortstop) and strove to be on the same level. Acquired by the Reds in 1967, Concepcion was assigned to the Florida State League. It was a taxing experience for the 21-year-old infielder, as he had a limited grasp of the English language and suffered from bouts of homesickness. He stuck it out, getting a call to Cincinnati in 1970.

Concepcion played in an era when shortstops weren't expected to hit, so no one was terribly alarmed when he managed a feeble .222 batting average in his first three seasons. He wore the number "13" on his jersey and found it amusing that several superstitious teammates had advised him to avoid it. He had worn the same number back home and joked that it was good luck for him.

Concepcion reached his peak years between 1973–1982, when he played on nine All-Star Teams and won five Gold Gloves. With batting averages ranging from .260 to .306, he collected no fewer than 60 RBIs on seven occasions. His stellar play drew lavish praise from some of the all-time greats. Pee Wee Reese remarked, "No one does everything as well as Concepcion. It's possible no one ever has."

Concepcion was a productive October hitter for the Reds, fashioning a .297 batting average in nine postseason series. He was especially successful against the Pirates in the NLCS, collecting 11 hits—two of them for extra bases—in 27 at-bats. The Reds won six of nine October showdowns with Concepcion in the lineup.

Concepcion was devoutly religious and could be seen making the sign of the cross during each at-bat. He hung around Cincinnati longer than any other member of the "Big Red Machine," playing his last season with the Reds in 1988. He developed a style of throwing to first base from deep in the hole by bouncing the ball when playing on artificial turf. The technique has been widely imitated throughout the years. The slick-fielding shortstop was elected to the Latino Baseball Hall of Fame in 2010. He garnered moderate support from Cooperstown voters, peaking at 16.9 percent in 1998. Sabermetric similarity scores compare him favorably to Hall of Famers Pee Wee Reese and his boyhood idol—Luis Aparicio.

GEORGE FOSTER, OUTFIELD

Born in Alabama, Foster moved to California with his family and became the only Leuzinger High School alumnus to reach the majors. He was selected in the third round of the 1968 amateur draft by the Giants. Called to San Francisco in 1969, he saw little playing time with Willie Mays, Bobby Bonds, and Ken Henderson patrolling the outfield. Foster was traded to the Reds in 1971, but hit just .234 in 104 games. He remained a part-time player until 1974, when Sparky Anderson began platooning him with Ken Griffey Sr. In 1975, Pete Rose was shifted to third base to make room for Foster in left field. Foster had a breakout year, hitting .300 and collecting 78 RBIs out of the lower half of the batting order. In the postseason, he collected 12 hits in 10 games with four runs scored and a pair of RBIs.

During the next five seasons, Foster was one of the most productive sluggers in baseball, averaging 35 homers and 116 RBIs per year. His signature campaign came in 1977, when he paced the NL in runs (124), homers (52), RBIs (149), and slugging percentage (.631). He was an obvious choice for NL MVP. Interestingly, the Rawlings Company supplied the majors with baseballs that year, which were manufactured in Haiti. Author Roger Angell joked that the balls had been "secretly polished there with applications of Haitian juju oil." Whatever the cause, the NL saw a dramatic increase in homers during the 1977 slate.

Foster had an unusual sense of humor. During his prime slugging years, he began using a black bat because he wanted to "integrate the bat rack" in Cincinnati. A productive postseason performer, he used the ebony-colored lumber to compile a .326 World Series average.

The Reds hung on to Foster through the 1981 campaign, before trading him to the Mets. The contract made Foster the highest-paid player in the majors. Without protection in the middle of the order, his batting average declined sharply. In four full seasons with New York, he never hit higher than .269. The Mets expected much more for their money and eventually released him in August 1986. He finished his major-league career with the White Sox.

Foster played in the Senior Professional Baseball Association in 1989 and 1990. He has remained active since his retirement. In addition to hosting his own radio show, he has worked as a motivational speaker. He also operates a nonprofit organization benefiting inner-city children. The foundation, which bears his name, is known as "Dream."

FAST FACT: The 1976 Cincinnati Reds had one representative from each infield station on the All-Star Team: first baseman Tony Perez, second baseman Joe Morgan, shortstop Dave Concepcion, third baseman Pete Rose, and catcher Johnny Bench.

18

NEW YORK YANKEES

1976–1978

George Steinbrenner was a difficult man to work for, as evidenced by the alarming number of team executives he used and discarded during his tenure as Yankees owner. Meddling, tempestuous, and fickle, Steinbrenner—known simply as the "Boss"—had absolutely no tolerance for failure. He expected the Yankees to win every year, and if they didn't, heads would roll. Although he was certainly not the warmest, fuzziest character, his insatiable drive for excellence propelled the Yanks to seven World Series titles and 11 pennants during his long reign.

In 1967, Steinbrenner became CEO of the American Ship Building Company. He tried to purchase the Cleveland Indians, but owner Vernon Stouffer wouldn't sell to him. Steinbrenner despised the word *no*, and in 1973, his aspirations of owning a baseball team became a reality when he assembled a group of financiers to purchase the New York Yankees from CBS. Three years and several transactions later, the Yankees were champions of the American League.

The previous owners had done Steinbrenner a tremendous favor when they acquired Graig Nettles from the Indians in November 1972. A slick-fielding, hard-hitting third baseman, Nettles received the nickname "Puff" for his ability to disappear immediately after playing a practical joke or otherwise making a nuisance of himself. During his 11 years in the Bronx, he gathered more than 20 homers on eight occasions, peaking at 37 during the 1977 slate. A two-time Gold Glove recipient, he frequently dazzled fans with his stupendous grabs at the hot corner.

Nettles joined an infield anchored by future team captain Thurman Munson. Munson was among the best catchers of the 1970s, renowned for his clutch hitting and defensive excellence. Still, he lived in the shadow of Carlton Fisk and Johnny Bench, who always seemed to garner more attention. Munson could be a bit prickly at times, admitting to one journalist, "I'm a little too belligerent. I cuss and swear at people. I yell at umpires. . . . I don't sign as many autographs as I should, and I haven't always been very good with the writers." Regardless of his shortcomings, he attained folk-hero status in the Bronx.

In 1974, Steinbrenner brought controversy to the Big Apple when he became embroiled in a political scandal. Prior to the start of the season, he was indicted on several criminal counts and later pleaded guilty to making illegal contributions to Richard Nixon's reelection campaign. He was fined a hefty sum by a U.S. district court and suspended for two years by Commissioner Bowie Kuhn. The suspension was later shortened considerably.

Meanwhile, the Yankees continued to build a powerhouse. In 1974, Chris Chambliss and Lou Piniella joined the club. Catfish Hunter and Billy Martin were added the following year. Mickey Rivers and Willie Randolph donned pinstripes in 1976, as Steinbrenner returned from exile. Celebrating his homecoming, a refurbished Yankee Stadium opened for business.

The Yankees attracted more than 2 million fans during the 1976 campaign—more than any other club in the AL. The tone of the season was set early on when Billy Martin stole a victory from the Milwaukee Brewers on April 10. After Don Money hit an apparent game-winning grand slam at County Stadium, the pugnacious Martin charged out of the dugout and confronted umpire Jim McKean, claiming that time had been called by first baseman Chris Chambliss prior to pitcher Dave Pagan's windup. Swayed by Martin's argument, McKean admitted he had approved the timeout. In a rare reversal ruling, the home run was discounted. Money flied out, and the Yanks held on for a 9–7 win. Shortly afterward, the Bombers moved into first place for good.

Returning to the postseason after an extended absence, the Yankees met the Royals in the American League Championship Series. They had fared somewhat poorly against Kansas City during the regular season, losing seven of 12 meetings. Among the biggest stories in the AL that year, Kansas City All-Stars George Brett and Hal McRae had staged a dramatic race for the batting crown that was decided on the last day of the season. After Twins outfielder Steve Brye appeared to lay up on a ball hit by Brett, McRae cried racism—insinuating that Minnesota skipper Gene Mauch had ordered Brye to play unusually deep so that the ball would drop in. Mauch emphatically denied the claim. Brett continued his hot hitting in the playoffs, posting a .444 average, but McRae lost his stroke, managing a meager .125 mark. The Yankees advanced to the World Series on a walk-off homer in Game 5 by Chris Chambliss.

The Yankees highlight reels more or less ended there, as Steinbrenner's rejuvenated club got annihilated by the "Big Red Machine" in the World Series. Game 2 was the only close contest, as the Bombers rallied from a 3–0 deficit to tie the game in the seventh inning at Riverfront Stadium. Catfish Hunter got two quick outs in the bottom of the ninth before Ken Griffey reached on a throwing error by shortstop Fred Stanley. National League MVP Joe Morgan was walked to get to Tony Perez—one of the Reds' most reliable RBI men. Perez delivered a clutch single to give Cincinnati a 4–3 win. The Yanks dropped the other three games by at least four runs.

In 1977, slugger Reggie Jackson brought his traveling sideshow to the Bronx. Within weeks of his arrival, he had managed to create a rift between himself and Thurman Munson. Speaking to a writer from *Sport* magazine, Jackson boasted, "I'm the straw that stirs the drink. Munson thinks he can be the straw that stirs the drink, but he can only stir it bad." (Several versions of the quote exist.)

Although Jackson carried the club at times, he also went into prolonged batting slumps. Still, he was Steinbrenner's most coveted player, and the "Boss" demanded he remain in the lineup even when he wasn't producing. On numerous occasions, Martin tried to hide Reggie at the bottom of the order, but he invariably heard about it later, with Steinbrenner insisting that the slugger bat third or fourth. Martin had strong ideas about how to run a ballclub, and he resented Steinbrenner's intrusive ways. He also resented Jackson's ego, and there was friction between the two from the start.

Martin had made no bones about the fact that Reggie wasn't his first choice. At one point, he had advocated for the acquisition of Joe Rudi, a decent hitter and an excellent defensive outfielder. Reggie was a subpar fielder, although he did possess a strong arm. Between 1968–1977, he led AL right fielders in errors numerous times. He also had a tendency to loaf after balls. In his book *The Bronx Zoo*, reliever Sparky Lyle writes, "Let's face it, Reggie's a bad outfielder. He has good speed to the ball, but the catching part is shaky."

On June 18, 1977, Reggie and Billy demonstrated their animosity toward one another on national television. The Yankees were visiting Fenway Park and trailing the Red Sox in the standings. As usual, Steinbrenner was griping that the team should be in first place. Martin had asked Jackson to shag some fly balls during batting practice, but the slugger had allegedly refused. This led to an epic showdown in the Yankees dugout.

The Bombers were behind, 7–4, in the sixth inning when Jim Rice hit a blooper to right field that dunked in for a hit. Reggie moved casually toward it and took his time getting it back to the infield. By then, Rice was on second base. Billy was fuming. He came out to the mound to remove pitcher Mike Torrez. He then sent Paul Blair out to replace Reggie. This was obviously an attempt to embarrass the egotistical outfielder, whom Billy had never wanted in the first place.

Sensitive about his public image, Jackson stormed into the dugout and demanded to know what he had done wrong. Martin snarled at him, "You know what you did!" Reggie then made the mistake of calling Martin an old man. Billy had never backed down from a fight during his career, and he wasn't about to start. It took three coaches to separate the two. Reggie yelled at Billy, "You better start liking me!" (An insinuation that if anyone was going to be fired, it would be Martin.)

Steinbrenner, who had watched the game on TV with millions of others, decided to get rid of Billy a couple of days later. But when the story was leaked by United Press International writer Milt Richman, the public reaction was overwhelmingly negative. George ultimately changed his mind, although he would fire and rehire Martin numerous times throughout the next few seasons.

In the 1977 World Series, all was forgiven, as Jackson earned the nickname "Mr. October" with his dramatic display of power against the Dodgers. After homering in Game 4 and Game 5, Reggie hit a two-run shot on the first pitch he saw from Burt Hooton in the fourth inning of Game 6. In the fifth, with a man on, Jackson again hammered the first pitch from Elias Sosa for a homer to put the Yankees up, 7–3. With fans chanting his name in the eighth, he connected with Charlie Hough's first offering, driving it 475 feet. Including his Game 5 blast, he had homered in four consecutive swings of the bat. The Yankees clinched the Series in dramatic fashion that night.

Before coming to New York, Jackson had bragged that a candy bar would be named after him. In 1978, Wayne Candies made good on the slugger's boast, marketing chocolate-covered disks with peanuts and caramel known as "Reggie!" bars. Catfish Hunter famously joked, "When you open a 'Reggie!' bar, it tells you how good it is."

In 1978, the Yankees made another important roster move when they added future Hall of Famer Rich Gossage to the mix. In an era when closers were often required to go more than an inning at a time, Gossage won 124 games and picked up 310 saves. "What these guys do today is easy compared to what we did," he said many years later. "It takes three guys to do what I did." The high-strung reliever spent portions of seven seasons in New York, leading the league twice in saves. Adding to the clubhouse drama, he got into a scuffle with teammate Cliff Johnson in 1979.

Turmoil between Billy and Reggie resurfaced in 1978, as the two clashed again during a July game against the Royals. The Yankees were mired in fourth place at the time, sitting 13 games behind the Red Sox. As Jackson came to bat in the bottom of the 10th with a runner on base, Martin flashed the bunt sign. Jackson's first attempt went foul, and Billy promptly ordered him to swing away. Inexplicably, Reggie tried bunting again—twice. He ended up popping out. Martin was livid, smashing things in his office and demanding that Jackson be suspended. Steinbrenner backed him up for once, and the Yankees won the next several games with Reggie out of the lineup.

Not long after the incident, Martin found out from White Sox owner Bill Veeck that Steinbrenner had been negotiating behind the scenes to arrange a trade of managers. Obviously upset, Martin spewed venom to reporters about Reggie and George. "They deserve each other," Martin said. "One's a born liar and the other's convicted." Steinbrenner dispatched Yankees president Al Rosen to fire Billy, but Martin beat him to the punch, resigning during a tearful press conference in Kansas City.

Under Bob Lemon, the Yankees turned their season around. For four straight days in September, the Bombers handed Boston a humiliating series of defeats at Fenway Park, moving into a first-place tie. (The series came to be known as the "Boston Massacre.") The Yankees built a three-and-a-half-game lead at one point, but the Red Sox went on a tear, winning 12 of their last 14 games. At the close of play on October 1, the two teams remained deadlocked atop the AL East. A one-game playoff in Boston pitted hurler Ron Guidry against Mike Torrez. The Sox were leading, 2–0, when light-hitting shortstop Bucky Dent lifted a three-run homer into the left-field screen. It was only his fifth home run of the season. The Yanks held on for a 5–4 win.

In the World Series, the Dodgers threatened to make quick work of the Yankees, taking the first two games by a combined score of 15–8. But the Bombers came storming back to win four in a row. The Series is best remembered for a controversial play in Game 4. Trailing 3–1 in the sixth, the Yankees had Munson on second base and Jackson at first when Lou Piniella hit a sinking liner toward Bill Russell at short. The ball glanced off of Russell's glove and dropped to the ground. Munson hesitated, believing Piniella's drive would be caught, and Russell—who could easily have tagged the Yankees catcher—opted to step on second to force Jackson and then throw to first to complete the double play. It was a bad decision. Seeing Munson on his way to third, Jackson froze about 20 feet between first and second, and stuck his hip out, redirecting Russell's throw into right field. The Yankees scored their second run of the inning. Dodger skipper Tom Lasorda argued strenuously for an interference call, but the play was allowed to stand. The Yankees tied the game in the bottom of the eighth and won it in the 10th. The Dodgers lost momentum, losing the final two games of the Series by a 19–4 margin.

After a disappointing fourth-place finish in 1979, the Yankees returned to the ALCS the following year. The Royals had their revenge, sweeping the series. In 1981, it was the Dodgers' turn to make up for past failures, eliminating the Yankees in yet another World Series rematch. The season was not without its share of drama, as Jackson and Nettles got into a fight at a party celebrating the clinching of the AL pennant. After a verbal altercation, Jackson knocked Nettles's beer out of his hand, and Nettles punched Reggie in the mouth. Both players tried to downplay the incident afterward. Reggie did not return for another season in the Bronx. The Yanks remained absent from the postseason until 1995.

The Yankee clubhouse was a simmering cauldron of combustible egos in the latter half of the 1970s. Writer Peter Golenbock collaborated with two former Yankees to create tell-all books about their experiences in New York during that era. *The Bronx Zoo*—Sparky Lyle's account—was released in 1979. *Balls*—written from Graig Nettles's perspective—followed a few years later. Anxious to get his own story out there, Reggie Jackson worked with Mike Lupica to produce an autobiography. More than two decades later, the drama still resonated with fans as an eight-part miniseries entitled *The Bronx Is Burning* debuted on ESPN. Based on a best-selling book by Jonathan Mahler, the show recounts the tale of the 1977 championship season, which was played amidst the backdrop of the infamous "Son of Sam" killings. It was watched by millions and received mostly positive reviews.

To date, three members of the 1970s championship squads have been inducted into the Hall of Fame (Jackson, Hunter, and Gossage). Numerous others have received their fair share of attention throughout the years. Both Nettles and Lyle have been recognized for their on-field excellence. Munson remains a highly respected figure in New York, and the colorful Martin has never been forgotten—although his name sometimes surfaces as a punch line. Steinbrenner, while viewed as a sinister figure by many, has made an ineffaceable mark on the sport. Other members of the lively 1970s crew are mentioned less and less as time goes by.

WILLIE RANDOLPH, SECOND BASE

Randolph donated 13 years of valuable service to the Yankees and remains one of the longest-tenured second basemen in club history. In an era of glaring disharmony, he was reliable, quiet, and consistent. Born in Holly Hill, South Carolina, Randolph attended high school in Brooklyn, New York. He was selected in the seventh round of the 1972 amateur draft by the Pirates and got his call to the majors in 1975. He entered 30 games and managed a meager .164 average before the Yankees obtained him in a trade prior to the 1976 slate.

With an immediate opening at second base, the Bombers offered Randolph a full-time job. He didn't disappoint, hitting .267 and getting named to the All-Star Team. Five more All-Star selections would follow.

Randolph was a stellar defensive player during his 18 years in the majors, leading the league in putouts and assists once apiece. He paced the loop in double plays twice, while finishing among the top five in fielding percentage six times. Unfortunately, Gold Glove Awards were dominated by Frank White and Lou Whitaker during Randolph's prime, and he was shut out.

The soft-spoken second baseman carried his own weight offensively, often hitting in the second slot. From 1977–1987, he posted a batting average of .270 or better 10 times. He had an excellent feel for the strike zone, drawing more than 1,200 walks during his career. He led the league in that category during the 1980 slate with 119. On the base paths, he had ample speed, stealing 30 or more bags on four occasions. He finished with double-digit totals for 12 straight seasons.

Randolph played in three World Series with the Yankees, enjoying his finest Fall Classic in 1981, against the Dodgers, when he compiled a stellar .464 on-base percentage. In Game 1 of the 1977 Series, he scored three of four New York runs, and his sixth-inning homer off of Hall of Famer Don Sutton tied the game at two apiece.

With turmoil constantly swirling around him, Randolph rarely fueled the fire. But in 1981, trouble finally caught up with him. In August of that year, he was fined for skipping an off-day workout ordered by an irate George Steinbrenner. Instead, Randolph kept a long-standing appointment to greet 1,000 youngsters for the New Jersey Mental Health Association. He was fined $500—the maximum penalty allowed by the Major League Baseball Players Association. Although Willie rarely mouthed off, he told the Associated Press, "This thing is so petty to me. George always talks about promoting the Yanks, and that's what I was doing. I didn't get paid, and the money went to charity." George quickly forgave his star second baseman, later naming him cocaptain of the Yankees.

Willie wore four different uniforms after 1988. In 1991, he joined the Brewers and experienced an offensive revival, recording a career-best .327 batting average. He finished his playing days with the Mets in 1992. A long career as a coach and manager followed.

In 2006, Randolph guided the Mets to a National League Division Series sweep of the Dodgers. The National League Championship Series went seven games that year, but the Mets ultimately ended up on the short end. Randolph was fired in June 2008, after the club got off to a 34–35 start.

ED FIGUEROA, PITCHER

Figueroa had four great seasons in the majors, spending three of them with the Yankees. Born in Ciales, Puerto Rico, the right-hander started playing ball at the age of nine. During his childhood, his Little League team won a national championship, and his Babe Ruth squad got to play in a World Series. Signed by the Mets in 1966, Figueroa kicked around the minors until the Angels gave him a permanent roster spot during the 1975 campaign. Pitching alongside Nolan Ryan, he collected 16 wins and posted a 2.91 ERA—fifth best in the league. That December, he was traded, along with Mickey Rivers, to the Yanks in exchange for speedy slugger Bobby Bonds. While Bonds had a handful of good seasons left in him, the Yankees got the better end of the deal.

Figueroa was not an overpowering pitcher. He had a decent sinking fastball and an assortment of breaking pitches. He kept the ball around the plate most of the time, using the corners to his advantage. From 1976–1978, he was one of the Yankees' most durable hurlers, finishing nearly 38 percent of his starts and averaging 18 wins per year. His finest season came in 1978, when he won 20 games and accrued an attractive ERA of 2.99. He was the first Puerto Rican pitcher to reach the 20-win threshold.

With a somewhat heavy workload, Figueroa was never terribly effective when the postseason rolled around. He coughed up 26 earned runs in 31 1/3 innings of work. His worst World Series start came against the Dodgers in Game 1 of the 1978 affair. He never made it out of the second inning, allowing five hits and three runs. The bullpen wasn't much better that day, as LA tacked on eight more runs off of three different relievers.

Figueroa was reportedly miffed when Billy Martin passed him over in the 1977 World Series. The hurler had suffered nerve damage in his right index finger that season, and Martin didn't feel he had fully recovered. "Figgy" was not overly fond of Martin and asked to be traded numerous times before the volatile skipper's 1978 resignation. "He treated me like dirt," Figueroa griped. "He has told people I'm gutless and cannot pitch under pressure."

Due to an awkward delivery that had him throwing across his body, Figueroa experienced serious arm problems in 1979. After posting a 7–16 record between 1979–1981, he was finished in the majors. In 1989 and 1990, he played in the Senior Professional Baseball Association and fared poorly. He also pitched for multiple teams in the Puerto Rico Winter Baseball League. Off the diamond, he owned a trucking company and two restaurants at different times. He served as a pitching coach for the Puerto Rican national team in 2003 and has appeared at numerous Yankees Old-Timers' Games.

CHRIS CHAMBLISS, FIRST BASE

Born in Dayton, Ohio, Chambliss's father was a U.S. Navy chaplain, and his family moved often. He ended up in Oceanside, California, where he caught the attention of Reds scouts while playing high school ball. He turned down two contract offers in 1967 and 1968, enrolling at UCLA instead. Drafted again by the Indians in 1970, he finally signed a professional contract. In 1971, he captured Rookie of the Year honors with a .275 batting average and 48 RBIs in 111 games.

Chambliss spent three full seasons in Cleveland and was off to a .328 start at the plate in 1974, when the Yankees acquired him in a trade involving seven players. He finished the season at .255 but placed among the league leaders in multiple defensive categories. Chambliss was an outstanding first baseman, leading the league in putouts, assists, double plays, and fielding percentage once apiece. He won a Gold Glove in 1978.

Chambliss exuded a quiet confidence, especially when it came to the offensive side of the game. "I never worry about my hitting," he told a reporter one day. "I've always been able to hit." He spent most of his career at the heart of the batting order, typically occupying the fifth slot. A line-drive hitter with some power, he fashioned a respectable .285 average with runners on base. He was especially dangerous with the bases loaded, compiling a .346 average in that scenario. Between

1976–1978, Chambliss was a major RBI producer for the Yankees, gathering no fewer than 90 per season.

In Game 5 of the 1976 ALCS, Chambliss delivered one of the most iconic homers in playoff history. The game had been delayed several times by unruly fans who were throwing firecrackers and garbage onto the field. Chambliss stepped to the plate leading off the bottom of the ninth with the game tied at six. In the on-deck circle, Sandy Alomar said nervously to the Yankees batboy, "He's got to hit one out because, if he doesn't, I'm on deck." Facing reliever Mark Littell of the Royals, Chambliss drilled his 11th hit of the Series on the first pitch he saw. It sailed over the right-field wall as pandemonium ensued. The big first-sacker motored around the bases, dodging jubilant fans like a football running back. He had tucked his helmet under his arm so no one would steal it. With people surrounding home plate, he wasn't sure if he had completed the circuit. Escorted by police, he returned to the field a bit later, only to find that the plate had been stolen. He touched the area where it had been.

Chambliss was a productive hitter for the Yanks in the postseason, hitting .308 with 12 runs, eight extra-base hits, and 15 RBIs in 27 games. The Bombers won five of the six October showdowns he appeared in. Chambliss maintained a positive attitude despite the drama that often surrounded him. "If you're not having fun in baseball, then you miss the point of everything," he once said.

In 1980, Chambliss traded in his pinstripes for a Braves uniform. He remained a regular in Atlanta until 1985, when he lost his starting first-base job to Bob Horner. Before then, he had prompted the following lines from a beat writer: "In the major league world of slumps and surges, breakdowns and comebacks, Chris Chambliss stands as a remarkable bastion of dutiful consistency." During his last season in Atlanta, he hit .311 in 97 games. Out of the majors in 1987, he served as Yankees hitting coach the following year. He later spent seven seasons as a minor-league manager and also coached for the Cardinals, Reds, and Mariners. He had a second stint as a Yankees coach during the club's glory years of 1996–2000.

MICKEY RIVERS, CENTER FIELD

Rivers is among the most colorful Yankees characters in history. Like Casey Stengel before him, he could leave audiences completely bewildered with his utterances. Quick-witted and carefree, he created an arsenal of amusing anecdotes throughout the years.

Born in Florida, Rivers attended Miami-Dade College—the same school that sent teammate Bucky Dent to the majors. Unusual incidents abounded during Rivers's college days. Minutes before the start of a game one afternoon, he was found in full uniform sleeping under a tree outside the ballpark. On another occasion, he bounded over the outfield fence during a game in progress to avoid some people he had seen entering the stadium.

After being sought by numerous teams, Rivers finally signed with the Braves. Traded to the Angels in a deal that included future Hall of Famer Hoyt Wilhelm, the speedy outfielder hit .320 in an August 1970 call-up. He shuffled between the majors and minors until 1974, which was his first season as a full-time player. Appearing in 118 games, he hit .285 and led the league with 11 triples. He added 13 more triples the following year (tops in the AL), while also leading the league with 70 stolen bases. Rivers's speed earned him the nickname "Mick the Quick," but it wasn't readily apparent. He hobbled to the batter's box as if he were nursing sore hamstrings. When he swung through a pitch or fouled one off, he twirled his bat like a baton.

Between 1976–1978, Rivers hit .301 at the top of the Yankees order, stealing 90 bases and averaging 84 runs per year. In six postseason series, he hit .308 and reached base more than 40 times. During the regular season, Rivers never drew more than 43 bases on balls—unusual for a leadoff man.

Rivers added significantly to the lore of the "Bronx Zoo." During a marital dispute in the Yankee Stadium parking lot one day, Mickey's wife deliberately ran her Mercedes into the Cadillac he had driven to the ballpark. Rivers's verbal clashes with Reggie Jackson became instant classics. When the arrogant slugger boasted that he had an IQ of 160 one day, Mickey quipped, "Out of what—a thousand?" On another occasion, Jackson told Rivers in front of reporters that he needed to read and write more often. Without missing a beat, Mickey shot back, "You need to stop reading and writing and start hitting." In one of the most infamous exchanges between the two, Rivers commented about Reggie's name (Reginald Martinez Jackson), saying, "No wonder you're all mixed up. You got a white man's first name, a Spanish man's middle name, and a black man's last name." (Multiple versions of this quote exist.)

In July 1979, Rivers was traded to the Rangers. He stayed with them through the 1984 slate. In his last major-league season, he hit an even .300 in 102 games. Rivers played in the Senior Professional Baseball Association in 1989. He has appeared at numerous Yankees Old-Timers' Games since then.

BUCKY DENT, SHORTSTOP

Dent played alongside Mickey Rivers at Miami-Dade College and was a first-round pick in the 1970 amateur draft. He spent portions of four seasons in the minors before getting a call to Chicago. He was starting shortstop for the White Sox for three full seasons until the Yanks acquired him in a trade for Oscar Gamble and LaMarr Hoyt before the 1977 campaign.

During his five-plus seasons in the Bronx, Dent didn't set the world on fire with his offense, but he hit respectably out of the bottom half of the order. His best regular-season showing came in 1980, when he assembled a .262 average with 33 extra-base hits and 52 RBIs. He received the second of three career All-Star selections that year. An unselfish hitter, he placed among the top 10 in sacrifice hits five times during his big-league tenure.

Dent was known more for his defense, topping the circuit in fielding percentage on three occasions. He paced the loop in putouts and assists once apiece and double plays twice. While the statistic was not often calibrated in his time, he posted the highest range factor among AL shortstops in 1975.

Dent is best remembered for his postseason heroics in 1978. His three-run homer in the one-game division playoff at Fenway Park earned him the epithet "Bucky Effin' Dent" among disgruntled Boston fans. More than 30 years later, he was still being razzed by the Beantown faithful. "Some people told me that I ruined their lives," Dent told a *Daily News* reporter in 2010. "But they are never rude or disrespectful. It's all in good fun." Dent's famous Fenway homer would likely have been caught in at least half a dozen other ballparks, but the "Green Monster" stands just 310 feet from home plate. His bloop homer did not hold up as the game-winner, but it erased a 2–0 Boston lead and shifted momentum in favor of the Yankees. In the Fall Classic that year, Dent hit .417 with seven RBIs, capturing Series MVP honors.

The handsome Dent was especially popular with female fans. In 1979, he posed for a pinup poster. That same year, he appeared in the TV movie *Dallas Cowboys Cheerleaders*, portraying the love interest of actress Jane Seymour's character. In September 1983, Dent donned a swimsuit for a *Playgirl* pictorial.

When Dent struggled at the plate in 1982, the Yankees traded him to Texas for Lee Mazzilli. Released by the Rangers in April 1984, he signed with the Yankees, only to be released after an unsuccessful minor-league stint. The Royals took a chance on him that year but ended up letting him go in October. He never played another major-league game after 1984.

The subsequent years were busy ones, as Dent managed in the Yankees minor-league system at Fort Lauderdale and Columbus. He took over for Dallas Green in New York during the 1989 campaign and held the job until June of the following year, when the fickle Steinbrenner replaced him with Stump Merrill. Dent coached for the Rangers and Cardinals between 1991–2001. His son Cody entered the Washington Nationals' minor-league system in 2013.

RON GUIDRY, PITCHER

Born in Louisiana, Guidry had Cajun roots. He was nicknamed "Gator" on account of those ties. He attended the University of Southwestern Louisiana and majored in architecture. After signing with the Yankees in 1971, he began a slow ascent to the majors.

By the time he joined the Yankees staff as a full-timer in 1977, his fastball was being clocked regularly at 95 miles per hour. He had also mastered a sharp-breaking slider, which he learned from watching reliever Sparky Lyle. Tall and lean, at 5-foot-11, 161 pounds, he was deceptively tough. "He fools you," said infielder Jim Spencer. "He's a lot stronger than people think. You wouldn't expect him to pop the ball like that."

Without Guidry in the rotation, it seems doubtful that the Yankees would have won back-to-back World Series titles in 1977 and 1978. In both seasons, he was the most productive starter on the club, posting a 41–10 regular-season record with a 2.21 ERA. In 1978, he turned in one of the most remarkable seasons ever by a left-hander, leading the league in wins (25), winning percentage (.893), ERA (1.74), and shutouts (9). He finished second in strikeouts (missing a Triple Crown by just 13 Ks) and was a unanimous choice for the Cy Young Award.

A remarkable postseason performer, Guidry started five games against the Dodgers and Royals in 1977 and 1978, going 4–0 with a 2.17 ERA. In Game 4 of the 1977 World Series, he tossed a complete-game four-hitter with seven strikeouts. Had he not hung a pitch to Davey Lopes in the third inning with a runner aboard, he might have ended up with a shutout. Instead, he wound up on the winning end of a 4–2 decision. Guidry was on the mound for New York during the one-game division playoff against the Red Sox in 1978. On short rest, he turned in 6 1/3 innings of solid work, picking up his 25th win of the season.

Guidry spent his entire 14-year career with the Yankees, retiring with 170 wins. His lifetime total is remarkable considering that he had only two pitches in his arsenal throughout most of his career. A five-time Gold Glove recipient, he finished among the top 10 in Cy Young voting six times. In 1978, he struck out 18 batters in a game, breaking a franchise record and setting an AL record for left-handers. Another crowning achievement, he completed an "immaculate inning" in August 1984, striking out Carlton Fisk, Tom Paciorek, and Greg Luzinski of the White Sox on nine pitches.

Beset by arm trouble in 1981, Guidry bounced back with a pair of 20-win efforts in 1983 and 1985. He hurt his arm again the following season and never fully recovered. He was finished in the majors after 1988.

In his prime, Guidry's pitches intimidated opponents and teammates alike. Reserve catcher Fran Healy commented, "I never wore a mask to warm up a pitcher until Guidry came along." Guidry was a cool customer on the mound. "I treat all games as they come," he once said. "I don't feel any pressure because I don't worry about a game until I get to the ballpark."

Guidry served as Yankees pitching coach in 2006 and 2007. He developed a lasting friendship with Yankees icon Yogi Berra that became the subject of a book by Harvey Araton entitled *Driving Mr. Yogi: Yogi Berra, Ron Guidry, and Baseball's Greatest Gift*.

LOU PINIELLA, OUTFIELD/DESIGNATED HITTER

Nowadays, Piniella is known more for his career as a manager, which spanned 23 seasons and included stints with the Yankees, Reds, Mariners, Devil Rays, and Cubs. In 1990, he led the Reds to their first world championship since the 1976 sweep of the Yankees. In 2001, he guided Seattle to a record-setting 116 victories. He was named Manager of the Year three times before he retired.

Long before his days at the helm, Piniella was a highly competent outfielder. Born and raised in Tampa, Florida, he was signed as an amateur free agent by the Indians in 1962. Months later, he was drafted by the Senators. He would eventually be shipped to Baltimore to complete a trade for Buster Narum—a pitcher of little note. Piniella's travels continued as he worked his way up the minor-league ladder. The O's traded him to the Indians in 1966, and the Seattle Pilots plucked him from Cleveland in October 1968. By then, he had gotten two cups of coffee in the majors, entering a total of 10 games.

In 1969, Piniella's career began properly when the Pilots dished him to the Royals. He captured Rookie of the Year honors with a .282 average, 38 extra-base hits, and 68 RBIs. He would remain a regular in Kansas City for five full seasons, topping the .300 mark at the plate twice.

Traded to the Yankees before the 1974 slate, Piniella began an 11-year run in the Bronx. Although his quick temper always seemed to land him in trouble on the field, he was approachable and accommodating off the diamond. He won awards in two consecutive seasons as a fan/media favorite. When he came to bat, the Yankee faithful would often chant his name: "L-o-u-u-u!!!" Anyone unfamiliar with the routine might have thought he was being booed.

Ever the hothead, Piniella did nothing to ease the bad blood between the Red Sox and Yankees in 1976. On a cool May night in New York, he plowed into Carlton Fisk at home plate. "He stuck his elbow in my eye and ran me over," Fisk complained to reporters after the game. Piniella didn't deny the charge. "I ran into Fisk pretty good," he said. "We ended up punching a little behind home plate. And then it escalated to a different level." Both benches emptied, and several side bouts took place. Graig Nettles ended up body-slamming Sox hurler Bill Lee, who was seriously injured in the scrape. "I just think that everybody was on edge then. If somebody got knocked down or something, it could become a brawl right away," said Don Zimmer, who managed the Red Sox in the second half that year. During the course of his career, Piniella punished the Red Sox with his bat, hitting .310 in 145 games with nine homers and 51 ribbies.

Piniella was among the most successful Yankees hitters during the postseason, scoring 15 runs and driving in 19 in 10 October showdowns. His finest performance came in the 1981 World Series against the Dodgers, when he hit .438. Despite his efforts, the Yankees dropped the Series in six games.

Defensively, Piniella was equipped with a strong arm and good instincts. He finished with double-digit totals for outfield assists three times. While Bucky Dent's homer often takes center stage, "Sweet Lou" (as he was known to many) may have single-handedly saved the division playoff game in 1978, with his glove. The Yanks were clinging to a 5-4 lead in the ninth. With one out and Rick Burleson on first, Jerry Remy hit a hard liner into a sun-drenched right field. Piniella froze Burleson when he pretended to be poised to make the catch. In reality, he had temporarily lost sight of the ball. At the last second, he made a lunging stab with his glove, snagging the ball on a hop to keep the runners at first and second base. Jim Rice and Carl Yastrzemski flied out, ending the game. Had Burleson moved to third on Remy's single, he would likely have scored to tie the game since Rice's fly was deep enough to move him up a base.

Piniella saw increasingly less playing time in the early 1980s. He ended his career in 1984, hitting .302 in 29 games. He served as Yankees GM briefly and also managed the club for portions of three seasons before moving on. During his long managerial career, he was ejected from more than 60 games. He is currently among the top 20 of all time in that category.

GRAIG NETTLES, THIRD BASE

In the 1976 and 1977 World Series, Nettles put on a defensive display that has rarely been equaled in the event's long and storied history. He joked about it afterward: "People recognize me wherever I go, where it used to be just New York. I guess people who aren't even baseball fans watch the World Series. I was driving down the freeway in Los Angeles over the winter and some guy pulled up next to me and gave me the finger."

Nettles began his career with the Twins, splitting time between the outfield and third base. He was traded after the 1969 slate in a deal that sent top-shelf hurler Luis Tiant to Minnesota. Nettles spent three seasons as the Indians regular third baseman. His power became evident as he averaged 24 home runs per year. He also proved what he could do defensively, setting single-season records for assists and double plays. In 1971, he led the league in nearly every defensive category, although the Gold Glove went to Brooks Robinson.

In 1973, Nettles was traded to New York, where he became a major star. "Some kids dream of joining the circus, others of becoming Major League Baseball players. I have been doubly blessed," Nettles later joked. "As a member of the New York Yankees, I have gotten to do both." While he never hit for high averages, he gathered 250 homers for the Yankees and retired with a lifetime total of 390. With the Yankees from 1973–1978, he drove-in 80 or more runs on five occasions. He earned MVP consideration three times in that span.

When Robinson retired after the 1976 slate, the Gold Glove was up for grabs. Nettles won it twice. He currently ranks second among third basemen in assists and double plays. In his book *The Bronx Zoo*, which was released in 1979, reliever Sparky Lyle offers glowing praise for Nettles's defensive prowess: "[He's] the best third baseman in baseball and will be for the next five years. Without him at third base, my years on the Yankees would not have been half as productive as they were."

Nettles could be a bit ornery at times. In the 1977 ALCS, he got into a fight with George Brett at third base after Brett delivered a RBI triple. Both benches emptied. Nettles later tangled with Reggie Jackson at a party celebrating the clinching of the 1981 pennant. Jackson didn't return for another season in the Bronx, while Nettles remained through the 1983 slate.

In 1984, Nettles helped the Padres to their first pennant in franchise history. He spent four more seasons in the majors after that with three different clubs. Following his retirement, he played in the Senior Professional Baseball Association. He tried his hand at managing for one season but failed, leading the Bakersfield Blaze of the California League to a last-place finish. The Baseball-Reference claims that Nettles is the all-time leader in home runs among players with last names that begin with the letter "N."

THURMAN MUNSON, CATCHER

Asked about Munson's moodiness, Sparky Lyle once quipped, "Nah. Thurman's not moody. When you're moody, you're nice sometimes. Thurman's just mean." Named captain of the Yankees in 1976, Munson was aware of his prickly nature. "Maybe they made me captain because I've been here so long. But if I'm supposed to lead by example, then I'll be a terrible captain," he said.

Munson could have gone to several colleges on a football scholarship. He ended up at Kent State, and after being chosen in the first round by the Yankees, he dropped out of school. He played in less than 100 minor-league games before earning a promotion to the Bronx. In 1970, he captured Rookie of the Year honors.

Munson appeared in various positions in the batting order during the early part of his career. In 1975, he was finally inserted in the heart of the order. His offensive production increased dramatically. From 1975–1977, he reached the century mark in RBIs each year. Although he peaked in several offensive categories during the 1975 campaign, he was named MVP the following year. His postseason performance was exceptional, as he gathered 19 hits in nine games for a .475 batting average. He remained a major October producer throughout his career, hitting .357 with 12 extra-base hits and 22 RBIs in six postseason series.

Short and stout at 5-foot-11, 190-plus pounds, he was referred to by various unflattering nicknames. "Tugboat," the "Squatty Body," and the "Walrus" were all used at various points in time. In spite of his appearance, he captured three consecutive Gold Glove Awards from 1973–1975.

Munson was suffering from knee and back problems by the late 1970s, which forced the Yankees to try him out at first base. Famous game footage of the Yankees captain shows him writhing in pain behind the plate and limping off the field. Munson was a proud man and fierce competitor, earning respect from both teammates and opponents.

In 1979, the seven-time All-Star purchased a Cessna Citation private jet. He had been flying since the previous spring. On August 2, 1979, he was practicing takeoff and landing procedures when his plane came up short of the runway. Two of Munson's friends tried to pull him from his seat but ended up having to flee for their own safety. The official cause of death was smoke inhalation; however, he also suffered a broken neck and spinal trauma.

SPARKY LYLE, RELIEF PITCHER

Lyle was born and raised in Pennsylvania. Since his high school didn't have a baseball team, he developed his skills in American Legion ball, striking out 31 batters in 14 innings during one tournament. He was granted a tryout with the Pirates but failed. The Orioles signed him in 1964, but lost him to the Red Sox in the November draft. Groomed as a reliever, Lyle crossed paths with the great Ted Williams, who told him he would never make it to the majors unless he established a slider. "I threw the pitch so that it would come straight at the batter until it got to within three feet of the plate. Then it would break down," said Lyle. "When Ted Williams told you to try something, you tried it."

Traded to the Yankees in 1972, Lyle had his best season to that point, assembling a 9–5 record, while leading the league in closing appearances and saves. He finished the season with a handsome 1.92 ERA.

Lyle once posed the question, "Why pitch in nine innings when you can get just as famous pitching two?" Between 1973–1978, he made quite a name for himself, finishing among the league leaders in saves almost every year. During his Cy Young season of 1977, he posted a 2.17 ERA in 60 closing appearances. He won 13 games and saved 26— numbers that may seem ordinary by today's standards but were exceptional in an era when relievers routinely worked more than an inning at a time. Lyle continued his success in the postseason with two wins over the Royals and another victory over the Dodgers in the World Series. Combined with his October stats from the previous year, he allowed just two earned runs in 17 2/3 innings of relief.

The Yankees made a curious move in the offseason, acquiring Goose Gossage from the Pirates. As the 1978 season progressed, manager Bob Lemon—Billy Martin's replacement—leaned heavily toward Gossage as a bullpen choice. Lyle made just eight appearances in September and October to Gossage's 11. In the postseason, Goose closed five games, while Sparky made just one appearance—a mop-up assignment in Game 2. The jilted Lyle feuded with Steinbrenner throughout the year.

With more time on his hands, Lyle began to record his observations. In 1979, the reliever's tell-all book, *The Bronx Zoo*, was released. In it, he exposes all sorts of sordid clubhouse details without apology. "The best soap opera was the team we had here in the 1970s," says pitcher Ron Guidry. "[People] couldn't wait to pick up the papers the next morning to see what was going on." Plenty of inquisitive fans picked up Lyle's book as it spent 29 weeks on the *New York Times* best-seller list.

Graig Nettles famously quipped of the hurler's departure before the 1979 campaign, "[Lyle] went from Cy Young to sayonara." His lackluster performance in 1980 resulted in another trade to the Phillies that September. He was never terribly effective again, retiring in 1982, with 99 wins and 238 saves. He received only moderate support for the Hall of Fame from baseball writers, getting 13.1 percent of the vote in 1988.

In 1990, Lyle released a follow-up book with coauthor David Fisher. Entitled *The Year I Owned the Yankees: A Baseball Fantasy*, the work jokingly reflects on Steinbrenner's tenure as Yankees owner to that point. Lyle returned to the game as a manager for the Somerset Patriots of the Atlantic League in 1998. He remained at the helm for 15 seasons, vacating the job after the 2012 campaign.

GOOSE GOSSAGE, RELIEF PITCHER

Selected in the ninth round of the 1970 amateur draft, Gossage spent two years in the minors before earning a spot on the White Sox roster. He was mediocre in his first two seasons, warranting a demotion to the minors in 1974. The following year, he became Chicago's closer, proving his worth with a 1.84 ERA and a league-leading 26 saves. He made his first All-Star appearance that year.

In 1976, Paul Richards took over as manager in Chicago and inserted Gossage into the starting rotation. He had one of the most forgettable seasons of his career, remarking later on, "I don't know if I have the patience to be a starter. I almost went nuts waiting five days to pitch." Traded to the Pirates in 1977, Gossage's career took off. He won 11 games and tied his personal high for saves with 26. He also recorded a brilliant 1.62 ERA, while working 133 innings.

Gossage was so upset when the Pirates didn't resign him in 1977, he broke down and cried. Signed by New York, he got off to a rocky start and began hearing boos at Yankee Stadium. In those days, relievers were driven onto the field by bullpen cars. Center fielder Mickey Rivers once jokingly jumped onto the hood of the vehicle in a satirical attempt to prevent Gossage from entering a game. Goose did regain his form, leading the league with 27 saves. In the one-game divisional playoff against the Red Sox, he survived 2 2/3 shaky innings, preserving a one-run lead. He got a win in the ALCS and later the World Series.

Gossage remembered his reliever's role as being grueling. "We were abused," he said. "No one worried about our arms falling off." Gossage had a lively fastball in the high 90s and a menacing persona on the mound. Immensely confident in his ability to dispose of hitters, he once bragged, "I was brought into situations God couldn't get out of and I got out of them."

Gossage's years in the Bronx were not without their share of controversy. In 1979, he missed three months after a clubhouse fight with Cliff Johnson. He also bickered with Steinbrenner constantly. The Yankees had a no facial hair policy, and Gossage deliberately grew a Fu Manchu moustache to (in his own words) "tick off Steinbrenner." In 1982, he exploded at reporters, declaring, "All you guys with pens and tape recorders, you can turn them on and take it upstairs to the fat man because I'm sick of all this negative stuff." Still, he loved the thrill of being a Yankee, telling a *Baseball Digest* reporter, "It's hard to explain what the feeling is when you first put that Yankee uniform on. . . . There's no other place like Yankee Stadium."

Before the 1984 slate, Gossage signed with the Padres and helped them to a World Series berth. He hung around the majors past his 42nd birthday and defected to Japan's Pacific League briefly. He finished with 310 saves. In 2008, he was enshrined at Cooperstown. The Yankees dedicated a plaque to him in Monument Park during the 2014 campaign.

FAST FACT: George Steinbrenner was notoriously fickle. Between 1973–1990, he went through 19 managers, 15 pitching coaches, and 13 general managers. Billy Martin was one of the "Boss's" favorite targets, getting hired and fired a total of five times.

19

OAKLAND ATHLETICS

1988–1990

After Charlie Finley's fire sale of the late 1970s, the A's posted sub-.500 records for three straight years. The 1979 campaign was particularly dreadful, as Oakland accumulated 108 losses and finished 34 games behind the division champion California Angels. Dismissed from his duties in New York, Billy Martin took over the helm in 1980, and turned the team around. Four Athletics starters posted at least 14 wins on Martin's watch as the club placed second with a respectable 83–79 record.

During the strike-shortened 1981 slate, Oakland captured the American League West and swept the Royals in the American League Division Series, earning the right to play the Yankees for the pennant. Billy Martin would have liked nothing more than to show his former employer that he could be a winner outside the Bronx, but his group of overachievers proved to be no match for George Steinbrenner's personal All-Star Team. Six New York hurlers limited the A's to a collective .222 batting average as the Bombers swept the series by a combined score of 20–4.

Martin couldn't stop the A's from plummeting to fifth place the following year. George and Billy ironed out their differences before the 1983 campaign, and Martin returned to his former post in the Big Apple. Without him, the Athletics struggled to find their way for several seasons. The most valuable member of the club during those lean years was Rickey Henderson.

Stories about Henderson's narcissism have circulated widely—some verifiably true and others greatly exaggerated. They make for interesting reading either way. Henderson was known to stand naked in front of a full-length mirror before games repeating the mantra, "Rickey's the best." Asked about talking to himself one day, he responded, "I just remind myself of what I'm trying to do. I never answer myself, so how can I be talking to myself?" Henderson had a peculiar habit of referring to himself in the third person and persisted at times even when it created grammatical confusion. Late in his career, he allegedly left a message on the answering machine of Padres GM Kevin Towers that said, "This is Rickey calling on behalf of Rickey. Rickey wants to play ball." (He later denied that this was true.)

Other odd tales about Henderson abound. He once fell asleep on an ice pack and got frostbite on his foot, which kept him out of three games. After receiving his $1 million check from the A's, he framed it and hung it on his wall instead of cashing it. This created havoc with the A's accounting department until team representatives suggested he cash it and display a photocopy of it. After breaking Ty Cobb's record for runs scored with a homer, Henderson added drama to the moment by sliding into home. He may not have been the most humble man ever to don a uniform, but he was undoubtedly among the greatest leadoff hitters in baseball history.

Henderson griped about being underappreciated until his lifetime numbers could no longer be ignored. In regard to statistics that matter most for leadoff men, he ranks first all-time in stolen bases (1,406), first in runs scored (2,295), second in walks (2,190), and fourth in times on base (5,343). He defected to the Yankees in 1985, but returned in time to help the A's to consecutive World Series berths in 1989 and 1990.

Things began to turn around for Oakland in 1986 with the arrival of Jose Canseco and Mark McGwire. The Cuban-born Canseco had made his debut the previous year at the age of 20, hitting .302 in 29 games. In his first full season, he captured Rookie of the Year honors with 63 extra-base hits and 117 RBIs. The A's felt his presence dramatically, placing third in the West—their highest finish since 1981. McGwire didn't help the club much in 1986, hitting .189 as a late August call-up, but in the next few seasons, he and Canseco would form one of the most potent offensive tandems of the era.

The story didn't end well. The reputations of both men were irrevocably tarnished due to their involvement with steroids. Canseco ended up outing himself and more than a dozen other players in two sets of memoirs. McGwire admitted his indiscretions to broadcaster Bob Costas in a tearful 2010 interview. Neither has a legitimate shot at being inducted into the Hall of Fame at this juncture. But for six exciting seasons, Canseco and McGwire took the game to a whole new level, ushering in an era of rippling biceps and tape-measure homers. In the 1989 playoffs, Canseco hit a ball into the fifth deck of the SkyDome in Toronto—a 480-foot blast by some estimates. During his 16-year career, McGwire reportedly hit at least 10 homers that traveled even farther, including a 538-foot clout at the Kingdome in Seattle. That one came at the expense of Mariners legend Randy Johnson.

McGwire and Canseco combined for no fewer than 50 homers and 152 RBIs per year from 1987–1992, earning the colorful nickname the "Bash Brothers." Their prolific power numbers are more dramatically expressed in tabular form (see table 19.1).

In 1987, the A's strengthened their roster considerably with the acquisition of future Hall of Famer Dennis Eckersley. The hard-throwing right-hander had come up with a lame arm in 1986, and the Cubs practically gave him away the following spring, offering to pay a portion of his substantial salary. Before joining the A's, Eckersley had accumulated 151 victories in 12 seasons as a starter. Placing him on a trajectory to Cooperstown, manager Tony La Russa (a future Hall of Famer himself) assigned the aging hurler to the bullpen. Eckersley—or simply "Eck," as he was known throughout the majors—tied for the team lead

Table 19.1. Home Runs and RBIs by Mark McGwire and Jose Canseco (1987–1992)

	1987	1988	1989	1990	1991	1992
Mark McGwire	49	32	33	39	22	42
Jose Canseco	31	42	17	37	44	22

	1987	1988	1989	1990	1991	1992
Mark McGwire	118	99	95	108	75	104
Jose Canseco	113	124	57	101	122	72

in saves during his first year with Oakland. After that, he became the most dominant closer in the AL for a five-year span. Using a nasty slider–fastball combination and a slingshot delivery, Eckersley saved 320 regular-season games for the A's between 1987–1995. A spirited competitor, he became known for his emotional reactions when he performed his job well.

On the heels of a third-place finish in 1987, the A's shored up their slugging corps with the acquisition of veterans Don Baylor and Dave Parker. Used exclusively as a DH, the 39-year-old Baylor was a former AL MVP, with more than 300 homers and 1,200 RBIs on his resume. He had a knack for leaning into pitches, getting hit 267 times in his career—fourth on the all-time list. Parker was two years younger with remarkably similar lifetime numbers. A two-time batting champion and National League MVP during his days with the Pirates, he was still available for light duty in left field and at first base.

With a reliable group of pitchers anchoring the rotation (many of whom are discussed in great detail later in this chapter), the A's began the 1988 campaign in first place. Aside from a brief stretch in mid-April, they occupied that position all season long. They met the Red Sox in the American League Championship Series, cruising to a four-game sweep. Although the Athletics were heavily favored to beat the Dodgers in the World Series, they ran into a brick wall.

The tone was set in Game 1, when Kirk Gibson emerged as an unlikely October hero. Gibson had injured both of his legs during the National League Championship Series and was reportedly ill with a stomach virus. Unable to start, he watched a good portion of the game in the Dodgers clubhouse while undergoing physical therapy. With the Dodgers trailing 4–3 in the ninth, Gibson was summoned to pinch hit against Eckersley with two outs and a runner on base. Eckersley later admitted to being irritated because it took Gibson a long time to get ready to hit. "When you've got your foot on their throat, you just want to get it over with," he said. With a full count, Gibson anticipated a back-door slider. He guessed correctly, lifting it into the right-field seats for a walk-off homer. Broadcaster Don Drysdale's call was as follows: "This crowd will not stop! They can't believe the ending! And this time, Mighty Casey did *not* strike out!" Every year since then, Gibson has been featured in World Series highlight reels, pumping his fist and hobbling around the bases.

The A's never knew what hit them. Coming off a record-setting streak of consecutive scoreless innings, Dodgers ace Orel Hershiser was virtually unhittable in both of his starts. While the A's were able to salvage a 2–1 victory in the third meeting, the Dodgers hardly broke a sweat in the next two games, clinching the Series at Oakland.

The 1989 campaign started on a sour note. Canseco suffered a fractured wrist during spring training. While recuperating, he was stopped by Fort Lauderdale police and fined for driving at speeds in excess of 100 miles per hour. Although he would return in mid-July to smash 17 homers and gather 57 RBIs, the A's soldiered on without him. In June, they added Rickey Henderson to the mix. The so-called "Man of Steal" helped the club tremendously, compiling an on-base percentage of .425 and scoring 72 runs in 85 games. By season's end, the A's had left their closest competitors (the Royals) seven games behind. After taking down the Blue Jays in the ALCS, it was on to the World Series against the San Francisco Giants.

The 1989 Fall Classic is among the most memorable in history—not for the events that transpired on the field, but for the natural disaster that preceded Game 3. The cities of San Francisco and Oakland are situated on opposite sides of the San Francisco Bay and connected by the vast expanse of the San Francisco–Oakland Bay Bridge. Fittingly, the Series was being billed as the "Battle of the Bay." After the events of October 17, it would forever be known as the "Earthquake Series."

The Giants were led by effervescent manager Roger Craig, who popularized the rallying cry "Humm Baby!" Making their first Fall Classic appearance since 1962, Craig's troops hardly put up a fight as Oakland won the first two games by a collective 10–1 margin. The Giants were looking to get back on track at Candlestick Park, sending 12-game winner Don Robinson to the mound against Bob Welch, a veteran of five previous postseasons.

At 5:04 p.m., as many fans were still settling into their seats, tremors shook the stadium. Light towers swayed, and concrete fell from sections of the upper deck. Communication systems were knocked out, and the scoreboard malfunctioned. After the quake subsided less than a minute later, broadcaster Al Michaels remarked, "That's the greatest opening in the history of television, bar none."

As news of the disaster began trickling in, baseball became insignificant. The quake had registered 7.1 on the Richter scale, bringing down a section of the Bay Bridge and an elevated stretch of Interstate 880. More than 60 people were killed and thousands injured. Game 3 of the Series would not be played until 12 days later—the longest delay in the history of the Fall Classic. The A's galloped to a 13–7 win and completed a sweep the following day with a 9–6 victory. The Series drew the lowest TV ratings of any October showcase that preceded it.

The A's picked up right where they left off the following year, winning 103 games and capturing their third straight AL pennant. The "Bash Brothers" stayed relatively healthy all season long, putting up one of their best combined efforts. Rickey Henderson hit .325 and stole 65 bases, moving ever closer to Lou Brock's coveted record. Meanwhile, the A's got some mileage out of 35-year-old veteran Willie Randolph, who was acquired from the Dodgers in a May trade. The former Yankees captain provided steady offense and was a reliable double-play partner at second base.

The 1990 Cincinnati Reds were a pitching-rich club that featured the "Nasty Boys"—a trio of flame-throwing relievers who combined for 44 saves, while sporting a major attitude. Rob Dibble, the most colorful of the three, landed himself in hot water multiple times during his career for angry outbursts on the diamond. The other two "Nasty Boys," Norm Charlton and Randy Myers, made more than 120 appearances between them during the 1990 slate. With Hall of Fame shortstop Barry Larkin anchoring the infield, the Reds eliminated the Pirates in the NLCS and wreaked havoc on the A's in the World Series.

The Athletics' big boppers, McGwire and Canseco, combined for just four hits in 26 at-bats. Canseco's only hit was a solo homer in Game 2 that tied the score at two apiece. The Reds ended up winning anyway in 10 innings, 5–4. Rickey Henderson was a ray of light for Oakland, hitting .333 with three walks and three steals, but the rest of the A's regulars lost their way, collectively hitting .207 in the four-game sweep.

Controversial Reds owner Marge Schott sullied the affair by slighting her star outfielder, Eric Davis. Davis was injured in Game 4 while diving for a ball. He suffered an injury to his kidney that required surgery. Upon his release from an Oakland hospital, he was forced to pay his own way home. He was less than happy about it, commenting to reporters that Schott treated her dog "Schotzie" (the owner's self-appointed team mascot) better than him. Schott would go on to make numerous racially charged statements that eventually forced her out of baseball.

The A's returned to the ALCS in 1992, losing to the Blue Jays in six games. Canseco was traded to Texas in late August of that year. The following season, McGwire suffered a serious injury that limited him to 27 games. Henderson departed for Toronto in a July transaction. Oakland slumped in the standings for the remainder of the decade. Unable to turn the team around, Hall of Fame skipper Tony La Russa took over the Cardinals in 1996. McGwire joined him in 1997. The "Bashing" years were officially over.

As is so often the case with the most dominant clubs in baseball history, the high-profile players soak up most of the glory. While the accomplishments of Canseco and McGwire are forever tainted, their names are inextricably linked to the success of the Oakland A's in the late 1980s and early 1990s. Dennis Eckersley was the first member of the squad to make it to the Hall of Fame in 2004. Rickey Henderson followed five years later. La Russa, enshrined in 2014, as a manager, was yet another Oakland alumnus to receive his just deserts. Others were not so lucky. Some have been forgotten. It's amazing what a couple of decades will do.

RICKEY HENDERSON, LEFT FIELD

At 5-foot-10, 180 pounds, Henderson had legs like tree trunks. He stood at the plate in a crouched position with his front leg extended. He had ample power at the top of the order, clubbing 81 leadoff homers during his career—a major-league record. He sang his own praises to teammates and the press, annoying some, while amusing others. In later years, he explained that what people perceived as "cockiness" was just his competitive spirit. Whatever the case, he was among the biggest showboats the game has ever seen—egotistical, brash, and highly entertaining.

Born in Chicago, Henderson grew up in Oakland. He was drafted in the fourth round by the A's in 1976, hitting .300 at each minor-league stop. During his first full season in the majors, he became the third modern-era player to steal 100 bases. He would exceed the lifetime mark for steals in 1991. After swiping base number 939 against the

Yankees, he uprooted the bag and held it aloft. The game was interrupted so he could address the cheering Oakland crowd. Showing off
his characteristic arrogance, he said, "Lou Brock was a great basesteal-
er, but today I am the greatest of all time." During his 25 years in the
majors, Henderson led the league in that category on a dozen occasions.
He defied the passage of time, swiping 66 bags at the age of 39.

The self-promoting outfielder made many stops during his career,
including four separate stints with Oakland. He went wherever the
money and the action were. Before the 1985 slate, he accepted a significant pay increase to join the Yankees. The team never finished higher
than second during his tenure, and his frequent squabbles with management did not endear him to fans in the Bronx. He returned to
Oakland in time for three consecutive pennants. With the A's out of
contention in the middle of the 1993 slate, he griped about wanting a
trade and got one. He hit just .170 in two postseason series with the
Blue Jays that year. As usual, the A's took him back. By the time he
retired, Henderson had spent time with nine different clubs.

In 2000, Henderson lost his swing and hung around too long trying
to get it back. He was 44 years old when he appeared in his last big-
league game. He spent portions of three seasons in independent ball,
trying to catch the eye of major-league reps. No one would take him.
With numerous statistical records to his credit, he received an overwhelming 94.8 percent of the Cooperstown vote in 2009.

JOSE CANSECO, OUTFIELD

Canseco is known to many as a cheater and a tattletale. His 2005 tell-all
book *Juiced* fingers a gaggle of high-profile players for steroid use and
was not well received by critics, peers, or fans. But in his second book,
Vindicated, the former slugger got to say "I told you so," as many of the
players he accused of wrongdoing ended up being brought up on PED
charges.

Born in La Habana, Cuba, Canseco left the country when he and his
identical twin Ozzie were in their infancy. He grew up in Miami, where
he caught the eye of scouts. In 1985, he hit .333 with 36 homers and
127 RBIs at the minor-league level. He was called to Oakland and fared
well in 29 games.

In his first full season, Canseco grabbed Rookie of the Year honors with great power numbers, although he hit just .240 and struck out 175 times. His best all-around season came in 1988, when he led the AL in homers (42), RBIs (124), and slugging percentage (.569), while hitting .307. He also became the 40/40 man in the majors, with exactly 40 steals. He was a unanimous choice for MVP. Injured the following year, he put up strong numbers in the second half. Injuries would be a common theme throughout his career, as he appeared in 150 or more games just five times in 17 seasons.

Canseco's regular-season success did not always carry over into October. In fact, two of the three World Series he appeared in with the A's were epic failures. Against the Dodgers in 1988, he went 1-for-19 at the plate, with five strikeouts. Facing the Reds in 1990, he had a 1-for-12 showing. He did maintain a productive home-run pace, slamming seven homers in 30 postseason games. When his bat went cold, he was of little use to the clubs he played for. A notoriously bad outfielder, he accidentally allowed a ball to bounce off his head and over the fence for a home run.

From 1992–2001, the often-injured Canseco played for seven different teams. He put up respectable numbers when healthy, particularly in 1998, when he cracked 46 homers with 107 RBIs for Toronto. He played in various independent leagues through the 2013 campaign in hopes of returning to the majors. He had his sights set on reaching the 500-homer mark but ultimately fell short, with 462.

Canseco's private life reads like a bad soap opera. In addition to numerous steroid infractions, he has been arrested for reckless driving, aggravated assault, and weapons violations. Divorced twice, he filed for bankruptcy in 2012. In 2014, he accidentally shot himself while cleaning his gun at his Las Vegas home, seriously injuring one of his fingers. He was eliminated from the primary Hall of Fame ballot in 2007, when he failed to get the minimum number of required votes.

MARK MCGWIRE, FIRST BASE

In 1998, McGwire told an Associated Press writer that he had taken androstenedione, an over-the-counter muscle enhancer that had already been banned by the National Football League. At the time, it was not prohibited by Major League Baseball and was not classified as an anabolic steroid. Nevertheless, McGwire was subpoenaed in 2005 to appear before a House Government Reform Committee. He refused to answer questions under oath, remarking, "If a player answers 'no,' he simply will not be believed. If he answers 'yes,' he risks public scorn and endless government investigations." Five years later, McGwire finally admitted to using steroids periodically during the course of a full decade. "It was foolish and it was a mistake," he said tearfully. "I truly apologize. Looking back, I wish I had never played in the steroids era." His confession rendered 12 All-Star selections, 3 Silver Slugger Awards, and 583 lifetime home runs virtually meaningless. In 2016, he made his tenth appearance on the Hall of Fame ballot, drawing just 12.3 percent of the vote.

For most of his career, McGwire was a highly regarded first baseman with tremendous power. Marlins coach Rich Donnelly remembered McGwire hitting a popup one day that sailed so high, every player on the field called for it. Before reaching the majors, McGwire had made a name for himself with the University of Southern California. He also played for Team USA in the Pan American Games and the 1984 Olympics.

McGwire set a rookie record in 1987 with 49 homers. During the A's stretch of dominance from 1988–1990, he averaged 35 long balls and 101 RBIs per year. The season was perhaps the best of his career in Oakland, as he won a Gold Glove, in addition to finishing among the league leaders in multiple slugging categories. His 110 walks were tops in the AL that year.

Like his fellow "Bash Brother," McGwire was not a reliable postseason performer. In three World Series with the A's, he managed an anemic .188 batting average with a single homer. Plagued by injuries throughout his career, he appeared in just 178 games between 1993–1995. During his last full season with Oakland, he launched 52 circuit blasts, while accruing a healthy .467 on-base percentage. Both were league highs.

Traded to the Cardinals in July 1997, "Big Mac" (as he came to be known) reached the peak of his slugging capacity, averaging one homer per eight at-bats in a three-year span. In 1998, he broke Roger Maris's single-season record for long balls, finishing the year with 70. He was challenged throughout the season by Cubs right fielder Sammy Sosa, who eclipsed Maris's mark with 66 clouts of his own.

After a 65-homer effort in 1999, McGwire's career wound down rapidly. He still went deep at a remarkable rate, but lacking the skills to be an everyday first baseman, he sat out more than 60 games in 2000 and 2001. He retired after the latter campaign. In portions of 16 seasons in the majors, McGwire averaged one homer per 10.6 at-bats. By way of comparison, Babe Ruth averaged one per every 11.8 at-bats. For Hank Aaron, that mark was 16.3, and for Barry Bonds it was 12.9.

Since his retirement, McGwire has served as a hitting coach for the Cardinals and Dodgers.

DENNIS ECKERSLEY, RELIEF PITCHER

Before moving to the bullpen, Eckersley had been a successful starting pitcher. He was resistant to the idea of working in relief. "I sure wasn't happy about it," he recalled. "I thought it was a demotion, and I hoped it would only be a part-time assignment. When I first came up, the bullpen was pretty much where they put guys who couldn't start."

During the course of his career, Eckersley developed funny names for his pitches, including "cheese," "hair," "cookie," and "yakker." He ascended to the majors with Cleveland in 1975. In his first start, he shut out the A's. His finest single-game accomplishment as a starter came in 1977, when he tossed a no-hitter against the Angels. The following year, he was traded to Boston, where he posted a 20–8 record and followed with a 17–10 effort. He began to lose his effectiveness, and the fans turned against him. Upon leaving a bar one night, he found his tires slashed.

Suffering from arm trouble in 1984, Eckersley was traded to the Cubs. He developed a drinking problem and sought help for it. By the time he was dealt to the A's before the 1987 slate for three minor-league players, he was clean and sober. A switch to the bullpen preserved his spiraling career. From 1988–1997, he averaged 37 saves per year. He would end up as the only pitcher in history with at least 100 saves and 100 complete games.

In the postseason, Eckersley had a few rough patches—particularly the walk-off homer he surrendered to Kirk Gibson in Game 1 of the

1988 World Series. He has been credited with coining the phrase "walk-off" but also referred to such gut-wrenching moments as those as "bridge jobs" (meaning it made a pitcher want to jump off a bridge afterward). Eckersley was always more efficient in the ALCS, posting a lifetime ERA of 1.50 in 14 appearances.

Eckersley's AL MVP Award in 1992 was questioned by some. Statistician Bill James writes, "Meaning no disrespect to Eckersley, who deserves to be a Hall of Famer, I just think giving a pitcher who faces 309 batters in a season an MVP Award is preposterous." Maybe so, but it's a distinction that "Eck" was immensely proud of. The right-handed fireman finished his career with the Red Sox and later moved on to a broadcasting career with the club. He was elected to the Hall of Fame in 2004.

DAVE HENDERSON, CENTER FIELD

Known for his broad grin and high-spirited play, Henderson (no relation to Rickey) was once referred to as the "Fans' Man" by *Sports Illustrated*. He was the Mariners' first-ever pick in the 1977 draft. A star linebacker in high school, he considered pursuing a college football career before receiving a lucrative signing bonus from Seattle. He had several decent slugging seasons in the minors before getting promoted in 1981. It took him a few years to realize his full potential as a major leaguer.

At 6-foot-2, 210 pounds, Henderson was somewhat slow afoot and lacked range in the outfield. When he got his hands on the ball, he was good with a glove and equipped with a strong arm. Still, his primary value to the clubs he played for was offensive.

Traded to Boston during the 1986 slate, he delivered one of the biggest homers in Red Sox history. With the Sox facing elimination in Game 5 of the ALCS against California, Henderson smashed a two-run ninth-inning homer off of Donnie Moore that ultimately sent the game into extra innings. In the 11th frame, he drove in the winning run with a sacrifice fly. The Sox ended up eliminating the Angels in seven games. In the World Series that year, Henderson continued his clutch hitting with a .400 batting average.

After getting off to a slow start in 1987, Henderson was traded to the Giants. He ended up in Oakland, where he entered his prime years. From 1988–1991, he averaged 80 RBIs and 21 homers per year. Although he slumped in the 1990 World Series, he hit over .300 in the 1988 and 1989 Fall Classics with seven runs scored. In Oakland's 13–7 Game 3 blowout against San Francisco in 1989, he was 3-for-4 at the plate with a pair of homers and four RBIs. In Game 4 of the 1988 Fall Classic against LA, he went 4-for-5. Teammate Dave Stewart once said of Henderson, "He is the definition of a money ballplayer. He gets the job done."

Henderson became extremely popular in Oakland for his enthusiasm on the field. Asked about the permasmile he always wore, he commented, "Playing professional baseball brings a smile to my face. I don't need much else to have a good time." In 1992, his numbers began to drop off sharply. He was traded to Kansas City in 1994, and played his last season there. He moved on to a career as a Mariners broadcaster beginning in 1998. He died of a heart attack in December 2015.

DAVE STEWART, PITCHER

In high school, Stewart was an All-American baseball and football star. He was drafted by the Dodgers in 1975, while attending Merritt Junior College. Originally selected as a catcher, he was converted to a pitcher in the minors. The Dodgers brought him up briefly in 1978, and again during the strike-shortened 1981 slate. He pitched well during the 1981 regular season but was a bust in the National League Division Series that year. In the opener against the Astros, he gave up a game-winning homer. In Game 2, he was charged with another loss. He bounced back in the World Series against the Yankees, finishing two games and yielding no runs.

Between 1983–1986, Stewart played for four different teams, serving a variety of roles. In January 1985, he generated negative headlines when he was arrested in a seedy section of LA engaging in sex with a prostitute. He pleaded no contest to a misdemeanor charge, ending up with a fine and a probation term. What was especially embarrassing about the arrest was the fact that the "woman" Stewart was with ended up being a transvestite. His troubles continued that year as he struggled on the mound for the Rangers, assembling an 0–6 record before a trade sent him to Philadelphia. He underwent surgery in the offseason for bone chips in his elbow.

Released by the Phillies in May 1986, Stewart landed a roster spot with his hometown A's. He had grown up a Giants fan and was a childhood friend of Rickey Henderson, who he described as being the "life of the party." Beginning in 1987, Stewart experienced a career revival. Using a highly effective forkball, he won 20 games in four straight seasons. He led the league in complete games twice in that span.

Stewart was among the Athletics' most reliable October performers. He was named MVP of the 1990 ALCS and 1989 World Series. While wearing an Oakland uniform, he assembled an 8–3 postseason record with a cumulative 2.22 ERA. In 1990, he added a no-hitter to his resume, beating the Blue Jays, 5–0, at the SkyDome in Toronto. He struck out 12 batters that day. Batterymate Pat Borders once said of the big right-hander, "He has total concentration and control. 'Stew' is even tougher in the big games."

In 1991, Stewart led the league in starts for the fourth consecutive season but wound up with an 11–11 record and cumbersome 5.18 ERA. He was a little better in 1992, but still failed to return to his old form. He signed with Toronto before the 1993 campaign and spent two seasons with the Blue Jays before making a final curtain call with Oakland in 1995.

Finished as a player, he worked for several organizations as a pitching coach and front-office executive. In 2014, the Arizona Diamondbacks announced that they were hiring him to fill the position of general manager.

BOB WELCH, PITCHER

Welch's career can be divided into two parts: the 10 seasons he spent with the Dodgers and the latter years, during which he played for the A's. Both legs of his major-league tour were highly successful and filled with multiple postseason opportunities.

Born in Detroit, Welch attended Eastern Michigan University and was drafted in the first round by the Dodgers in 1977. He spent portions of two seasons in the minors before getting the call to LA in 1978.

He entered 23 games—13 as a starter—and won seven of 11 decisions, while posting a highly efficient 2.02 ERA. He gained national attention in the World Series that year, making a ninth-inning appearance in Game 2 against the Yankees. With one out and two runners on, he retired Thurman Munson on a fly to right field and Reggie Jackson on a strikeout after an extended at-bat. The Dodgers won, 4–3. He would appear in seven postseason series with LA, enjoying varying degrees of success. In the 1981 World Series, he joined the "infinity club," allowing two runs and three hits without retiring a single batter.

Welch's 1979 campaign was derailed by a sore arm. During the offseason, he sought treatment for alcohol abuse and began a successful recovery. His book *Five O'Clock Comes Early: A Young Man's Battle with Alcoholism* was published in 1982. He invested quite a bit of time promoting the book and encouraging other alcoholics to seek help for the affliction.

On the mound, Welch became known for his dramatic leg kick. He had an above-average fastball, a decent breaking ball, and a split-finger pitch. He later added a forkball to his repertoire. Between 1980–1987, he won no fewer than 14 regular-season games for the Dodgers five times. He was included in a three-team trade before the 1988 slate that landed him in Oakland. Most insiders agree that he became a more complete pitcher with the A's.

"If you understand what pitching is all about," said manager Tony La Russa, "you'll know some pitchers pitch and other pitchers throw. Bob's a pitcher." Former Dodgers coach Ron Perranoski described Welch as a "little impetuous and hyper" when he was with LA. He saw a dramatic change in Welch after he departed for Oakland. "He's older and more mature," Perranoski said. "He's developed all his pitches."

Welch averaged 18 wins for the A's in a four-year stretch. He reached the summit of his career in 1990, when he led the league with 27 wins and a .818 winning percentage. He beat out Roger Clemens in a tight Cy Young race that year, earning 15 first-place votes to the "Rocket's" eight.

In six October showdowns with the A's, Welch notched a 2–0 record with a slightly inflated ERA. He ended up with a lifetime postseason mark of 3–3. Faced with personal problems and injuries after the 1990 campaign, Welch pitched his last game in relief during the 1994 slate—the day before players went on strike. He retired at the age of 37.

After his playing days, he coached for the Diamondbacks and Ogden Raptors, a Dodgers affiliate. He died of a heart attack in June 2014. "I wish there were more teammates like him throughout the game today. He was a fierce competitor," said Mark McGwire. "I don't think there was a player who knew him who didn't care for him."

CARNEY LANSFORD, THIRD BASE

Born in San Jose, California, Lansford played in the 1969 Little League World Series. His brothers Jody and Phil were both professional players, but Carney was undoubtedly the most talented of the brood. Lansford bypassed college to play in the Angels farm system. He was a third-round selection in 1975. He had a breakout year in 1977, hitting .332 for El Paso of the Texas League. By 1978, he was wearing an Angels uniform.

In his major-league debut, Lansford hit .294 and finished third in Rookie of the Year voting behind Lou Whitaker and Paul Molitor. It was an excellent rookie class, as Alan Trammell finished fourth. Lansford had three good seasons in California before getting traded to Boston. He prospered in the cozy confines of Fenway Park, capturing the 1981 batting title with a .336 average. He would break the .300 mark at the plate five times during his career, including a run of four straight seasons from 1981–1984.

Lansford was used most often as a second-slot hitter, but he also appeared fifth in the order fairly regularly. He was remarkably efficient with men on base, accruing a .294 batting average in that scenario in portions of 15 seasons. He had excellent speed on the bases, swiping 20 or more bags five times, with a high of 37 in 1989. Despite his positive attributes, he received just one All-Star selection.

In addition to wielding a productive bat, Lansford was an excellent fielder. He led AL third basemen in putouts twice and fielding percentage four times. Still, he never won a Gold Glove. Describing Lansford's style, one columnist remarked that he played "with his chin 10 inches off the ground at third base on every pitch. He chased every pop foul with vigor whether his team was eight runs up or eight runs down. His uniform was always the dirtiest." Hall of Fame skipper Sparky Anderson once referred to Lansford as a "coal miner" for his tireless work ethic. "When I leave the park, I can always feel that I've given my best effort," Lansford told reporters one day. "I've never said that I could have played harder, and I never want to say it."

Despite injuries in 1983 and 1985, he was one of Oakland's most productive players for several years. His best regular-season effort with the A's came in 1989, when he matched his career-best .336 batting mark. He missed a second batting crown by four percentage points as Kirby Puckett trumped him with a .339 mark that year.

Lansford handled the pressures of October rather well, fashioning a .305 career postseason average. He did his best work in 1989 and 1990, logging a total of six multihit games. At one point, he compiled an 11-game hitting streak in postseason play. He retired with 39 hits and 10 walks in eight series.

Lansford suffered a serious knee injury before the 1991 campaign and appeared in just five games. He hit .262 the following year and then retired. He moved on to a long career as a major-league coach, working for the A's, Cardinals, Giants, Blue Jays, and Rockies. Lansford had a small role in the 1994 film *Angels in the Outfield*.

FAST FACT: The term white elephant *refers to a burdensome possession that creates more trouble than it is worth. In the early days of the AL, Giants manager John McGraw used the expression in reference to the A's. The original owners found McGraw's remark so amusing they adopted a white elephant as a team logo. The emblem has appeared on the sleeves of A's jerseys periodically throughout the years—particularly in the championship season of 1989.*

20

TORONTO BLUE JAYS

1991–1993

In January 1976, Giants owner Horace Stoneham made plans to sell the club to a syndicate fronted by Don McDougall—president of the Labatt Brewing Company. The team would have played its games in Exhibition Stadium and carried the moniker the Toronto Giants. The deal ended up being squelched by a U.S. court. Shortly afterward, real estate magnate Robert Lurie purchased the club with the intent to keep it in San Francisco. As city officials in Toronto continued to push for a major-league franchise, their efforts were rewarded.

The Blue Jays received their moniker after a "name the team" contest produced more than 4,000 entries. They joined the American League in 1977, and were the laughingstock of the Eastern Division for nearly a decade. During their first three years of existence, they piled up more than 100 losses per season. They would wallow in the basement until 1982, when future Hall of Fame skipper Bobby Cox led the team to a sixth-place showing—their highest finish to that point.

Cox remained with the club through the 1985 campaign, and improvement was evident each year on his watch. During his last season in Toronto, he guided the team to a playoff berth. The Jays met the Royals in the American League Championship Series and jumped out to a 3–1 advantage before dropping three straight games. Cox was named AL Manager of the Year. When the Braves offered him the GM position in

1986, he readily accepted it. He would return to the dugout in Atlanta during the 1990 slate, continuing his path to Cooperstown.

With big shoes to fill, the Jays hired Jimy Williams as manager—a veteran of six minor-league seasons. Although the club would finish well above the .500 mark in each of Williams's first three campaigns, the AL East was a notoriously tough division, and the Blue Jays failed to make the playoffs. By 1989, patience among team executives was wearing thin. When the club got off to a sluggish 12–24 start, Williams was fired and replaced with Cito Gaston.

Gaston had spent 11 seasons in the majors as an outfielder for three different teams. A lifetime .256 hitter, he reached the high point of his playing career in 1970, slamming 29 homers and driving in 93 runs for the Padres. He earned his only All-Star selection that season. He retired as a player after the 1980 slate and served as Blue Jays hitting coach from 1982–1989. When he took the reins from Williams, he had no managerial experience. While the move was expected to be temporary, Gaston guided the Jays to a division title, ensuring himself a job in 1990.

In later years, Gaston would be criticized as a "push button" and "do-nothing" manager. In all fairness to his detractors, he did have an extremely laid-back approach. One sportswriter classified Gaston as a "yup-and-nope guy." Regardless of those denunciations, he presided over the most fruitful period in franchise history. The A's made quick work of the Jays in the 1989 ALCS, eliminating them in five games. Acknowledged for his efforts, Gaston finished second in Manager of the Year voting.

By 1990, the Toronto clubhouse was packed with talented veterans and budding stars. The Blue Jays were especially strong in the pitching department, with 32-year-old right-hander Dave Stieb anchoring the pitching corps, along with future Yankees standouts Jimmy Key and David Wells. Most of the heavy hitting was done by corner infielders Fred McGriff and Kelly Gruber, with left fielder George Bell contributing significantly as well. Despite their efforts, the Jays finished two games behind the Red Sox.

In 1991, the roster was strengthened considerably with the addition of future Hall of Famer Roberto Alomar. Alomar had spent three seasons with the Padres, showing off his superior defensive skills and considerable speed on the base paths. In 1990, he earned the first of 12 consecutive All-Star selections. Ten Gold Gloves and four Silver Slug-

ger Awards would follow. The Puerto Rican–born second baseman became a bona fide superstar in Toronto, placing among the top 10 in
MVP voting each year from 1991–1993.

Although the Jays encountered stiff resistance from the Red Sox in
1991, they spent a total of 157 days in first place and eventually finished
seven games ahead of their New England rivals. In late August, Gaston
left the club to undergo back surgery. In his absence, former World
Series hero Gene Tenace took over, steering the team to a 19–14 finish.
In the ALCS, Toronto proved to be no match for Kirby Puckett and the
Twins. The Blue Jays won just one of five meetings, losing the last three
by a combined score of 20–10. Minnesota ended up with a World Series
victory over the Braves in one of the most hotly contested showdowns in
history.

Reinforcing an already solid lineup, the Jays added 40-year-old slugger Dave Winfield to the mix in 1992. With 12 All-Star selections and
seven Gold Gloves to his credit, the seasoned veteran was approaching
two career milestones—500 doubles and 3,000 hits. Proving he was still
a viable offensive presence, he hit .290 with 62 extra-base hits and 108
RBIs.

The pitching staff was bolstered considerably in 1992, with the addition of Tigers great Jack Morris. The gruff, ultracompetitive right-hander had won 15 or more games 10 times while playing in Detroit. He
enjoyed his last successful season north of the border, posting a career-
high 21 wins. At the end of August, the Jays orchestrated another blockbuster deal, wrestling David Cone away from the Mets. Coming off of
his second career All-Star selection, Cone carried a 13–7 record. His
five shutouts were tops in the National League. After two rocky outings
with Toronto, he turned in five consecutive quality starts, finishing the
season with 17 wins and a 2.81 ERA.

With a star-studded roster, the Jays clinched the AL East and rolled
to a win over the A's in the ALCS. The World Series pitted them against
the powerful Braves. The showdown was not as hotly contested as the
previous year's matchup in terms of games played, but four of the six
meetings were decided by a single run. The final game meandered into
the 11th inning, when Winfield delivered a two-run double to break a
2–2 tie. The Braves did not go quietly, answering with a score of their
own before stranding the tying run at third base. The Blue Jays had
finally come full circle—from pathetic losers to world champions.

The first team outside the United States to capture a World Series title, the Jays were invited to the White House for a celebration. President George H. W. Bush told reporters he wished Carla Hills, who had negotiated the North American Free Trade Agreement, were present. "I thought she understood that our free trade agreement with Canada did not mean that the United States would trade away the world championship," Bush jibed.

Toronto suffered a major loss when Winfield signed with the Twins before the 1993 slate. But team executives imported another future Hall of Famer to take his place. In Milwaukee, it was considered one of the worst front-office moves in history. Brewers GM Sal Bando waited too long to offer Paul Molitor arbitration and defended his actions by contending that the aging superstar was "only a DH." Maybe so, but Molitor led the AL with 211 hits and finished second in the batting race to teammate John Olerud, posting a .332 average.

With the departure of David Cone in December 1992, the Jays acquired former Oakland ace Dave Stewart, who was on the downside of his career at the age of 36. He proved to be a highly useful retread, winning 12 regular-season games and earning MVP honors in the ALCS. Toronto executives pulled off another epic late-season trade in 1993, when they lured Rickey Henderson into the fold. Unfortunately, he put up numbers unbecoming of his vast talents, hitting .215 in 44 regular-season games.

After the Blue Jays had claimed their third straight division title and polished off the White Sox in the ALCS, Molitor put on quite a show in the World Series. He gathered 12 hits (six for extra bases) in 24 at-bats, extending his postseason hitting streak to eight games. In the finale, he went 3-for-5 at the plate with a homer and a pair of RBIs. Outfielder Joe Carter stole Molitor's thunder, blasting a three-run walk-off homer that clinched the Series for the Jays. While Carter ended up in World Series highlight reels forever after, it was Molitor who walked away with MVP honors. "When I chose to come to Toronto, it was a difficult choice," Molitor said after the game. "Once it was made, I had the vision of Toronto becoming the first team in 15 years to win back-to-back titles." (The Yankees were the last team to turn the trick in 1977 and 1978.)

A three-peat was not in the cards. The Blue Jays slid to third place in the standings in 1994, posting a 55–60 record before a strike wiped out the rest of the season. By the time play resumed in 1995, Toronto had retooled the pitching staff. Several position players had moved on as well, and the new-look Blue Jays tumbled even further in the standings. Gaston absorbed a lion's share of the blame for the team's downfall. He ended up losing his job near the end of the 1997 slate.

Although the Blue Jays carried numerous prominent stars on their roster during their three-year run of dominance in the early 1990s, the club owed much of its success to a core group of average Joes who peaked at about the same time. To be certain, there were many players on the 1992 and 1993 championship squads whose names were never of the household variety. Nevertheless, they helped the Jays evolve into the greatest Canadian team in baseball history.

ROBERTO ALOMAR, SECOND BASE

Baseball was a popular pastime among members of the Alomar family. Roberto's father Sandy forged a 15-year major-league career with several clubs. His brother Sandy Jr. was a six-time All-Star for the Indians. As a kid playing sandlot ball, Roberto told his father, "I'm going to be better than you." As it turned out, he was the best of the bunch.

Elected to Cooperstown in 2011, it wasn't an easy road to the Hall for Alomar. More than a decade earlier, he had gotten into a heated argument with umpire John Hirschbeck and spit in the arbiter's face. Although Alomar publicly apologized and became friendly with Hirschbeck, the ugly incident haunted him for years. Overlooked for the Hall in his first year of eligibility, he received a resounding 90 percent of the vote on his second try. Before then, Hirschbeck had personally rallied for Alomar's induction.

Born and raised in Puerto Rico, Alomar started his minor-league career at the age of 17. He joined his brother on the Las Vegas Stars of the Pacific Coast League in 1988, and after appearing in just nine games, he was called to the majors by the Padres. He had a solid rookie effort and was determined to become an even better player. During his first spring training, he grabbed the attention of coaches and peers by hauling a bag of baseballs off to an unoccupied diamond and hitting off a tee for an hour He once proclaimed, "I'm not only a player of the game—I'm a student of the game. I watch and learn."

By the time he joined the Blue Jays in 1991, Alomar was one of the best second basemen in the majors. He had great range and a strong arm. He was adept at going deep in the hole, sliding to snare grounders and springing back up to release rifle throws to first base. His 10 Gold Gloves are more than any player at his position.

A lifetime .300 hitter, he combined speed and moderate power. Alomar slammed 40 or more doubles on four occasions and finished in double digits for homers nine times. Between 1988–2001, he stole 30 or more bases in eight seasons. By the time he retired, he was among a select group of players with 500 doubles, 200 homers, and 400 stolen bases.

In his 17-year career, Alomar helped three different clubs reach the postseason. His only two World Series appearances were with the Blue Jays. He gathered 12 hits in six games during the 1993 Fall Classic and forged a .347 lifetime batting average in Series play.

Alomar's downfall came quickly. After hitting .336 in 2001 with Cleveland, he was traded to the Mets. He put up mediocre numbers in the next three seasons and left the game behind. Of all the compliments Alomar received, perhaps the most ringing endorsement came from Hall of Famer Orlando Cepeda. "I've seen a lot of second basemen in my time," Cepeda said, continuing,

> My father played in the Negro Leagues and the Caribbean Winter League, where I saw Cool Papa Bell play. I played with Julian Javier, Felix Millan, and Cookie Rojas. I played against Bill Mazeroski and Joe Morgan. In All-Star Games, I saw Rod Carew. As good as they were, none of them were as good as Roberto Alomar. I've been watching baseball for 60 years, and he's the best I've ever seen.

JOHN OLERUD, FIRST BASE

In his first year of eligibility, Olerud captured less than 1 percent of the vote for Cooperstown and was eliminated from the ballot. The argument among baseball writers was that Olerud's career was above average but not spectacular. Examining his numbers, it's difficult to disagree with that assessment. But there were flashes of brilliance along the way. One of his most productive spans occurred while he was playing for Toronto.

Olerud's father was a minor-league catcher who never made it to the majors. Olerud was a major-league first baseman who never played in the minors. Olerud suffered a brain aneurysm while attending Washington State University. The experience prompted him to wear a protective batting helmet at his defensive post. It became his trademark. Selected in the third round of the 1989 June draft, Olerud was ranked by *Baseball America* as the nation's number-three prospect. The Toronto brass felt that he was ready for prime time and promoted him instantly. His acquisition resulted in a trade that shipped Fred McGriff and Tony Fernandez to San Diego in exchange for Joe Carter and Roberto Alomar.

Olerud had far less power than McGriff but was always a reliable fielder, capturing three Gold Gloves. He currently ranks among the top 40 in putouts and the top 20 in assists, as well as fielding percentage.

With no minor-league conditioning, Olerud got off to a slow start in Toronto. The Blue Jays wanted him to swing for the fences, and his batting average suffered at times. In 1991, he generated 17 long balls and 30 doubles but hit a career-low .256. His struggles continued in the ALCS against the Twins that year, as he managed just three hits in 19 at-bats.

In 1992, Olerud boosted his batting average to .284, while producing similar power numbers. He had a great postseason, hitting .333 in 10 games. In Game 4 of the ALCS versus Oakland, his 4-for-5 performance helped lift the Jays to a 7–6 win in 11 innings.

Out of nowhere, the tall, lanky first sacker (6-foot-5, 205 pounds) became one of the most formidable hitters in baseball during the 1993 slate. He captured a batting title with a .363 average. He flirted with the .400 mark into early August, prompting many comparisons to Ted Williams's storied 1941 campaign and George Brett's valiant run in 1980. On his way to the batting crown, Olerud clubbed a league-leading 54 doubles and topped the circuit with a robust .473 on-base percentage. He stayed hot in the postseason as opposing hurlers attempted to pitch around him. He collected 12 hits and eight walks in 11 games, scoring 10 runs while driving in five.

Olerud was not colorful or flashy, and he rarely generated clever quotes for the press. In fact, one source referred to him as "laconic." There was immense pressure on Olerud to repeat his 1993 performance, and when his numbers came crashing back to earth the next several seasons, the Blue Jays traded him to the Mets. He had one more exceptional season, hitting .354 in 1998. He finished second in the batting race that year to Larry Walker of the Rockies, who benefited tremendously from hitter-friendly Coors Field. Olerud topped the .300 mark with Seattle in 2001 and 2002. He maintained a keen batting eye throughout his career, drawing 80 or more walks nine times and retiring with a commendable .398 on-base percentage—among the top marks of all time. "I've always been the type of hitter who likes to get deep in the count—see all of the pitcher's pitches," he once said. "I felt like if I got a chance to see all his pitches, then I would be able to react better." A lifetime .295 hitter, his reactions were more than adequate. He retired after the 2005 campaign.

TOM HENKE, PITCHER

When Henke was a kid, he spent most evenings pitching to his father, who reportedly caught his offerings while sitting on a five-gallon bucket. When the hurler got a bit older, he was encouraged by friends to have his abilities professionally evaluated. It was a life-changing event, as he ended up getting drafted by multiple teams before finally signing with Texas.

Henke began his pro career with the Gulf Coast Rangers in 1980. Various managers at the minor-league level experimented with Henke as a starter. During the 1981 slate, he was groomed as a closer. He owed a large measure of his success to his sizable repertoire. Henke employed a fastball, splitter, slider, and forkball—ample tools for a reliever.

After two cups of coffee with Texas in 1982 and 1983, he spent a large chunk of the 1984 slate in the majors. He got hit fairly hard, prompting a transfer to Toronto in 1985. He started the season in Syracuse, picking up 18 saves, while compiling a 0.88 ERA. Joining the Jays on July 29, he yielded no runs in his first 11 appearances. He finished the season with 13 saves.

During the next seven seasons, Henke was one of the Jays' most reliable firemen, finishing among the top 10 in saves six times, while compiling a cumulative 2.51 ERA. He appeared in five postseason series for Toronto and pitched commendably, emerging with five saves, two wins, and a 1.83 ERA. Beginning in the 1989 ALCS, the right-hander was charged with no runs in 11 consecutive appearances. Unfortunately, his final October outing was a blown save against the Braves in Game 6 of the 1992 World Series. Staked to a 2–1 lead in the bottom of the ninth at Atlanta, he yielded the tying run on a single to Otis Nixon. The Jays rallied in the 11th to clinch the Series.

At 6-foot-5, Henke towered over many opponents and was even more imposing standing on the mound. He carried the nickname the "Terminator" in his prime. Still, he was not always brimming with self-confidence. He admitted to being uncomfortable in big cities during his career—particularly New York. Bob Elliott, dean of Canadian sports-writers, said of Henke, "He could come off as a golly-gee type, but he was usually the smartest guy in the room."

In 1993, Henke joined the Rangers (again) for a slight salary in-crease. He picked up a career-high 40 saves, although his ERA rose more than 60 points. He struggled to regain his form the following year and ended up with the Cardinals in 1995. Henke had a spectacular season, collecting 36 saves, while recording a 1.82 ERA in 52 appearances. He retired at the top of his game. He was only the seventh hurler in history to reach 300 saves. He was later inducted into the Canadian Baseball Hall of Fame.

DEVON WHITE, CENTER FIELD

There have only been a handful of Jamaican-born players in the majors. Aside from Chili Davis, Devon White was the most successful. White's family moved to the United States during his formative years, and he attended high school in New York City. Enamored with his talents, the Angels signed him in the 1981 draft. White played for several minor-league clubs between 1981–1986, finally earning a full-time slot with the Angels during the 1987 slate. He had a great season all around, collecting 62 extra-base hits and 87 RBIs, while stealing 32 bases. In a rookie class that included Mark McGwire and Mike Greenwell, White finished fifth in Rookie of the Year voting.

White demonstrated a pleasing combination of speed and power. He hit at least 17 homers on five occasions during his career, while gathering 30 or more doubles the same number of times. He finished with double-digit stolen base totals each season from 1987–1999. He swiped 30 or more bags in five of those campaigns. He was proficient in his attempts, retiring with a lifetime success rate of 77.9 percent (placing him in the top 100 of all time).

White did not get along with Angels manager Doug Rader, and when he slumped to .217 at the plate in 1990, he was shipped to Toronto. His production increased dramatically—especially in 1991, when he accumulated a career-high 67 extra-base hits. He also captured the third of seven Gold Glove Awards. White was an outstanding defensive center fielder with wide range. He moved with long, loping strides, leading the AL in putouts three times and range factor twice. "There are going to be plays that I make look routine that aren't routine," he once said self-assuredly. Teammate Al Leiter echoed that confidence, stating, "He'll get the balls that most guys don't. He's always there."

Unintimidated by postseason pressure, White was among Toronto's most productive postseason hitters between 1991–1993. Appearing at the top of the order, he gathered 41 hits and 12 walks in 29 games. His finest postseason series came against the White Sox in the 1993 ALCS. He hit at a robust .444 clip with a slugging percentage of .667.

White was granted free agency after the 1995 campaign. The Jays had begun to slide in the standings by then. Looking for a change of scenery, he signed with the Marlins. He would make three more stops, in Arizona, Los Angeles, and Milwaukee, before calling it quits at the age of 38. In 2001, his last campaign, he hit .277 and stole 18 bases in 21 attempts. According to Baseball-Reference, White made more than $36 million during his major-league career. One can assume he is rather comfortable in his retirement.

JOE CARTER, OUTFIELD

Carter played in the 1979 Continental Cup, helping the United States capture a Bronze Medal. He attended Wichita State University and was the Cubs' first-round pick in the 1981 draft. Chicago executives clearly saw his potential, sending him to Cleveland in a trade that brought top-shelf hurler Rick Sutcliffe to the Windy City.

Carter spent six seasons with the Tribe, becoming one of the most productive sluggers in the AL. In 1986, he hit .302 and drove in a league-leading 121 runs. The Indians used him as trade bait to wrangle catcher Sandy Alomar and infielder Carlos Baerga away from the Padres. Both players would be instrumental in Cleveland's rise to contention. After one successful season in San Diego, Carter was again involved in a blockbuster deal that sent him to Toronto along with Roberto Alomar. He would spend the next seven seasons wearing a Blue Jays uniform.

A model of consistency, the right-handed slugger collected 98 or more RBIs 11 times between 1986–1997. He joined an elite group of players to reach the century mark on 10 occasions. Other names on that list include Babe Ruth, Willie Mays, and Hank Aaron. Although Carter didn't generate as much power as the aforementioned players, he gathered no fewer than 21 homers in 12 consecutive campaigns.

Carter's most memorable clout came in Game 6 of the 1993 World Series. The Jays were trailing, 6–5, in the bottom of the ninth inning when the slugger stepped in to face Philly bullpen ace Mitch Williams. Rickey Henderson had drawn a walk, and with one out, Paul Molitor had singled. Carter was ahead in the count, 2–1, when Williams threw him a slider for strike two. Carter was expecting another slider but got a fastball instead. "When I made contact, I never saw the ball. All I saw was the bank of lights," he reminisced years later. "I knew I hit it good, but I didn't know if I hit it high enough to get it over the fence." It was only the second World Series-ending homer in history (Bill Mazeroski of the Pirates hit the first one against the Yankees in 1960). Interestingly, the 1993 World Series was the second most sparsely watched Fall Classic in history to that point, with a lukewarm Nielsen rating of 17.3.

Carter enjoyed several productive seasons after that before slumping to .234 at the plate in 1997. A free agent, he signed with the Orioles for a reported $3.1 million. The O's traded him to the Giants in July 1998. It was his last season in the majors.

While Carter provided one of the brightest World Series moments of all time, he got little respect from baseball writers after his retirement. In his first year of eligibility, he received less than 5 percent of the Cooperstown vote—below the cutoff for future consideration. He remains a hero to many—especially in Canada. "People talk about that home run as if it happened yesterday," Carter told a reporter in 2013. "I'm very elated that they still remember that."

DAVE WINFIELD, DESIGNATED HITTER

Winfield spent the majority of his career outside of Toronto. A first-round pick of the Padres in 1973, he never played a single game in the minors. He emerged as one of the top outfielders in the NL, making four straight All-Star appearances and capturing a pair of Gold Gloves. Unable to meet his salary demands, the Padres lost him to the Yankees in 1981.

Winfield played well in New York but ended up on the bad side of George Steinbrenner and Billy Martin. Martin said that Winfield had the "softest bat" he had ever seen for a player of that height (Winfield was 6-foot-6 and had been drafted by the NBA's Atlanta Hawks). When Winfield infamously killed a seagull at Exposition Stadium in Toronto with a warm-up throw, Martin quipped, "They say he killed that gull on purpose, [but] they wouldn't say that if they'd seen the throws he's been making. . . . First time he's hit the cutoff man all year."

Steinbrenner pegged Winfield as a "selfish athlete" and, after the slugger's poor showing in the 1981 World Series versus the Dodgers, mockingly labeled him "Mr. May" in comparison to Reggie Jackson, who had earned the distinction of "Mr. October." Steinbrenner later conspired with gambler Howard Spira to dig up dirt on Winfield, and the ruse backfired. The Yankees owner ended up being placed on baseball's "permanently ineligible list" by Commissioner Fay Vincent (although only for a short while). Winfield sat out the entire 1989 season with a herniated disk and left the club in May 1990. He later requested that his Cooperstown plaque picture him with a Padres cap—a request that was granted.

Winfield was 40 years old by the time he reached the Blue Jays in 1992. He had his best season in several years. Occupying the cleanup spot, he hit .303 with runners in scoring position and collected more than 100 RBIs for the eighth and final time in his career. In the postseason, he gathered 11 hits and six more ribbies. His two-run double in the 11th inning of Game 6 was the series-clincher. In December of that year, he signed with the Twins.

Since his retirement, Winfield has served as executive vice president, a senior advisor, and a spring training instructor for the Padres. In 2013, he joined the staff of the Major League Baseball Players Association. He is also author of numerous books.

PAUL MOLITOR, DESIGNATED HITTER

Unlike Winfield, Molitor hung around Toronto for two more years after winning a world championship. Granted free agency by the Brewers in October 1992, he waited until December to sign with the Jays. Although the Toronto brass knew they were getting a good player, they had no idea just how good the 36-year-old Molitor would be. During his three-year stint north of the border, he hit .315, while averaging 53 extra-base hits per year. After tearing up the ALCS against the White Sox in 1993, he went 12-for-24 in the World Series with a pair of doubles, triples, and homers. He was fittingly named Series MVP.

Before then, Molitor had been a top-notch infielder for the Brewers, leading the AL in runs scored on three occasions. In 1987, he assembled a 39-game hitting streak—the longest since Pete Rose's 44-game skein in 1978. In the 1982 World Series with Milwaukee's fabled "Brew Crew," he had seven consecutive base hits, including a five-hit effort in Game 1. A daring baserunner, Molitor stole home 11 times during his career. Often injured in the field, he is second among Hall of Famers in designated-hitting assignments. Only Frank Thomas appeared in that capacity more often.

When Molitor's average dropped to .270 in 1995, the Jays let him go. He led the league with 225 hits the following year as a member of the Twins. Molitor closed out his career with 3,319 hits—10th on the all-time list at the time of this writing. After his retirement, he served as a bench coach and hitting instructor with the Twins and Mariners. In 2015, he succeeded Ron Gardenhire as manager in Minnesota.

FAST FACT: The 1970s were a dreadful era for Canadian baseball. Playing their inaugural season in 1969, the Montreal Expos finished below .500 in each of their first ten seasons. The Blue Jays experienced some growing pains of their own, averaging 106 losses per season from 1977–1979.

21

ATLANTA BRAVES
1991–1996

Like most avid followers of the Buffalo Bills, Atlanta Braves fans know about the agony of defeat. The Bills made four consecutive Super Bowl appearances from 1990–1993, coming up empty each time. While the Braves' record for futility is not as extreme, they did manage to lose three of four World Series between 1991–1996. By strict definition, Atlanta never built an actual dynasty. But few would deny the fact that they were one of the best teams in the National League (and perhaps all of baseball) for six years running. Sometimes the best teams don't win. The Braves have the numbers to back this up.

The saga of the "tomahawk chop" began in 1990, when the Braves finished in last place, 26 games behind the division-leading Reds. In his third year at the helm, manager Russ Nixon guided the club to a 25–40 start. Unable to sit idly by in the front office any longer, Bobby Cox dusted off his uniform and returned to the dugout. Cox had managed the Braves from 1978–1981, before taking the reins in Toronto. In 1986, he accepted the general manager's position in Atlanta, suffering through four full seasons of mediocrity. Nixon was not the first skipper to be fired on Cox's watch. Chuck Tanner had received his walking papers just 39 games into the 1988 campaign. The Braves responded positively to Cox's managerial return, winning four of five games during the final days of June. But by the end of July, they were still in the basement and headed nowhere fast.

There were numerous deficiencies in the Atlanta lineup, and Cox immediately set out to fix them. A two-time MVP and perennial long-ball threat in his prime, fan favorite Dale Murphy was 34 years old and no longer breaking down fences in 1990. Recognizing this weakness, Cox moved budding slugger David Justice from first base to the outfield and endorsed Murphy's August transfer to the Phillies. Justice won Rookie of the Year honors in 1990 and remained one of Atlanta's most productive hitters for several seasons.

Multiple changes would follow in 1991. Shoring up the infield, Terry Pendleton was acquired from the Cardinals and installed at third base in place of Jim Presley—a former Mariners slugger who had never realized his potential in Atlanta. Cox then created a middle-infield platoon, with Mark Lemke backing up incumbent second baseman Jeff Treadway and utility man Jeff Blauser splitting time with the light-hitting Rafael Belliard at shortstop. Sid Bream, formerly of the Pirates, was signed as a free agent to fill the first-base slot vacated by Justice. Although the pitching rotation remained the same, dramatic improvement was evident all around. In addition to a top-notch performance from 21-year-old Steve Avery, Tom Glavine emerged as one of the best left-handers in the NL.

Glavine could have played two sports professionally. A hockey star in high school, he was selected by the Los Angeles Kings in the fourth round of the 1984 NHL Entry Draft. After carefully considering his options, he chose baseball. Glavine had one of the best changeups in the majors and made a living off of painting the corners. By the second or third inning of most games, he had dramatically expanded the strike zone. He enjoyed 12 dominant seasons in Atlanta, leading the league in starts six times and reaching the 20-win threshold on five occasions.

Among the game's most successful multisport stars, outfielder Deion Sanders joined the Braves in 1991, after two seasons with the Yankees. Throughout his baseball career, he moonlighted as a defensive back in the NFL. Sanders had spent his college days at Florida State University, where fans often engaged in a cheer called the "Seminole Chop." Sanders's followers began using the same motion during spring training games in 1991, and the Braves' organist took to playing the accompanying music. Before long, foam tomahawks were one of the top-selling items at Atlanta-Fulton County Stadium. Players responded positively to the chanting and chopping. "I just felt that you couldn't come into Atlanta and beat us," said Justice.

The Braves collected 94 victories in 1991, and came out on the winning end of a seven-game showdown against the Pirates in the National League Championship Series. Atlanta was trailing three games to two when Avery and Smoltz handcuffed the Pittsburgh offense in consecutive starts. In an article he penned for the *Pittsburgh Press*, Barry Bonds commented, "I'm not going to tell you they were the better team, but I'm going to tell you I'll be rooting for them in the World Series. I'll be doing the tomahawk chop."

During a 100th anniversary countdown, ESPN selected the 1991 World Series as the greatest of all time. Five games were decided by a single run, four came down to the last at-bat, and three required extra innings to decide the outcome. The home team emerged victorious in each contest. Game 7 was among the tightest pitching duels in the history of the Fall Classic.

The Twins had won the American League pennant with quality pitching and timely hitting. The offense was led by future Hall of Fame outfielder Kirby Puckett, first baseman Kent Hrbek, and designated hitter Chili Davis. After Puckett's 11th-inning homer in Game 6 necessitated a final showdown between the two clubs, Series MVP Jack Morris took the mound against 14-game winner John Smoltz. Morris had issued a challenge to the Braves the night before, telling reporters, "In the words of Marvin Gaye: 'Let's get it on.'" Smoltz was lifted in the eighth after a brilliant performance, while Morris went the distance. With the crowd noise in Minnesota's Metrodome reaching deafening levels, the game remained scoreless until the bottom of the 10th. Dan Gladden led off with a double for the Twins and was sacrificed to third. Following intentional walks to Puckett and Hrbek, pinch-hitter Gene Larkin delivered the biggest hit of his career, chasing Gladden across the plate with the winning run. "I think I'm going to have an ulcer," Puckett said after the game.

It was more of the same in 1992, as Atlanta won the NL East with a 98–64 record and disposed of the Pirates in the NLCS. The World Series didn't have as many twists and turns as the 1991 affair, but it ended with an identical outcome—another epic failure for the Braves. Looking for answers, Atlanta executives made one of the smartest transactions in franchise history.

A right-hander, Greg Maddux had spent seven seasons polishing his craft on a Cubs team that contended only once. The 1992 campaign was his best effort yet, as he posted 20 wins and a sterling 2.18 ERA. A free agent at seasons' end, the Braves offered him a substantial raise and signing bonus. He spurned a larger offer from the Yankees to play for Atlanta. More than a decade of excellence would follow.

Maddux was among the greatest pitchers of his era and perhaps of all time. Using a sinker, curve, circle change, and cutter, he captured four straight Cy Young Awards from 1992–1995. Additionally, he won four ERA titles and led the league in shutouts five times. The most defensively decorated moundsman in history, only Jim Kaat came close to matching Maddux's 18 Gold Glove Awards. Never an overpowering pitcher, Maddux explained his strategy as follows: "I could probably throw harder if I wanted, but why? When they're in a jam, a lot of pitchers try to throw harder. Me, I try to locate better." Hall of Famer Wade Boggs once griped, "When he knows you're not going to swing, he throws you a straight one. He sees into the future. It's like he has a crystal ball inside his glove."

It didn't take a crystal ball to predict future success for the Braves. Maddux became a principal member of Atlanta's "Big Three"—an often unhittable combination that included Glavine and Smoltz. Smoltz, a big right-hander with four effective pitches in his arsenal, collected more than 200 wins and 150 saves for the Braves during his long career—a unique combination in the modern era. Discounting the strike-shortened 1994 slate, Atlanta's preeminent trio posted no fewer than 47 victories between them each year from 1993 to 1998. Their efforts guided the Braves to a long succession of playoff appearances.

The "Big Three" posted their highest single-season victory total in 1993, as both Maddux and Glavine were 20-game winners. Outfielders Ron Gant and David Justice put up industrious offensive numbers, combining for more than 70 homers and 200 RBIs. After winning a tight division title race over the Giants, which was decided on the last day of the season, the Braves seemed destined to go all the way. And then something completely unexpected happened.

They lost to the Phillies in the NLCS.

After dropping the opener at Philadelphia in 10 innings, Atlanta bounced back to win the next two contests by a 23–7 margin. Games four and five were decided by a single run as the Braves fell into a 3–2 hole. In the finale, Maddux could not subdue the Philly assault. The 6–3 loss sent Atlanta home early for the first time in three years.

The 1994 strike left a permanent blemish on the face of the sport. It was the eighth work stoppage in the game's history, and it led to the cancellation of more than 900 games. More importantly, it led to the cancellation of the World Series—the first time in 90 years that this had happened. Commenting on the agreement that was reached to resume play in 1995, sportswriter Michael Farber remarked, "Two hundred and eighty six million letters of apology, one for every Canadian and U.S. citizen, might have been a start, but the players and owners have decided to make peace in their own way." Since then, World Series TV ratings have steadily declined.

The Braves fielded one of the best teams in decades during the 1995 campaign. The pitching staff was phenomenal, posting the lowest ERA in the majors, while leading both leagues in strikeouts. Third baseman Chipper Jones finished second in Rookie of the Year voting. Outfielder Ryan Klesko and catcher Javy Lopez had breakout seasons, combining for 37 homers and a .313 batting average.

When Major League Baseball expanded from two to three divisions in 1994, the wild-card format was introduced (it had made a brief appearance during the strike-shortened 1981 season). In just their third year of existence, the Rockies grabbed the extra playoff spot but bowed to Atlanta in four games. The Reds didn't fare any better against the Braves in the NLCS, getting swept by a combined score of 19–5.

In a Native American-themed World Series, Atlanta squared off against Cleveland. Both clubs were trying to shake off the ghosts of past October failures. The Indians hadn't been to a Fall Classic since 1954, when they compiled an incredible .721 regular-season winning percentage, only to be swept by the underdog Giants. For the Braves, memories of Series letdowns were far fresher.

Atlanta finally ended five years of bitter disappointment with a stirring 1–0 victory in Game 6. Owner Ted Turner walked around Atlanta-Fulton County Stadium with the World Series trophy on his head. Steve Avery completed a celebratory lap around the bases and slid into home. David Justice, who delivered the game-winning homer in the sixth, told reporters, "I really had a good feeling that it was our time. We had suffered enough." Interestingly, Justice had criticized fans in Atlanta two nights earlier for their lack of enthusiasm.

The Braves made a convincing run at a repeat in 1996, but ultimately came up short. When Justice went down with a shoulder injury, 22-year-old rookie Jermaine Dye rose to the occasion, hitting .281 in 98 appearances. John Smoltz turned in one of the best seasons of his career, capturing Cy Young honors with a league-leading 24 wins and 276 strikeouts. Glavine and Maddux added 30 wins of their own.

The Yankees, who were returning to the World Series for the first time since 1981, didn't know what hit them in the first two games. On the heels of a 12–1 blowout win in the opener, Greg Maddux took the Bombers to school in the second contest, using just 82 pitches (62 for strikes) to breeze through eight scoreless innings. Closer Mark Wohlers struck out to side in the ninth, completing the 4–0 shutout. Things appeared to be well in hand for the Braves. But as had happened so many times before, they allowed a convincing advantage to slip through their fingers. Resilient Yankee southpaw Andy Pettitte bounced back from a disastrous start in the opener to give New York a 3–2 Series edge in Game 5. In the finale, a ninth-inning Atlanta rally fell short (yet again) as the Yankees brought a championship back to New York.

In 2005, the Braves completed a run of 14 consecutive playoff appearances—the longest streak of its kind to date and a remarkable accomplishment to say the least. At the same time, it was a badge of failure, as the team lost five division series, four league championship series, and four Fall Classics in that span. Few major-league clubs have come close to matching Atlanta's track record of postseason futility.

Despite their penchant for October collapse, the Braves were undoubtedly among the greatest teams of the 1990s. In 2014, Bobby Cox, Greg Maddux, and Tom Glavine were enshrined at Cooperstown. John Smoltz was duly recognized the following year. There is a chance that Chipper Jones may join the quartet at some point in the future. Among the greatest switch-hitters of all time, Jones's name appears on a short list of players who have scored more than 1,600 runs, while collecting as many RBIs.

Some of the nameless, (relatively) faceless others who helped the Braves dominate the NL during the 1990s are also remembered on the pages that follow.

GREG MADDUX, PITCHER

When Maddux became eligible for the Hall of Fame in 2014, it was a no-brainer. In addition to his four consecutive Cy Young Awards, he is the only pitcher to collect 15 wins in 17 straight seasons. His 18 Gold Gloves are the most for any player at any position. Polishing off a stellar resume, he finished among an elite group of hurlers with 300 wins and 3,000 strikeouts. Of the 10 men on that list, Maddux is the only one to have issued fewer than 1,000 walks.

Born in San Angelo, Texas, Maddux spent a large portion of his childhood in Madrid, Spain, where his father was stationed in the U.S. Air Force. He and his older brother Mike (who would turn professional first) honed their skills under the tutelage of Ralph Meder—a former major-league scout. Meder taught Maddux to locate his pitches precisely and change speeds often. In crisis situations, he instructed Maddux to throw softer rather than with higher velocity.

Chosen in the second round of the 1984 amateur draft, Maddux made his debut with the Cubs two years later. He got off to a disastrous start, compiling an 8–18 record in his first two seasons. The right-hander's first winning effort came in 1988, when he went 18–8 with a 3.18 ERA. He reached the high point of his career with the Cubs in 1992, when he won 20 games and captured his first Cy Young Award.

Between 1993–1996, Maddux posted the lowest ERA in the NL on three occasions and paced the loop in wins twice. When his streak of consecutive Cy Young Awards ended in 1996, he finished among the top five contenders four more times. Maddux's pinpoint control allowed him to post fewer walks per nine innings than his NL counterparts during nine seasons. In 1995, he went 51 straight innings without issuing a free pass. His mastery of opponents drew elaborate praise from contemporaries. Expos scout Phil Favia said, "Maddux is so good, we all should be wearing tuxedos when he pitches." Teammate John Smoltz remarked, "I swear, he makes it look like guys are swinging foam bats against him."

In 2004, Maddux returned to the Cubs. He spent portions of three more seasons in Chicago before landing in Los Angeles and San Diego. He retired in 2008. Since then, he has served as assistant to the GM of the Cubs and Rangers. He also worked as a pitching coach for Team USA in the 2013 World Baseball Classic.

TOM GLAVINE, PITCHER

Glavine grew up in Billerica, Massachusetts. Not only did he excel at sports, but he was also a member of the National Honor Society in high school. In 1984, he was chosen in the NHL Draft ahead of Hall of Famers Brett Hull and Luc Robitaille. Ultimately, he chose a career on the diamond. Commenting on his decision to pursue the more gentlemanly sport, Glavine pointed out, "Being a left-handed pitcher, I had a huge advantage. . . . In hockey, I didn't have that type of advantage."

Glavine got off to a rough start in the majors, posting a 9–21 record with a 4.76 ERA in his first two seasons. By the time the 1990s arrived, he had perfected his art. His win total during that decade was exceeded only by teammate Greg Maddux. From 1991–1996, Glavine led the league three times in wins and once apiece in shutouts and complete games. He was a Cy Young Award winner in 1991 and 1996.

In World Series play, Glavine accrued a 4–3 record. His most dominant performance came in Game 6 of the 1995 Series, when he tossed a one-hit shutout over the Indians. In the 1992 Fall Classic versus the Blue Jays, he compiled a 1.59 ERA.

Glavine was dealt to the Mets before the 2003 slate. He was in his late 30s by then and looking for his 300th win. During the 2004 campaign, the veteran southpaw was involved in an accident while riding in a New York taxi. While his arm was left uninjured, he lost both of his front teeth. "That was my pride and joy—that I made it through all those years of junior hockey without losing any of my teeth," he joked. "So I end up losing my teeth, but not in the glamorous fashion I envisioned."

Glavine's 300th victory finally came in 2007. The following year, he returned to Atlanta to close out his career. He retired with 305 wins. Fittingly, he was elected to the Hall of Fame the same year as longtime staffmate Greg Maddux. With pitchers making fewer starts these days and limited by pitch counts, there are many who believe that Glavine and Maddux may be among the last 300-game winners. At the end of the 2015 campaign, the only active players with at least 200 career wins were aging out.

JOHN SMOLTZ, PITCHER

Smoltz got started in the Tigers organization. He was traded for Doyle Alexander in 1987. Alexander went 9–0 for Detroit down the stretch and helped the club to the American League Championship Series. Smoltz didn't even make his major-league debut until 1988. But he would go on to set the franchise record for strikeouts.

Among the greatest October performers in history, Smoltz's numbers are mind-boggling. In 25 postseason series, he posted a 15–4 record with a 2.67 ERA. The Braves won 28 of the 41 games he appeared in.

In 2001, Smoltz was moved to the bullpen after undergoing successful Tommy John surgery. Before then, he had been used almost exclusively as a starter. He set the NL record with 55 saves in 2002, and is the only pitcher to retire with 200 wins and 150 saves. Commenting on his shift to the bullpen, Smoltz said, "Not everyone can be a great starting pitcher, but anyone can start. Anyone can't close. It's a completely different animal. . . . I think it's the most challenging thing in the game." In need of reliable arms, the Braves moved Smoltz back into the rotation after four years as a closer. He continued to be successful in that role, compiling a 44–24 record from 2005–2007.

During the course of his long career, Smoltz led the league in wins and strikeouts twice apiece. With several effective pitches in his arsenal, he averaged eight strikeouts per nine innings. During his Cy Young season of 1996, that number soared to 9.8. Recognized for his excellence, he was named to eight All-Star Teams—two as a reliever.

In 2009, the mileage finally caught up with Smoltz and he lost his effectiveness. He made his last appearance that year. He was a member of the 2015 Hall of Fame class. His number "29" was retired by the Braves. He has appeared as an analyst for Fox Network.

CHIPPER JONES, THIRD BASE

Jones grew up in Pierson, Florida, receiving the nickname "Chipper" during his childhood. He was the Braves' first-round pick in 1990. Within three years, he was the nation's number-one prospect, but injuries delayed his ascent to the majors. He missed the entire 1994 campaign with knee issues. He played his first full season with the Braves in 1995, finishing second to pitcher Hideo Nomo in Rookie of the Year voting.

Jones stuck around for 19 big-league seasons, spending his entire career with one team—an unusual occurrence nowadays. His lifetime accomplishments were numerous. Among switch-hitters, he holds the NL single-season record for homers (45), along with the career mark (468). In 2007, he tied a record for consecutive games with an extra-base hit (14). Other achievements include eight All-Star selections, two Silver Slugger Awards, and an MVP Award in 1999. He seemed to get better with age, as he won a batting title at the age of 36.

Jones played in 21 postseason series and hit .287 with 13 homers and 47 RBIs. In the 1995 and 1996 Fall Classics, he collected a total of six doubles, while scoring six runs. Through no direct fault of Jones, the Braves won just one of the three World Series he appeared in.

After winning the 2008 batting title, Jones was slowed by injuries. He averaged just 111 appearances per year from 2010–2012. When he retired after the latter campaign, he said he had been involved in baseball for more than two decades and it was time "to do something else." He pointed out that he had kids at home who were getting to be "at a fun age" and wanted to concentrate on being a full-time father.

Early in his career, Jones had an affair with a Hooters waitress, and it destroyed his first marriage. He divorced from his second wife in 2012, after he began dating former Playboy Playmate Taylor Higgins. Although his love life was sometimes messy, he gave back to the community at large. His charity—the Chipper Jones Family Foundation—has raised substantial funds for youth baseball programs in Florida and Georgia. Jones's number "10" was retired by the Braves in 2013, and he was inducted into the team's Hall of Fame. His sabermetric scores put him on target for the more prestigious Hall in Cooperstown.

FRED MCGRIFF, FIRST BASE

While McGriff's name has faded from prominence with the passage of time, he was among baseball's elite sluggers for more than a decade. Born in Tampa, Florida, he set multiple records at Jefferson High School. Those records would later be broken by future Yankee great

Tino Martinez. McGriff began his pro career with the Yankees in 1981. He spent two years in their minor-league system before a trade sent him to the Blue Jays. After a cup of coffee in 1986, Toronto recalled him for good the following year. By then, he had perfected his unique batting style. After making contact with a pitch, McGriff would release his top hand and whirl his bat through the air in a tight circle. Since it worked for him, none of his coaches suggested he change his mechanics.

McGriff had a breakout season in 1988, clubbing 34 homers and gathering 82 RBIs. He would exceed the 30-homer threshold each year for the next six seasons, leading each league once apiece. After the 1990 slate, he was traded to the Padres with Tony Fernandez in exchange for Roberto Alomar and Joe Carter. The Braves acquired him in July 1993, for three players of little note. He helped the club tremendously down the stretch, hitting .310 in 68 games with 19 homers and 55 RBIs. Atlanta's NLCS loss to Philadelphia had little to do with McGriff, as he raked Philly pitching at a .435 clip and compiled a robust .519 on-base percentage.

A big man, at 6-foot-3, 215 pounds, McGriff wasn't loud or flashy, but he exuded a quiet confidence. He never set out to hit home runs. "A lot of times, hitting home runs is not good for you because it really makes you start trying to yank the ball," he told a reporter one day. According to McGriff, the key was to "forget about hitting home runs, go make hard contact, try to hit .300."

McGriff's name was similar to a cartoon character created by the Ad Council to enhance crime awareness among children. The character, a basset hound named "McGruff the Crime Dog," educated kids about drugs, bullying, and the importance of staying in school. Although McGriff was slightly resistant to being saddled with the nickname "Crime Dog" at first, he eventually became rather fond of it.

The lefty slugger enjoyed four and a half successful seasons in Atlanta. Between 1994–1997, he averaged 28 homers and 98 RBIs per year. He was a stable postseason presence in that span, gathering 44 hits (18 for extra bases) in 39 games. McGriff was a patient hitter, drawing 90 or more walks during the regular season five times during his career. For eight consecutive seasons, his on-base percentage never dipped below .375.

After the 1997 campaign, McGriff signed with the Tampa Bay Devil Rays. He would reach the 30–homer and 100-RBI threshold in the same season three more times before retiring. He finished with 493 long balls. After his playing days, he worked as a special advisor to the Rays and also hosted a radio show. So far, McGriff has received moderate support from Cooperstown voters, peaking at 23.9 percent of the vote in 2012. Sabermetric scores place him right on the cusp for the Hall of Fame. His share of votes has been slowly dwindling during the last couple of years, and he remains a long shot for induction.

MARK LEMKE, SECOND BASE

Lemke grew up in Utica, New York. He was picked by the Braves in a late round of the 1983 draft. Prior to that, he had been considering academic pursuits at Purdue University. He passed on college to join the Braves' minor-league system and ended up waiting seven years to earn a permanent roster spot in Atlanta.

Lemke's hustle and determination inspired teammates, who referred to him as the "Lemmer." An Associated Press writer once joked that, if the flashy and vastly overrated Deion Sanders could carry the nickname "Prime Time," then the hard-working, underappreciated Lemke should be referred to as "Grime Time." "He's an original dirt player," manager Bobby Cox said of Lemke. "He's always at the ballpark looking for someone to play catch with him."

Lemke earned the nickname "Little Mr. October" in 1996, when he compiled a 13-game postseason hitting streak. He hit safely in all but three of the Braves' playoff games that year. The hustling second baseman also compiled October hitting streaks of eight games (from 1991–1992) and seven games (in 1995). In the 1991 World Series against the Twins, he rapped out 10 hits (four for extra bases) and accrued a handsome .417 batting average. He was even better in the 1996 ALCS versus the Cardinals, gathering 12 safeties (including his only postseason homer) and emerging with a .444 batting mark.

During the regular season, Lemke's batting record was far more prosaic, but he played with gusto. "When I go out on the field, I try to give it everything I have," he once said. "I'll do whatever it takes, and I feel like that's what gotten me to the big leagues." Often serving as a backup infielder, he was known for his reliable glove and wide range. He led NL second baseman in putouts, double plays, and fielding percentage once apiece. His lifetime range factor (average putouts and assists) per nine innings places him among the top 100 second baseman of all time in that category.

A free agent after the 1997 slate, Lemke spent his last season in Boston, failing to bring his batting average above the dreaded "Mendoza Line." After his major-league days were over, he joined the New Jersey Jackals of the independent Northern League and attempted a career as a knuckleball pitcher. Also serving as an infield coach, he posted a 5–1 record with an astronomical ERA in 1999. He was released the following year after setting a league record with wild pitches in nine consecutive at-bats. Lemke later hosted a Braves pregame radio show in Atlanta. He has also done color commentary.

DAVID JUSTICE, OUTFIELD

Born in Cincinnati, Justice was a precocious child who skipped the seventh and eighth grades and graduated at the age of 16. He attended Thomas Moore College in Kentucky and began his pro career with the Braves in 1985. A left-handed hitter with power, he toiled in the Atlanta farm system until 1990, when he captured Rookie of the Year honors with 28 homers, 78 RBIs, and a .282 batting average.

Justice would spend portions of eight seasons with the Braves, nursing injuries a great deal of the time. When he was healthy, he was one of the most productive hitters on the club. In 1993, he made a career-high 157 appearances, slugging 40 homers and gathering 120 RBIs. He also drew 78 walks that year, finishing third in MVP voting.

Justice appeared in 112 postseason games during his career. Although he rarely hit for average, he provided plenty of power with 33 extra-base hits (14 homers) and 63 RBIs. His homer in Game 6 of the 1995 Fall Classic clinched the Series for the Braves. His teams won 13 of the playoff series he appeared in.

Traded by the Braves in the spring of 1997, he played for the Indians, Yankees, and A's before calling it quits in 2002. His best season outside of Atlanta came in 2000, when he blasted 41 long balls and gathered 118 RBIs while splitting time with Cleveland and New York. Each team Justice played on made it to the postseason at least once.

Justice's personal life was even more interesting than his exploits on the diamond. In 1992, he appeared on an episode of *The Young and the Restless*. In 1994, he was named one of *People* magazine's "50 Most Beautiful People." Justice was married to alluring actress Halle Berry from December 1992 to February 1996, when Berry made claims of physical abuse and sought a restraining order. The couple divorced in 1997, and the ordeal tarnished Justice's reputation to an extent.

In 2007, the slugger was inducted into the Atlanta Braves Hall of Fame. Eligible for Cooperstown the following year, he was taken off the ballot after receiving just one vote. In the infamous Mitchell Report, former Mets clubhouse attendant Kirk Radomski claimed to have sold Justice human growth hormone when he was playing for the Yankees. Justice said that this was an outright lie and insisted that he had never even met Radomski. He did admit to discussing the use of HGH with Yankees strength coach Brian McNamee. McNamee allegedly obtained some for the ailing slugger, who was suffering from shoulder problems, but Justice claimed he never used it. He encouraged any players wrongfully accused in the Mitchell Report to publicly refute the claims made against them. Justice served as an ESPN commentator for two seasons. He also worked for the YES Network.

FAST FACT: When the 1995 Braves captured a World Series title, they became the first team to be crowned champions in three different cities. The club had previously won championships in Boston (1914) and Milwaukee (1957).

22

NEW YORK YANKEES

1996–2000

After the "Bronx Zoo" era of the late 1970s and early 1980s, the Yankees experienced one of the longest postseason droughts in franchise history, going more than a decade without a playoff berth. In an effort to rebuild a winner, owner George Steinbrenner consistently maintained a bloated payroll, importing dozens of high-priced prospects and established stars. Among the biggest names to wear pinstripes during those lean years were Hall of Famers Dave Winfield, Rickey Henderson, and Phil Niekro. Beginning in 1984, fan favorite Don Mattingly more or less carried the club until chronic back trouble started to slow him down in 1990. The Bombers posted their lowest winning percentage since the Deadball Era that year.

As the team continued to flounder in the standings, Yankees fans needed a scorecard just to keep up with the influx of managers and coaches. During the 1980s, the Bombers went through a dozen managerial changes. Several men had multiple stints at the helm, including Gene Michael, Billy Martin, and Lou Piniella. When Buck Showalter survived four straight seasons as Yankees skipper from 1992–1995, he became the longest tenured skipper since Ralph Houk, who had completed a run of seven uninterrupted campaigns in 1973.

Several positive changes began to take place during the 1990s. In 1991, Bernie Williams joined the club. Although he would not realize his full offensive potential right away, he made an immediate impact with his glove. Using long, graceful strides, there didn't seem to be a ball hit to center field that he couldn't track down. He became a more complete player in 1995, when he began a run of eight consecutive .300 seasons at the plate. The pinnacle of his career came in 1998, when he won a batting title and a Gold Glove, while earning his second All-Star selection.

In November 1992, the Yankees made a key transaction when they acquired right fielder Paul O'Neill from the Reds. Among the most intense competitors ever to step onto the diamond, O'Neill was known to many as the "Warrior." He expected perfection from himself and often went into angry tirades when he failed to deliver in the clutch. There wasn't a bat rack or water cooler that was safe from his wrath. In Cincinnati, he had been encouraged to swing for the fences, and his batting average suffered because of it. In New York, he became a more disciplined hitter, exceeding the .300 mark in six straight seasons. He won a batting title during the strike-shortened 1994 campaign with a .359 average. O'Neill had one of the strongest arms in the majors, and few baserunners chose to test it. He finished among the top five in assists at his position seven times, leading the National League in 1990. He tied a record (never to be broken) in 1996 with a perfect fielding percentage. He led both leagues three times in that category.

In 1993, the Yankees continued to strengthen their roster with the addition of third baseman Wade Boggs. A man of rituals, Boggs woke up at precisely the same hour and ate only chicken on game days. Before each at-bat, he traced the Hebrew symbol for "life" (known as "Chai") in the dirt—an extremely odd practice considering that he wasn't Jewish. Because of his quirks—or perhaps in spite of them—Boggs gathered more than 3,000 hits and compiled a stellar lifetime on-base percentage of .415. He maintained a .300 average in four of his five seasons with New York. He also captured two Gold Gloves—an award that had previously eluded him.

While George Steinbrenner's blueprint for success had always relied heavily on the acquisition of established stars, that mold was finally broken in 1995, with the arrival of the so-called "Core Four." Called up from Triple A Columbus in late April, Andy Pettitte was the first to arrive, bringing with him a variety of pitches and a deceptive pickoff move. Using his signature cutter, along with a slider, curve, and change, he became one of the most successful left-handers in franchise history, gathering more than 200 wins in pinstripes. He kept runners close to the bag with 100 successful pickoffs during his career.

Another Columbus standout, Mariano Rivera joined the Yankees a few weeks after Pettitte. Originally groomed as a starter, he was moved to the bullpen permanently in his sophomore year. His success in the majors was somewhat surprising considering the fact that he had only two effective pitches in his arsenal—a straight fastball and a cut fastball with late movement. The cutter tailed in on left-handed hitters with the effect of a buzz saw. Rivera broke more bats in 19 seasons than perhaps a dozen relievers combined. He retired with 652 career saves—an all-time record. He picked up 42 additional saves in the postseason—more than twice the total of his closest competitor at the time of his retirement.

In May 1995, the Yankees continued to pick the Columbus roster down to its bare bones, calling up Derek Jeter. While he hit just .250 in his debut, he would blossom into the greatest shortstop in Yankees history. When people talk about Jeter, they talk about the intangibles— his reassuring presence in the lineup, his almost supernatural ability to rise to the occasion. But immeasurable attributes aside, he compiled a pretty impressive batch of statistics throughout the years: more than 3,400 career hits, 13 seasons with at least 100 runs scored, more than 4,700 times on base—the list goes on. Named captain in 2003, he carried himself with dignity both off and on the field. Literary journalist Gay Talese marveled at Jeter's class: "In this era of boorish athletes, obnoxious fans, greedy owners, and shattered myths, here's a hero who's actually polite. . . . You can't compare him to Joe DiMaggio for DiMaggio didn't have bad manners—he had no manners."

Rounding out the quartet that would lead the Yankees to multiple world championships, Jorge Posada made his Bronx debut in September 1995. He would spend one more season with the Columbus Clippers before earning a permanent roster spot in New York. After playing backup to Joe Girardi in 1997, Posada became the Yankees' full-time catcher the following year. With above-average power and a keen batting eye, he held his own offensively. Behind the plate, he had a knack for working with difficult hurlers—especially Orlando Hernandez, a temperamental, junk-throwing import who was at one time among the top pitchers in Cuba. Posada was equipped with an accurate, powerful arm, placing among the top five in runners caught stealing nine times during his career. When he retired in 2011, the Yankees spent several seasons looking for an adequate replacement.

The Bombers were sitting atop the American League East with a six-and-a-half-game lead when a strike ended the 1994 campaign. They enjoyed a triumphant return to the playoffs the following year via a wild-card berth. Playing in his last season, ailing captain Don Mattingly went off on a tear in the American League Division Series, blasting four doubles and a homer, while driving in six runs. It wasn't enough, as the Bombers squandered a two-game advantage to the Mariners, losing the series in five hard-fought games.

Anything less than a world championship was considered a failure in the mind of George Steinbrenner. Instead of rewarding manager Buck Showalter for a job well done, the "Boss" went out and hired Joe Torre to pilot the club in 1996. Torre had spent his playing days as a catcher and had been a good one at that. In 1971, he had won a batting title and a MVP Award with St. Louis. Before taking the reins in the Bronx, he had spent 15 years at the helm of the Mets, Braves, and Cardinals. The mild-mannered Brooklyn native was accommodating to the press and respectful of his players. He rarely lost his temper. He also had a knack for making the right decisions at the right times. He proved this definitively in 1996, by guiding the Yankees to their first pennant in more than a decade.

The 1996 American League Championship Series contained one of the most controversial calls in playoff history. In Game 1, the Yankees were trailing the Orioles, 4–3, in the bottom of the eighth when Derek Jeter hit a deep fly to right field. Tony Tarasco settled under the ball and appeared to have a shot at catching it before a 12-year-old fan named Jeffrey Maier reached over the wall and grabbed it. Umpire Rich Garcia declared it a game-tying homer despite the protests of Baltimore manager Davey Johnson. The play proved to be pivotal, as the Yankees won in 11 innings on a memorable walk-off homer by Bernie Williams.

With the formidable pitching trio of Greg Maddux, Tom Glavine, and John Smoltz, the defending world champion Braves were favored to win the 1996 Series over the Yankees, who had gotten a fair amount of mileage out of former crosstown greats Darryl Strawberry and Dwight Gooden. It was a feel-good story, as "Straw" and "Doc" (as they were affectionately known to some fans) overcame substance abuse issues to become productive members of the club. Gooden tossed his first career no-hitter in May and won 11 games. Strawberry collected 11 homers during the regular season and added three more in the ALCS against Baltimore. Another former Met, David Cone, had been added to the Yankees roster in July 1995. After getting off to a 4–1 start in 1996, he developed a career-threatening aneurysm in his pitching arm and underwent surgery. It was another triumphant tale, as the resilient junkballer returned in September and finished the season with a 7–2 record.

The Yankees fell into a 2–0 hole after dropping the first two games of the Series by a combined score of 16–1. But a strong outing from Cone in Game 3 and an Atlanta bullpen meltdown in the fourth contest helped knot the Series at two games apiece. The last two meetings were pitching duels. A costly error by center fielder Marquis Grissom (his third of the postseason) made Braves ace John Smoltz a tough-luck loser in Game 5. Maddux went to the mound in the finale and the Yankees finally figured him out, breaking through for three runs in the third inning. It was all the offense they would need in a Series-clinching victory.

The Yankees started the 1997 campaign with their roster essentially intact. They dropped to second place in the East, settling for their second wild-card berth in a three-year span. Facing the Indians in the division series, the Bombers jumped out to a two games to one advantage, only to watch it evaporate. The finale was played at Jacobs Field. Before a frenzied throng of Cleveland supporters, New York stranded the tying run at second base in the ninth, losing a nail-biter, 4–3.

Disgruntled with the loss, George Steinbrenner reached deep into his wallet during a flurry of offseason activity. Notable signings included third baseman Scott Brosius (acquired from the A's), designated hitter Chili Davis (formerly of the Royals), and second baseman Chuck Knoblauch (obtained in a trade with Minnesota). The club didn't meet with much resistance in 1998. After finishing 22 games ahead of the Red Sox, Torre's crew breezed to a sweep of the ALDS and World Series. The playoffs were rendered all the more dramatic when Darryl Strawberry was diagnosed with colon cancer in October. Playing in his fourth season with the Yanks, he had blasted 24 homers and played in 100 games for the first time since 1991. The Yankees played inspired ball, setting an all-time record with 125 total wins. The previous mark had been held by the 1986 Mets.

The 1999 campaign began on a sad note with the passing of Joe DiMaggio on March 8. Things took another bleak turn when Joe Torre was diagnosed with prostate cancer. Remarkably, he remained at the helm for most of the year as the Bombers won 98 games and cruised through the playoffs with an 11–1 record. David Cone provided the most memorable regular-season moment when he tossed the 16th perfect game in major-league history on Old-Timers' Day at Yankee Stadium. In the postseason, Mariano Rivera stole the spotlight, allowing no runs in eight appearances. He was credited with two wins and six saves, capturing World Series MVP honors.

Before the 2000 slate, there hadn't been a subway series in New York since the 1950s. With the introduction of interleague play in 1997, the Yankees and Mets locked horns each year—often with little more at stake than inner-city bragging rights. In July 2000, the friendly rivalry turned ugly when tempestuous hurler Roger Clemens (acquired from Toronto before the 1999 campaign) hit catcher Mike Piazza in the helmet with a pitch. Piazza sustained a concussion and missed the All-Star Game. Prior to that at-bat, the hard-hitting backstop had accrued a bloated batting average against Clemens. According to multiple sources, Clemens had told his trainer that he intended to "do something about it." As the two clubs became front-runners in their respective leagues late in the season, numerous sportswriters waxed poetic about a potential postseason showdown between Piazza and the "Rocket."

That confrontation took place in Game 2 of the World Series. With a 1–2 count on Piazza in the first inning, Clemens delivered a 97-mile-per-hour fastball that shattered Piazza's bat on contact. The barrel end flew toward Clemens, who inexplicably threw it in Piazza's direction as the ball rolled foul. Still holding the bat handle, the flabbergasted Mets backstop pointed it at the hurler and said, "What is your problem?" The two were separated, and upon returning to the mound, Clemens induced a harmless groundout to second base. The rest of the Series was tightly contested as the Yankees came away with their third consecutive world championship. Derek Jeter earned MVP honors with a .409 performance at the plate.

In 2007, the Yankees completed a run of 13 straight playoff appearances. By then, Bernie Williams had retired and the "Core Four" were aging out. The quartet would have one more taste of October glory in 2009, winning the World Series in six games over the Phillies. George Steinbrenner passed away the following year, leaving the team in the hands of his sons. Jorge Posada retired after the 2011 campaign. Andy Pettitte and Mariano Rivera threw their last pitches two years later. Derek Jeter bid a fond farewell to the Big Apple in 2014. Joe Torre, who left the Yankees before the 2008 campaign, was inducted into Cooperstown as a manager that same year.

New York has always been a media hotbed. With the Yankees fielding winning teams year after year during the late 1990s and beyond, few, if any, talented players escaped the spotlight. To date, the Yankees squads of that era represent the last bona fide dynasty in baseball history. Their extended run of dominance would not have been possible without the contributions of the following men.

DEREK JETER, SHORTSTOP

Few players have meant more to the Yankees and to the sport itself than Jeter. He was a model of consistency and integrity for 20 major-league seasons. His youthful appearance and charismatic presence on the diamond made him one of the most marketed players in the game's history. The Yankees shortstop endorsed Nike, Gatorade, Fleet Bank, MasterCard, Visa, and Skippy Peanut Butter—among numerous other products.

Outfielder Tim Raines once said, "Hanging out with [Jeter] sucks because all the women flock to him. . . . He's been on the cover of GQ, is rich and famous, hits for average and power, and is a helluva nice guy." Raines wasn't kidding, as Jeter has been linked to multiple A-list starlets throughout the years, including Mariah Carey, Jessica Alba, and Scarlett Johansson. But despite all the attention he received, the Yankees icon was actually rather bashful. "He's basically shy," said manager Joe Torre. "And I know most people don't see him that way. He's so fluid among people. He knows what he is as far as the matinee idol stuff, and he wears it well. He has no pretenses. He's real."

Engaging personality aside, Jeter compiled an impressive set of statistics during his career. The accolades began early, as he was named minor-league player of the year in 1994 by the *Sporting News*. When he arrived in the majors, pitchers tried to work him inside, but he perfected an inside-out swing that directed balls toward the opposite field. At the end of the 2015 slate, he ranked sixth on the all-time hit list. Incredibly, he added 200 more hits in the postseason—more than any player in the game's history.

Perhaps because Jeter was so popular and overexposed, he had his share of detractors throughout the years. In particular, a group of statisticians used various number-crunching methods to back up the claim that Jeter was a weak defensive player. The Yankees shortstop won five Gold Gloves despite that criticism and currently ranks among the top 10 of all time in assists and double plays. Two of his defensive gems have appeared on Yankees highlight reels for more than a decade. During a midseason game at Fenway Park, Jeter ran all out in pursuit of a foul ball and ended up crashing headfirst into the stands. He came up bloody with the ball in his possession. During Game 3 of the 2001 ALDS, he strayed far from his defensive post to snare a bad throw from outfielder Shane Spencer. He flipped the ball to home plate in time to nail Jeremy Giambi by a hair, preserving a 1–0 win for the Yankees over the A's. His relay to home is often referred to as "The Play."

Jeter collected more hits at old Yankee Stadium than any player in history—surpassing Lou Gehrig to claim the record. Like Gehrig, Jeter had a long stint as team captain. When the title was bestowed upon him in 2003, he commented humbly, "This is a great honor. Captain of the Yankees is not a title that is thrown around lightly. It is a huge responsibility and one that I take very seriously. I thank Mr. Steinbrenner for having such confidence in me."

Few players have provided the kind of high drama that took place at Yankee Stadium in September 2014. Playing in his final home game, the 14-time All-Star and beloved Yankees icon came to bat in the bottom of the ninth against Baltimore with the score tied at five. The Yankees had been mathematically eliminated from the playoffs, and the original plan was to remove Jeter from the game. He had already delivered a clutch double in the first inning and circled the bases with the tying run. A sellout crowd had saluted him during the middle innings with the thunderous chant "Thank you, captain!" Their words had brought Jeter to tears. After Yankees closer David Robertson blew a three-run lead in the top of the ninth and Brett Gardner sacrificed pinch-runner Antoan Richardson to second in the bottom of the inning, manager Joe Girardi figured no better script could be written. He allowed Jeter to bat one last time in the Bronx cathedral that had been the site of so many of his career-defining moments. Jeter rose to the occasion yet again, delivering a single to center field that scored the winning run. It was his first walk-off hit in several years. "It was sort of an out of body experience for me," he said after the game. "I was just trying not to cry." Three days later, in his final career at-bat in Boston, Jeter rapped another one of his trademark singles, scoring Ichiro Suzuki and ending his career with a lofty total of 3,465 hits.

Since his retirement, Jeter has put his energy into his own publishing company, which is affiliated with Simon & Schuster. The company has an adult division and children's division. Jeter has received writing credit for two children's titles to date, *Hit and Miss* and *The Contract*.

MARIANO RIVERA, RELIEF PITCHER

During an appearance on the YES Network TV series *Kids on Deck*, Rivera explained his job as follows: "I get the ball, I throw the ball, and then I go take a shower." Rivera certainly made it look simple throughout the years. With little more than a cut fastball in his arsenal, he mowed down opposing hitters with astonishing efficiency for nearly two decades, setting the all-time record for saves in the regular season and postseason.

Talking about Rivera's devastating cutter, infielder Tony Womack complained, "When he throws it, you think it's straight and the next thing you know, it's on your thumbs." Teammate Alex Rodriguez sang Rivera's praises: "To me he's the greatest modern-day weapon I have seen or played against. He has the heart and soul of the New York Yankees dynasty."

In addition to being a top-notch closer, Rivera was jovial and approachable to both fans and teammates. Before games, he was known to linger near the stands, signing autographs for extended periods of time. His Yankees peers were greatly comforted whenever he entered the game. Hall of Fame reliever Rich Gossage remarked, "When Rivera takes the mound, the other team is sitting in the dugout thinking 'We've got no chance. It's over.' This guy walks into the game and they are done."

According to Rivera, the key to his success was a short memory. He rarely, if ever, thought about past failures and never looked terribly rattled on the mound. He also maintained a sense of humor about himself. After a succession of rocky appearances at Fenway Park, he was greeted with a sarcastic ovation as he entered a game one day. While jogging to the mound, he smiled and acknowledged the mock cheers with a tip of his cap.

Whenever Rivera came into a game at Yankee Stadium, the song "Enter Sandman" by hard-rock group Metallica would blare over the loudspeakers, making the moment all the more dramatic. He rarely spoiled the moment, converting 94 percent of his lifetime save opportunities and retiring with an all-time record 652. He added 42 more saves in the postseason. During the Yankees' era of dominance from 1996–2000, Rivera gave up just five earned runs in 38 October appearances.

Rivera sustained a fluke injury while shagging fly balls during batting practice in 2012. He missed most of the season. He returned the following year, announcing prior to the start of the season that it would be his last. He went out with a bang, saving 44 games and posting a 2.11 ERA. In 2014, the Yankees honored Rivera by visiting his home country of Panama to play a pair of exhibition games against the Marlins. Major League Baseball honored Rivera by naming a new AL award after him to honor the league's best reliever. Rivera's autobiography was published that same year.

BERNIE WILLIAMS, CENTER FIELD

Williams's family lived in the Bronx until Bernie was one year old. They moved to Puerto Rico after that. Williams excelled at track and field while growing up, taking four gold medals in the CAV Junior Championships in San Juan. He was a standout baseball player as well, getting signed by a scout on his 17th birthday. He had aspirations of becoming a doctor before choosing a career on the diamond.

Making his first appearance in the Yankees lineup in 1991, Williams became New York's starting center fielder in 1993. Interestingly, George Steinbrenner tried to trade him that year, and a deal to obtain Expos slugger Larry Walker was discussed. The trade never materialized, as Williams ended up proving himself, hitting .268 while playing stellar defense.

From 1995–2002, Williams's batting average never dropped below .305. A switch-hitter, he generated more power as his career progressed, peaking at 30 homers in 2000. He played in 121 postseason games with the Yankees—smashing 22 homers and driving in 80 runs. Many of those RBIs were quite memorable, as he drove home the winning run in nine postseason games. Two of his October homers were of the walk-off variety. Radio announcer John Sterling was known to add drama to these moments, shouting, "Bern, baby—bern!" The phrase began to appear as a graphic on the scoreboard at Yankee Stadium.

In the outfield, Williams had good speed and wide range. He finished among the leaders in fielding percentage nine times and won four Gold Gloves. Despite his multidimensional talents, he appeared on less than 10 percent of Hall of Fame ballots in 2012, and was eliminated the following year when he failed to generate the minimum number of votes.

Since retiring, Williams has forged a career as a jazz guitarist. He was nominated for a Latin Grammy in 2009. He supports multiple charities and has his own website, "Bernie Williams: From Center Field to Center Stage." His number "51" was retired by the Yankees in May 2015.

PAUL O'NEILL, RIGHT FIELD

O'Neill grew up in Columbus, Ohio, as a fan of the Reds. Drafted by his favorite team in 1981, he made his big-league debut four years later. Assuming full-time playing status in 1988, he provided one of the most memorable bloopers in baseball history when he fielded a base hit but couldn't hang onto the ball. He ended up kicking it back to the infield in time to hold Phillies baserunner Steve Jeltz at third base. One play-by-play announcer joked, "The Cincinnati Bengals are on the phone!" The popular sports show *This Week in Baseball* added the play to its "Hall of Fame."

Highly personable off the field, O'Neill was known for his intensity on the diamond. He threw tantrums when he failed to deliver in the clutch and made his displeasure known to umpires when he disagreed with a call. Before the 1991 season, Cincinnati manager Lou Piniella asked O'Neill to change his batting style to generate more homers. O'Neill objected and was eventually traded to the Yankees in November 1992. George Steinbrenner later gave him the nickname the "Warrior" on account of his passion for the sport.

From 1993–2001, O'Neill was one of the Yankees' most reliable run producers. Occupying the third slot in the batting order, he drove in 90 or more runs in six straight seasons, reaching the century mark four times. He compiled a lifetime .303 batting average during his nine seasons in pinstripes and won a batting title during the strike-shortened 1994 slate.

Defensively, O'Neill was among the best in the game. While he never won a Gold Glove, he led players at his position in fielding percentage six times. In 1996, he completed 146 outfield assignments without committing a single error. His lifetime fielding percentage is fifth on the all-time list. Equipped with a strong, accurate arm, he was rarely tested by runners. He led NL right fielders in assists during the 1990 slate and finished with double-digit figures in four other seasons.

O'Neill had an extensive postseason career that included 30 extra-base hits, 39 RBIs, and 39 runs scored in 85 games—most of them spent with the Yankees. He retired after the 2001 slate and later became a member of the YES Network broadcasting team. In 2015, he created some controversy when he left his post in the middle of a game to have his picture taken with talk show host Jimmy Fallon. The year before, he was honored with a plaque in Yankee Stadium's Monument Park.

O'Neill is the only player to have played on the winning team in three perfect games—Tom Browning in 1988, David Wells in 1998, and David Cone in 1999.

ANDY PETTITTE, PITCHER

Born in Baton Rouge, Louisiana, Pettitte is of Italian and Cajun descent. In high school, he played football and baseball. A late-round Yankees draft pick in 1990, he put off signing to attend junior college. He officially joined the organization the following year. In 1995, he was called to New York and assigned to the bullpen. A slew of injuries to Yankees starters gave him an opportunity in the rotation. He made the most of it, winning six of his last seven starts and finishing the season at 12–9.

Pettitte was one of the winningest pitchers in franchise history, posting 219 victories during his career as a Yankee. He is the franchise leader in strikeouts. He never finished a season with a record below .500 and has more postseason wins than any pitcher in history (19). He was all business on the mound and became known for pulling the brim of his hat down low and staring intensely at his catcher.

A left-hander, Pettitte had a sweeping curve and an evasive cutter. He liked to paint the corners of the strike zone. He also had one of the best pickoff moves of his generation, nailing 100 baserunners during his 18-year career. His best season with the Yankees came in 1996, when he led the league with 21 wins and finished second in Cy Young voting. He enjoyed his finest postseason in 2000, logging a 2–0 record with a 2.84 ERA in five starts. The Yankees won every game he appeared in. He was MVP of the ALCS the following October.

After the 2003 slate, Pettitte was convinced by friend and teammate Roger Clemens to sign with the Astros. Injured for most of the year, he bounced back in 2005, going 17–9 with a career-best 2.39 ERA. He made one quality start in the World Series that year with Houston but ended up with a no-decision.

In 2007, Pettitte was implicated in the infamous Mitchell Report for taking human growth hormone. He admitted to using it in 2002 and again in 2004. He also divulged that Clemens had used it. Unlike Pettitte, who admitted his indiscretion and took his lumps, Clemens maintained his innocence. The two became estranged.

Pettitte returned to the Yankees in 2007 and compiled a 70–49 record through the 2013 slate, which was his last in the majors. Together, he and Mariano Rivera set an all-time record for win–save combinations by a pitching duo. In 2015, the Yankees announced that Pettitte's number would be retired and a plaque dedicated to him in Monument Park.

JORGE POSADA, CATCHER

Posada was born in Santurce, Puerto Rico. In high school, he was an all-star shortstop. He played college ball at Calhoun Community College in Alabama, where he encountered racism from various classmates. His teammates accepted him warmly, naming him cocaptain in 1991.

Posada was not yet a catcher when he began his minor-league career with the Yankees. That transformation took place in 1992. While playing for Greensboro in the South Atlantic League, he worked with Andy Pettitte for the first time. By 1994, he had worked his way up to Triple A Columbus, but a collision at home plate left him with a broken leg and dislocated ankle. Although Posada played in an era when major-league catchers were allowed to block the plate, the injury made him extremely hesitant to do so.

Following brief call-ups in 1995 and 1996, Posada played backup to Joe Girardi the following year. He hit .250 in 60 games and fielded his position above the league average. He became the Yankees' primary receiver the following year.

The switch-hitting Posada put up excellent power numbers for his position, smashing 275 homers and 379 doubles during his career. Being a catcher, he had a sharp batting eye—drawing 70 or more walks five times. He enjoyed his finest season at the plate in 2007, when he hit .338, drove in 90 runs, and compiled a stellar .426 on-base percentage. By the time he retired, he had captured five Silver Slugger Awards.

Defensively, Posada was more than adequate, leading the AL three times in putouts and twice in assists. He was extremely durable behind the plate, rarely losing significant playing time to injuries. By 2011, Posada was 39 years old and slowing down. He appeared primarily as a designated hitter, while Russell Martin did most of the catching. He announced his retirement in January of the following year. Posada's sabermetric numbers put him on the cusp of the Hall of Fame. But similarity scores compare him favorably to Cooperstown alumni Gabby Hartnett, Gary Carter, and Bill Dickey.

Off the field, Posada founded his own charity—the Jorge Posada Foundation—which sponsors research for a disease known as craniosynostosis. The condition results in abnormal bone growth in the skulls of infants. Posada's son is afflicted.

SCOTT BROSIUS, THIRD BASE

Born and raised in Oregon, Brosius was selected in a late round of the 1987 draft by the A's. He puttered in the minors for portions of seven seasons before finally attaining full-time status in Oakland. He was given lengthy trials between 1991–1993. Brosius had a promising debut, landing on a short list of players to homer in their first major-league game.

During the course of his career, Brosius was hot and cold at the plate, putting up excellent numbers one year and slumping the next. He hit .262 in 1995, and followed with a .304 effort in 1996. When his average fell more than 100 points in 1997, the A's traded him to the Yankees for pitcher Kenny Rogers and cash.

Brosius became a better player all around in New York. In 1998, he reached career highs in hits (159), runs scored (86), and RBIs (98), while hitting an even .300. He made his first and only All-Star appearance that season, going 1-for-2 with a run scored in a 13–8 AL blowout. His defense really came around the following year, as he led the AL with a .962 fielding percentage and captured a Gold Glove.

In the postseason, Brosius had a knack for rising to the occasion. In 1998, he gathered 18 hits in playoff action and drove in 15 runs. In Game 3 of the World Series, he almost single-handedly led the Yankees to victory, slamming a pair of homers that accounted for four of five New York runs. His .471 Series average netted him MVP honors. "There's nothing more fun than this," he said after his Game 3 performance. "When you grow up, you want to get a chance to play in the World Series. This is what you play for."

In September 1999, Brosius suffered a personal tragedy when his father died of colon cancer at age 55. He turned sorrow into triumph during the Fall Classic, hitting .375 and helping the Yanks to a sweep of the Braves. Joe Torre praised his ability to remain focused. "He had a tough year emotionally. Nobody else had to live with what he did. And he was still the same guy." Brosius cemented his reputation as an October hero when he blasted a ninth-inning homer in Game 5 of the 2001 Fall Classic off of reliever Byung-Hyun Kim. The two-run shot sent the game into extra innings. Brosius ended up with a lifetime batting mark of .314 in World Series play.

Brosius had a solid season all around in 2001, but announced his retirement at season's end so he could spend more time with his family. "I was surprised about Scott," said Steinbrenner when he got the news. "But he wanted to retire a Yankee. He's a great warrior. I hate to lose him."

Brosius took a job as assistant coach at Linfield College in Oregon. He eventually became head coach in 2008, guiding the club to three Division III College World Series appearances. In 2013, the school finally captured a championship. Brosius was elected to the Oregon Sports Hall of Fame in 2005.

ORLANDO HERNANDEZ, PITCHER

Hernandez was one of Cuba's top pitchers, playing for such teams as Industriales, Ciudad Habana, and Habaneras. During his 10-year career in the Cuban National Series, he compiled the highest winning percentage in league history. He was also a regular on the Cuban national team, aiding the squad to a gold medal at the Barcelona Olympics in 1992.

In 1995, Hernandez's half-brother, Livan, defected from Cuba (he would later become a successful major-league pitcher). Some time after Livan's departure, Orlando was detained by government officials and questioned about his ties to an American sports agent. He was banned from Cuban baseball. In 1997, he followed his half-brother's example, defecting from the city of Caiberien. He and several others were picked up by the U.S. Coast Guard in the vicinity of the Bahamas. Within two months, the Yankees had arranged for him to enter the United States on a visa. He signed a four-year contract with the club.

In early June 1998, Hernandez joined the Yankees. He made 21 starts and won seven of his last eight decisions, posting a 12–4 record with a 3.13 ERA. He enjoyed his best season the following year. Although his ERA rose nearly a hundred points, he averaged close to seven strikeouts per nine frames and notched a 17–9 record. Beset by injuries in 2000, he missed a few starts and would never appear in more than 24 games during the rest of his tenure in New York, which ended after the 2004 campaign.

Hernandez was nicknamed "El Duque" (literally "The Duke") in deference to his status as Cuban baseball royalty. He was known for his high leg kick. When he arrived in New York, his papers had been forged by his agent to make him appear younger. He is believed to have been 32 years old in his rookie year. On the mound, he used an assortment of slow junk pitches, throwing them from various arm angles and release points. He was a painfully slow worker, fiddling with his cap and uniform constantly before shaking off multiple signs—especially when he was in a jam. The Yankees assigned the Spanish-speaking Jorge Posada to work with him, and the two sometimes squabbled like brothers.

From 1998–2000, "El Duque" was among the Yankees' most successful postseason performers. In 1998, he yielded just one earned run in 14 innings. In 1999, he limited the opposition to four runs in 30 frames. The following year, he had a quality outing against the A's in the ALDS, running his postseason record up to 6–0. He won two more games in the ALCS before the Mets finally saddled him with a loss in Game 3 of the 2000 World Series. That game remained tied until the bottom of the eighth, when the Mets broke through with the winning run.

Granted free agency in 2004, Hernandez signed with the White Sox and won another World Series ring. He retired in 2007, at the age of 41. In October play, he was 9–3 with a handsome 2.55 ERA. He appeared at the 67th annual Old-Timers' Game at Yankee Stadium in 2013. The following year, he rejoined the team as a minor-league spring training instructor.

DAVID WELLS, PITCHER

Born in Torrance, California, Wells grew up in San Diego. He described himself as a "gym rat" who spent most of his time hanging out at a local recreational center or playing ball. His major-league debut came in 1987, with Toronto. A left-hander, he would not become a full-time starter until the age of 30. In six seasons with the Blue Jays, he ran up a middling record of 47–37 with an ERA slightly below the 4.00 mark. He earned his first World Series ring in 1992, and was cut by Toronto the following spring. He ended up in Detroit, where he became a top-notch hurler. In 1995, he went 10–3 with the Tigers before a July trade landed him in Cincinnati. He finished the season at 16–8 with an ERA of 3.24—his best season to that point.

Wells arrived in New York for the 1997 slate. He was an avid fan of Babe Ruth and took the uniform number "33" in honor of the Babe's retired digit. Wells got himself a tattoo of Ruth and even purchased one of the slugger's original game-worn hats for a reported sum of $35,000. He was reprimanded and fined by Yankees management for wearing it during one of his starts (it did not conform to the team's dress code). A big man at 6-foot-3, 200-plus pounds, Wells carried the nickname "Boomer." He had a fondness for beer and motorcycles. On the mound, he had an above-average fastball, a great curve, and pinpoint control.

In 1997 and 1998, the self-proclaimed rebel compiled a 34–14 regular-season record. He led the AL with a .818 winning percentage in the latter campaign, while tossing a league-best five shutouts. One of those was a perfect game—the 15th in major-league history. After completing the historic 4–0 win over the Twins, he claimed that he was hung over when he threw it. He describes his condition as "half-drunk" in his book *Perfect I'm Not*, which was released in 2003. In September 1998, he came fairly close to tossing a second perfect game against the A's. He retired the first 20 batters in order before Jason Giambi singled with an 0–2 count. Wells ended up with a two-hitter.

The big southpaw was virtually unhittable in the postseason during his first stint with the Yankees, winning all five of his starts. He was named MVP of the 1998 ALCS against the Indians. Traded to the Blue Jays in 1999, he would return to New York for another successful two-year run beginning in 2002. He finished his Yankees career with a stellar 68–28 regular-season record. He was 7–2 for the Bombers in postseason play.

In 2007, Wells was diagnosed with type 2 diabetes. He was released by the Padres that year and finished the season with the Dodgers. It was his last major-league campaign. Finished as a player, he served as a broadcaster for *MLB on TBS*. He also was host of *The Cheap Seats* on FOXsports.com. When Joe Torre's memoir *The Yankee Years* was released, Wells called him a "punk" for revealing clubhouse secrets and said he would like to punch him in the face or have someone else do it.

TINO MARTINEZ, FIRST BASE

A native of Tampa, Florida, Martinez attended Jefferson High School, breaking numerous baseball records set by fellow alumnus Fred McGriff. Martinez moved on to the University of Tampa and was selected to play for Team USA in 1987. He was among the squad's leading hitters in the Pan American Games and the World Cup. He ended up getting selected by the Mariners in the first round of the 1988 draft.

Martinez spent portions of six seasons in Seattle, slowly developing into a reliable power hitter. His first great season came in 1995, when he collected 69 extra-base hits (including 31 homers) and 111 RBIs. In the ALDS that year, he punished the Yanks, hitting .409 with a homer and five ribbies. Enamored with his talents, the Yankees arranged a five-player trade that also brought pitcher Jeff Nelson to the Bronx.

Martinez endeared himself to Yankees fans with his lively personality and productive bat. Between 1996–2001, he reached the century mark in RBIs each year but one (he finished with 91 in 2000), while averaging 29 homers. He enjoyed his finest offensive campaign in 1997, when he slammed a career-high 44 long balls and knocked in 141 runs. He even won baseball's annual Home Run Derby that year.

A fine defensive first baseman, Martinez finished first or second in fielding percentage seven times during his career. He led the league in assists during the 1999 slate. Despite those numbers, he never captured a Gold Glove.

The World Series was often Martinez's finest hour. In 25 Fall Classic games, he scored 11 runs and drove in 14 more. Two of his Series homers were quite memorable. In Game 1 of the 1998 Fall Classic, he hit a 3–2 pitch from San Diego's Mark Langston into the upper deck at Yankee Stadium for a grand slam. In Game 4 of the 2001 affair, his two-out, ninth-inning homer off of Diamondbacks hurler Byung-Hyun Kim tied the score in a game the Yankees won in extra innings.

Granted free agency in 2001, Martinez signed with the Cardinals. He spent two seasons in St. Louis and one with his hometown Tampa Bay Devil Rays before returning to New York for one last hurrah in 2005. He retired as a Yankee, later serving as a YES Network analyst. He had a brief stint as a Marlins hitting coach in 2013, but resigned when certain players complained that he had been verbally and physically abusive to them. He apologized, contending that his harsh comments had been intended as constructive criticism. He also admitted to having grabbed one player angrily. "I just thought with some young players you needed to be a little firmer and try to get them on track," he told the Associated Press. "Right now, I'm disappointed in myself. I'm embarrassed." A plaque dedicated to Martinez currently resides in Monument Park at Yankee Stadium.

DAVID CONE, PITCHER

Cone was a native of Kansas City. In high school, he played quarterback and led his team to a district championship. Rockhurst High had no baseball program, and Cone got his early experience in the Ban Johnson Amateur Baseball League during the summer. He was drafted in 1981, by the Royals, after attending an open tryout.

An injury in 1983 slowed Cone's path to the majors. He was converted to a relief pitcher at Triple A Omaha, joining the Royals in 1986. In 11 games, he was hit pretty hard, and Kansas City ended up trading him to the Mets. He put up unremarkable numbers in 1987, and followed with a breakthrough season, posting a 20–3 record with a 2.22 ERA. He earned the first of five All-Star selections and finished third in Cy Young voting.

Cone developed a large following in New York. Calling themselves "Coneheads," many of his fans came to Shea Stadium wearing pointy rubber skullcaps like characters from the old Dan Aykroyd sketches on *Saturday Night Live*. The right-hander won 75 games for the Mets between 1988–1992, before a trade sent him to Toronto. He pitched well, helping the Jays to a world championship in 1992.

Cone ended up with the Royals again and captured Cy Young honors in 1994, on the strength of a 16–5 record and a 2.94 ERA. A nomad, he began the following season with Toronto and ended up getting shipped to the Yankees in a July trade. Cone's return to the Big Apple was highly successful, as he compiled a 9–2 record in 13 starts. In the ALDS, the Mariners treated him rather roughly, but the Yankees had the offense to back him up in the opener. He was not on the mound when the Yankees lost the series, leaving in the eighth inning with the score tied at four.

In 1996, Cone was off to a 4–1 start before developing a career-threatening aneurysm in his pitching shoulder. He underwent surgery and bravely returned in September to win three of four decisions. Careful not to put too much stress on his arm, Joe Torre used him once in each round of the playoffs. He went six innings in each outing and turned in a pair of quality starts. In Game 3 of the World Series, he scattered four hits and allowed just one run as the Yankees began an improbable comeback against the Braves.

Cone's best pitches were his split-fingered fastball and slider. His offerings had dramatic movement, often dropping sharply in or out of the strike zone. They darted so remarkably at times that he didn't always get the benefit of umpire's calls. He averaged a manageable 3 1/2 walks per nine frames, yielding 80 or more free passes in seven seasons.

Cone had three more excellent years with the Yankees after the 1996 campaign, earning two All-Star selections and finishing among the top 10 in Cy Young voting twice. He led the AL with 20 wins in 1998—landing on a short list of pitchers to reach that total in both leagues. The defining moment of his career came on July 18, 1999, when he threw a perfect game against the Expos. Interestingly, it happened on Old-Timers' Day, with Don Larsen—author of a perfect game in the 1956 World Series—throwing out the ceremonial first pitch.

In 2000, Cone pitched well below expectations and looked uncomfortable on the mound at times. Torre stuck by him anyway as his ERA ballooned to 6.91 and his record sank to 4–14. The Yankees granted him free agency at season's end, and he departed for Boston. He never completely regained his old form. Out of the majors in 2002, he made a comeback attempt in 2003, with the Mets. It was unsuccessful.

In 2001, Cone became a color commentator for the YES Network. When he returned to the mound for the Mets, George Steinbrenner became highly irritated, assuring Cone that he was no longer welcome in the Bronx. The Mets offered him a broadcasting job after his retirement as a player, but he turned it down to spend time with his family. In 2008, he returned to the YES Network working as an analyst and a host of *Yankees on Deck*.

FAST FACT: From 1998–2000, the Yankees compiled an incredible 33–8 record in postseason play. This included consecutive Series sweeps in 1998 and 1999.

23

HONORABLE MENTIONS

CHICAGO WHITE SOX (1917–1919)

History will never know how many Hall of Famers the White Sox could have produced during the second decade of the twentieth century. Three players who did not participate in the 1919 World Series fix made it to Cooperstown (Ray Schalk, Red Faber, and Eddie Collins). Of the eight men who were banned for life by Judge Kenesaw Mountain Landis for throwing games, at least three would have received serious consideration—especially "Shoeless" Joe Jackson, who is generally considered to be one of the greatest players outside the Hall of Fame. In 1917, the White Sox finished nine games ahead of the Red Sox and vanquished the Giants in the World Series. The club slumped to sixth place the following year when several marquee players were lost to the war cause. By 1919, the stars had returned. On paper, the ChiSox were a better team than the Reds and had a good chance at winning the World Series had everyone played fairly.

Key Players

Eddie Collins, Second Base

The educated Collins didn't associate with the band of delinquents who hijacked the 1919 Series, so his Hall of Fame career continued uninterrupted. Arguably the greatest second baseman in history, he is the all-time leader in multiple statistical categories among players at his position. He hit .302 in the two World Series he appeared in with Chicago.

Joe Jackson, Outfield

Born in rural South Carolina, the naïve and illiterate Jackson had some adjustment problems when he first reached the majors. One sportswriter referred to him as a "wide-eyed and gullible yokel." He was worldly enough to post a .356 lifetime batting average in 13 seasons. His involvement in the throwing of games was minimal, as he collected 12 base hits during the 1919 Fall Classic—more than any player on either club.

Buck Weaver, Third Base

Had Weaver not fallen in with the wrong crowd, he might have completed a glorious career. Although defense was not his strong point, he hit .305 between 1917–1920, including a personal-best .331 showing in the latter campaign. Weaver was entering the prime of his career when he was banned from the sport. With the so-called Lively Ball Era in full swing, his offensive numbers would presumably have gotten even better.

Eddie Cicotte, Pitcher

Cicotte used a wide array of trick pitches, including a knuckleball, emery ball, and spitball. He won 57 games during Chicago's two pennant-winning seasons. At the start of the 1919 World Series, he was instructed to hit the first batter he faced to indicate that the fix was on. Morrie Rath was the victim. Cicotte reportedly hammed it up so much in one of his starts that he drew suspicion from fans and sportswriters.

PITTSBURGH PIRATES (1925–1927)

After a World Series victory in 1909, the Pirates fell out of contention for some time, placing fourth or lower in eight consecutive seasons. But owner Barney Dreyfuss had a marvelous eye for talent and continued to import a steady stream of able-bodied players to Pittsburgh. The club returned to glory in 1925, finally unseating the Giants as National

League champions and ending a long championship drought with a victory over the Senators in the World Series. A late September slump sank the Pirates' pennant hopes in 1926, but they came out on top again the following year. The 1927 squad was among the best in franchise history. Unfortunately, the Yankees had the most powerful team of the decade. With Babe Ruth, Lou Gehrig, Earle Combs, and Tony Lazzeri in their prime, the "Murderers' Row" Yankees made quick work of the Bucs, sweeping the World Series. While the Pirates would carry a number of Hall of Famers on their roster, the club would not see postseason action again until 1960.

Key Players

Pie Traynor, Third Base

Traynor supposedly received his unusual nickname for his love of pies as a kid. He didn't generate many homers, but he hit for high average and had decent speed on the base paths. Most of his contemporaries considered him to be the best at his position defensively. A lifetime .320 hitter in regular-season play, he hit more than 20 points higher in the 1925 World Series. Yankees hurlers handcuffed him in the 1927 Fall Classic, but he finished his postseason career at .293. His numbers eventually landed him in the Hall of Fame.

Kiki Cuyler, Outfield

It was a difficult task keeping Cuyler off the base paths in 1925. He piled up 220 hits, drew 58 walks, and got hit by 13 pitches that year. Polishing off a stellar campaign, he raked three doubles and a homer in the World Series. During the 1927 slate, Cuyler got into a dispute with manager Donie Bush and ended up getting benched. He missed more than 60 games, including the World Series. Traded to the Cubs before the 1928 campaign, he continued on a trajectory to Cooperstown.

Max Carey, Outfield

The switch-hitting Carey was nearing the end of his Hall of Fame career when the Pirates won the World Series in 1925. It was his last great season, as he hit .343 and led the NL for the fourth straight year with 46 steals. He swiped three more in the World Series and hit .458.

Traded to Brooklyn after he got off to a .222 start the following year, he ended his playing days in Flatbush. Carey retired with 10 stolen-base titles to his credit.

Paul Waner, Outfield

Had the award existed then, Waner, also known as "Big Poison," would likely have been named Rookie of the Year in 1926, when he hit .336 with a league-leading 22 triples. He followed with the greatest season of his career, pacing the circuit in hits (237), triples (18), and RBIs (131), while capturing a batting crown with a .380 average. He stayed hot in the World Series that year while most of his teammates cooled off. At least he had a NL MVP Award to show for his efforts. Known for his fondness for alcohol, Waner once received a facetious compliment from Casey Stengel regarding his base-running skills. "He had to be a very graceful player because he could slide without breaking the bottle on his hip," said Stengel.

Lloyd Waner, Outfield

Lloyd was three years younger than his brother Paul and carried the nickname "Little Poison." He was undeniably toxic to opposing pitchers in his 1927 debut, hitting .355, while leading the league with 133 runs scored. Creating havoc at the top of the batting order, he reached base in eight of 18 trips to the plate during the World Series that year. The five runs he scored didn't help the Pirates to a single victory. There was no rivalry between siblings, as Paul insisted that Lloyd was a better player. Said Paul, "He can spot me 25 feet and then beat me in a sprint. A batter's got to knock a fly over the fence to keep him from reaching it, and he doesn't miss 'em either." In the sprint to the Hall of Fame, Paul arrived first in 1952. Lloyd was elected via the Veteran's Committee in 1967.

ST. LOUIS CARDINALS (1942–1946)

After the bombing of Pearl Harbor, major leaguers began joining the armed forces in large numbers. By 1943, more than 200 players were serving in the military. In 1945, that figure nearly doubled. Although the pennant races that took place during the war years were competitive in their own right, the level of play was significantly diminished. This fact became readily apparent when the lowly St. Louis Browns suddenly rose to contention in 1944, after serving as perennial doormats during the previous four decades. The Cardinals were the most dominant club during the war era; however, their success can only be taken in light of the conspicuous absence of talent in the majors during World War II. From 1942–1944, the Redbirds captured three pennants and two world championships. Silencing their detractors, they came away with a creditable Series victory over the Red Sox after most of the stars had returned to action in 1946.

Key Players

Mort Cooper, Pitcher

The right-handed Cooper was a decent pitcher before the war, but he became a superstar after the talent pool was depleted. From 1942–1944, he won at least 21 games each year. In 1942, he was named MVP on the strength of his 22–7 record, 1.78 ERA, and league-leading 10 shutouts. His best postseason work came in Game 5 of the 1944 World Series against the Browns, when he tossed a complete-game shutout. In three Fall Classics, he compiled a 3.00 ERA. He later defected to the Braves in the wake of a bitter salary dispute.

Marty Marion, Shortstop

Marion was known to many as "Mr. Shortstop." He was never more than an adequate hitter, but his glove work was exceptional. He finished atop the NL leaderboards in various defensive categories for a full decade. He enjoyed his most memorable season in 1944, when he captured NL MVP honors. Marion played in four World Series with the Cardinals, gathering nine extra-base hits and 11 RBIs. His name remained on the primary Hall of Fame ballot until 1973, and recently reappeared on the Veteran's Committee list. Many of Marion's teammates felt that he was a worthy candidate the first time around.

Stan Musial, Outfield

Musial was undoubtedly the greatest player in franchise history. At the time of this writing, he ranked second on the all-time list in total bases, third in doubles, fourth in hits, and seventh in RBIs. He was also a consummate gentleman to fans, sportswriters, and teammates. Dedicating a statue to Musial outside of Busch Stadium, Commissioner Ford Frick declared, "Here stands baseball's happy warrior. Here stands baseball's perfect knight."

Walker Cooper, Catcher

During his prime, the 6-foot-3, 210-pound Cooper was an intimidating presence at home plate. He had a longer and more productive career than his older brother Mort, whom he worked with frequently as a batterymate. Walker was an All-Star each year from 1942–1944, posting a .300 average twice in that span. In 1943, he was a runner-up for the NL MVP, with 43 extra-base hits and 81 RBIs, to complement his outstanding defensive play. Cooper had a strong arm, placing among the top five in runners caught stealing five times. In three World Series with St. Louis, he hit an even .300 with six RBIs.

NEW YORK YANKEES (1955–1958)

With several chapters of this book already dedicated to memorable Yankees squads, it seems only fair that a couple of Bronx powerhouses should end up on the cusp of inclusion. After completing a five-year championship run in 1953, the Yankees continued to dominate the American League for another decade. They met with mixed results in the postseason, however. From 1955–1958, the Bombers carried the World Series to a Game 7 each year. They lost two of those deciding contests—to the Dodgers in 1955 and the Braves in 1957. During that four-year span of AL supremacy, men in pinstripes accounted for more than 25 percent of the available AL All-Star spots.

Key Players

Mickey Mantle, Outfield

When the mid-1950s arrived, Mantle was just entering his prime. He referred to the 1956 campaign as his "favorite summer" since it was his Triple Crown year. He finished the season with 52 homers, 130 RBIs, and a career-high .353 average. From 1955–1958, he clubbed seven World Series homers and drove in 10 runs.

Yogi Berra, Catcher

Berra was a fine hitter during the regular season but always raised his game to another level on the October stage. His most productive World Series by far was the 1956 affair, when he slugged three homers and drove in 10 runs. He also caught Don Larsen's perfect game. "[Larsen] didn't shake me off once," Yogi remembered. "He was throwing pretty hard and had a good breaking ball that day. Everything was working for him."

Whitey Ford, Pitcher

Interestingly, Ford was at his best during the Yankees' Series losses of 1955 and 1957. Against the Dodgers, he was 2–0 with a 2.12 ERA. Facing the Braves, he surrendered just two runs in 16 innings of work. Supremely confident, Ford appeared on the *Ed Sullivan Show* along with Mickey Mantle and staffmate Tommy Byrne on the night before Game 6 of the 1955 Fall Classic. Asked who was pitching the following night, Ford said, "I am and Tommy's pitching the seventh game."

Moose Skowron, First Base

Although he never really became a household name, Skowron was of immense value to the club in the postseason. His three-run homer in Game 6 of the 1955 World Series lifted the Yankees to a 5–1 victory. The following October, he blasted a grand slam in Game 7. He was at it again in 1958, homering in Game 1, driving in the winning run in Game 6, and launching a three-run shot in the deciding contest. Mickey Mantle once paid Skowron an immense compliment when he said,

> People used to look at our lineup and concentrate on the guys in the middle of the order. Moose might have been batting sixth or seventh, but he made our lineup deep and more dangerous. You didn't want to give him too much around the plate. He was like Yogi Berra. He could hit bad pitches out and beat you.

NEW YORK YANKEES (1960–1964)

No era of baseball history would be complete without a slew of World Series appearances by the Yankees. By the time the 1960s arrived, some of the fan favorites were aging out, particularly Yogi Berra, who saw increasingly less playing time behind the plate before taking over as manager in 1964. Lesser stars of the 1950s, for example, Hank Bauer, Joe Collins, and Jerry Coleman, were gone. But a new crop of October heroes emerged as the Bombers made five straight World Series appearances from 1960–1964. They won just two, compiling an uncharacteristic 14–16 postseason record in that span.

Key Players

Roger Maris, Outfield

Maris's story has become a cautionary tale—how the pressures of the Bronx nearly destroyed this quiet, unassuming, small-town boy. For three glorious seasons, Maris's name was mentioned in the same breath as Mickey Mantle. The lefty-swinging outfielder captured back-to-back MVP Awards in 1960 and 1961, and made four consecutive All-Star appearances before injuries and personal issues slowed him down. In five World Series with the Yankees, he gathered 20 hits, including five homers and three doubles. After breaking Ruth's single-season record for home runs in 1961, he was threatened with an asterisk.

Elston Howard, Catcher/Outfield

By the end of the 1954 slate, the Yankees had still not added an African American player to their roster. They had originally targeted slick-fielding first baseman Vic Power but found him to be too outspoken and controversial. In the end, they chose Howard. "They couldn't have done better," said teammate Norm Siebern. "He had great morals, personality, and character. He was an outstanding individual." He was an outstanding player as well. A catcher by trade, he was moved to the outfield until Yogi Berra started to wear down. Howard made the All-Star team each year from 1957–1965, and captured a MVP Award in 1963. From 1960–1964, he hit .280 in World Series play with nine extra-base hits and nine RBIs.

Ralph Terry, Pitcher

Terry is remembered for giving up a walk-off homer to Bill Mazeroski in Game 7 of the 1960 Fall Classic. Many fans forget that he redeemed himself with a series-clinching shutout over the Giants in 1962. Toiling in relative anonymity beside Whitey Ford, the right-handed Terry posted a 66–38 record from 1960–1963, while keeping his ERA in the low threes each year. In 1962, he led the league with 23 wins and received his only All-Star selection. Discounting his ill-fated performance in the 1960 World Series, he compiled a lifetime ERA of 2.52 in the postseason.

Whitey Ford, Pitcher

Plagued by shoulder issues in 1960, Ford won just 12 regular-season games. Casey Stengel saved him for Game 3 of the World Series instead of starting him in the opener. After winning his second start in Game 6, he was unavailable for the deciding contest. Ford stated that it was the only time he was ever angry with Stengel. He refused to speak to Casey during the somber ride home to New York after the crushing Game 7 defeat. Ralph Houk took over as manager the following year, and Ford had two of his best seasons ever, winning 25 games in 1961, and 24 in 1963. He was MVP of the 1961 Series versus the Reds.

Mickey Mantle, Outfield

There are many who believe that Mantle would have broken Ruth's single-season home-run record in 1961 before Maris. The "M&M Boys" were neck and neck in the chase before Mantle came down with a severe cold. At the suggestion of broadcaster Mel Allen, he visited an East Side physician, who, clad in a soiled smock, injected Mantle with an elixir that made him even sicker. The area around the injection site became so inflamed that it had to be cut open and lanced. Mantle sat out several games as Maris broke the record in 76 more at-bats. The "Mick" finished with 54—the highest total of his career. Injuries continued to plague Mantle in the early 1960s, but he put up great numbers when he was healthy.

BOSTON RED SOX (2004–2007)

Entering the 2004 campaign, the Red Sox had experienced the second longest championship drought in major-league history, going more than 80 years without a World Series title. Making the situation especially frustrating, the club finished second in the AL East behind the Yankees each year from 1998–2003. The 2004 season ended in familiar fashion, with the Red Sox sitting in second place. They entered the playoffs with a wild card berth and fell behind the Yankees in the American League Championship Series—another hauntingly common scenario. But the script would be rewritten that year, as Boston rallied from a three-game deficit to win the AL pennant. Following the Game 7 victory, fans at Fenway Park got out of control, and a college student named Victoria Snelgrove was killed by police after being shot with a pepper-spray ball. BoSox outfielder Trot Nixon said ruefully, "I'd give Game 7 back to have her back." The World Series was anticlimactic, as the Sox rolled over the Cardinals in four games. After losing the American League Division Series to the White Sox in 2005, and missing the playoffs the following year, Boston completed its second Series sweep in a four-year span with a triumph over the Rockies. The Boston roster was relatively unstable from 2004–2007, but there were a few core players who contributed heavily to both Series victories.

Key Players

Manny Ramirez, Outfield

Ramirez loved to stand near home plate admiring his tape-measure home runs. He was also accused of loafing in the outfield. Late in his career, he was suspended twice for using banned substances. These incidents came to be known as "Manny Moments." In 2004 and 2007, Ramirez slammed 63 homers and drove in more than 200 runs for the Red Sox during the regular season. His .412 batting average earned him World Series MVP honors in 2004.

David Ortiz, Designated Hitter

Ortiz is still active at the time of this writing. Emminently likeable, he carries the warm and fuzzy nicknames of "Big Papi" and "Cookie Monster." There are many who consider him to be the best DH of all time. He certainly has the numbers to back it up. Among the greatest clutch players in baseball history, Ortiz launched 12 walk-off homers between 2003–2013 (including postseason play). He currently holds the record for most hits and RBIs by a DH. Additionally, he owns multiple franchise records, including the single-season mark for homers (54 in 2006). That's quite an accomplishment considering that Ted Williams once called Fenway Park home.

Ortiz's value to the club has been immeasurable. "I know that great players are great, are supposed to be great in any moment," said Red Sox GM Ben Cherington, "but it's hard to see [Ortiz] in those moments and not think there's something different about him. . . . I can't add anything more to the legend that's already there. He keeps writing more chapters on his own." One of those chapters came in 2013, when the husky slugger captured World Series MVP honors with 11 hits, six RBIs, and a .760 on-base percentage in six games.

Jason Varitek, Catcher

A solid defensive catcher, Varitek was behind the plate for four no-hitters—a feat duplicated by just one other player in baseball history. In 2004, his competitive spirit and leadership skills inspired the Red Sox to promote him to team captain. He spent his entire 15-year career in Boston, averaging 19 homers and 70 RBIs per year between 2003–2007. During his two World Series appearances, he drove in seven runs in eight games.

Curt Schilling, Pitcher

The right-handed Schilling spent most of his career outside Boston, piling up 163 wins and more than 2,500 strikeouts with four different teams. He enjoyed one of his best seasons ever with the Red Sox in 2004, compiling a 21–6 record with a 3.26 ERA. During the first game of the ALDS, he seriously injured his right ankle and underwent a surgical procedure to temporarily repair it. In Game 6 of the ALCS, he beat the Yankees with blood conspicuously soaking through his sock. He continued his success in the World Series, winning his only start against the Cardinals. In 2007, Schilling made just 24 regular-season appearances due to nagging injuries. By the time the postseason rolled around, he was back in top form, going 3–0 with a 3.00 ERA in four appearances. He had previously been named MVP of the 2001 World Series with the Diamondbacks.

PHILADELPHIA PHILLIES (2007–2011)

The Phillies are among the least successful franchises in baseball history, with a cumulative won–loss percentage below .500 and just two World Series titles to their credit in more than 130 years of existence. After fielding strong teams during the 1970s and early 1980s, the club fell out of contention for many years. Aside from a World Series berth in 1993, the Phillies remained absent from postseason play for more than two decades. In 2007, a core group of talented players began to gel. A loss in the National League Division Series was followed by a series victory in 2008—the first since 1980. The club returned to the Fall Classic in 2009, but fell to the Yankees in six games. Two more playoff appearances would follow—a six-game loss in the 2010 National League Championship Series and a five-game defeat at the hands of the Cardinals in the 2011 divisional series.

Key Players

Ryan Howard, First Base

From 2006–2011, Howard was one of the premier sluggers in the NL, gathering no fewer than 31 homers each year and peaking at 58 long balls in 2006. He was named Rookie of the Year in 2005, and MVP the following season. He led the league in RBIs three times in a four-year span. In the postseason, Howard was one of the Phillies' leading run producers, drilling six homers, while driving in 26 runs in 2008 and 2009. He was named MVP of the latter NLCS. He ruptured his Achilles tendon in the 2011 playoffs. Upon returning in July 2012, his season was prematurely ended due to a freak incident in the on-deck circle. He dropped one of the weights he was using to warm up with on his toe, fracturing it. He has not been the same player since.

Chase Utley, Second Base

Utley made five straight All-Star appearances beginning in 2006. He began his career as a five-tool player, hitting for power and average, while demonstrating speed on the bases and a strong arm at second base. Unafraid to take one for the team, he got hit by more pitches than any National Leaguer in three consecutive campaigns. He smashed five homers in the 2009 World Series against the Yankees, scoring seven runs and driving in eight more. Plagued by a series of injuries since 2010, his numbers have been on a downward spiral ever since.

Jimmy Rollins, Shortstop

Rollins spent 15 years in Philly prior to departing for Los Angeles before the 2015 slate. With remarkable speed, he led the NL four times in triples, while stealing 30 or more bases on 10 occasions. His best season came in 2007, when he captured NL MVP honors with 139 runs scored and 20 triples. A solid defensive shortstop, Rollins claimed four Gold Gloves between 2007–2012. On the downside, he is known for swinging at the first pitch—not always a good policy for a leadoff hitter.

Cole Hamels, Pitcher

Hamels was a top-shelf hurler in 2007 and 2008, posting a 29–15 record in that stretch. He was Philly's postseason hero in 2008, going 4–0 in five starts. He was named MVP of the 2008 NLCS and World Series. After struggling in 2009, he straightened himself out the following year. Through the 2014 campaign, he had a 7–4 postseason record and a 3.09 ERA. The left-hander generated controversy in 2012, when he admitted to hitting Washington Nationals slugger Bryce Harper for being too "cocky." He was called "gutless" and "classless" by Nationals GM Mike Rizzo.

Shane Victorino, Outfield

The Hawaiian-born Victorino was a key player on three pennant-winning squads. After helping the Phillies to consecutive World Series appearances, he was a vital cog in Boston's world championship run of 2013. Still active through the 2015 slate, Victorino has good speed on the bases. He has led the NL in triples twice, while stealing no fewer than 25 bases on five occasions. Although he was moderately unproductive in the World Series with Philadelphia, he was a strong offensive presence in other rounds of the playoffs—particularly in the 2009 NLCS, when he hit .368 with two homers and six RBIs. The Red Sox traded Victorino to the Dodgers partway through the 2015 campaign.

SAN FRANCISCO GIANTS (2010–2014)

The Giants had an interesting run from 2010–2014. In that span, they won three NL pennants and were shut out of the playoffs twice. In 2014, they spent half of the season in second place, emerging with a last minute wild-card berth on the heels of a September collapse by the Brewers. The cast of characters was diverse during the Giants' five-year stretch of quasi-dominance, with only three positional players maintaining full-time status for at least four seasons. The club employed five full-time left fielders, four second basemen, and three center fielders. The pitching staff was unstable as well, with three different closers anchoring the bullpen. At times, the Giants were bad—especially in 2013, when they posted a 76–86 record and finished 16 games behind the division-leading Dodgers. But through it all, they managed to add three world championships to the club's modest collection. No Giants squad had ever won as many championships in such a short span.

Key Players

Buster Posey, Catcher

Regardless of whether Posey ends up in the Hall of Fame, he will forever be remembered for the grisly season-ending injury he suffered in a collision at home plate in 2011. His leg buckled at a grotesque angle, resulting in an ankle dislocation and broken bone. Major league rules were later changed to allow baserunners a clear path to the plate on close plays. Considered one of the best catchers in the major leagues, Posey was Rookie of the Year in 2010, and NL MVP in 2012. He was a significant postseason contributor as well, hitting .300 in the 2010 World Series and .389 in the 2014 NLDS. His similarity scores through the 2015 campaign compare him favorably to Hall of Fame catcher Gabby Hartnett at the same age.

Pablo Sandoval, Third Base

Sandoval's nicknames "Kung Fu Panda" and "Round Mound of Pound" pertain to his portly stature. At 5-foot-11, 255 pounds, he looks like he can't get out of his own way. But Sandoval runs the bases surprisingly well and has excellent range at third base. During his seven seasons in San Francisco, he hit .294 and averaged 15 homers and 66 RBIs per year. In the postseason, he kicked it up a notch, fashioning a .344 batting mark in 39 games. He was MVP of the 2012 World Series. Moving to Boston in 2015, he slumped mightily at the plate for extended periods of time.

Brandon Crawford, Shortstop

For the time being, the Giants don't have to worry about the shortstop position. Crawford has been carrying out his duties commendably for the better part of five seasons. Although he strikes out a lot and hits for mediocre averages, his power numbers have increased steadily each year. In two World Series, he has fashioned a .286 batting average. Defensively, he displays wide range and a strong arm. While it's too early to tell, there are many who believe he is on the way to bigger and better seasons.

Hunter Pence, Right Field

Pence had his breakthrough seasons with the Astros, slamming 25 homers each year from 2008–2010. Traded to the Giants in late July 2011, he collected 35 RBIs in 54 games. He has been a reliable run producer in San Francisco ever since. In 11 World Series games with the Giants, he has raked opposing pitching at a .390 clip, while driving in six runs. Defensively, he has led NL right fielders in assists five times.

Madison Bumgarner, Pitcher

On an inconsistent pitching staff, Bumgarner has given the Giants the most stability in the past few years. Between 2011–2014, he averaged 15 wins per year. His ERA never exceeded 3.37 in that span. Solidly built at 6-foot-5, 235 pounds, the left-hander hits well for a pitcher and is proud of that distinction. During the Giants' 2014 championship run, he accrued a .258 regular-season batting average with four homers and 15 RBIs in 34 games. In the World Series, he was an irrepressible force on the mound. After winning both of his starts, he was called on to finish Game 7. He held the Royals to two hits in five innings, picking up a save and a World Series MVP Award. He was also MVP of the NLCS that year. Through the 2015 slate, he owned a 4–0 record with a preposterous 0.25 ERA in three World Series.

BIBLIOGRAPHY

"8-in-a-Row Predicted by Yankee Players." *United Press International*, October 6, 1953.

Aaron, Hank, et al. *The Hall: A Celebration of Baseball's Greats*. Boston: Little, Brown and Company, 2014.

Acocella, Nick. "Finley Entertained and Enraged." *ESPN*, http://espn.go.com/classic/biography/s/Finley_Charles.html (accessed November 24, 2015).

Ahrens, Art. *Chicago Cubs: Tinker to Evers to Chance*. Chicago: Arcadia, 2007.

Akin, William. "Steve Brodie." *Society for American Baseball Research*, http://sabr.org/bioproj/person/cffef117 (accessed November 24, 2015).

"All Tied Up! Braves Win, 1–0, 'Dirt Player' Comes through for Atlanta." *Associated Press*, October 11, 1991.

"Allie Reynolds, Star Pitcher for Yankees, Is Dead at 79," *New York Times*, December 27, 1994.

Anderson, Ron. "Bullet Joe Bush." *Society for American Baseball Research*, http://sabr.org/bioproj/person/30a2a3bd (accessed November 24, 2015).

Angus, Jeff. "Jim Gilliam." *Society for American Baseball Research*, http://sabr.org/bioproj/person/3c15c318 (accessed November 24, 2015).

Armour, Mark. "Dave McNally." *Society for American Baseball Research*, http://sabr.org/bioproj/person/11d59b62 (accessed November 24, 2015).

———. "Frank Howard." *Society for American Baseball Research*, http://sabr.org/bioproj/person/789d55a7 (accessed November 24, 2015).

———. "Sam Leever." *Society for American Baseball Research*, http://sabr.org/bioproj/person/3cf96cc4 (accessed November 24, 2015).

———. "Tommy Leach." *Society for American Baseball Research*, http://sabr.org/bioproj/person/ba1b7d5b (accessed November 24, 2015).

"Art Nehf Started Baseball under Tutelage of St. Pete Grid Coach." *St. Petersburg Times*, October 4, 1924.

"Art Nehf, Pitcher for Giants, Dead." *New York Times*, December 20, 1960.

"Auto Crash May Doom Career of Campanella." *Associated Press*, January 28, 1958.

"Barnes Gets into Line with Giants." *New York Times*, February 22, 1921.

"Batters Often Tip You on What They Intend to Do, Says Gardner." *Palm Beach Post*, June 27, 1922.

Bedingfield, Gary. "Billy Cox." *Baseball in Wartime*, April 12, 2007, http://www.baseballinwartime.com/player_biographies/cox_billy.htm (accessed November 24, 2015).

Beitiks, Edvins. "Steinbach Enjoys New Reputation." *San Francisco Examiner*, July 13, 1988.

Berger, Ralph. "Earle Combs." *Society for American Baseball Research*, http://sabr.org/bioproj/person/62bcbcbd (accessed November 24, 2015).

Bernstein, Sam. "Barney Dreyfuss." *Society for American Baseball Research*, http://sabr.org/bioproj/person/29ceb9e0 (accessed November 24, 2015).

Berra, Yogi, with Tom Horton. *Yogi . . . It Ain't Over*. New York: HarperTorch, 1990.

"Big Crowd Sees Braves Win Over Yankees, 3–2." *Associated Press*, March 17, 1935.

"Billy Cox, 58, a Dodger Standout as Third Baseman in Early 50s." *New York Times*, April 1, 1978.

Birch, Ray, "Everett Scott." *Society for American Baseball Research*, http://sabr.org/bioproj/person/365591cd (accessed November 24, 2015).

Bishop, Bill. "Casey Stengel." *Society for American Baseball Research*, http://sabr.org/bioproj/person/bd6a83d8 (accessed November 24, 2015).

Blair, Sam. "Forgotten Tragedy: Saga of Ross "Pep" Youngs—1920s Baseball Star's Career Often Overlooked." *Seattle Times*, May 3, 1992.

Blankstein, Andrew. "Former Dodger Willie Davis Found Dead in Burbank Home." *Los Angeles Times*, March 9, 2010.

"Blue Jays Honored at White House." *Associated Press*, December 17, 1992.

"Blue Jays Win Second Straight World Series." *Associated Press*, October 22, 1993.

Bogen, Gil. *Johnny Kling: A Baseball Biography*. Jefferson, NC: McFarland, 2006.

Bolfe, Bob. "We Carry a Message of Good News." *Palm Beach Post*, February 4, 1940.

Bonds, Barry. "It's Tough to Understand the Negativism." *Pittsburgh Press*, October 18, 1991.

"Boog Powell Bests Frank Robinson in Contest." *Associated Press*, September 3, 1985.

"Boy Pitcher Beat Giants Easily." *New York Times*, October 10, 1913.

Braucher, Bill. "Bing Miller Thanks Cub Manager for Leaving Malone on Mound in Final Game of Last Series." *NEA News Service*, April 18, 1930.

Byron, Bennett. "Union Park: Home of the World Champion National League Baltimore Orioles." *Deadball Baseball*, February 9, 2012, http://deadballbaseball.com/?p=1343 (accessed November 24, 2015).

Calcaterra, Craig. "Maury Wills Thinks He Should Be a Hall of Famer for Some Reason." *NBCsports*, July 12, 2012, http://mlb.nbcsports.com/2012/07/12/maury-wills-thinks-he-should-be-a-hall-of-famer-for-some-reason/ (accessed November 24, 2015).

Carrol, Dink. "Playing the Field: Late Innings for Walter Johnson." *Montreal Gazette*, August 21, 1946.

Ceresi, Frank. "The History of the Temple Cup." *Baseballlibrary*, September 25, 2008, (accessed November 24, 2015).

"Champion A's Manager Dick Williams Dies at 82." *SFGATE*, July 7, 2011, http://www.sfgate.com/sports/article/Champion-A-s-manager-Dick-Williams-dies-at-82-2355363.php (accessed November 24, 2015).

"Charles O. Finley, Baseball Team Owner Who Challenged Traditions, Dies at 77." *New York Times*, February 20, 1996.

"Chris Chambliss Showed He Was Ready." *Associated Press*, April 11, 1981.

Christie, Bill. "Met Dream Turns to Reality." *Pittsburgh Press*, October 17, 1969.

"Cochrane Agrees Pepper Martin Caused It All." *International News Service*, October 4, 1931.

"Collins, Hooper, and Gardner Are the Greatest Money Players in Major Baseball Leagues." *Ottawa Citizen*, October 2, 1920.

"Connie Mack to Spring New Team." *New York Times*, September 22, 1915.

Corbett, Warren. "Earl Weaver." *Society for American Baseball Research*, http://sabr.org/bioproj/person/0cfc37e3 (accessed November 24, 2015).

———. "Red Ruffing." *Society for American Baseball Research*, http://sabr.org/bioproj/person/7111866b (accessed November 24, 2015).

Corcoran, Cliff. "Reggie Jackson's Year in Orange and Black: A Lost Classic." *Camden Chat*, January 18, 2013, http://www.camdenchat.com/2013/1/18/3889674/reggie-jackson-baltimore-orioles-year-in-orange-and-black-a-lost-classic (accessed November 24, 2015).

Costa, Gabe. "By the Numbers: Gil McDougald—A Quiet Yankee Legend." *CBS*, January 21, 2011, http://newyork.cbslocal.com/2011/01/21/by-the-numbers-gil-mcdougald-a-quiet-yankee-legend/ (accessed November 24, 2015).

Costello, Rory. "Ed Figueroa." *Society for American Baseball Research*, http://sabr.org/ bioproj/person/750a1e46 (accessed November 24, 2015).

———. "Joe Rudi." *Society for American Baseball Research*, http://sabr.org/bioproj/person/ 59c2abe2 (accessed November 24, 2015).

"Costly Heinie Groh Has Proved Small Factor in Giants' Success This Season." *International News Service*, October 2, 1922.

"Curt Flood Act of 1998: Application of Federal Antitrust Laws to Major League Baseball Players." *Congressional Research*, http://congressionalresearch.com/98-820/document. php?study=Curt+Flood+Act+of+1998+Application+of+of+Federal+Antitrust+Laws+to+ Major+League+Baseball+Players (accessed November 24, 2015).

"Dave Stewart Sentenced." *Associated Press*, January 30, 1985.

Davis, Ralph. "Remember Ginger Beaumont?" *Pittsburgh Press*, February 22, 1922.

"Dodgers Jubilant after Win." *Associated Press*, October 4, 1955.

"Dodgers Still Wondering How to Beat Yankees." *United Press International*, October 6, 1953.

Donaghy, Jim. "Henderson Takes over as Mr. October for A's." *Associated Press*, October 5, 1989.

Doyle, Pat. "Minor League History: A Look Back." *Baseball Almanac*, http://www.baseball-almanac.com/minor-league/minor0.shtml (accessed November 24, 2015).

Dwyre, Bill. "Sal's Spitter: Here's the Scoop." *Milwaukee Journal*, August 30, 1979.

Dykes, Jimmy, and Charles O. Dexter. *You Can't Steal First Base*. Philadelphia: J. B. Lippincott, 1967.

"Earl Credits Blass, Frank: Best Loss." *Associated Press*, October 18, 1971.

"Ebbets Field Demolished." *Brooklynbeforenow.blogspot*, February 23, 2011 (accessed November 24, 2015).

Evans, Billy. "Mark Koenig Is Key to Yankees' Chances." *Milwaukee Journal*, May 11, 1927.

"Even Chance by Doctors." *United Press International*, May 27, 1937.

"Experts Choose Jack Barry of Athletics as King of All Big-League Shortstops." *Edmonton Journal*, April 2, 1914.

Faber, Charles. "Sadie McMahon." *Society for American Baseball Research*, http://sabr.org/ bioproj/person/5e6054fa (accessed November 24, 2015).

"Fagan, Ryan. "Terry Pendleton Roughs up Chris Johnson over Slide into First." *Sporting News*, September 28, 2013.

Fainaru, Steve. "Gamble Paid Off." *Associated Press*, July 23, 1982.

"Faker Assumes Murphy Role." *Associated Press*, December 24, 1929.

Flood, Curt, and Richard Walker. *The Way It Is*. New York: Trident Press, 1971.

"Frank Crosetti, 91, a Fixture in Yankee Pinstripes, Is Dead," *New York Times*, February 13, 2002.

Gannon, Pat. "They Say in New York." *Milwaukee Journal*, May 30, 1937.

"Gashouse Gang's Pepper Martin Dies." *Associated Press*, March 5, 1965.

"George Earnshaw Hero of Series." *Associated Press*, October 9, 1930.

"George Earnshaw Ordered to Retire by Manager Mack." *Associated Press*, August 31, 1933.

Gergen, George. "05-20-76: The First Brawl in the Bronx." *NYYFans* (accessed February 9, 2014).

"Gil McDougald Shows His Weird Batting Stance." *Associated Press*, April 22, 1952.

Glueckstein, Fred. "Tony Lazzeri." *Society for American Baseball Research*, http://sabr.org/ bioproj/person/1b3c179c (accessed November 24, 2015).

Gold, Eddie, and Art Ahrens. *The Golden Era Cubs: 1876–1940*. Chicago: Bonus Books, 1985.

Goldstein, Richard. "Clem Labine, All-Star Reliever, Dies at 80." *New York Times*, March 4, 2007.

———. "Mike Cuellar, Star Pitcher for Orioles, Dies at 72." *New York Times*, April 4, 2010.

Golenbock, Peter. *The Spirit of St. Louis: A History of the St. Louis Cardinals and Browns*. New York: Spike, 2000.

Goodwin, Doris Kearns. *Wait 'Til Next Year: A Memoir*. New York: Touchstone, 1997.

Gould, Alan. "St. Louis Cardinals Defeat Macks for World's Title." *Associated Press*, October 11, 1931.

Grayson, Harry. "They Played the Game: Everett Scott Wore Padded Shoes to Escape Being Cut by Sliders." *NEA News Service*, July 1, 1943.

———. "Wally Schang, One of Catching Greats, in Six Fall Series." *NEA News Service*, September 18, 1943.

"Great Scott! Brosius Blasts Padres, Twice." *Associated Press*, October 21, 1998.

Gregor, Chisolm. "After Two Decades, Carter's Homer Resonates." *MLB.com*, October 22, 2013, http://m.mlb.com/news/article/63211856/ (accessed November 24, 2015).

Gugger, John. "Phillips: Most Valuable Pest." *Toledo Blade*, August 17, 1991.

Hagberg, David. "Baltimore Baseball and Beer: Baltimore's Brewers and Their Early Ties to Baseball." *Baltimore Bottle Club*, http://www.baltimorebottleclub.org/articles/baltimore_baseball_n_beer.pdf (accessed November 24, 2015).

Herness, Glen. "Rube Walberg." *Society for American Baseball Research*, http://sabr.org/bioproj/person/87b589bc (accessed November 24, 2015).

Hertzel, Bob. "Braves Fall in a Classic Series, but There Were No Losers." *Pittsburgh Press*, October 28, 1991.

"Irish Meusel Sent to Giants in Trade." *New York Times*, July 26, 1921.

Jaffe, Chris. "40th Anniversary: The Orange Baseball Experiment." *Hardball Times*, March 29, 2013, http://www.hardballtimes.com/tht-live/40th-anniversary-the-orange-baseball-experiment/ (accessed November 24, 2015).

James, Bill. *The New Bill James Historical Baseball Abstract*. New York: Free Press, 2001.

Jensen, Don. "Tris Speaker." *Society for American Baseball Research*, http://sabr.org/bioproj/person/6d9f34bd (accessed November 24, 2015).

"Jimmy Dykes, Big-League Star and Manager, Succumbs at 79." *New York Times*, June 16, 1976.

"Jimmy Key Retires after 15 Years, 116 Victories." *Associated Press*, January 30, 1999.

"Joe Page Yankees' Man of Hour Again This Year." *Portsmouth Times*, April 22, 1950.

"Johnny Murphy Is Dead at 61, General Manager of the Mets." *New York Times*, January 15, 1970.

Jones, David. *Deadball Stars of the American League*. Dulles, VA: Potomac Books, 2006.

"Justice, Gooden Fire Back at Radomski." *ESPN*, January 28, 2009, http://sports.espn.go.com/mlb/news/story?id=3862988 (accessed November 24, 2015).

Kahn, Roger. *The Boys of Summer*, reissue edition. New York: Harper Perennial Modern Classic, 2006.

Kates, Maxwell. "Brooks Robinson." *Society for American Baseball Research*, http://sabr.org/bioproj/person/55363cdb (accessed November 24, 2015).

Keenan, Jimmy. "Joe Kelley." *Society for American Baseball Research*, http://sabr.org/bioproj/person/17b00755 (accessed November 24, 2015).

"Ken Boyer Loses Cancer Battle." *United Press International*, September 8, 1982.

"Ken Holtzman Alive and Happy with A's." *Associated Press*, October 13, 1973.

Kiesewetter, John. "How Dick Williams Fooled Johnny Bench." *Cincinnati.com*, July 8, 2011 (accessed November 24, 2015).

Korte, Tim. "Manager in the Making." *Associated Press*, February 24, 2003.

Lahman, Sean. "Heinie Groh." *Society for American Baseball Research*, http://sabr.org/bioproj/person/b90e80de (accessed November 24, 2015).

Leavy, Jane. *Sandy Koufax: A Lefty's Legacy*, reissue edition. New York: Harper Perennial, 2010.

Ledman, Gary. "This Veteran Gets No Respect." *Evening Independent*, March 7, 1979.

Leggett, William. "Manager of the Money Men." *Sports Illustrated*, October 7, 1968.

Leventhal, Josh. *The World Series: An Illustrated Encyclopedia of the Fall Classic*. New York: Blackdog and Leventhal, 2001.

Levy, Sam. "Rube Walberg Worries Too Much." *Milwaukee Journal*, April 12, 1935.

Lieb, Frederick C. *The Baltimore Orioles*. New York: G. P. Putnam's Sons, 1955.

"Living Dangerously, Klesko Finds Happiness off the Field." *Associated Press*, February 29, 1996.

Lowenfish, Lee. *Branch Rickey: Baseball's Ferocious Gentleman*. Lincoln: University of Nebraska Press, 2009.

Lyle, Sparky, with Peter Golenbock. *The Bronx Zoo: The Astonishing Inside Story of the 1978 World Champion New York Yankees*. New York: Triumph, 2005.

Madden, Bill. "Johnny Podres Dead at 75." *New York Daily News*, January 14, 2008.

"Marlins' Tino Martinez Resigns." *Associated Press*, July 29, 2013.

Martinez, Michael. "It Looks like Jimmy's Going to Be a Real Key in New York." *New York Times News Service*, March 20, 1993.

Mason, Ward. "William Carrigan's Last Game." *Sporting Life*, December 1916.

Mathewson, Christy. *Pitching in a Pinch*. Lincoln: University of Nebraska Press, 1994.

McCollister, John. *The Bucs! The Story of the Pittsburgh Pirates*. Boulder, CO: Taylor Trade, 1998.

McLain, Denny, with Dave Diles. *Nobody's Perfect*. New York: Dial, 1975.

McMillan, Ken. *Amazing Tales from the New York Yankees Dugout: A Collection of the Greatest Yankees Stories Ever Told*. New York: Sports Publishing, 2012.

McMinn, Fred. "Farm Boy Mike Moore Top Draftee." *United Press International*, June 9, 1981.

McMurray, John. "Amos Strunk." *Society for American Baseball Research*, http://sabr.org/bioproj/person/e0df08f4 (accessed November 24, 2015).

———. "Joe McCarthy." *Society for American Baseball Research*, http://sabr.org/bioproj/person/2c77f933 (accessed November 24, 2015).

Miller, Richard. "Gary Nolan." *Society for American Baseball Research*, http://sabr.org/bioproj/person/dd89241b (accessed November 24, 2015).

Moffett, Dan. "Mr. Consistency: Changes Bypass Chambliss." *Palm Beach Post*, March 2, 1984.

Moore, Terrence. "Driessen's Career to Culminate in Reds Hall of Fame." *MLB.com*, June 22, 2012, http://m.mlb.com/news/article/33735040/ (accessed November 24, 2015).

Neft, David S., et al. *The Sports Encyclopedia: Baseball 2000*. New York: St. Martin's Griffin, 2000.

Neil, Edward J. "Eager, Enthusiastic, and Willing, Pepper Martin Is Ideal Player to Manager of Big-League Team." *Associated Press*, October 13, 1931.

"New York Dynasty Built on Hustle." *United Press International*, October 10, 1949.

"Newcombe Reveals Alcohol Problems of Brooklyn Title Team." *Associated Press*, May 14, 1986.

Newhouse, Dave. "Carney Lansford Is 'Charlie Hustle' of Oakland." *Lodi News-Sentinel*, August 6, 1992.

O'Brien, Don. "Rube Waddell." *Society for American Baseball Research*, http://sabr.org/bioproj/person/a5b2c2b4 (accessed November 24, 2015).

O'Keeffe, Michael, "Ex-Yankee Bucky Dent Still Drivin' 'em Wild in Boston," *New York Daily News*, July 21, 2010.

"Old-Time Ruth Mate Defends Babe's Mark." *Associated Press*, September 6, 1961.

"Orioles' Outfielder Earned Eight Gold Gloves." *Los Angeles Times*, December 28, 2013.

"Orlando Hernandez Rejoins Yankees as Minor League Spring Training Instructor." *Associated Press*, March 3, 2014.

"O's Bauer Makes Like Diplomat." *Associated Press*, October 10, 1966.

Pepe, Phil. *The Ballad of Billy and George*. Guilford, CT: Lyons Press, 2008.

"Pepper Martin Arrested for Punching Fan." *Associate Press*, August 15, 1951.

"Pepper Martin Is Suspended for Choking Umpire." *Associated Press*, September 2, 1949.

Pietrusza, David, et al. *Baseball: The Biographical Encyclopedia*. New York: Sport Classic Books, 2003.

"Players Sorry for Ken Boyer." *Associated Press*, June 10, 1980.

Potter, Chris. "Why Is Our Baseball Team Called the Pittsburgh Pirates?" *Pittsburgh City Paper*, August 14, 2003, http://www.pghcitypaper.com/pittsburgh/why-is-our-baseball-team-called-the-pittsburgh-pirates-what-do-pirates-have-to-do-with-pittsburgh/Content?oid=1335541 (accessed November 24, 2015).

Pyette, Ryan. "Henke Inducted to Canadian Baseball Hall of Fame." *Toronto Sun*, June 19, 2011.

"Raines Admits He Spent $40,000 on a Cocaine Habit in Nine Months." *United Press International*, November 16, 1982.

"Red Rolfe, Yankees' Star Third Baseman, Dies at 60." *New York Times*, July 9, 1969.

Reeves, Grant T. "Echoes from the Field and Clubhouse." *Baseball Magazine*, September 1915.

"Revisiting the Frank Robinson Trade." *Red Reporter*, November 23, 2013, http://www. redreporter.com/2013/11/23/5133726/revisiting-the-frank-robinson-trade (accessed November 24, 2015).

Ritter, Lawrence. *The Glory of Their Times: The Story of the Early Days of Baseball Told by the Men Who Played It*. New York: Macmillan, 1966.

Rogers, C. Paul. "Lefty Gomez." *Society for American Baseball Research*, http://sabr.org/ bioproj/person/94f0b0a4 (accessed November 24, 2015).

———. "Whitey Ford." *Society for American Baseball Research*, http://sabr.org/bioproj/ person/fca49b7c (accessed November 24, 2015).

"Ron Guidry's 18 Strikeouts Thrill Fans." *Associated Press*, June 19, 1978.

Rygelski, James, and Robert Tiemann. *10 Rings: Stories of the St. Louis Cardinals Championships*. St. Louis, MO: Reedy Press, 2011.

"Scott Brosius Could Be the Yankees' New Mr. October." *Associated Press*, October 15, 1999.

"Series Veteran to Oppose Lefty." *Associated Press*, October 17, 1993.

Simon, Tom. *Deadball Stars of the National League*. Washington, DC: Brassey's, 2004.

———. *Green Mountain Boys of Summer: Vermonters in the Major Leagues, 1882–1993*. Shelburne, VT: New England Press, 2000.

Siner, Howard. "Why Fred McGriff Likes What He Sees." *McCook Daily Gazette*, August 13, 1993.

———. "Why John Olerud Is a Real Big Hit." *Calhoun Times*, July 10, 1993.

Skipper, Doug. "Connie Mack." *Society for American Baseball Research*, http://sabr.org/ bioproj/person/3462e06e (accessed November 24, 2015).

Smizik, Bob. "Tenace A's Ace in Series Victory." *Pittsburgh Press*, October 23, 1972.

———. "Verdict Is In: Cincinnati Is World's Best." *Pittsburgh Press*, October 23, 1975.

Spatz, Lyle. "Jack Doyle." *Society for American Baseball Research*, http://sabr.org/node/6666 (accessed November 24, 2015).

Stout, Glenn. "When the Yankees Nearly Moved to Boston." *ESPN*, July 18, 2002, http:// static.espn.go.com/mlb/s/2002/0718/1407265.html (accessed November 24, 2015).

"Stuffy McInnis Startles Fans, Uses First-Base Mitten on Third." *Telegraph Herald*, June 2, 1918.

Swaine, Rick. "Jackie Robinson." *Society for American Baseball Research*, http://sabr.org/ bioproj/person/bb9e2490 (accessed November 24, 2015).

———. "Roy Campanella." *Society for American Baseball Research*, http://sabr.org/bioproj/ person/a52ccbb5 (accessed November 24, 2015).

Tan, Cecilia. *The Fifty Greatest Yankee Games*. New York: John Wiley and Sons, 2005.

"'That's America,' Says Sal Bando." *United Press International*, April 12, 1977.

Thomson, Cindy. "Sparky Anderson." *Society for American Baseball Research*, http://sabr. org/bioproj/person/8762afda (accessed November 24, 2015).

Thorn, John. *The Relief Pitcher: Baseball's New Hero*. New York: Dutton, 1979.

"Tommy Henrich May Retire from Baseball." *Warsaw Times Union*, November 9, 1950.

Triscuit, Zack. "Ned Hanlon." *Society for American Baseball Research*, http://sabr.org/ bioproj/person/1e360183 (accessed November 24, 2015).

Tusa C., Alfonso L. "Cito Gaston." *Society for American Baseball Research*, http://sabr.org/ bioproj/person/946b8db1 (accessed November 24, 2015).

"Umpire Ashford Quits in Wake of Javier Row." *Lodi News-Sentinel*, January 25, 1965.

Vaughan, Manning. "Much Depends on Rube Walberg." *Milwaukee Journal*, January 12, 1931.

Vecsey, George. "Oakland's Other Hometown Hero." *New York Times News Service*, October 11, 1989.

Vesparian, John. "Johnny Murphy." *Society for American Baseball Research*, http://sabr.org/bioproj/person/f236db6a (accessed November 24, 2015).

Voelker, Robert. "Delirium Grips City as Bucs Win." *Pittsburgh Post-Gazette*, October 18, 1971.

Walsh, Davis J. "Bob Meusel Fools Fans by Easy-Going Look on Field." *International News Service*, June 28, 1926.

Ward, John J. "Baseball's Premiere Catcher." *Baseball Magazine*, January 1916.

Weinreb, Michael. "The Origin of the Seven-Game Series." *Society for American Baseball Research*, October 24, 2011, http://sabr.org/latest/origin-seven-game-series (accessed November 24, 2015).

Wells, David, with Chris Kreski. *Perfect I'm Not: Boomer on Beer, Brawls, Backaches, and Baseball*. New York: William Morrow, 2003.

White, Bill. *Uppity: My Untold Story about the Games People Play*. New York: Grand Central Publishing, 2011.

White, Roy, and Darrell Berger. *"Then Roy Said to Mickey . . ." The Best Yankees Stories Ever Told*. Chicago: Triumph, 2009.

"Why Cardinals Career Had Sour Ending for Julian Javier." *RetroSimba*, March 18, 2012, http://retrosimba.com/2012/03/18/why-cardinals-career-had-sour-ending-for-julian-javier/ (accessed November 24, 2015).

Willey, Ken. "Bob Meusel." *Society for American Baseball Research*, http://sabr.org/bioproj/person/f8d53553 (accessed November 24, 2015).

Williams, Joe. "It's a Lie!" *Pittsburgh Press*, October 6, 1939.

Wills, Maury, and Mike Celizic. *On the Run: The Never Dull and Often Shocking Life of Maury Wills*. New York: Carroll and Graf, 1992.

Wine, Steven. "Devon White: The Glide in his Stride." *Associated Press*, March 5, 1998.

"Yankees Fine Willie Randolph after Charity Event." *Associated Press*, August 22, 1981.

Zingg, Paul, and E. A. Reed. "Harry Hooper." *Society for American Baseball Research*, http://sabr.org/bioproj/person/4f4206c6 (accessed November 24, 2015).

WEBSITES

Ballparks of Baseball, http://www.ballparksofbaseball.com/
Baseball Almanac, http://www.baseball-almanac.com/
Baseball Knoji, https://baseball.knoji.com/
Baseball Library, http://baseballlibrary.com
Baseball Reference, http://www.baseball-reference.com/
Charles Stoneham Archives, New York Historical Society, http://sports.nyhistory.org/tag/charles-stoneham/
Chicago Cubs, http://chicago.cubs.mlb.com
Deadball Era: Where Every Player Is Safe at Home, http://thedeadballera.com/
Mark McGwire's 10 Longest Home Runs, http://www.mcgwire.com/tenlongest.html
Mickey Mantle: The American Dream Comes to Life, http://www.themick.com/
Mickey Rivers, http://mickeyrivers.com
Retrosheet, http://www.retrosheet.org
Toronto Blue Jays, http://toronto.bluejays.mlb.com/tor/history/

INDEX

ABOUT THE AUTHOR

Jonathan Weeks is a card-carrying member of the Society for American Baseball Research and has written several books on the topic of baseball, including *Cellar Dwellers: The Worst Teams in Baseball History* (Scarecrow Press, 2012). He resides in Malone, New York, where the weather in winter is about as hospitable as the surface of Mars. During the offseason, Weeks spends his time looking up baseball stats and rambling on about players who have been overlooked for the Hall of Fame. He also moonlights as a football and hockey fan, although his favorite teams disappoint him year after year and he prefers not to discuss it.